中央軍事政治學校出版　每星期出版一次

OP52   30 —

G

The Northern Expedition

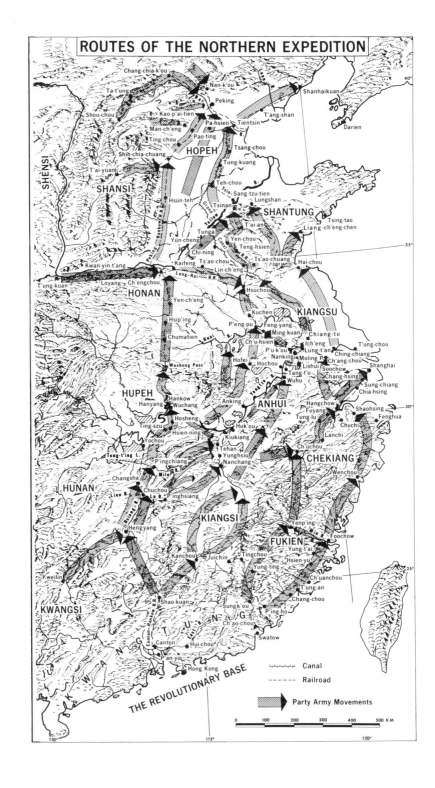

ROUTES OF THE NORTHERN EXPEDITION

SHENSI

SHANSI

HOPEH

SHANTUNG

HONAN

KIANGSU

HUPEH

ANHUI

HUNAN

CHEKIANG

KIANGSI

FUKIEN

KWANGSI

KWANGTUNG

THE REVOLUTIONARY BASE

Chang-chia-k'ou · Nan-k'ou
Ta-t'ung · Shanhaikuan
Shou-chou · Peking
Kao-p'ai-tien · T'ang-shan
Man-ch'eng · Pa-hsien · Tientsin · Darien
Ting-chou · Pao-ting
Shih-chia-chuang · Tsang-chou
T'ai-yuan · Tung-kuang
Hsün-teh · Teh-chou · Tsin-Sang-tzu-tien · Lungshan
Tsinan · Tsing-tao
T'ai-an · Liang-ch'eng-chen
Tunga · Yen-chou
Yün-cheng · Teng-hsien
Chi-ning · Ts'ao-chuang · Hai-chou
Kaifeng · Ts'ao-chou · Lin-ch'eng
Kwan-yin-t'ang · Lung-Hai R.R.
T'ung-kuan · Loyang · Ch'engchou · Hsuchou
Yen-ch'eng
Kuchen
Hsip'ing · Feng-yang
P'eng-pu · Ming-kuan · Chiang-tu
Chumatien · Ch'u-hsien · Ich'eng · T'ung-chou
P'u-k'ou · Lung-t'an · Ching-chiang
Nanking · Moling P. · Ch'ang-chou · Shanghai
Wusheng Pass · Hofei · Hochow · Lishui · Soochow
Tang-t'u · Chang-hsing · Sung-chiang
Wuhu · Chia-hsing
Hankow · Anking · Hangchow · Shaohsing
Hanyang · Wuchang · Fuyang · Fenghua
Hosheng · Tung-lu · Chuchi
Ting-szu · Huk'ou · Lanchi
Yochou · Kiukiang · Ch'uchou
Tung-t'ing L. · Tehan · Wenchou
P'ingchiang · Yunghsiu · CHEKIANG
Changsha · Nanchang
Chuchou · P'inghsiang
Hengyang · Yenp'ing · Foochow
Kweilin · Kanchou · Juichin · Tingchou · FUKIEN · Yung-t'ai
Yung-ting · Hsien-yu
Ch'uanchou
T'ung-an
Shao-kuan · Sungk'ou · Chang-chou
Ch'ao-chou · P'ing-ho
Canton · Hui-chou · Swatow
'an-yu · Hong Kong

Canal
Railroad
Party Army Movements

0 100 200 300 400 500 K M

THE NORTHERN EXPEDITION
CHINA'S NATIONAL
REVOLUTION OF 1926-1928

DONALD A. JORDAN

The University Press of Hawaii
Honolulu

Manufactured in the United States of America

Book design by Roger J. Eggers

Cover design by Russell D. Fujita

Library of Congress Cataloging in Publication Data

Jordan, Donald A   1936-
   The northern expedition.

   Bibliography: p.
   Includes index.
   1. China—History—Northern Expedition, 1926-
1928. I. Title.
DS777.47.J6   951.04'1   75-40309
ISBN 0-8248-0352-3

Contents

Maps

Preface

What was the Northern Expedition? Was it, as some acclaimed, the Great National Revolution? For some Marxists, the term "national" referred to a phase of necessary bourgeois development that would precede the more significant work of the Social Revolution. For Kuomintang members and others influenced by the West, nationhood was a state of community togetherness that strengthened the modern world powers. The goals of the Northern Expedition of 1926-1928 are as encompassing as was Chinese nationalism in the 1920s. The arguments favoring nationhood differed then widely according to individual levels of education, "modernization," and politicization. It may be easier to describe what it was against than what nationalism was for. Those promoting the expedition and the national movement were opposed to the status quo. Dismal decades of defeat as the Ch'ing regime fell apart had shattered the Chinese self-satisfaction. The failure of the revolutionaries after 1911 to reintegrate and reorder the Chinese state led to continuing disappointment and disillusionment. Both idealistic Chinese youth and their elders craved some improvement from the enervating disunity. The many military governors in their provinces marched their mercenaries and seemed more bent on grabbing from fellow Chinese than they were anxious over the greed of foreign imperialists. China's "loss of face" in the world community was sensed mainly by those most aware of the outside world. Keeping fresh the disgrace of Japan's gains from Yuan Shih-k'ai, the nationalists who commemorated National Humiliation Day were not the peasants hoeing in the field. By the launching of the expedition in 1926, the National Revolution was an inclusive multilevel movement.

In order to achieve national reunification, the Northern Expedition of necessity became a "many splendored thing," gathering in as many dissident elements as possible. Judging the success or tragedy of such a union was left to a later period. The only demand shared by all the participants was for a new, more integrated political system for China, one that would replace the existing, defenseless, kaleidoscopic patchwork of warlord satrapies.

The young elite educated in modern ways who gathered in the treaty ports were among the most aware of nationalism. Although but a tiny part of China's millions, they were articulate, enthusiastic, and idealistic—if rather inexperienced and impractical. But in the search for new alternatives, even this elite element lacked homogeneity, for some saw strength in national unity while others envisioned a social struggle among Chinese that would revitalize China. The symbol of their common desire for a stronger China and their divergence over means to that end was the United Front of the Kuomintang and Chinese Communist Party from 1923 to 1927.

Also wanting a new chance for their plans were republicans, federalists, constitutionalists, and provincial autonomists. They, too, generally chafed under warlord rulers who were too strong for civilians to oust but too weak to resist the demands and bribes of foreign powers. Frustrated with his own impotence in Chinese politics, Sun Yat-sen had learned through bitter experience and forced exile that he would have to attract allies of all stripes. Although a symbol of nationalism for many, Sun allied himself with Kwangtung militarist Ch'en Chiung-ming and made overtures to regional overlords, such as Chang Tso-lin. Desperate to find means to pull Chinese together in a common cause, Sun had espoused provincial autonomy in federalism in 1921, but rejected them as the tide of nationalism swelled. In 1926 Chiang Kai-shek and other patrons of the military campaign resurrected them once again. With his experience in the outside world, Sun sought patronage from the United States, Great Britain, Japan, and finally from the Soviet Union. Sun then accepted Russia's offer of aid free of imperialistic demands, but did not exclude the possibility of a rapprochement with the others.

The controversy as to whether Sun was a socialist, Communist, or a hybrid will be outside the scope of this study. Adherents of those ideological variants were gathered into the ranks of the national revolutionaries. The point to be introduced here is that the so-called National Revolution and its military phase, the Northern Expedition, cannot be labeled neatly as entirely nationalistic, socialistic, or opportunistic. Instead, the movement was a loose coalition of Chinese elites who were at least nationwide in their origins, if not nationalized according to Western specifications. They did share a righteous indignation over the treatment meted out to the disunited Chinese people by the foreign powers and their merchants. Only reunification could return to China the strength to determine her own destiny. Since it had become apparent that the armed forces of the warlords could only be overcome by military means, a new war would have to be waged to remove them as obstacles to reunification. Those militarists who would recognize the authority of the Kuomintang in *national* affairs could be eased into the movement as representing the interest of the people in their provinces.

The advantage of such an inclusive approach was its ability to quickly incorporate any who could contribute to the rapid reunification of China. Its weakness was to be the lack of a dynamic ideology that could keep the participants united and this led to misunderstanding and factionalism. Beyond the facade formed by these multifarious elites lay the vast masses of Chinese peasantry and the smaller clusterings of urban proletariats. How deeply did the desire for nationhood penetrate among them? Were the Chinese people as a whole responsive to the modern slogans of nationalism? The role of these peasants and workers received much publicity from Marxists and Trotskyites, which was what initially attracted my attention to the expedition. My evaluation of their role in the National Revolution is the most revisionistic or iconoclastic aspect of this study.

Differentiating the Kuomintang's campaign of 1926-1928 from several prior abortive efforts by Sun Yat-sen was the more consolidated base in Kwangtung from which it was launched. Part 1 of this introductory survey of the expedition outlines the main features of the Revolutionary Base, where developed the Kuomintang's Whampoa Academy and from where its Party Army spread Party rule in that key southern province. Although the Chinese Communists were part of the United Front, operating first in Kwangtung and then in the opening phase of the expedition, this study will not feature their parallel development as a party in those years. Instead, the focus will center on the Kuomintang as the promoter of the military campaign, albeit the Russian military advisors were ubiquitous once they were resigned to its commencement.

There has been no military account of the progress of the expedition available in the West, and even the Kuomintang's chronicle is quite limited in its scope, and so Part 2 will describe the geographic parameters and the combatants, and will evaluate the intensity of the civil war. It became apparent during my research that the conflict was bloody and desperate at points, although this aspect had been ignored by political observers antagonistic to the military leadership. Initially I had searched for evidence to support the fascinating polemic of Harold Isaacs, *The Tragedy of the Chinese Revolution*, from which I assumed that Communist-led mass organizations had overcome warlord forces ahead of the Party Army. Had the reunification been accomplished by peasant and worker propagandists rushing north? Had this political success set the style for the victories of Asian Communists later? If the masses were so all-powerful under Communist direction, then how can we make sense of their successive uprisings that failed from the spring of 1927 in Shanghai, through the summer in Hunan, at Nanchang, Swatow, and finally to the debacle at Canton in December? Had the Marxists been overly optimistic as to the politicization of the peasantry in their rush to apply political formulas to Chinese conditions? As my research progressed, especially in Communist materials, I found that while the mass organizations had aided the Party Army at particular points in 1925 and 1926, there had been a side to the mass movement that had been disruptive to the goal of military reunification of China. If the masses had been so crucial to the rise of Chiang Kai-shek in 1925, then why had he lost his initial enthusiasm for mass organizations? Less publicized was the success of the Party Army's friendly approach toward the *un*organized civilians of the countryside through which it fought.

Part 4 deals with these political efforts of the National Revolutionary Army, which evolved from the Party Army. The Political Departments of army units indoctrinated Kuomintang troops in correct ideology and behavior toward civilians, combining practical Chinese means with the latest Comintern techniques. Western concepts blended with the nineteenth-century practices of Tseng Kuo-fan, admired by Mao Tse-tung as well as by Chiang Kai-shek. Among the future Chinese Communist leaders who gained experience in political work at Canton and then on the expedition were not only Mao, but Chou En-lai, Liu Shao-ch'i, Li Li-san, Chu Teh, Lin Piao, and many others. The lessons learned both by the Communists and the Kuomintang influenced their later responses.

Taoists claimed, "In victory there is defeat, and in defeat there is victory." This seems particularly suited to the Northern Expedition where the contributions made by warlord defectors speeded the national reunification but left the Kuomintang with one cause of its later decline. Part 5 outlines the Kuomintang's tactics to subvert warlord subordinates and entice them into the ranks of the expansive National Revolutionary Army. One Party leader whom I interviewed, Sun Fo, explained to me that the gathering of these military forces increased the military potential of the Kuomintang and allowed the expeditionary forces to reach the Manchurian border within two years. This timetable, according to Sun Fo, was more dependent on the defections than on any other single factor.

Researching the Northern Expedition and the myriad of related topics reveals a skeletal outline, but one thin on details in many places. The problem of inaccessibility and loss of materials has been frustrating. Crates of Party records and reports were lost during the rapid retreat from Nanking in 1937. The Communists likewise lost much in quick departures from Shanghai, Canton, and elsewhere in 1927 and then in the Long March across the wilds of western China to Yenan. Also, despite the military victory of the Kuomintang by 1928, the collection of oral history from the survivors is hampered by either their malodorous connections with warlords or their involvement in the factional struggles that wracked the Kuomintang, leaving scars still tender, however well hidden. Thus, ex-Political Department workers are reluctant to recall their cooperation with Communists before 1927, or their participation in the mass movements that became taboo from mid-1927 on. Strangely enough, Kuomintang agencies supplied me more data on the Communist version of the expedition than on their own. Perhaps when some of the key participants have passed from positions of leadership, both in Taiwan and Peking, really useful materials may be more "conveniently" released.

In the meantime, this study has been based on a wide variety of official and private memoirs, published documents, archival materials, observations in Chinese and foreign newspapers, and oral history. As an outline it provides clues and questions, if not all the answers. Although these materials from university libraries, Hong Kong's Supreme Court Library, centers in Taiwan, publications from Peking, the Hoover Institution's East Asian Collection, the National Archives and Library of Congress in Washington, records of the British Foreign Office, and French archives may be only the visible portion of the iceberg, some tentative conclusions can be made. Hopefully, this "draft outline," as a Chinese scholar should classify his work, will stir enough controversy to stimulate further study.

Acknowledgments

I wish to thank those who have provided so much help in the innumerable hours and years of research, and with translation, writing, and revision. Chinese friends and associates have been invaluable in translating difficult passages and terms and in leading me to useful materials. In Taiwan they provided me with introductions that led to interviews and access to collections. The staff and librarian at Taipei's research center for Chinese Communist Studies under the Bureau of Investigation were helpful beyond any expectation. The Fulbright Foundation in Taipei aided in countless vital ways my research there. Scholars at Academia Sinica, and Chengchih University deserve my gratitude. Walter Gourlay must be thanked for recommending the Hong Kong newspapers, which he had already researched, and the British White Paper on Shameen. He and the Harvard East Asia Research Center scholars also provided editorial advice. As a scholar steeped in the period of this study, C. Martin Wilbur made valuable suggestions in Taiwan and helped immensely through his *Documents on Communism, Nationalism, and Soviet Advisors in China, 1918-1927*. Crucial to the beginning of my study was Eugene Boardman who directed it through the dissertation phase at the University of Wisconsin, where Leonard Gordon also encouraged my work and aided me in gaining Fulbright and NDEA grants. Later at Ohio University, the Research Committee, Graduate College, and International Studies Center provided financial support for further research and travel. At the Hoover Institution, John Ma and David Tseng were inspiring in their patient cooperation. Saving me considerable time through his efficiency was J. Taylor at the National Archives, Military Records Division. For suggestions and encouragement in seeking a publisher, I thank Samuel Chu and David C. Wilson. Most difficult to express in words is my dependency on my wife, Mary Kaye, who was a partner in all phases of the project and should be titled something between a patron saint and the coauthor.

Abbreviations

CA	Collective Army
CCP	Chinese Communist Party
CEC	Central Executive Committee of the Kuomintang
C-in-C	Commander-in-Chief
GLU	Chinese National General Labor Union
KGLU	Kwangtung General Labor Union
KMT	Kuomintang
NRA	National Revolutionary Army

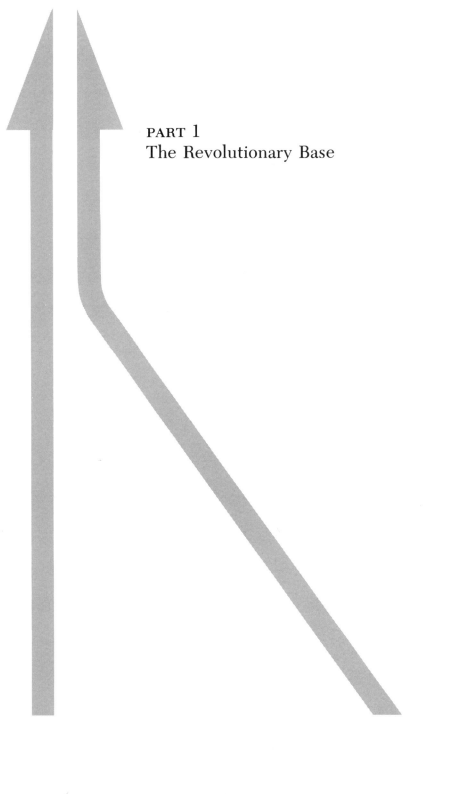

PART 1
The Revolutionary Base

CHAPTER 1

Building the Model

Emerging from the wreckage of an empire badly mauled by foreign powers and decomposed internally, Chinese nationalism had by the 1920s begun to spread beyond the new urban elites to the proletariat of the treaty ports and out into the countryside. Although the antiforeign racialism of 1911's revolutionaries had helped to topple the decadent Manchus, the feelings of nationhood had grown slowly among the Chinese and had meaning primarily for the modern educated. The civilian visionaries of the anti-Manchu movement were ill prepared for the frustrating realities that befell the infant republic. Their dreams vanished as the ex-military lieutenants of the Manchus rose in power, sparring among themselves for territory, while the foreign imperialists continued their rapacious exploitation of the defenseless ghost republic. The political idealism of those Chinese educated in Anglo-American values seemed irrelevant in a world where at Versailles the Western democracies sold China's interests in Shantung to an expansive Japan in return for satisfaction of their own desires.

Frustrated parliamentarians, republicans, and ex-revolutionaries who had worked for the end of the old regime, groped impotently for some means to reintegrate the shattered economy, society, and body politic. By the 1920s, the debates of modern intellectuals turned away from complete Westernization toward a reappraisal of what China really needed. Even the greediest military governor, a warlord, might mouth "saving China"—but what then was China? Neither the idealistic rhetoric of thinkers nor the raw armed force of the warlords had been sufficient, separately, to pull China

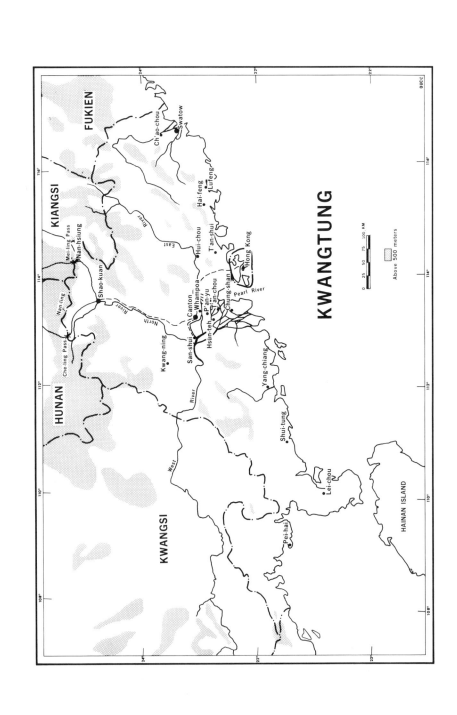

KWANGTUNG

FUKIEN

KIANGSI

HUNAN

KWANGSI

HAINAN ISLAND

Ch'ao-chou
Swatow
Hai-feng
Lu-feng
Hui-chou
T'an-shui
Hong Kong
Nan-hsiung
Mei-ling Pass
Shao-kuan
Nan-ling
Che-ling Pass
Kwang-ning
Canton
Whampoa
P'an-yu
Fan-chou
Chung-shan
San-shui
Hsün-teh
Pearl River
Yang-chiang
Shui-tung
Lei-chou
Pei-hai

East River
North River
West River

0 25 50 75 100 KM

Above 500 meters

back together. Sun Yat-sen, the quixotic leader of the Kuomintang (KMT), and his faithfuls had been able to reflect on this lesson while exiled abroad after successive losses to warlord forces.[1]

Underestimating his military strength, Sun had promoted expeditions, beginning in 1900 and continuing until 1924, shortly before his death in early 1925, which he hoped would sweep northward from Kwangtung to reunite China under his leadership. Through these abortive starts in South China, Sun and his younger followers learned that the creation of a Chinese nation would require discipline, unifying goals, and considerable military power. In the early 1920s, Sun failed in his solicitation of support from Japan and the United States[2] and so began to listen to the new Russian dream of a "Brotherhood of Oppressed Nations" and offers of military and financial aid. Along with a Russian alliance, these could help to implement Sun's vision of building his home province of Kwangtung into a "revolutionary base" from which to launch his military campaign for the reunification of China. Until this could be realized, in place of China there would remain a shifting scene of warring states too distracted by civil wars to defend or lift up the suffering Chinese people.

To the strategists in the new Soviet Union, suffering China held great potential. Anti-imperialist action there could shut off sources of raw materials from the leading capitalist countries, as well as the markets and cheap labor for their factories that the powers had found in China. While Soviet "missionaries" had helped to organize a group of Chinese radicals into the Chinese Communist Party (CCP) in mid-1921, it remained a small body of intellectuals. They studied and trained for mass leadership, but were frustrated by warlord power from recruiting followers. In 1923 when Stalin's leadership promoted the alliance with the Kuomintang, the CCP, which was pressured into the collaboration, only numbered several hundred members.[3] The Russians, seeking influence in China, saw more immediate potential in the thousands of nationalistic bourgeois in Sun's party, who were placed throughout China. At the same time the Russians wooed such warlords as Wu P'ei-fu and Feng Yü-hsiang, and dabbled in national minority movements within China's northern border. The Soviets already had proved quite effective in the central Asian portion of the old Russian empire by subsidizing revolutionaries within newly created republics, coming to their aid upon invitation, and then welcoming the republics into the Union of Soviet Socialist Republics. In Peking's current terminology, this is labeled Socialist Imperialism, but in the 1920s many Chinese were impressed by the logic of Soviet anti-imperialism against the foreign powers and China's desperate need of foreign aid. However, in the ensuing collaboration, Russian political, military, and ideological models were to prove as crucial to the Kuomintang national revolution as did Russian material aid.

Consequently, 1923 saw the genesis of a Russian-influenced national political and military structure at Canton, the revolutionary capital. The city's long access to modern influences and its anti-Manchu experience made it a natural choice. Progress was slow but young men joined the movement. Their resourcefulness built muscle for Sun's visionary plans by means of a modern military academy, Whampoa, which would feed into a Party Army. This would be the nucleus of the National Revolutionary Army (NRA), which would move north to conquer the many warlord regimes into which China had disintegrated. A modern administrative apparatus created for Canton would be expanded gradually to manage the province of Kwangtung, and ultimately the nation. Kwangtung would be the Revolutionary Base.

In late 1924, Sun's national movement was still dangerously dependent on warlords in Kwangtung. Surrounded by this host of armed opportunists, Sun lacked security even within Canton. Although Yunnanese militarists Liu Chen-huan and Yang Hsi-min had aided Sun in ousting the disloyal warlord Ch'en Chiung-ming two years earlier, they themselves now menaced Sun's plans. Sun's municipal agents efficiently collected taxes and the contributions of overseas Chinese only to see the funds siphoned off to keep the support of Generals Liu and Yang. Whenever Ch'en Chiung-ming, still at large in the East River uplands, would move on Canton, Liu and Yang would requisition from Sun a sum of 10,000 silver yuan* for the defense of Canton, or C$100,000 to force Ch'en back up the East River to Huichou. This protection racket further emphasized the vulnerability of the KMT at Canton until the Party could muster its own military forces.[4] By late 1924, a frustrated and ailing Sun traveled north to Peking, hoping to negotiate for some wider political arena for the KMT.

When Sun Yat-sen died in March 1925, he deprived the struggling KMT of his catalytic charisma, which had drawn together a party of diversity. But, though his party suffered divisions, Sun had left behind a legacy. Somehow the KMT not only survived his loss but began to nurture what had been sown. The structures Sun had helped to create at Canton were the seeds from which the National Revolution could develop. Sun's death transmitted his nationalistic zeal to at least the modern elites of China, for whom Sun came to symbolize a new, stirring, selfless, patriotism. Wherever the news traveled in 1925, memorial services eulogized Sun's enduring efforts. As a symbol, Sun was perhaps even more inspiring than he had been as man. During his life, this senior revolutionary had overshadowed his younger followers, but after his death these disciples at Canton lost their inhibitions. Although the diversity endangered their cohesiveness, it also stimulated creative potential. Challenged by the hostile surroundings and realizing the opportunities for leadership, Sun's survivors blossomed forth with a broad range of modern political and military programs.

Experimenting with modern political techniques, the KMT government at Canton appealed beyond the usual intellectual and military elites, to the broader masses of Chinese society. Some members, impressed by Marxist progress in creating a new Russia from another ancient, agrarian system,

---

*The Chinese silver yuan was then worth approximately US$.50 and will hereafter be abbreviated as C$.

hoped to apply similar methods in China by means of the small, rising urban proletariat. Other partisans believed that the modern-educated youth and their merchant families with economic power in the ports were best prepared to democratize and industrialize China. Ready to join a movement for change were frustrated students of modern schools, educated Chinese women, and the downtrodden, ubiquitous footsoldiers. A few saw the potential in the yet unorganized peasantry. In Sun's reorganization of the KMT in 1924, his party had borrowed heavily from Russian Communist political methodology, but members also showed the influence of liberal Anglo-American education and that of earlier Confucian progressives like Tseng Kuo-fan—a hero of both Chiang Kai-shek and young Mao Tse-tung. Later, with some insight, panicking European businessmen of Shanghai blamed the revolutionary "red" menace on the insidious influence of American Christian mission schools.

The national revolutionary movement envisioned by the KMT needed the spark of a radicalizing issue to attract mass support. In a China still disintegrated, Sun Yat-sen's death on March 12, 1925, gained the attention of the urban elites, but they had to be energized into taking action. Just such a politicizing incident, made to order for the Canton nationalists, as Michael Borodin, the Comintern agent, later observed, occurred on May 30 in Shanghai. A demonstration of several thousand young students, workers, and city people protesting the death of a Chinese worker marched on a British-commanded police station in the International Settlement. Among the instigators were KMT students and merchants. With the crowd surging toward the station, the police in their panic fired into the crowd, killing a dozen Chinese and wounding twice that number. At Canton the KMT, with their Russian and CCP strategists, immediately capitalized on the new martyrs by planning what became the Hong Kong-Kwangtung Strike.

Perhaps counting on growing support from throughout China, the Canton group felt ready to test its military muscle. On June 12, 1925, various local KMT military allies, including units under Whampoa Academy's superintendent, Chiang Kai-shek, with support from Canton unions, forced uncooperative Yunnan and Kwangsi troops out of the Pearl River lowlands where they might have collaborated with British Hong Kong. A committee of revolutionaries at Swatow coordinated the action and appointed Chiang commander. Sun Yat-sen had earlier appointed Chiang Canton garrison commander.[5] The student division from Whampoa had fought with spirit under fire and the workers had proven their usefulness. By June 18, the KMT was ready to publicize a protest against the May 30 "massacre" through a massive strike in Kwangtung against firms run by British imperialists, a boycott of all goods from Great Britain and Hong Kong, and a blockade of all intercourse with that crown colony, which had taken over so much of Canton's sea trade. On June 21 some workers in Canton began the walkout from British firms. This matched with the KMT's nationalistic aim to throw out the oppressive and exploitive imperialists and their warlord "running dogs." The events of June 1925 in the Revolutionary Base, with their anti-imperialist and antiwarlord fervor, forecast in the microcosm the great Northern Expedition to come.

Among the first workers brought into the Hong Kong-Kwangtung Strike were those Chinese employed in the foreign concession on Shameen, a sandbar island separated from Canton by narrow Shaki Creek. Where the Shanghai Incident may have erupted from the police's overreaction, the events that followed at Shameen seem less spontaneous. On June 21, British Consul General J. Jamieson noted that Shaki Creek had been blocked by innumerable sampans, and rumors circulated of impending trouble. On the twenty-second, Jamieson warned C.C. Wu, Canton's Foreign Secretary, that he had heard of a planned provocation that would martyr "dare-to-die" youth from the Kwangtung University Student Association. Since the British would defend the concession if attacked, Jamieson said, the individual and collective responsibility would lie with the Canton government. As tension heightened, a French bank transferred its valuables from Shameen onto a French gunboat, one of the several foreign gunboats anchored in the stream. The promotion of the strike depended partly on the support given the KMT by Russia and the "united front" with the CCP. The movement became linked with the ascendancy of Chiang Kai-shek, considered by Western consuls at Canton to be an "uncompromising . . . anti-imperialist and an ardent Bolshevik."[6]

The leadership at Canton responded to Jamieson's warning by requesting permission to stage a protest march *through* Shameen Island, which was summarily refused on June 22. On the morning of the twenty-third, units began to assemble along the Canton Bund for a long parade in protest of the Shanghai Incident and British and Japanese imperialism. Opposite the Shameen concession, the street was cleared and cadet propagandists from Whampoa circulated anti-British leaflets that drew attention to the parade that afternoon. Purposely to avoid antagonizing masses of Chinese nationalists with the sight of gleaming British bayonets, Consul Jamieson set up a defense line that would be out of sight from the Bund. Across the Shameen bridge, Canton police moved into posts at regular intervals and a company of soldiers withdrew from the hot southern sun to stations under the arcades along the parade route.

That afternoon the parade of 60,000 included members of unions, peasant associations, student associations, and soldiers (thus representing the KMT's social ideal of an "all-class" union). The marchers, with placards raised and flags flying, stretched a half mile along the route from east Canton west toward Shameen Island. Most of the parading units barraged Shameen with shouted slogans. What followed may have been the work of a particular KMT element. After one student group, chanting slogans against the British, had passed the Shameen bridge, it was followed by units of Whampoa cadets and KMT army political workers, which halted, drawing a loud response from the paraders and bystanders. Then, according to foreign observers, numbers of the marchers fell out of formation opposite

Shameen, whereupon the Whampoa unit let loose a volley of pistol shots followed by a barrage of rifle bullets that rained on the bridge.

At that point Consul Jamieson and several British officials dashed from their vantage point for better cover. The foreign troops on Shameen returned the fire, which quickly included sniper fire from the building opposite Shameen. After ten minutes of firing, the British passed the order to cease fire and stay under cover. During this exchange, casualties fell on both sides; one French civilian was killed and eight Europeans and Japanese were wounded. Accounts of Chinese casualties varied widely, from the protest from the Canton government's Foreign Secretary C.C. Wu against the death of over 100 Chinese due to unprovoked British, French, and Portuguese "savagery" to the later CCP count of 52 killed and 170 wounded.[7] A high-ranking British naval officer claimed his people had seen only one Chinese fall in the firing.

The official British concensus was that the firing had begun from the Chinese side and that "no doubt they were Russian-trained Whampoa Military Academy soldiers."[8] Some argued that the British did not stand to gain from another bloody incident. However, there were those who had pressed for a firm show that would end Chinese militancy. Since such high Whampoa leaders as General Ho Ying-ch'in accompanied the Whampoa element,[9] it seemed unlikely that the Chinese fired without forethought. Considering the political methods popular at Whampoa and the well-utilized effect of the "massacre" on Kwangtung society, the KMT-CCP strategists may very well deserve the credit for engineering such a successful provocation. These *ts'an-an* (atrocious incidents) ignited the KMT national movement and scattered its sparks far beyond the Revolutionary Base of Kwangtung. Baiting the foreign bear proved so effective in manipulating antiforeign emotions that the device earned a permanent place in the anti-imperialist arsenal of the CCP and, for a time, the KMT Left.

Before the furor over Shameen had abated, Canton's strategists used the welling up of nationalistic emotions to turn the nominal Hong Kong Strike into a reality. From June 23 on, the strike attracted true "mass" support, which during 1925 and 1926 was organized into a structured and responsive body. With their ideological emphasis upon the proletariat and their political training, the CCP apparently saw most clearly the opportunity present and sought to lead the strike, albeit in the *name* of the KMT and the United Front. The CCP Central of Shanghai immediately ordered specialists in organizing to Canton, where thousands of striking workers began to congregate. By July 6, 1925, these CCP members were on hand at a meeting of Hong Kong and Canton union representatives where they were nominated and elected to positions of leadership. The successful takeover of strike leadership was eased greatly by the strategic position of CCP member T'an P'ing-shan, who headed the KMT's Organization Department.

T'an had the authority to request that CCP member Su Chao-cheng, just arrived from Shanghai, take the position of chairman of the new Strike

Committee. Su's credentials were quite correct in the eyes of fellow Marxists and also appealed to the strikers. Son of a Kwangtung peasant, Su had shipped out of Hong Kong as a sailor in 1905, and in Hong Kong he came into contact with nationalistic ideas. Fellow Cantonese sailors drew him into the *T'ung-meng hui* in 1908, after which he is alleged to have joined in the 1911 revolution in Kwangtung. Later Su gravitated to that sanctuary for all sorts of political movements, the Shanghai concessions, where he joined the CCP. His training there and experience in the Seamen's Strike of 1922 in Hong Kong led him to the chairmanship of the Strike Committee at the age of forty.[10] Directing the mushrooming movement demanded diverse abilities—a burden lessened considerably by supervision from the Comintern's ranking man in Canton, Michael Borodin.

The strike apparatus grew to include an 800-man representatives' assembly under the Strike Committee. The Assembly followed the model for democratic centralism and spoke for tens of thousands of striking workers—both unionized and unaffiliated. The Strike Committee was fitted into the CCP's broadest Chinese labor organization, the Chinese National General Labor Union (GLU). Su Chao-cheng's operation included a large headquarters compound, Canton's abandoned East Park amusement center, appropriated by the Labor Department of the KMT. The complex included strikers' dormitories, a school, a prison for "strikebreakers," an armory, and facilities for a multitude of subcommittees. KMT control over Canton was invaluable in institutionalizing the strike. Liao Chung-k'ai, at the apex of the KMT hierarchy, sympathized with the Communist emphasis on social revolution and proved quite helpful in the organizational phase until his assassination in August 1925. In tagging KMT "Rightists" with that crime, those least cooperative with the strike were forced into exile. A military arm strengthened the Strike Committee through a force of over 2,200 uniformed, drilled, and disciplined pickets. Since the pickets implemented the wide range of committee decisions, they strengthened the hand of the strike organization immeasurably.[11]

In the summer of 1925, during the early months of the Hong Kong-Kwangtung Strike, cadets, faculty from Whampoa, and Russian advisors helped to train the pickets into paramilitary units.[12] Divided into corps and detachments, the committee assigned them to wherever it needed muscle. At Canton and smaller ports with Strike Committee branches, the picket units had the authority to seize goods and foods suspected of either originating in, or bound for markets in Hong Kong. Marine pickets patrolled Kwangtung's harbors and rivers. Pickets had the power to confiscate goods on the spot, fine offenders, and arrest violators for imprisonment at the strike headquarters.

Under the committee structure was a legal bureau and a court that tried the apprehended who worked for the British or traded with them. Besides the prison, the headquarters also had offices that examined contraband and then sold the items at its auctions—thus adding to its revenue. Another source of income was the transportation passes, which a committee office could issue to merchants and travelers upon their payment of a fee.[13]

The Hong Kong Strike married several issues into a popular movement. That the cause was popular with the provincial proletariat was evidenced by the 30,000 workers who initially streamed into Canton from various ports and from Hong Kong immediately in response to the Shameen Incident.[14] By the peak of its influence in mid-1926, the strike had attracted thrice that number, many of whom became dependent on the Strike Committee for daily bread and housing in its dormitories.

In accord with Comintern strategy, the strike attacked British capitalism at its East Asian markets. The Comintern, a patron organization to chief Russian advisor Borodin, began to subsidize the Strike Committee shortly after its creation with at least 6,000 rubles arriving monthly in the name of various Russian labor organizations.[15] Probably of greatest significance was the opportunity presented for the CCP to organize the proletariat into a base of political power, a goal that the KMT sought for a time but failed to realize. As a part of the KMT-CCP United Front, the Strike Committee did use its armed pickets in the consolidation of Canton as the seat of the KMT's "National Government," formalized there on July 1, 1925. The activists in Canton proclaimed their structure to be more representative of China than was the shadowy Peking Government, which was manipulated by a succession of warlords who had sold out to various foreign powers. KMT and CCP members claimed to speak for a nationwide constituency by means of party branches. Implementing their national aspirations first meant expansion of political control outward into the Revolutionary Base of Kwangtung. The securing of political and military power in a defensible riverain basin from which all of vast China might be "pacified" followed an ancient pattern suited to the land's divided topography and politics.

The effects of the Hong Kong Strike on the economy were mixed. Canton, temporary capital of the KMT National Government and center of the Revolutionary Base, was significantly dependent on international trade. British shipping and the revenues related to that trade dropped 60 percent the first month of the strike. Although the regime lost this major source of income as commerce declined, the take-over of numerous, small coastal ports where fees could be collected meant new sources of revenue for the KMT National Government.[16] Diverting attention from the loss of trade and related livelihood, the Strike Committee publicized the losses to the British imperialists—allegedly C$1.8 million per day.[17] Another expense for Canton was the sum of at least $80,000 monthly in maintenance funds that the KMT doled out to the Strike Committee.[18]

During the fall of 1925, the pickets and groups of strikers aided in the offensive led by the NRA against local militarist Ch'en Chiung-ming throughout the East River area of Kwangtung. At that time strikers, union members, and peasant associations organized by the CCP supported the fighting potential of the KMT's military arm by carrying its supplies and weapons, providing medical services, and propagandizing in newly conquered areas.[19] The mass organization certainly gave the NRA greater mobility than Ch'en Chiung-ming possessed, and thus speeded the taking of Huichou and made possible the close pursuit of Ch'en's retreat. Less than one year later, Chiang Kai-shek gave a speech on this Eastern Expedition in which he acknowledged that his forces had

> . . . achieved victory quickly with the help of peasants and workers. From my past experience I realize the benefit of the cooperation of peasants and workers with the revolutionary army. . . . if the soldiers of an army are not friendly to the people, that army will unquestionably be defeated.[20]

The KMT's military consolidation of Kwangtung as the Revolutionary Base directly benefited the CCP and its Hong Kong Strike apparatus. Strikers fanned out *behind* the victorious NRA, set up branches of the strike organization, and stationed pickets to enforce the anti-British boycott. By the completion of the Eastern Expedition of the fall of 1925, branches functioned from the port of Swatow in easternmost Kwangtung through to Peihai on the Gulf of Tonkin. Brigades of 200 pickets were stationed at small ports throughout the Pearl River estuary, and smaller units saw duty at coastal towns and on Hainan Island. In the same capacity, a small fleet of boats patrolled the Kwangtung coast hunting for strikebreaking smugglers.[21]

During the consolidation of the Revolutionary Base in Kwangtung, both the KMT and the CCP benefited from the United Front and from the expansion of the mass organization.

CHAPTER 2

Human Resources

'O

When the KMT established on July 1, 1925, its "National Government" in opposition to Peking, it counted on several sources of power, which added up to an increasingly viable operation. Less dramatic than the Hong Kong Strike but vitally important were the *jen ts'ai*, men of ability, who came to Canton to help build a new China. Most noticeable among these were students returned from abroad with their newly acquired modern economic and political know-how. These urban elites were the rationalizers and systematizers who the KMT believed could build a modern national system. An example of the new technocrat was T.V. Soong whose role in creating a fiscal foundation was crucial.

He was born into the energetic Soong merchant family. Educated at Shanghai's mission-run St. John's College and then at Harvard in business administration, Soong then had gained experience by working for three years at the large International Banking Corporation of New York. He returned from New York to serve Sun Yat-sen as an English secretary and financial advisor.[1] Soong's credentials were enhanced by the family tie to Sun Yat-sen's wife Soong Ch'ing-ling, also T.V.'s sister. Against nepotism as an evil of Chinese ways, Sun had hesitated in 1924 to appoint his talented brother-in-law to any post higher than that of head of Canton's Central Bank. That post, however, for Soong at the age of thirty-four was a demanding and rewarding challenge.

The Central Bank soon exemplified to practical Chinese observers the soundness of the national revolutionary movement. Up to that point regional militarists, like Wu P'ei-fu, with no education in rationalized finances solved financial problems by carting away the silver reserves of banks in their newly conquered territories. Sun Ch'uan-fang in the southeast and Chang Tso-lin in the northeast forced merchants to accept payments in overissued scrip. In contrast, at Canton the Central Bank was accumulating one of the largest silver reserves of any official bank in China of the 1920s. Backed by these reserves, Canton's currency and fiscal integrity became increasingly respected by the treaty port elites. Carefully husbanded capital met payroll needs and underwrote the military machine that later was to roll north.

Soong accepted appointment as Finance Minister in the new National Government in September 1925. Backed by the Party and its army, the Finance Minister revamped and collected taxes with vigor and efficiency. The struggle to pull China back together again and oust the foreign powers could not be waged on antiforeign rhetoric or ideology alone. The Boxer's attempt had proven this earlier. Soong and other technocrats helped provide a material base for the revolution. His rationalized procedures greatly curtailed traditional "squeeze" and official profiteering, thereby more than quadrupling Canton's revenue from about C$800,000 for July 1925 to C$3,616,000 for October of that year.[2]

The selection of Kwangtung as a base for a national revolution was not surprising in that the city of Canton faced the sea, and the Cantonese had been among the first Chinese drawn into the trade-born currents of the modern world of nation states. According to reserved northerners, the Cantonese were considered rather impetuous and pushy, but certainly innovative. With the environs secure under the KMT military, the Party leaders moved the old city toward modernization. Other examples of the modern elite at Canton who aided the KMT would be the mayors who administered the municipal government in 1925 and 1926—Sun Fo, only son of Sun Yat-sen, and C.C. Wu (Wu Ch'ao-ch'u).

Sun Fo had studied municipal administration at Columbia University where he received a master's degree in 1917 following his undergraduate work at the University of California.[3] C.C. Wu was another returned student who served first as Sun Fo's aide and then as mayor. Wu was the son of the famous diplomat and scholar, Wu T'ing-fang, and had been educated first in Washington, D.C., and then at Harvard. He had also earned a law degree in London in 1911. At twenty-six, quite familiar with the West, Wu gained experience with the Peking Government's Foreign Ministry and then with the Constitutional Drafting Committee. Joining Sun Yat-sen's movement in 1917, Wu participated as one of Canton's representatives at the frustrating Versailles Peace Conference where the Western powers sold out China to an imperious Japan. By his mid-thirties Wu had served as Canton's Vice-Minister and then full Minister of Foreign Affairs.[4]

Both Sun and Wu exemplified the energetic returned student eager to apply his modern training to China's pressing needs. They were also sons of revolutionaries, the postrevolutionary generation coming into its own.

However, as modern as they seemed, their status was also dependent to some extent on their family ties. Sun Fo promoted razing Canton's ancient city walls and replacing them with paved boulevards despite considerable resistance from the residents. However, when property values rose along the new, wider thoroughfares, burghers came with petitions to widen other ancient, narrow streets. Once securely in power in Canton, such KMT leaders promoted programs for sanitation, road construction, flood control, dredging Canton's waterways, social reform, and labor unionization. All these programs for urban modernization had to share a limited budget dominated by the needs of the expanding Party Army. Thus, it was mandatory that the leadership rationalize Canton's finances, planning monthly expenditures and accounting for municipal revenues through both stringent daily and monthly audits.[5] The experts with national aspirations who ran Canton could not afford the luxury of "squeeze." These young leaders of Canton typified the modern elite of the treaty ports who were attracted to Canton by its aura of hope and accomplishment. Elsewhere in China hung the pall of frustration permeated by stagnation and regressive warlord leadership, which ignored modern skills and slowed China's return to unity and an ability to defend herself. Inland from the modern ports were rural problems that were to test severely the new capabilities of the modern urban leaders—both KMT and CCP.

By 1925 much of the rapid rate of change at Canton could be traced to the tighter organization of the KMT after its restructuring and rationalization along Russian lines. "Democratic centralism" apparently supplied the political cohesion that Sun Yat-sen had found lacking. During China's disappointing experiments with Western-style parliamentary democracy after the Revolution of 1911, Sun had observed that Chinese society was like a dish of sand—it needed something to bond it into a solid entity. Earlier KMT efforts at gathering popular support through labor unions had been slowed by warlord suppression and lack of coherent issues and ideology. After 1923, with the incorporation of Comintern experts and Chinese Communist Party organizers trained in organizational technique, the KMT labor movement expanded at a faster pace.[6]

In Kwangtung, the unionization of labor turned from the rather limited gathering in of skilled workers to one based on a broader industry-wide appeal. In Canton's new National Government, the organizers created departments that dealt with workers, peasants, women, merchants, and soldiers. Significantly, the overseas Chinese, who had been long-time supporters of the revolutionary movement and the KMT, rated a separate department. The talent of the returned students and the modern-educated urban elite were very much in evidence within these agencies.

Heading the Workers' and Peasants' departments from late 1925 until his departure on the Northern Expedition in mid-1926 was Ch'en Kung-po. Although earlier an associate of the new CCP at Peking University, Ch'en apparently severed formal ties with that party before leaving China to enroll at Columbia University as a student of economics. His chosen field typified the emphasis placed by modern Chinese students upon the study of *practical* fields that would elevate China materially. Having earned a Ph.D., he joined the ranks of returned students when he came back to Canton following Sun Yat-sen's death.[7] There he became a protégé of Russian-oriented Liao Chung-k'ai and Wang Ching-wei, both closely associated with Sun and counseled by Michael Borodin of the Comintern.[8] Ch'en and his associates in the KMT and CCP spurred on the organization of workers in Canton by means of strikes, interunion conflicts, and demands for higher wages. This approach was a cause of intraparty dispute since it strained the KMT theory of a "union of classes," which stressed in some degree harmony between workers and their employers.

In the coming contest for China with the warlords, military leadership was to be crucial and, here again, the modern elites dominated Canton's military. Sun Yat-sen and other Western-influenced followers had learned well, as they endured their odyssey of exile, that democratic institutions were quite vulnerable and defenseless in China, and that military power was needed if they were to grow. The military system of the KMT also emulated Russian models and received daily direction from hundreds of Russian military advisors assigned to Canton. The success of the Red Army during Russia's civil war was proof that an army could mean life and death to political power.

The Party Army of the KMT, as it was first called, began to show promise in 1924 almost immediately after the creation of the officer's academy at Whampoa, across the river from Canton. The graduates, cadets, and their enlisted trainees served as the model for an expanding number of "armies" led by militarists allied with the KMT movement. This nucleus was known also as the Student Army through its student membership and ties with the Whampoa Academy,[9] and then as the First Army when the KMT began to gather military allies as newly numbered "armies" that were integrated into the National Revolutionary Army of the Northern Expedition. However, only the First Army could be labeled a truly Kuomintang army. Initially it had been formed by the KMT's Military Council from units and regiments of Whampoa cadets; but by late 1925 preparatory branch academies at Huichou and Ch'aochou, Kwangtung, also fed into the First Army, and KMT agents recruited volunteers in Shanghai and other cities.

Manifesting the KMT's enthusiasm for Whampoa and the Party Army was the use of high Party leaders as instructors in academy courses. Chairman Wang Ching-wei taught Party history, Hu Han-min taught the Three Peoples' Principles, Finance Minister Liao Chung-k'ai was the administrator, and Chiang Kai-shek—Sun's closest military follower—was the superintendent of the academy. The aim of the academy was to forge a zealous, politically indoctrinated force loyal to Sun's ideals and obedient to Party discipline. Since it was to serve the new Chinese nation, the Party strove to recruit for its army on a nation-wide scale.

These efforts in army recruitment also reflected the rationalized, organized approach of the young leadership. Sun had set up a recruiting committee in 1923 and then committee branches, the first of which was in that sanctuary of revolutionary subversion, the foreign enclave of Shanghai. Ch'en Kuo-fu headed the Shanghai operations,[10] which drew in the first cadet recruits not only from the surrounding Kiangsu, Anhui, and Chekiang areas, but, surprisingly, twice as many from upriver in the Hunan-Kiangsi region.[11]

Farther north, recruiting was carried on through Party branch headquarters, such as the one in Peking where Lu Yu-yü contacted fellow Shantung provincials studying in various universities in the metropolis.[12] Even Mongolian, Tibetan, and Thai party members brought in army recruits. Thus the national scope of the movement proved more attractive to potential recruits than did the regional orientation of its opponents. The inclusion of various ethnic elements also lived up to Sun's ideal of integrating non-Chinese minority groups in the nation-to-be.

The success in recruiting both for the KMT's civilian and military organizations involved capturing the imaginations of the young students of Chinese middle schools and universities. The propagandizing by teachers and professors won over many; others read of the movement in the writings of sympathetic or partisan journalists.[13] Some Whampoa recruits gave Shanghai newspapers as their addresses in Shanghai.

The minds of many Chinese intellectuals were ripe for the nationalistic movement and KMT leadership. Modern colleges and universities had attracted the ambitious youth of a society in a state of degeneration. Public institutions, however, faced hard times as warlord administrations cut educational funds in order to pay military expenditures. At one point in the mid-twenties, Ts'ai Yüan-p'ei, president of prestigious Peking University, resigned over cuts in funding, and the nonpayment of coal bills nearly closed the institution. Faculties were underpaid and overburdened. The expanding student bodies, crammed into shoddy dormitories, seethed with discontent and frustration. Among the graduates, even the elite found their talents wasted in warlord bureaucracies or in the drudgery of translating for arrogant foreigners, or they were unemployed. The premodern, largely rural, economy of China could not absorb the skills of these graduates, a problem common to developing nations anywhere, but exacerbated by the effects of foreign economic exploitation in China. Naturally, many of these educated youths found themselves in agreement with the KMT's goals of urban modernization.

Under the influence of KMT educators, some universities became centers of the national revolutionary movement. Shanghai University's president and Party faithful, Yü Yu-jen, brought partisan intellectuals into the faculty and furthered recruitment of students for Whampoa and the movement in Canton.[14] As modern as the movement may have appeared, its recruitment practices incorporated the timeless Chinese awareness of provincial ties. President Yü at Shanghai recruited students and youth from his native Shensi, just as some of those bound for Canton included students recruited by Mao Tse-tung entirely from his home province of Hunan. Other collaborators at Shanghai University included such famous Communists as Ch'en Tu-hsiu and Ch'ü Ch'iu-pai in the Sociology Department.[15]

The partisan newspaper *Min-kuo jih-pao* [Republic daily] certainly aided the work of Ch'en Kuo-fu's recruiting agency in Shanghai. The involvement of the press in Chinese politics was typified by its editor, Yeh Ch'u-ts'ang, who in 1925 was concurrently an administrator of the KMT-oriented Shanghai University, a member of the Party's Shanghai Executive Committee, and a member of the Central Executive Committee (CEC) at Canton.[16] Yeh's ties reveal the common interaction in national movements among members of the press, universities, and political parties.

Thus, a variety of KMT-allied bodies in the Shanghai area gathered Party recruits and channeled the young talent of the vast Yangtze basin into Ch'en Kuo-fu's recruiting agency, which then arranged for temporary lodging, stipends, and transportation to Canton. Northern Chinese, recruited through Party agencies in Peking, slipped past warlord police and out through the foreign concessions at Tientsin where they boarded Russian steamers, most of them bound for Canton via a screening process at the Shanghai office.[17] Most of the zealous young modern elite went to officer training at Whampoa from educational institutions. Of those from lower socioeconomic levels who had flocked to Shanghai seeking any manner of employment, some were attracted by the NRA's promise of regular meals and pay, as well as rapid promotions up through its ranks. Such operations at Shanghai processed over 5,000 recruits during 1925, the year preceding the Northern Expedition. There, too, the financial stability of Canton counted since each recruit cost the agency an average of C$21 for a steamship ticket, pocket money, and canned rations for the voyage, in addition to the bribes to local warlord officials and KMT informants.[18]

As vital as was recruiting work outside Kwangtung, some in the KMT who promoted a quick commencement of the Northern Expedition to reunite China could not wait for the trickle of individual volunteers to fill out the numbers needed in the Party's military system. The decision was made to attract wholesale defections of units and to include defeated troops into KMT ranks. Earlier, in 1924, a KMT force had defeated near Canton a "merchant corps," which was partially absorbed, as were units of Ch'en Chiung-ming and later the Yunnan-Kwangsi soldiers of the warlords Liu Chen-huan and .Yang Hsi-min, who were defeated in June 1925. These were grouped into the Second Division of the First or Party Army.[19] Thus, even within the purest partisan military unit, there were elements that had entered without politically correct motives. More defeated troops had swelled the ranks in October 1925 after the victories of the Second Eastern Expedition against Ch'en Chiung-ming and the conquest of southern Kwangtung. The KMT military leadership had come to feel that the sheer force of numbers would be crucial to success (an attitude common in Chinese armies throughout history). The inclusion of these forces would also deprive an opponent from fielding them against the NRA.

At Whampoa this concern with moving forward the start of the Northern Expedition caused Chiang to order that the academy's entrance requirements be lowered, if necessary, to enroll enough officer candidates. The Whampoa graduates were in great demand to help indoctrinate and train the influx of newcomers, a task that continued into 1928. By late 1925, having drawn from various sources of soldiery, the KMT's First Army had grown to a force of over 10,000, dominated by Whampoa's superintendent, Chiang Kai-shek.[20] Supporting this military army were other sources of KMT strength—political and administrative leadership, rationalized organization, and nation-wide efforts. The priority given to military means in the coming struggle for national power was evidenced in the KMT budget, the lion's share of which in 1925 and 1926 went into military buildup. Even in Kwangtung, the KMT military had been vital in consolidating the province as the Revolutionary Base.

RUSSIAN AID

This expanding demand on the Party coffers to cover military expenditures heavily strained the resources of a single province. KMT resources had to cover the arms, ammunition, clothing, food, transportation, salaries, and a variety of equipment (even to aircraft) that made for a relatively modern fighting force. Expenditures stretched to the limit the innovative talents and efficiency of the Finance Ministry's tax collectors. Overseas Chinese contributed to meet a part of the need. Despite their efforts, the young KMT administrators could not eliminate a partial dependence on foreign aid. Sun Yat-sen had been forced to solve this need earlier, first by seeking aid from the West, the United States in particular,[21] and then by taking from Russia what was offered through the Comintern. The extent of this aid from 1924 to the break in KMT-Russian relations in 1927 is still open to speculation. Neither the KMT nor Kremlin archives on this period are available. The USSR is understandably reluctant to divulge its role in the KMT's national revolution—the leadership of which it sought hard after but lost. Even during the alliance, Russia was discreet in sending aid to Canton so as not to provoke the anti-Communist warlords with which Russia was dealing, nor to incur a blockade of such aid by anti-Communist powers.

In October 1926, when Russian Ambassador L.M. Karakhan was pressed on the matter by Western reporters, he retorted that Canton had received ". . . not one ruble! . . . It is all talk!"[22] However, Karakhan's military attaché had earlier informed V. Galen (also known as Bluecher or Blyukher), the chief Russian military advisor at Canton, that the USSR had from 1924 to December 1925 delivered on credit to the KMT materiel valued at 2 million rubles.[23] Thus, indeed, Canton may not have received any *rubles*. Contemporary Western observers in their anxiety over the revolutionary movement probably exaggerated Russia's material involvement in it. Just months before the July 1926 launching of the Northern Expedition, the foreign press in the treaty ports alleged that Russian aid totaled $40 million, including $12 million credit to back Canton's Central Bank.[24] The account admitted, however, that "so far there are no exact figures in Kuomintang journals." Part of this materiel aid was in the form of arms and ammunition *sold* on credit, the quality of which has been criticized by surviving KMT members. A similar credit arrangement between

Russia and Canton allowed Cantonese purchase of oil at a low price; Canton's National Government in turn retailed the oil products as a profitable monopoly.[25] The Russian aid gave Borodin, as head of the Russian advisory mission, considerable leverage in influencing KMT decision-making.

The advisory effort was invaluable during and after the creation of Canton's self-proclaimed National Government, formally instituted on July 1, 1925. In 1925 there were as many as 1,000 Russians in Kwangtung advising the KMT on programs that ranged from the organizing and leading of mass organizations to the teaching of aviation. Earlier, in 1923, Sun Yat-sen had dispatched Chiang Kai-shek to Russia to evaluate the Russian military system, after which Chiang requested that Moscow assign as an advisor to the KMT General Galen, who became for a time the head of the military and technical advisory effort.[26] Between Chiang and Galen, Chiang's junior by two years, there developed mutual respect and a valuable rapport.[27] In their capacity as advisors and instructors at the Whampoa Academy, Galen and other Russians undoubtedly raised the military standards of both the academy and the expanding KMT military establishment.[28] Ironically, that improved force was to be used within less than four years to prevent CCP dominance.

As the leader of the mission to Canton, Moscow had appointed Michael Borodin—an agent with a fascinating background in international intrigue and revolutionary activity on both sides of the Atlantic. Specifically, Borodin provided expertise in the organization of the masses, in propaganda, political work in the military, and the development of the Hong Kong Strike apparatus.[29] Madame Borodin, an American, assisted in the active women's movement of the KMT. The two "universities" in Moscow created to train selected Chinese students in political technique and Marxist history contributed to Canton's pool of human resources.[30] Borodin's presence at Canton also represented Russia's support to Canton's National Government, a psychological and diplomatic asset for the KMT. Another intangible aid was the use of official Russian steamers in transporting KMT agents and recruits back and forth along the China coast in diplomatic immunity.[31]

Any listing of the resources available at Canton must include Canton's arsenal. Although the KMT had to purchase arms and munitions abroad, in addition to the Soviet military aid it received, the Canton regime hoped to become self-sufficient. In the mid-twenties, the leaders of the various opposition regional regimes centered their armies around their arsenals. In 1925 the Canton Arsenal was one of the five major arms producers in China. Many of the arsenals could be traced back to the self-strengthening efforts of the late Ch'ing restoration leaders. Rebuilt in 1921 to incorporate new U.S. machinery, the Canton Arsenal publicly claimed to produce 700,000 bullets and 750 rifles monthly, but this was still obviously inadequate to meet the needs of a proliferating NRA seeking to conquer all the opposing warlords of China.[32]

The arsenal, too, gained from the KMT's nation-wide recruiting efforts.

Ch'en Kuo-fu's Shanghai agency helped by hiring scarce experts, who worked alongside Russian advisors in the production of small field cannon and trench mortar, weapons which Canton was able to produce in limited numbers by 1925.[33] These middle-range weapons were well suited to the NRA's operations in the rugged ranges of South China, where weapons had to be carried by coolies along footpaths to circumvent the heavy firepower of the warlords' railroad cannon in the valleys. Restricted as the KMT was to its Revolutionary Base in Kwangtung, it lacked the resources to expand the production of the arsenal to the point of self-sufficiency.

To the north in Hupei, Wu P'ei-fu's British-patronized regime depended on its Hanyang Arsenal, which boasted an output triple that of Canton's.[34] In far-off Manchuria, Chang Tso-lin's Mukden arms industry also flourished, supported in part by Japanese aid. By 1926, the dream of self-sufficiency in armaments first drew the attention of Chiang and other promoters of national military reunification to Wuhan's Hanyang Arsenal and to the great Kiangnan Arsenal of Shanghai downriver. Although observers have made a strong case for Chiang's attraction to Shanghai's banks, the large arsenals there and at Nanking were equally prized.

CHAPTER 3

The KMT Military:
Party Army, Confederation, or Hegemony?

Although the Whampoa Academy had been created to provide the nucleus for the Party Army, Sun Yat-sen and some of his disciples concluded that the KMT needed military muscle more quickly than could be generated solely from the new academy. In the past, the conquest of China's disintegrated vastness forced dynastic founders to depend on alliances of military forces. For the same reason, the Canton regime sought to gather military allies outside the Revolutionary Base. In the early 1920s Sun had allied himself with Ch'en Chiung-ming and other southern militarists, and after Sun's death the gathering in of military allies accelerated. The only element spiritually and materially tied to the KMT was the First Army, or Party Army. In 1925, after the establishment of the KMT's National Government at Canton, its heterogeneous military system proliferated.

On August 26, 1925, four separate provincial forces, each built around an individual leader, joined with the Party Army under the new name of the National Revolutionary Army. At this time the Party Army was officially numbered the First Army, and the other units each received a number as an "army." These first four allied armies and their leaders exemplify the diversity that characterized the KMT military camp at this time. The stories of these commanders are as complex as the era and will be outlined only briefly.

The Second Army, a force of about 15,000 Hunanese, joined the NRA through a KMT stalwart—T'an Yen-k'ai. At the age of forty-nine in 1925,

T'an's career reflected China's experience of the past half century. He had entered the Ch'ing bureaucracy through the Imperial Examinations as a *chin-shih* degree holder and was appointed a compiler in the Hanlin Academy. Although his upward mobility would have been prohibited under a strong dynasty, T'an managed to rise in his own province, a sign of the decline in Peking's authority. Pressed by reformers, the Ch'ing conceded to the formation of provincial assemblies in 1909, and in 1910 T'an Yen-k'ai became chairman of the new Hunan Provincial Assembly. It was in this position that he came under KMT influence. After the 1911 revolution, T'an stayed on in his home province where he led an armed revolt against Yüan Shih-k'ai when Yüan attempted to become the new monarch of the province. By 1918 T'an was the civil-military governor of Hunan in control of a Hunan militia,[1] and a proponent of provincial autonomy within a federation—as was Mao Tse-tung in the early 1920s.[2]

When ousted by stronger northern military forces, T'an and his troops gravitated across the border into Kwangtung to join with Sun Yat-sen. Although, in 1922, T'an had supported Sun in vain against the "rebellion" of Ch'en Chiung-ming, his military potential and political prestige were such that he soon was elected to the KMT's Central Executive Committee. At this time, he managed to incorporate into his force a defeated Hunanese unit. By the time his troops became the Second Army, T'an had been appointed to the KMT's high-level Political and Military councils.[3] In late 1924 when Sun Yat-sen went to Peking to seek cooperation from the northern militarists, T'an attempted a supportive campaign to conquer Kiangsi and Hunan, but failed.[4]

The Third Army, like the Second and most of the other corps in China, was composed of fellow provincials—in this case from Yunnan. As was endemic in China, provincialism had risen while central authority disintegrated. Topography, self-sufficiency, dialects—all had played a role in the breaking apart of China; but then, in 1925, it was, ironically, provincial armies that helped to recentralize politics at the expense of the provinces. The Yunnanese of the Third Army took orders from Chu P'ei-teh, and included some who defected to the KMT during its victories in Kwangtung in mid-1925. Others had been absorbed into the corps after their defeat in June.[5] Chu had been educated at the Yunnan Military Academy and then had gone on to a command in the provincial military system. Chu's loyalty to Sun had been demonstrated when he brought Yunnanese troops to Sun's aid during the struggle with Ch'en Chiung-ming. Considered reliable, Chu rose in status through his appointment as commander to the Third Army and membership in the Party's Central Executive Committee.

A Kwangtung force controlled by Li Chi-shen became the Fourth Army. Favoring Li were his connections with Kwangsi military leaders Li Tsung-jen and Huang Shao-hsiung, as well as his continuing membership in the KMT and his experience as dean of Military Instruction at Whampoa Academy.[6] When, in late 1925, the Hong Kong Strike organization was temporarily cut back, some strikers were transferred to the Fourth Army. Later in March 1926 when Chiang cleared Communists from the First

Army and the academy, these, too, found themselves enrolled under Li's supervision. Perhaps it was due to Li's reliability in the eyes of Chiang that the Fourth Army in both cases received the CCP elements. Li's chief of staff was Yeh T'ing, destined to become a founder of the future Red Army, who gained command of his Independent Regiment in the Fourth Army, a unit made up primarily of ex-Hong Kong strikers.[7] Yeh, a Kwangtung native, had graduated from the prestigious Paoting Military Academy; he later served with Sun Yat-sen's guards at Canton in 1922, and then went to Moscow to study in 1924. While at the University for the Toiling Workers of the East and at a military school, Yeh joined the Chinese Communist Party. Upon Yeh's return to Canton, at the age of twenty-seven, he was appointed Li Chi-sen's chief of staff.[8] The Fourth Army saw early and continuous action in the Northern Expedition, and Yeh's regiment has been immortalized in CCP histories as part of the vanguard of the future Red Army.

The Fifth Army of the NRA was commanded by Li Fu-lin, a Cantonese with experience as an anti-Manchu "bandit" leader. Li joined the *T'ung-meng hui* in 1908, and participated in the abortive revolt preceding the Revolution of 1911. In the postrevolutionary political flux, he gathered together a force of Fukienese and some Cantonese that operated in the Pearl River delta.[9] Li also had ties with a non-KMT Merchant Corps, which made him suspect in the eyes of the Russian advisors of 1925.[10] By that year, although Li's Fifth Army ranked as the largest "army" in the NRA, he had managed to block the entry into it of Russian advisors and the KMT's required Party Representatives. It was not until six months after the incorporation of the Fifth Army that Li accepted a Party Representative of his choice who was to set up the system of Political Departments. In March 1926, the KMT appointed as Party Representative to the Fifth Army Li Lang-ju, a Cantonese merchant who dealt in medicines.[11] With Li Fu-lin's influence centered on Honan Island across from Canton, the Fifth Army was probably most useful to the Canton regime as a means of controlling the rapacious bandits and pirates of the estuary and nearby coast.

As KMT victories expanded Party control in Kwangtung, the NRA added defeated and defected forces. On November 14, 1925, the Sixth Army, made up of Hunanese, was reorganized from forces defeated in the Second Eastern Expedition and put under the command of a fellow provincial, Ch'eng Ch'ien.[12] Ch'eng, trained in his native province's Hunan Military Service School, had also studied in Japan. In 1916 he fought with the Hunan militia against Yüan Shih-k'ai.[13] From 1923 on, Ch'eng was an officer in Sun Yat-sen's General Military Headquarters; when appointed to head the Sixth Army he was forty-three.[14]

The incorporation of a force of 30,000 Kwangsi troops as the Seventh Army in February 1926 was but a part of the broader strategy of bringing neighboring Kwangsi into the KMT fold. By then, Chiang Kai-shek was emerging as the KMT's leading military man and, as he became less and less compliant to the influence of Borodin and the CCP, they felt the KMT-CCP alliance to be threatened. By the time Borodin discreetly left

Canton in early February, the CCP had begun spreading rumors that Chiang was dealing with the northern warlords and the Japanese.[15]

Chiang's rise forced the KMT and their allies to a decision on the military reunification of China, which Chiang fervently promoted. Chiang Kai-shek had pushed the expansion of the KMT's military "confederation" and the centralization of authority necessary to integrate such a heterogeneous force for the conquest of China. In mid-February, agents of the Kwangsi military leaders, Li Tsung-jen, Huang Shao-hsiung, and Pai Ch'ung-hsi, negotiated with Canton, as did T'ang Sheng-chih who led a division in nearby southern Hunan.[16] An important aspect of the bargaining was the amount of provincial autonomy the KMT could promise to potential military governors.

This expansion of KMT influence outside Kwantung favored Chiang since it added to his military machine and forced the Party to commit its support to a northern expedition in the near future. Since the northern warlords would respond defensively, Chiang and those who wanted to speed up the timetable for moving north out of the Revolutionary Base also sought in February 1926 to bring the Hong Kong Strike under closer control so as not to prejudice production of goods necessary for the military campaign. On the twenty-fourth, the same day that the National Government set up a committee for the unification of Kwangsi and Kwangtung, Chiang asked the CEC to ". . . decide as soon as possible the matter of plans for the Northern Expedition and whether to assist the Kuominchün [Feng Yü-hsiang's army] in the northwest."[17]

National Government chairman Wang Ching-wei apparently went to Kwangsi to represent Canton in the negotiation to bring that province into the KMT orbit. To the Kwangsi generals, Wang promised military and financial aid as an incentive for the joining of the two provinces. The Provincial Government Committee, required by KMT practices, that was to administer Kwangsi was to be a compromise between provincial autonomy and centralization under KMT's National Government. This willingness on the part of Canton to compromise with provincial autonomists set a precedent for dealings with provincial leaders later—a policy born of exigency but inconsistent with the goals of nationalization. Thus, the committee membership included two civilian officials, three KMT generals, and three Kwangsi generals (Li, Pai, and Huang). The agreement made Canton predominant in all judicial, diplomatic, and financial affairs. For Canton and especially for Chiang, there were the advantages of increased military potential, security from a Kwangsi attack, and through Li and Pai a wider range of possible connections with Paoting classmates, such as T'ang Sheng-chih in Hunan.[18] The unification of the two provinces reached formalization on March 15, 1926, when Huang Shao-hsiung took an oath of office as a member of the National Government Committee.[19]

Shortly after the incorporation of the Seventh Army of Kwangsi, agents of the KMT met with T'ang Sheng-chih, whose three brigades in southern Hunan were supposedly allied with Wu P'ei-fu. Since T'ang's units made him the strongest single elment in the four-division Hunan Army under

Wu's governor Chao Heng-t'i, he was a valuable point of entry for Canton into Hunan—and thus to the Yangtze basin. Politics in Hunan were rather confused, as were warlord politics elsewhere, in that Governor Chao held the province through Wu, the overlord of Central China, but local military power was divided between T'ang's Fourth Division and the Third Division of his provincial rival, Yeh K'ai-hsin.[20] Chao hoped to centralize provincial affairs under his own direct control.

The KMT's contact with T'ang exemplifies the advantages in a nationwide membership combined with the traditional personal ties within the Party. Canton assigned Liu Wen-tao, like T'ang a Hunanese graduate of Paoting, to be special emissary between the Party and T'ang. Their negotiations were further eased by other Paoting alumni, Li Tsung-jen and Pai Ch'ung-hsi.[21] By February 18, 1926, T'ang's anxieties over his ambitious superior, Governor Chao Heng-t'i, as well as some interest in the National Revolution, prompted him to send his agents to Canton to discuss terms.[22] By the time that T'ang forced Governor Chao to retreat from Changsha, the Hunan capital, to Hankow in Hupei on February 24, the affiliation with Canton must have been completed. On the same day, Chiang ordered plans for the Northern Expedition, and Canton set up the committee to unite Kwangsi with Kwangtung.[23] Continuing to expand his foothold in Hunan, T'ang attacked rival General Yeh K'ai-hsin at Yüehchou on the twenty-eighth. When he suffered reverses against Yeh in early March 1926 it was to the KMT that T'ang telegraphed for reinforcements.[24] In particular T'ang appealed to T'an Yen-k'ai's Second Army—the Hunanese element in the NRA—in a tactic intended to smooth over future rivalry in Hunan.

In order to fill T'ang's request for aid, the KMT not only had to be willing to commit its resources in Hunan, but also to open hostilities against Hunan's overlord, Wu P'ei-fu. In early March, the KMT had not so committed its support, nor had T'ang formally submitted to Canton's authority in Hunan. At that point, within the KMT, the factions split over the Northern Expedition and decision-making was slowed. The CCP, under Russian direction and supported by some KMT Leftists, opposed placing national reunification ahead of local social revolution. Chiang's March 20 coup checked the CCP and others opposed to the expedition and reopened the way toward a final agreement between Canton and T'ang in Hunan. That coup will be outlined later. Within but a few days, on March 25, T'ang accepted the position of acting governor of Hunan from supporters in Hunan's Provincial Assembly. It was not until early June, when Canton had fulfilled its earlier promise of providing reinforcements, that he finalized his alliance with the KMT. Upon this accomplishment, T'ang exchanged the title of commander of a division for commander of the NRA's Eighth Army, the KMT's reward for defection. T'ang was also able to rise in the Hunan political structure from acting governor and head of the provincial Department of the Interior to the provisional governor of Hunan through the authority of the KMT's National Government at Canton.[25]

In late March 1926, T'ang commenced an attack against Yüehchou,

Hunan, in the name of the KMT, an action that committed Canton in Central China and pushed the Party to launch the Northern Expedition. At that time the KMT opened its campaign of propaganda against Wu P'ei-fu. In Hunan his subordinates warned Wu to reinforce his southern flank against the KMT; however, the KMT was able to take advantage of Wu's absence from Hunan-Hupei and his preoccupation with an on-going struggle in North China.

CHAPTER 4
Centralization of Canton's Power

By the time of the Northern Expedition, Chiang Kai-shek, its commander-in-chief, had gathered considerable power into his own hands—much more than Sun Yat-sen had ever been able to realize. This had been a result partly of the emergency nature of the war on which they were about to embark, partly due to the restructuring of the KMT, which Sun had begun, and partly because of Chiang's vision of the role of a Chinese leader. Prior to his death early in 1925, Sun Yat-sen had concluded that the Anglo-American style of democracy could not be transplanted whole to the China of the 1920s and had collaborated with the Russian Marxists in concentrating KMT powers, both political and military, for the duration of an indefinite phase of "party tutelage," or democratic centralism. To pull China back together would demand tremendous power—in all the military and political shadings of its meaning. The creation of the Whampoa Academy and a Party Army were parts of this program. The Russian model, in whose image both the KMT and CCP were created, included Party control of the military through a network of Party Representatives in Political Departments attached to all military units from army down to company size. Although Chiang disliked aspects of the Russian system he had observed in Moscow in 1923, in agreement with the Russian advisors he had stated that "if the army is not to become a warlord army it must first of all become the army of the Party."[1] Beginning with the establishment of Whampoa, the Party's Central Executive Committee agreed that a Party Representative was to countersign all orders and regulations within military units.[2]

Training in discipline was a means of reinforcing the centralization of authority. When the expedition did finally move north, the behavior of the NRA soldiers contrasted with the less-disciplined troops of the opponents. Belief in the cause of nationalism and hope for social betterment certainly strengthened discipline and morale. Discipline was further stiffened when Canton proclaimed the Joint Responsibility Law in January 1925. Under this law, a commanding officer and his unit's Party Representative could be executed if they withdrew their unit from battle without an order to do so. If subordinates and their units deserted their commanding officer, the subordinates could be executed. The allied armies as well as the "pure" First Army came under this discipline and influence of the head of the NRA.

In 1925, the year preceding the Northern Expedition, the contenders for Party leadership worked to centralize KMT authority. If there was to be a military reunification of China, as a military man Chiang's credentials were advantageous. Not only had Chiang been singled out by Sun to head the Whampoa system, but Chiang had been trained before the 1911 revolution at Tokyo's Shikan Gakko (Army Officers' Academy). By mid-1925, the victories in the Second Eastern Expedition throughout Kwangtung against the traitorous Ch'en Chiung-ming had given Chiang experience and yielded prestige for his cadets. Still threatened by the Yunnan and Kwangsi forces camped about Canton, the Party Headquarters had appointed Chiang as garrison commander of Canton on June 12, 1925. The next day Chiang's troops and associated units had attacked and defeated their opponents, who were then disarmed and incorporated into KMT units. When the Central Executive Committee did meet on June 15, it confirmed Chiang's new post and mapped out a strategy for Party organization that would further increase Party power.

The CEC claimed itself to be the highest KMT organ and created at Canton the new National Government Committee and its National Revolutionary Army, which involved rationalization of Party and military income and expenditures. The program and decisions fit the Marxist model of Party dictatorship.[3] Approval must have been given for the Kwangtung-Hong Kong Strike, which began June 18, and for the demonstration that resulted in the Shameen Incident on June 23. Both effectively attracted mass sympathy and support, which were vitally needed to invigorate the Party structure. Welcoming the tens of thousands of Cantonese strikers who returned to their Cantonese homes, the KMT and CCP integrated them into the *KMT* framework—in theory (in practice the CCP won control of them).

The formal institution of Canton's National Government, which was to act as the more viable alternative to the Peking National Government, took place on July 1, 1925. Expanding from the Party Army, the Russian-style Political Departments with Party Representatives (commissars) were introduced into all the associated forces of the new military confederation, the National Revolutionary Army. This act more distinctly defined the chain of command within the Party's military machine, an improvement over the KMT's earlier amorphous nature. At this point it was still unclear just who would grasp the new reins of power.

Within what the Russians called the KMT Left were those who supported the ubiquitous Russians and their aid program and the associated KMT-CCP United Front and Hong Kong Strike organization: Liao Chung-k'ai, Wang Ching-wei, and Chiang Kai-shek, all of whom in turn were strengthened by the above elements and the Party Army.[4] Finance Minister Liao, a strong promoter of the United Front and the Russian alliance, had cooperated in the appointment of CCP member Su Ch'ao-cheng to head the powerful Strike organization. Chiang held military status as superintendent of Whampoa and the garrison command and had the loyalty of the Whampoa cadets and graduates who went out to lead units in the NRA. They respected him as the Chinese had traditionally respected their teachers, or as disciples respect their masters. Wang Ching-wei thrived on his charisma, which during his stirring speeches kept audiences spellbound.

In that it reduced the number of potential leaders, the mysterious assassination of Liao Chung-k'ai on August 20, 1925, speeded the centralization of power in the KMT hierarchy. The same day, a united meeting of the CEC, the National Government Committee, and the Military Council focused Party power in a triumvirate over political, military, and police affairs. The three-man committee included the leading contenders at Canton—Wang Ching-wei, Chiang Kai-shek, and Hsü Ch'ung-chih.[5] At that point Hsü, who had commanded a force under Sun Yat-sen, retained the posts of Minister of War, head of the KMT's Military Department, Military Councilman, Kwangtung Military Commissioner, and chairman of Kwangtung's Provincial Affairs Committee.[6]

The centripetal pull gained momentum and on August 26 the KMT's Military Council decided to support a reorganization of the Party's military apparatus so that the Party's Military Council would control the NRA. It was at that point in the centralization process that the five KMT-affiliated "armies" became integrated, theoretically, into one body, the NRA. However, General Hsü Ch'ung-chih was neither featured in the leadership of the NRA nor was his own Kwangtung unit brought into it as a numbered army.

On September 18, 1925, Chiang secretly maneuvered loyal military units and strike pickets against Hsü's force. Chiang accused Hsü of manipulating the threat of Kwangtung warlord Ch'en Chiung-ming and of making deals involving truce arrangements. On September 19, Chiang wrote to Hsü recommending that Hsü take a trip out of Canton. Two days later, Hsü was still in Canton, and Chiang acted through the Party's Political Council, which ordered Ch'en Ming-shu to put Hsü on a steamer to Shanghai.[7] High-ranking contender Hu Han-min was next in line.

Hu, a party stalwart of long standing, was labeled a Rightist by the Russians, which generally meant that he was not cooperative to their "advice." Hu and a clique of Kwangtung members of the KMT opposed the United Front and were the objects of Russian efforts first at isolation and then elimination. Rumors, so influential in Chinese politics, linked Hu

Han-min to the August assassination of Liao Chung-k'ai. By September 1925 the resulting rancor was such that a consensus among the KMT hierarchy indicated Hu would best serve the KMT abroad—as an official emissary to Moscow where he would be safely under surveillance. Hu's exile particularly profited those promoting the KMT-Russian alliance, who bade Hu farewell aboard a Russian steamer on September 23. The power of what Borodin labeled his KMT Left, composed of Chiang and Wang Ching-wei, thereupon expanded, unchecked by General Hsü and Hu Han-min.

In the fall of 1925, with this centralization of power, Kwangtung could be brought more under Party influence as the Revolutionary Base. During the last week in September, the Military Council ordered Chiang to rid Kwangtung, once and for all, of Ch'en Chiung-ming's rival military power. As general commander of a Second Eastern Expedition, Chiang set forth with his troops on October 6, 1925. He took Ch'en's stronghold, the walled city of Huichou, by mid-October, and in early December he finally scattered the enemy into the ranges bordering Fukien and Kiangsi. Within the month, NRA elements had swept through Kwangtung to the west and south from Canton, securing the Revolutionary Base. As already noted, the Hong Kong-Kwangtung strikers and pickets contributed to and profited from this expansion of KMT power into Kwangtung.[8] Chiang and the strike organization still enjoyed their symbiotic relationship.

The rise of the KMT influence in the province paralleled the ascension of Commander Chiang, who by December 18 had gained the approval of the National Government Committee to set up a branch of the Whampoa Academy at newly liberated Ch'aochou, the dominant city of eastern Kwangtung. Chiang achieved the appointment of an associate in the Whampoa hierarchy, acting First Army Commander Ho Ying-ch'in, as Branch Academy director at Ch'aochou. Having by that time sufficient influence, Chiang appointed associates he considered reliable—a group that came to be known as the Whampoa Clique.

He astutely sensed the importance of centralizing education under Party leadership, especially military education. To the school ties that cemented Chinese elites was added obedience to military discipline. In December 1925, Chiang argued persuasively for the consolidation of the various academies run by KMT-affiliated armies. He reasoned with the Military Council that "the organizations educating the military should try to unify. . . . Their waste and ineffectiveness from duplicating the same work is laughable. If all the cliques are at odds this makes it even worse. If we want to unify the administration of the military then we must first plan to unify military education."[9]

Chiang's proposal passed shortly after when the Second National Congress of the KMT met in January 1926 in Canton—convened once the Second Eastern Expedition had consolidated the Revolutionary Base. The KMT changed the official name of Whampoa Academy to the Central Military and Political Academy and designated the other military academies as preparatory branches under its aegis.[10] The National Congress thus was one in which the KMT Left and its Communist patrons clearly dominated. Of 250 delegates to the Congress, 100 had "dual membership" (CCP-KMT) and of the powerful nine-member CEC Standing Committee, three were Communists.[11] The CCP role in the KMT had obviously expanded since the union with Sun in 1923. The Congress elected the symbol of the KMT Left, Wang Ching-wei, as Party chairman. At this time the leading KMT military leader, Chiang, spoke to the assembly of the world revolution against imperialism. Easing the way for the centralization of power was the absence of the opponents of the KMT alliance with the Russians and CCP. These Rightists (sometimes called the Western Hills faction) had quit the Canton regime earlier. They took their name from a meeting they held together in November over Sun Yat-sen's coffin near Peking's Western Hills, at which time they claimed among their numbers eleven CEC members, which sufficed as a quorum.

In early 1926, there had emerged from this turbid political arena at Canton a shaky balance of power that included Wang Ching-wei, Chiang Kai-shek, and the CCP members in high posts in the KMT. Wang had benefited when the military and mass organizations had ousted several other contenders. With Russian patronage, Chiang had managed to rise as the leading military figure and had profited from the support of the CCP-led strike organization in the Eastern Expeditions. Borodin and Stalin in Moscow could analyze their strategy as having borne fruit as the numbers of Hong Kong-Kwangtung strikers and organized peasants under CCP influence swelled and CCP membership jumped from 1,000 to 10,000 between May and September of 1925. CCP members held high posts in the KMT hierarchy. Thus, the dominant factions at Canton were the KMT Left, the CCP, and a military bloc around Chiang.

Among those high-ranking CCP members in the KMT was T'an P'ing-shan, who headed the Organization Department—a strategic post that oversaw the creation and leadership of mass organizations. CEC standing committeeman Lin Tsu-han led the Peasants' Department and Mao Tse-tung ran the Political Department de facto. Other CCP members were in the military system as concurrent Party Representatives and heads of the NRA's Political Departments.[12] In this manner Chou En-lai dominated the political work in the First Army, Li Fu-chün in the Second Army, and Lin Tsu-han in the Sixth Army.[13]

At the Congress, as delegate from Whampoa and the NRA, Chiang acted as the leading military spokesman. On January 6, 1926, he presented a military report to the Congress calling for raising the "livelihood" of officers and soldiers—a proposal that certainly enhanced his image among the military. Elected to the CEC and chosen as one of its powerful nine-man Standing Committee, Chiang's status was obvious.[14] He enjoyed sufficient influence so that when he brought up the need to plan for a Northern Expedition, chairman Wang Ching-wei felt constrained to concur, but the aura of unity was quite evanescent. The controversies over the expedition and the Hong Kong Strike so strained the fragile coalition that the KMT was forced toward further centralization.

The Russians, and therefore the CCP, feared that the Northern Expedition would not serve their goal of social revolution if it were led by the KMT military. On the other hand, with CCP membership booming and mass organizing expanding phenomenally in Kwangtung, the province could become a *Communist* base with a bit more patience, if the expedition were called off. However, Borodin avoided openly antagonizing Chiang and the KMT armies by opposing the campaign.[15] On January 27, Leftist Wang Ching-wei opened the official excoriation of Wu P'ei-fu, the first warlord opponent astride the route north.[16]

Chiang continued building authority after the Congress with his appointment from the Military Council on February 1, 1926, as inspector general of the NRA charged with overseeing war preparations.[17] In February, Wang apparently collaborated with Chiang to bring leaders of neighboring military regimes into the KMT sphere. Wang traveled to Wuchou, Kwangsi, to gather in the three generals there, while Chiang negotiated with agents of warlord Sun Ch'uan-fang, whose domain included Kiangsi and Fukien on Kwangtung's border.[18] Both Chiang and Sun were classmates from Tokyo's Shikan Gakko and discussed the benefits of mutual nonaggression. On February 25, Canton again issued propaganda criticizing nearby Wu P'ei-fu and the discreetly distant Chang Tso-lin as "running dogs" of the imperialists, but carefully avoided provoking neighboring Sun Ch'uan-fang.[19] The following day, mustering its mass organizations for a demonstration, Canton revealed popular support for an offensive against Wu and praised a potential ally in the north, Feng Yü-hsiang.[20] Borodin at that moment had traveled north to rendezvous with Feng at Urga, Mongolia. There they discussed the cooperation of the forces of Canton with those of Feng—both subsidized by the USSR. Russian strategy desired their combination against the warlord collaborators of imperialist Great Britain and Japan.[21] Chang Kuo-t'ao, a leading Chinese Communist at that time, recalled that this Russian promotion of a combination between Feng Yü-hsiang and Canton was not handled tactfully, and that Chiang and the military at Canton were made to feel subordinate to Feng, who was closer to Peking and thus capable of rapidly changing the leadership of China in Russia's favor. Advisor N. Kisanka (whose real name was Kuybyshev) allegedly proposed in February 1926 that Chiang collaborate with Feng by attacking Tientsin from the sea, and that after this was accomplished Chiang should help train Feng's many troops.[22]

However consciously or subconsciously, Stalin's faction in Moscow must have initially shied from promoting the reunion of the several parts of China into a strong whole. For Moscow, supporting tractable, dependent satellites was the safest course. Trotsky and his internationalists probably feared a China united under Chiang's bourgeois NRA.[23] Although the KMT did need unity and centralized power, Chiang in early 1926 already presented too many uncertainties to his Communist patrons to receive their approval to attempt the conquest of China. Ironically, outside observers at that time labeled Chiang "the Red General."

CHAPTER 5

Breaches in the Revolutionary Base

The solidarity of the Canton regime had been from the start more apparent than real. At various stages the alliance between the KMT and the Russian-CCP bloc had more foes and reluctant supporters than friends. Ultimately the responsibility for the alliance lay with Stalin. As the long-discussed Northern Expedition became a possibility, the Russian mission at Canton became increasingly wary of the power that would have to be given to its commander. By February 1926, there were some 100,000 assorted allied troops under NRA hegemony. In China it had become obvious that military power created political power. There is evidence that some Russian advisors and high-ranking Kisanka, in particular, had begun a campaign to neutralize Chiang's authority and postpone the military buildup. Kisanka, possibly at Stalin's order, criticized the planned expedition to reunite China through conquest and found fault with Chiang before his Whampoa cadets and division commanders.[1] It was later claimed that the anti-Chiang strategy included pamphlets attacking him, which circulated both in Canton and across the river at Whampoa.[2] Russian-CCP political support seemed to be shifting to Wang Ching-wei in order to check Chiang's further rise.

Chiang sensed that a reshuffling and purging of leadership, such as had earlier removed Hu Han-min and Hsü Ch'ung-chih, seemed to be directed at removing him, making Wang the sole receiver of Russian aid. To force the issue Chiang confronted Wang on February 8, 1926,[3] by offering his resignation if the Northern Expedition were not promoted and its Russian opponents returned to Russia. Although Chief Military Advisor Kisanka remained, General Victor Rogachev did resign from the NRA's general staff.[4] Chiang was not satisfied and petitioned successively for the dissolution of his Eastern Expeditionary Command, to make way for the CEC's formation of a new command to lead the Northern Expedition.[5] The KMT's Standing Committee did concede the issuing of a manifesto against Wu P'ei-fu and Chang Tso-lin, but Kisanka remained and there were rumors that he was inciting division commanders to rebel against Chiang.[6] On February 27, Chiang went again to KMT chairman Wang to gain the recall of Kisanka. This time Chiang's petition was reinforced by the offers of resignation from Canton Mayor C.C. Wu and Police Commissioner Wu T'ieh-ch'eng.[7] Although Chiang received assurances that the Northern Expedition would take place, by March 1926 the Party seemed polarized between those who supported Chiang and the *military* offensive and those who favored deepening the *social* revolution within Kwangtung. The diverging aims were worsened by conflicting viewpoints on the usefulness of the Kwangtung-Hong Kong Strike.

By early 1926, the strongest source of KMT support—the rising commercial element in the modern ports—was becoming disenchanted with the anti-British strikes and boycott. Although the strike had expressed some of their resentments against arrogant foreign exploitation so evident in the treaty ports, the merchants' livelihood depended on trade with foreigners. Their most significant customers were the British. Furthermore, the strike had expanded from an attack on British capitalism in China to strident propagandizing by strike-affiliated unions on the oppression of workers and peasants by *Chinese* capitalists and landlords, thus promoting class struggle among Chinese.

Originally, KMT strategists promoting national reunification had given priority to the fight against the foreign imperialists and their Chinese "running dogs," the warlords, and had hoped to harmonize support for the National Revolution through a *union* of *all* classes. In emphasizing the negative effects of foreign economic imperialism, the KMT propaganda pointed out that Chinese merchants *and* workers were both at the mercy of the foreign traders and factory owners protected by the hated Unequal Treaties. This stance took account of the vital financial support from the merchants in urban chambers of commerce and their gentry cousins of the countryside. After the strike organization began its work, both merchants and rural gentry had come under attack from the new unions and the CCP-sponsored peasant associations. By 1926, donors to the KMT treasury felt anxiety over the proliferating activities of the strike organization.

Although the strike apparatus was a temporary means of gathering workers around an issue, it channeled new personnel into more permanent labor organizations of the CCP. The Strike Committee was listed by the CCP as subordinate to its higher, most inclusive labor body—the Chinese National General Labor Union. Aside from supporting the Hong Kong Strike, new strike organization branches along the Kwangtung coast recruited striking sailors home from Hong Kong shipping concerns. These men also became members of the CCP's new Chinese Seamen's Union, which set up branches alongside the strike offices. By January 1926 the Seamen's Union lauded the growth in its periodical, *Chinese Seamen*, stating that: ". . . previously the Seamen's Union had been only an empty name but now it has already become organized like an army." The union slogans proclaimed: "Long Live the United Seamen of the World!" "Long Live the Proletariat and the Liberation of the Oppressed Masses!" "Long Live the World Revolution!" and "Knock Down the Capitalist Class!"[8]

Among the diverse KMT leaders, some elements were not long in deciding that the strike organization was too potent a force and confirmed their fears over the KMT-CCP coalition. Any attempts to curtail the Hong Kong-Kwangtung Strike, however, opposed the aims of Russian patrons, who could withhold their aid to both the KMT and the CCP. The Comintern promoted and subsidized the strike, which damaged British capitalism through its Asian markets and sources of raw materials, thus implementing the international strategy against capitalism. Not only was British trade in South China suffering greatly, but also the benefits accrued in terms of the recruitment and organization of the masses by the CCP were beyond all expectations. Moscow would not readily support a halt to the strike.

Besides rivaling the KMT in political authority, the strike organization cost the Canton regime in other ways. KMT coffers were the source of about 60 percent of the Strike Committee's budget—a pledged sum of C$80,000 monthly. Cantonese merchants "donated" another portion.[9] While the budget did cover a multitude of activities, and Chiang had used strikers in the Eastern Expeditions, he was quick to recognize that the portion doled out to the strikers was nonproductive. In mid-1925, only one month after the strikers began to flock to Canton, Chiang proposed to the Military Council that the strikers be put to work by the National Government building roads in Kwangtung and a proposed deepwater port at Whampoa capable of attracting sea trade away from Hong Kong.[10] The Strike Committee understandably lacked enthusiasm for any scheme that would transfer strikers from its authority, although it did reluctantly form a road construction subcommittee of around 3,000 workers.[11]

As a commercial entrepôt, Canton's economy suffered from the loss of sales to British Hong Kong and the British market. Tariff revenue dropped by 60 percent at Canton the first month of the strike, which indicates the extent of the dependence on British trade.[12] Although tariff revenues from newly conquered small ports in Kwangtung did help to compensate the government's loss, Canton producers sorely missed the loss of trade.

Production suffered along with trade as the Strike Committee promoted strikes throughout Canton as part of its campaign to unionize Kwangtung labor. Using the picket corps, the committee promoted strikes in a particular industry by "encouraging" the workers to leave their jobs and by preventing strikebreaking with the armed picket corps. Workers, who were generally persuaded to strike for economic incentives, were then enrolled in unions. The CCP then welcomed these new unions into its GLU. They were represented also through democratic centralism on the strike assembly. With some industries already unionized by the KMT or independently, Canton labor experienced the pull of rival union factions. Antagonism and violence between contending unions erupted into the open as they struggled to control recruits and employment. In this competition, the unions affiliated with the Hong Kong strike organization could call on the armed strike pickets. The other unions often called on the KMT's municipal police for protection. In this manner the Party military system came into confrontation with the strike organization. By early 1926, as preparations for the Northern Expedition prompted the tightening of KMT authority, the autonomy of the Strike Committee became one major source of argument between the KMT and their supposed collaborators.[13]

The Strike Committee's independence confused and frustrated numbers of the KMT hierarchy and provincial administrators. Those KMT diplomats exploring the possibilities of negotiations with the British were stymied as the strike apparatus and the Russian alliance checked their moves. The division of authority is illustrated by an incident in December 1925 when strike pickets imprisoned two Indian employees of a British firm. Although the British Consul at Canton directed a request for their release to the KMT's Foreign Ministry, in embarrassment Foreign Minister C.C. Wu had to admit that he was unable to supercede the authority of the strikers' court.[14]

Although the Hong Kong Strike should have given the Canton government leverage to make demands of the British, the divergent goals of the Strike Committee hampered the use of bargaining points. Significantly, Foreign Minister Wu became a most outspoken critic of the strike and the organization built around it. His opposition was related also to his own patronage of the KMT's Kwangtung Mechanics' Union, which was in violent contention with the unionization being carried on by the Strike Committee. Similarly, Canton Police Commissioner Wu T'ieh-ch'eng crossed the Strike Committee when he chose to protect KMT unions when interunion struggles erupted.[15]

Chiang remained ambivalent toward the Russian alliance in early 1926, which allowed him maneuverability as a centrist. When tensions did crest in March 1926, Chiang was caught between these two polarized forces but was yet flexible enough to take advantage of what might have been a disastrous cross fire.

The conflict became open in March 1926, stirred by the highly visible issue of the strike and its ubiquitous armed and uniformed pickets. In January, the KMT's Second National Congress had decided that planning for a Northern Expedition should be started, which necessarily brought into question the Hong Kong-Kwangtung Strike. According to a Communist history of the strike, it was at that point that even KMT proponents of the United Front with the CCP "wavered" in their support of the strike.[16] Were the KMT to provide materially for a military reunification of China, it would have to rein in the strike apparatus. Increased spending of what was to become 90 percent of its income on the military buildup meant the KMT had to *nurture* sources of provincial revenue that fed the national revolutionary movement.[17] This expansion necessarily required *more* trade rather than its restriction by the strike; nor was the plethora of economic strikes a stabilizing factor in the Revolutionary Base. Many felt that Canton had to choose between allowing the CCP to deepen the social revolution *within* Kwangtung and preparing for the military needs of an offensive into the rest of China.

In early March 1926, repeating his proposal of the first week of the strike in 1925, Chiang tried to bring the strikers under Party discipline by employing them on public projects. The Strike Committee resisted by claiming a large number of strikers as being occupied with committee projects. It sent others back to Hong Kong out of KMT jurisdiction by means of the railroad travel privileges granted them by the Canton government.[18] The Russian-CCP combine continued to oppose any change in the favorable situation for them in Kwangtung. They neither wished to give up the autonomy by which they had made such spectacular gains, nor did they favor the recognition of military leadership that would be brought by the fighting of a dangerous campaign against the millions of warlord troops to the north, a campaign that would threaten the existence of their privileged sanctuary in Kwangtung. However, feelings against the strike organization's power and the CCP were running high and may actually have carried Chiang along on a ground swell of reaction. Although the coup of March 20, 1926, still presents many moot questions, it is a fact that much of the action during the coup did revolve around the Hong Kong Strike headquarters.

As March began, work toward launching the Northern Expedition had been set in motion. The KMT press had officially attacked Wu P'ei-fu, and the Party had already attracted the Hunanese military leader T'ang Sheng-chih toward the brink of defection. But, while Chiang nagged the Party to support T'ang's rebellion in Hunan, the opponents of an expedition also gathered their resources. March was to be a critical watershed for the expedition.

The KMT and the NRA were diverse conglomerates that were highly susceptible to controversy and fractionation. Within the military, Chiang tried to consolidate and unite. However, during the first week of March there had been rumors of mutiny against the KMT Left, and even within the First Army more propaganda against Commander Chiang was circulated by mail.[19] Chiang shifted from their troops those commanders suspected of plotting against the rising CCP power in Canton. He replaced First Army Second Division Commander Wang Mao-kung with Liu Chi, and placed the division under surveillance. In the military supply system, Chiang buttressed his authority by appointing loyal Chu P'ei-teh as its head.[20] On March 8, Chiang went again to Chairman Wang Ching-wei to warn of the danger of losing power to the Russian-CCP combine and to request the withdrawal of Kisanka. He was partly trying to placate the most vociferous anti-Communists among his officer cadre[21] and the Sun Yat-senist Society.

Canton's navy became intimately involved in the polarization between the Communist and KMT goals when pickets of the strike organization seized two Canton navy gunboats. Alleging that the ships' commanders had acted in a counter-revolutionary manner by violating the strike blockade, the pickets turned those commanding officers over to the head of the Navy Bureau's Political Department, CCP member Li Chih-lung. When Li next moved to arrest the captain and officers of the navy's flagship, the *Chung-shan*, the CCP seemed to have gained the upper hand.[22] The murky details of the struggle that ensued have not been clarified with time, but the struggle likely swirled around the leadership of the National Revolution. Chiang and the Party members in power feared a take-over either by the Communists, or the anti-Communists. Early in March these anxieties were evidenced in the curfew placed upon Canton's government buildings and enforced by police patrols. By the second week of March, cadets on special guard across the river on Whampoa's bund peered toward Canton anxiously awaiting any sign of trouble.[23]

THE ANTI-COMMUNISTS MOVE FIRST

The March 20 Coup, or the *Chung-shan* Incident, was *not* unanticipated. The polarized factions were tensed for a blow of some sort. Was the affair master-minded or a spontaneous ignition of tensions? Which side actually moved first? Did the Russian-CCP combine or one of its factions under Kisanka plot to take over Canton (as they did less than two years later)? Or, was the attempt to kidnap Chiang an anti-Communist's prevarication to force a purge?[24] The orders given may never become known, but what took place on March 20 can be surveyed. At 4:00 A.M., following news of an alleged attempt from the gunboat *Chung-shan* to kidnap him, Chiang placed Canton under martial law by use of his authority as garrison commander. Moving police and cadets into strategic points about the city, his forces occupied government buildings, and marched through the eastern suburban headquarters of the Hong Kong Strike organization and the area where most of the Russian advisors lived. The cadets and police quickly surrounded and arrested many strike leaders and Russian advisors.[25]

During the day it became obvious that a combination of military and anti-Communists dominated Canton and favored launching the Northern Expedition as soon as possible. The most vocal Russian opponents of an expedition were out of Canton within the week.[26] Li Chih-lung, the naval Political Department head, and all other Party Representatives who were also heads of Political Departments in military units were questioned intensively at Whampoa as to their political affiliations and were kept for "retraining."[27] The First Army, upon which Chiang depended for reliable support, thus lost Chou En-lai and all known Communists.[28] The Canton press, a vital clarion for the National Revolution, was disciplined through the suspension of CCP-affiliated newspapers and censorship by the Military Council.[29] Before March 25, by which time Chiang faced Chairman Wang Ching-wei, the removal of selected CCP members from a number of KMT agencies was a *fait accompli*, for which Chiang requested appropriate punishment[30] because he had not gone through the proper CEC channels for authorization. The sympathetic Political Council that met on March 26 disapproved Chiang's means but judged the outcome warranted.[31] The success of the coup supports evidence that it had considerable backing. Quite possibly if Chiang had not taken on the leadership of the Rightists on March 20, those such as the young Sun Yat-senists would have carried out a coup without him—perhaps sweeping Chiang out as well.

Without organized resistance, the sudden move was carried out without bloodshed. Those ousted either left Canton for Russia or Shanghai, or submitted to retraining. Chiang explained the coup as one aimed at un-cooperative *individuals* rather than at the entire Russian-CCP presence or the alliance.[32] He presented his reasoning on March 20 to a Russian advisor along with an apology for the temporary house arrest of Russians in their East Mountain suburban compound.[33] On the twenty-second, Chiang reiterated his story to Canton's Russian Consul along with his request for the continuance of the alliance with Russia, but on a more equitable basis. As a conciliatory gesture, Chiang granted permission to the controversial Strike Committee to reopen its headquarters, which had been closed on the day the coup occurred. Within two days the Whampoa cadets ceased their open surveillance of the strike headquarters and ended the curfew that had been imposed.[34] At the same time, Kisanka and his supporters, Rogachev and Razgon, quietly boarded the *Pamyat Lenina* bound for the Soviet Union.[35]

CHAPTER 6
Mending the United Front in Kwangtung

Since the March 20 Coup had been bloodless, there remained many controversial persons and issues. One was the Hong Kong-Kwangtung Strike and its organization, which polarized the pro-Communist and anti-Communist members of the KMT, and thus severely tested the solidarity of the United Front. Those participating in the coup generally agreed that an expedition would require the resumption of trade with Hong Kong for economic purposes, and the restraint of the Strike Committee for political purposes. To them the Strike Committee presaged a Communist take-over of the Revolutionary Base. The same day that the Whampoa cadets moved against the strike headquarters, a note reportedly signed by Chairman Wang Ching-wei went from Canton to Hong Kong's British governor, Sir Cecil Clement, proposing that he and Canton each appoint three representatives to negotiate the settlement of the strike (by then in its ninth month).[1]

During the rest of March and into April 1926, representatives of Canton and Hong Kong reviewed the major obstacles to a settlement. What had begun as a political maneuver in 1925 took on strong economic colorings in order to retain the participation of Kwangtung labor. By spring 1926, the demand most difficult to resolve concerned retroactive payment of the nine months of wages lost by the tens of thousands of strikers.[2] This strike Committee demand bespoke Russia's keen interest in hampering British trade in China as well as in developing a broad base of mass support for the CCP. Diverse KMT leaders proposed ways of reining in the strike and its mass organization. By the spring of 1926, the KMT Center and Right wanted an end to the strike—but could not afford to prejudice the Russian aid program. From the March 20 Coup until the July launching of the expedition, various KMT luminaries confronted the Strike Organization, and the tensions within the KMT-CCP coalition can be seen through their experiences.

In the search for a *modus vivendi* after the coup, there emerged compromises that were typically Chinese. Although Chiang had forced out of key positions a group of CCP members, his faction in turn had to give in to the pressure of the Russian-CCP bloc demanding a similar ousting of the most active anti-Communists for the good of the United Front. Thus, the CCP attacked Wu T'ieh-ch'eng, the chief of the Canton police, commander of the First Army's Eleventh Division, and CEC member. He had collaborated with Mayor C.C. Wu in the use of police to curtail the armed strike pickets in the Communist union movement. The police had been called out to reinforce non-Communist unions during conflicts with rival CCP unions directed by the Strike Committee. Wu's police did not resist the coup of March 20, but joined with Chiang's Whampoa elements and then afterward provided the surveillance force around the Strike Organization. From his police headquarters had come the order preventing unions from: 1) arming members, 2) arresting workers, or 3) forcibly settling disputes among unions without National Government orders.[3] However, the KMT was not yet ready or able to disarm the CCP unions. When violence broke out between strikers and the police, Wu had to call off his police. In such a confrontation on March 29, 1926, at the memorial service for the KMT's seventy-two martyrs of the 1911 revolution, two mounted police had moved against a group of strikers only to find themselves in the hands of the Strike Committee and under investigation.[4]

Encouraging the committee were its Russian patrons and also the political power of the tens of thousands of affiliated, disciplined union members. Only a week after Chiang's coup, the strikers operated as usual in preventing communications with Hong Kong. They continued to demand travel passes to and from Hong Kong. Rumors even circulated that the committee planned a general strike to protest against the search and seizure of strikers at the headquarters during the coup.[5]

The restraining of Wu T'ieh-ch'eng could be seen by early April when the order to disarm the unions became modified to pertain to all unions *except* the strike pickets (the police did retain a measure of control through the requirement that all unions register their meetings, ahead of time, at police headquarters).[6] Not only was Wu forced to rein in his police from intervening against the CCP labor movement, but also in his compromise with the Communists, Chiang used the police to prevent *anti*-Communists from holding a planned demonstration.[7]

One significant outcome of the March 20 Coup was the concentration of power around centrist Chiang, at the expense of both the Communists and the KMT Rightists, or anti-Communists. (At that point the Right could be defined as anti-Communist.) To the Russia-CCP bloc, Wu T'ieh-ch'eng symbolized the avowed anti-Communist and enemy of "red" unions. But to Chiang, Wu also represented a focal point of military and police power, of which Chiang's rivals in the KMT Right might make use. In the settlement demanded of Chiang in return for continuance of Russian aid, Wu T'ieh-ch'eng, a sponsor of the militant Sun Yat-senists, became a sacrificial offering that saved "face" for the demoted CCP and undermined rivals of Chiang. Apparently Wu was not able to prove to Chiang that his loyalties were not tied to the Rightists. On April 24, Wu found himself dismissed as police chief and from First Army divisional command, and by late May he was confined first at his own police headquarters and then at Whampoa.[8] In recognition of the new locus of power, Wu's replacement took his orders from Chiang's Military Council rather than from the municipal and provincial governments.

C.C. Wu, diplomat for the KMT as well as mayor of Canton, earlier had been frustrated by the recalcitrant Strike Committee while negotiating with the British. Shortly after the March 20 Coup, British-educated Wu resumed informal talks with representatives from Hong Kong in hopes of using the strike as bargaining leverage with the British. On the matter of paying the strikers' lost wages, the British indicated a willingness to allow Hong Kong merchants to settle with the Strike Committee.[9] There was even talk of a British offer to finance the completion of the Canton-Hankow railway.[10] Less dependence on Russian aid would certainly have appealed to the anti-Communist element in the KMT with which C.C. Wu had close ties. However, Wu's optimism over a strike settlement was premature.

The postcoup compromise, while removing the Russian-CCP bloc from military leadership, had allowed it to retain a primary role among the mass organizations and in the strike. Once removed from NRA leadership and its Political Departments, the CCP and the strike apparatus were expected to concede their tacit support to the Northern Expedition and direct the supportive cooperation of the peasants and workers. C.C. Wu was apparently not a party to the deal, since but one week following the coup he blasted the Strike Committee as "troublemakers" and their pickets as "bribe-takers." Then, at the Kwangtung Labor Conference, Wu staged a walkout of KMT union delegates in protest against the affair as a CCP-dominated sham.[11]

Although C.C. Wu had not bolted Canton in 1925 with the anti-Communist Western Hills faction, he worked as a Sun Yat-senist against the Russian alliance and the coalition with the CCP. The pressure of these anti-Communists at Canton was sufficient to force the Strike Committee to make at least some show of subordination to the KMT. Stalin also insisted that the CCP uphold the United Front. In early April 1926, the Strike Committee responding to Wu's charges did publicize an investigation of alleged corruption and extortion among pickets enforcing the boycott.[12] However, conflict between the strikers and the nonaffiliated unions went on and the committee pressed the KMT to remove the most influential enemies of the strike from positions of authority. This was a trying time for the KMT, still tending its own wounds from the coup as well as trying to coexist with its CCP partner. Another of the points of compromise was the neutralization of the two most antagonistic political organizations—the CCP's Communist Youth and the KMT's Sun Yat-senists (Sun Wen Chu-i Hsüeh-hui). When the antagonists in the CCP and KMT agreed to disband these groups, the leading sponsor of the Sun Yat-senists, C.C. Wu, must also have been threatened along with his associate, Wu T'ieh-ch'eng.

By the end of April, Wu realized that his role was that of scapegoat and exiled himself from Canton, only avoiding arrest by a well-timed departure for Shanghai to visit the tomb of his father, Wu T'ing-fang.[13] He left the posts of Canton mayor, CEC member, National Government committeeman, and Military Councilman. In the last group, membership was narrowing to those amenable to Chiang's leadership. Of the eight men appointed in July 1925 to the Military Council, only Chiang, T'an Yen-k'ai, and loyal Chu P'ei-teh remained by late April 1926. Out, via a number of means, were: ex-chairman Wang Ching-wei, who was superceded in the coup; Liao Chung-k'ai, who was assassinated in 1925; Hu Han-min, discredited and exiled to Moscow by that assassination; Hsü Ch'ung-chih, ousted the preceding fall as the alleged collaborator of warlord Ch'en Chiung-ming; and C.C. Wu, anti-Communist casualty of the postcoup reconciliation. On April 16, 1926, Chiang received the powers of chairman of the Military Council from the CEC and the National Government.[14]

As quick as was the turnover in KMT leadership, the actual purging of the Sun Yat-senists proved to be a temporary show. Chinese politicians have Taoist resiliency, as well as flexibility. With the reconciliation efforts that preceded the launching of the expedition, exiled anti-Communists gravitated back to Canton. Later, following the KMT's split with the CCP in 1927, both ousted Wus returned to positions of Party leadership. One month after the Shanghai purge of April 1927, C.C. Wu emerged as Foreign Minister of Nanking. For Wu T'ieh-ch'eng, his release came after eight months' confinement, strangely enough through the intercessions of Leftist Mme. Sun Yat-sen (Soong Ch'ing-ling). She pled with Chiang that Wu T'ieh-ch'eng had performed innumerable services for Sun during their long association and acted as a guarantor that Wu would not interfere in politics.[15] Later Wu rose within the Party as mayor of Shanghai and then governor of Kwangsi.

Chiang's rise in the KMT during the spring of 1926 was dependent partly on his abilities and also on the pivotal nature of his role as a centrist at Canton. As military leader and head of the key Whampoa Academy, Chiang could expand his influence outward among the allied "armies" in the NRA. As commander of the First Army, Chiang already controlled the force best trained and most responsive to Party interests. He managed to dominate the KMT's military establishment, and because of his Party experience he was able also to attract civilian support. Up to the time of the coup, Chiang had stayed close enough to pro-Communist elements that when he curtailed the Sun Yat-senists, he convinced Stalin, Ch'en Tu-hsiu, and other CCP members that he was still useful.[16] Chiang appeared to be the strong man most capable of providing the centripetal force needed to weld together the fragile United Front and revolutionary movement.

At that stage Stalin still hoped to utilize the KMT's "national bourgeois revolution," though he did not really expect its success in reuniting China. Russian efforts elsewhere in China had not come to fruition. In early April 1926, Feng Yü-hsiang's troops, despite Russian advisors and aid, were in retreat from North China into the northwest hinterland following a series of defeats. Russian diplomats were creating a conciliatory image in Peking with the ephemeral government there. At Canton the Russians continued to dole out aid and thus were able to demand concessions for the CCP by threatening to call due all loans to the KMT and to cut off aid.

By the time the Second Congress of the KMT's CEC met in mid-May, it could approve the compromises achieved between the anti-Communists, Chiang, and the Russian mission. The anti-Communists had gained the removal of CCP influence in the military and the dissolution of the Communist Youth. Aside from Kisanka and his aides who left immediately after Chiang's coup, another dozen of the most "uncooperative" members of the Russian mission departed Canton on April 14, and Chiang demanded successfully that those remaining in Canton act strictly as advisors and not as policy makers.[17] On the other hand, the Communists had been placated by the removal of several outspoken anti-Communists and the dissolution of the militant Sun Yat-senists. Chiang also helped quiet anxious Russian advisors by his assertion that the coup had not been an attack on the alliance or on the Russian mission, but that it was an act against individuals. It remained for the Second KMT Congress to redefine the United Front.

When the sessions began on May 15, Chiang proposed making the CCP more subordinate to the KMT. The CEC drafted a declaration reiterating the KMT ideal of the union of classes rather than class conflict and redressing the CCP for misusing the coalition. The tone was conciliatory, probably as a result of the prior day's discussion between Chiang and Borodin who had returned to Canton from North China.[18] At Stalin's recommendation, Borodin agreed to continue Russian aid and to hold the CCP in line with the decisions of the forthcoming CEC meetings. On May 16 when Borodin gathered together the CCP leaders at his East Mountain quarters, the Russians reproached the leaders for their: ". . . obvious measures to enlarge the CCP which they consider the main purpose of their work. They want to monopolize authority everywhere. This causes jealousy in KMT members and the KMT will thus be torn apart."[19]

Next the CEC regulated against CCP domination of the KMT organizational apparatus. CCP membership on key KMT committees was to be limited to one-third. Thus, on the key nine-man Standing Committee of the CEC, there could be no more than three "dual members," CCP members who had entered the KMT as individuals.[20] The lower-level Party headquarters were also to achieve the same ratio of KMT to CCP members. To ensure the validity of the membership ratio, the CCP was asked to turn over to the CEC chairman a list of all dual members.[21]

To implement these regulations checking CCP influence, five KMT members (Chiang and his allies T'an Yen-k'ai, Chang Ching-chiang, Wu Chih-hui, and Sun Fo) and three representing the CCP (T'an P'ing-shan, Yu Shih-teh, and Ku Meng-yü) were to function on a bipartisan committee.[22] This committee was to see to it that the KMT Central Headquarters authorized all political meetings, that KMT members did not join "another party," and that Comintern orders to dual members be reviewed by KMT Headquarters.[23] Later, Chiang's Military Council, under the authorization of the CEC, ruled that CCP membership and service as an officer in the NRA be mutually exclusive. Thus, the "compromise" was much less favorable to the side of the Communists, although the Russians at that point felt sure that Chiang needed their support desperately.[24]

The Russian mission and aid program continued, and the CCP went on freely in its work with the proletariat and peasants, but the Russian-CCP partners did lose much of their influence within the military at Canton. This loss became clear the following year when the highly prized mass organizations failed to overcome the KMT military. In early 1926, CCP headquarters in Shanghai had a military department of only two minor members and little work.[25] By May 1926, in compensation for this loss of military presence in NRA Political Departments, the CCP had armed peasant associations for defense against "bandits" and had trained a corps of peasant experts in political techniques and ideology.[26] The diversion of CCP energy into mass organizing was evident a week after the coup. An example was Mao Tse-tung, until then active in the KMT Propaganda Department, who turned his attention to the peasants' movement as the secretary of the KMT Peasants' Department. In late March, Mao directed the Peasants' Movement Institute, enrolling over 300—mainly radicalized rural elite.

The institute had originally been a KMT organ, but, when it convened in late March 1926, its Communist reorientation was obvious. Besides Mao, the other five instructors were all CCP members who taught students from nineteen provinces Marxist techniques of rural revolution and ideology. The work at the institute signified the concentration of CCP energies on mass organization after the coup. Rather than CCP movements withering after March 20, the organizing of Kwangtung peasants blossomed during the spring and summer of 1926. As a flexible centrist, Chiang had to balance these mass organizations under CCP influence against the pressures from uncompromising anti-Communists—especially from within the ranks of the military. In the meantime, the CCP's mass organizing expanded rapidly in the then permissive surroundings of the Revolutionary Base. (See chapter 18.)

The CCP benefited from their predominance over the mass organizations of Kwangtung, which seemed to prove the practicality of Stalin's strategy of temporary compromise with the KMT. As soon after the coup as April 3, Ch'en Tu-hsiu acknowledged Chiang in the CCP organ, *Hsiang-tao*. Criticizing the "propaganda of the Right," which had implicated the Communists in a plot to overthrow Chiang and set up a Workers' and Peasants' Soviet—thus precipitating the coup—Ch'en argued that: "the CCP is not mad. . . . Chiang Kai-shek is . . . the pillar of the Chinese National Revolutionary Movement. The policy of the CCP is . . .

not only against the splitting up of Kwangtung's revolutionary power but also hopes to unite all revolutionary power in all China."[27]

The French Communist Party newspaper *L'Humanité* gave the official Comintern pronouncement that the "noise reported in the press of a conflict between the Kuomintang and the Communists is unfounded."[28] With the return of Borodin from the north to Canton in late April came more tangible evidence of Moscow's conciliatory stance. Within a matter of days Russian freighters off-loaded shipments of war materiel, including nine aircraft accompanied by Russian trainers assigned to the NRA's Aviation Bureau.[29] This provided leverage, exemplified during the decisive CEC meetings in mid-May when the Russian leaders embarrassed Finance Minister T. V. Soong over the matter of repaying Russia's loans. This move forced propitiatory responses from the KMT and underlined the practical rewards of maintaining amicable KMT-Russian relations.[30]

RECONCILIATION WITHIN THE KMT

The March 20 Coup involved more than a purge of Communists and uncooperative Rightists. If Chiang's long-dreamed-of Northern Expedition was to materialize, he had to reconcile the KMT factions to each other and to his ascension. He could not conduct the offensive against the warlords by himself.

After the coup, on March 29, the Western Hills faction of the Kuomintang's CEC convened in Shanghai what they claimed to be the Second National Congress. They decided to support Chiang's coup against the CCP and wired him of their approval.[31] To reinforce his centrist position, Chiang wired back his disapproval of the "Congress," calling instead for the upholding of the Party Central in Canton to purify the Party and launch the Northern Expedition.[32] Further negotiations took Sun Fo to Shanghai as Canton's representative.[33] Sun returned with a covey of exiled Rightists. One was Yeh Ch'u-ts'ang, the chief editor of the Rightist newspaper *Kuo-min jih-pao* [National people's daily], who in May became the CEC's appointee to the post of Party Secretary General.[34] Yeh replaced CCP's T'an P'ing-shan, Lin Tsu-han, and Yang Pao-an. An associate of Yeh Ch'u-ts'ang was Shao Yüan-chung who came to head the KMT's Youth Department. Both Yeh and Shao had been among the Western Hills rebels who had split with Canton over the issue of the Russian alliance and the United Front.

But the reconciliation was not limited to anti-Communist Western Hills men. Ku Meng-yü, ex-dean of Peking University and a leader of its student movement, who had been labeled by the Russians and CCP members as a KMT Leftist, replaced Mao Tse-tung in the strategic Propaganda Department.[35] Chiang gained for himself the post of acting head of the Organization Department. And what of the constitutional leader of the Canton regime at the time of the coup—its National Government Committee and Party chairman, Wang Ching-wei? Wang, who had promoted the alliance with the Communists, had benefited most from the support received from the Russians and CCP. The proponents of the coup must have been strong considering that a gathering of forces behind Chairman Wang did not materialize. Wang's opposition to Chiang's usurpation of authority was passive. Superceded by the anti-Communist coalition, Wang was isolated along with his Communist patrons. Rather than becoming the focus of a Leftist KMT-CCP campaign against Chiang, Wang waited in the wings for the results of the post coup compromise. His high rank did not guarantee him security. Neither army elements nor mass organizations rose against the coup.

By the mid-May meeting of the CEC, Wang Ching-wei had quietly left Canton "for his health." Then, when the CEC held an election for the chairmanship of the Party, Wang received two votes for that position out of thirty-five cast—as did Chiang. The CEC that had approved the curtailment of the CCP and the reconciliation of the KMT factions elected as Party chairman Chang Ching-chiang, nominated by Chiang Kai-shek, by a majority vote of nineteen.[36] Thus, neither Wang nor Chiang really dominated the KMT membership following the coup.

As Chiang's compromise candidate, at the age of sixty-three Chang Ching-chiang was no newcomer to Party service, but had been associated with Sun Yat-sen and his movement from before the 1911 revolution. Chang's home province was Chekiang just over the border from Shanghai, where his family had made its fortune as merchants (a background similar to that of his younger fellow provincial Chiang Kai-shek). Chang had participated in the leadership of revolutionary movement in Kiangsu.[37] During the long struggle of Sun's party before and after 1911, Chang had donated a large proportion of his family capital to the revolutionary cause—thus exemplifying a source of the KMT's financial power. Although Chang was a civilian, he had close ties with the KMT military through Chiang Kai-shek, and he had not been tainted as a patron of the United Front. Although a cripple and in poor health, his persuasive powers were notable and sorely needed by the divided party.

In its May sessions, the CEC sought to placate the disaffected factions in hopes of counteracting the KMT's endemic centrifugal tendencies—which mirrored a problem common to China. It was agreed to wire a plea to Wang Ching-wei and Hu Han-min (theoretically the symbols of the Left and the Right) for their return to Canton and to their work. A committee was to persuade Hu in Shanghai of the Party's need for his presence. Since many in the CEC felt that the terms "Right" and "Left" were meaningless and divisive, Sun Fo proposed, unsuccessfully, that the terms be banned from use in the Party.[38]

However, the differences separating KMT members and those that existed between the KMT and CCP were deep. The anti-Communists remained fearful of collaborating with the CCP and the Russians. The CCP and the KMT Left were rankled by new regulations that, in theory, restricted their dominance. Those outside Chiang's clique had to face the *fait accompli* of his rising influence and his unyielding demand for the Northern Expedition. The traditions of concensus and loyal opposition were absent in China, so that the joining of hands in the spring of 1926 was temporary, and more apparent than real. Factionalism, so common to Chinese politics where nationhood was still in its infancy, was to remain a fatal weakness of the KMT, which was not galvanized by an overriding ideological unity. Perhaps more basic was the traditional tendency to include and synthesize approaches that are not really compatible.

Without an adequate power base of its own, the leadership at Canton had to do the best with what it had, and gambled that a course of action was preferable to further delay. While the coup had slowed the jockeying for leadership, it had not truly eliminated the rivalries. The parallel with the leadership of the Taipings' northern expedition is striking. As summer warmed at Canton the question was: Would the political energy explode outward against the warlord enemies or inward in self-destruction?

CHAPTER 7

The Simmering Revolutionary Movement at Canton

The anti-Communists had accepted Chiang's compromises only with the greatest reluctance. As the mid-May 1926 CEC gathering commenced in Canton, rumors of an anti-Communist military take-over were so rampant that Chiang had doubled the guard in the city. Once the KMT was committed to its support of the Hunan rebel T'ang Sheng-chih and when Wu P'ei-fu's allies were threatening to invade from Hunan, the anti-Communists did give in to Chiang's dominion. However, they continued to propagandize within the Revolutionary Base. Whampoa remained a hotbed of anti-Communism even though its Sun Yat-senists had been formally disbanded. A Russian advisor then in Canton claims that the Sun Yat-senists merely changed their name to the Society of Young Chinese Comrades led by Yü Chih-huan.[1] The May issue of Whampoa's *Ko-ming hua-pao* [Revolutionary pictorial] was unequivocal. Cartoonist Liang Yu-ming of the Political Department caricatured the CCP as a large rat gnawing through the pillars of the KMT structure. The cartoon caption read: "The pillars have been eaten by rats. If new pillars aren't put in, the house will fall. If the various levels of Party Headquarters are ruined by the CCP then the KMT must reorganize again so that the danger will be removed." Another cartoon depicted Russia as a fat, fanged imperialist hunting with his "running dogs" on the leash—one a warlord and the other the CCP. Allegations were that Russia was then seeking recognition for Chang Tso-lin's autonomy in Manchuria in return for Japan's acceptance of

Russia's control of the Chinese Eastern Railroad. By 1926, the KMT anti-Communists, especially the Western Hills faction, had concluded that the Russians were still imperialists in East Asia—a view shared forty years later by Mao Tse-tung. The cover of the same issue illustrates the KMT concept of a harmonious union of classes in the national revolution (see endsheets to this book).

As auxiliaries of the parties in Canton, the labor unions exemplified the partisan rivalry. Despite the propaganda of conciliation in the spring of 1926, the unions, Communist and non-Communist, remained locked in convulsive contention for membership and power. The KMT-CCP compromise had actually promoted an intensification of Communist efforts among the workers. The ambitious leadership of the Hong Kong Strike Committee in creating new unions to join in the Communist labor structure did so with the knowledge that there would be an increase in strikes and conflicts between rival unions in all sectors of the economy. After the purging of anti-Communist police chief Wu T'ieh-ch'eng, one disorder threatened to expand into a large riot.[2] (See chapter 18.) During April 1926, the Strike Committee created a new United Association of Kwangtung Carriers, which included the stevedores and all workers in transportation for the province.[3]

Then a struggle developed over whether the CCP-oriented Chinese National General Labor Union (GLU) should dominate the KMT-oriented Kwangtung General Labor Union (KGLU). On May 7, when the KGLU held a ceremony dramatizing National Disgrace Day, the GLU tried to move the ceremony to its own headquarters at Kwangtung University. A melee erupted in which GLU members tore down the flags of the KMT and National Government. The KMT union then demanded a public apology from the GLU and the Strike Committee.[4]

Similar struggles took place in Canton between student unions of the CCP, KMT, and independents. When student union leaders gathered at Kwangtung University on April 4, a squabble over centralization grew into a student riot when the active Communist Youth claimed their own student union to be the only legal one.[5] At Canton's Kung Yi Medical College, interunion violence interfered with the running of the college and its hospital.[6] From Canton and Kwangtung, the conflict spread into Kwangsi, new KMT territory, where the student body at the Kwangsi Normal School became torn between the existing KMT student union and the new CCP one.[7]

In the spring of 1926, few business or commercial firms went untouched by the effects of the Hong Kong-Kwangtung Strike as the number of affiliated unions increased. Armed pickets in uniforms arrested, judged, and fined shopkeepers or detained them in the East Park prison. Pickets confiscated what they claimed to be contraband from Hong Kong. Manufacturers alleged that they purchased import permits from the committee, only to find their ordered materials seized upon arrival anyway.[8] Since the GLU hoped to unionize *all* workers, even small shops and crafts were hit by strikes. Pickets blockaded shops and demanded benefits for newly unionized personnel. In one case where demands for cash were not met, the pickets drove out the shop clerks, confiscated goods designated as contraband, and, with an armed guard, locked out the owners and customers.[9] Although the union in question was not registered by the KMT Workers' Department as was required and the pickets were armed in defiance of the compromise, the appeals of owners to the National Government committee went unheeded.[10] At that time, the Strike Committee was nicknamed "the second CCP municipal committee."[11]

Commerce at Canton slowed while strikers confiscated shipments of suspected Hong Kong origin and auctioned them. Critics of the strike, more vocal after the coup, claimed the pickets seized goods indiscriminately and alleged that they gathered considerable wealth from this "daylight banditry." In the T'ai-shan area pickets seized coal en route to a branch railroad, which disrupted rail communications with Canton for a time.[12] Even in the summer of 1926, while the Canton government strained to transport growing numbers of troops north to Shaokuan on the Hunan border, a strike on the line from Canton north to Shaokuan slowed troop movement for two weeks.[13]

Most frustrating to the Canton regime were the strikes that the Strike Committee engineered in the public sector. Since, by mid-1926, the strike organization and the GLU had integrated many unions, when one union protested or struck, other unions, sometimes in public services, went out on sympathy strikes.[14] Various governmental agencies tried futilely to stabilize the economy and society during the buildup for the expedition. Even in August 1926, with the Northern Expedition extended deep into Hunan, strikes in Canton affected postal communications and the Shih-ching Arsenal producing ammunitions for the front.[15] This seemed proof to those promoting the *national* revolution that a *social* revolution could not be carried on simultaneously.

Another in the KMT hierarchy who tried to function within the framework of the KMT-CCP compromise was Eugene Ch'en (Yu-jen), who returned to Canton after the coup to replace anti-Communist C.C. Wu. As the KMT's new Foreign Minister, Ch'en's dynamism and familiarity with Western international law proved invaluable to Canton's National Government. Born and raised as a British citizen of Cantonese parents in the West Indies, then educated in London, Ch'en was barely conversant in Kuo-yü and could not write Chinese. However, as a diplomat it was his knowledge of the English language and his understanding of Western law that was needed in negotiating with the British and other Western powers.[16] (Similarly, it was in part Borodin's English that gained for him the appointment to deal with the Western-educated Chinese at Canton.[17]) During May 1926 when Ch'en accepted his appointment from the CEC, his greatest challenge was to settle the dispute with the British and Hong Kong so that the eleven-month-old strike and boycott could end. The frustrations he faced in his role further illumine the contradictions in the KMT-CCP United Front.

Handicapping Ch'en as Foreign Minister was the fact that although the Canton regime had initially called the strike (which it continued to fund), it had lost the leadership of the strike to the Communists on the Strike Committee. Protected by the Russian mission and its aid program, the Strike Committee refused to contribute to KMT efforts at strike settlement. A difference in goals separated Foreign Minister Ch'en and strike chairman Su Ch'ao-cheng.

Another KMT negotiator from May on was Finance Minister T.V. Soong, an ally of Chiang who had the responsibility of doling out a *daily* stipend for the strikers' maintenance, which varied from C$6,000 to C$10,000, as well as of nurturing a stable financial base for the revolutionary movement. In response to the strike chairman's vow to prolong the strike in order to intensify the social revolution, Soong threatened to end the dole as a luxury Canton could ill afford in light of its massive military expenditures, which consumed well over one-half of Canton's governmental income. As the negotiations continued into June, leaders of the NRA also urged settlement so that they could purchase needed war materiel in Hong Kong. Although popular support had peaked earlier and few friends of the strike remained in the Canton government, on June 19, 1926, the Strike Committee held a large anniversary celebration honoring the strike at its East Park headquarters. On that occasion propaganda units circulated through Canton to drum up enthusiasm for the continuance of the strike.[18] It seemed that as long as Moscow promoted the strike, the KMT had to submit. While its resource base was restricted to Kwangtung, the KMT had to depend on the Russian mission and its aid.

By mid-July 1926, after the Northern Expedition had been officially launched, Chiang himself claimed to be waiting in Canton for a satisfactory strike settlement before moving up to the front.[19] From July 15 to 23, Eugene Ch'en presided over five meetings between the British of Hong Kong and Canton's agents, which included Finance Minister Soong and Propaganda Department head Ku Meng-yü.[20] The talks snagged on one thorny concession in particular, demanded by strike chairman Su at some of the sessions. This was the payment of back wages lost during the strike, a reward that the Strike Committee had apparently promised to the strikers. Both sides offered concessions related to the Shameen Incident but neither the Strike Committee nor the British would modify their stand on the compensation of lost wages.[21]

The Hong Kong delegation offered an alternative incentive—a loan to the Canton government for the development of communications in the province that included completion of the Canton-Hankow Railroad.[22] Although the negotiations failed, Foreign Minister Ch'en's rational diplomacy did gain British respect for Canton in its search for international recognition.

Ch'en appealed to the British to realize at that crucial time ". . . the developments in Chinese society and politics and the necessity for the Chinese to save themselves . . . and consider China as an independent country among other countries."[23] Within Canton, speeches and propaganda continued to stir up xenophobic bitterness and outraged pride against the British "Imperialists" and their "running dogs," the warlords, who were the immediate object of the military campaign. For his part Foreign Minister Ch'en, away from the rhetoric of the streets, sought in vain to work around the power of the Strike Committee and to negotiate as the National Government's plenipotentiary in circumstances ". . . free from labor interference."[24] Thus, in July when the Strike Committee held another rally to gather support for the strike, Ch'en refused to participate in the movement that frustrated his diplomacy.

Another KMT official upon whom fell the burden of strike-related problems was the Minister of Workers and Peasants, Ch'en Kung-po (see chapter 2). The March 20 Coup and the ensuing compromise moved Ch'en into the Ministry of Workers and Peasants through his association with both Wang Ching-wei's Left and the CCP. However, Ch'en's primary loyalties lay with the KMT and he soon felt frustrated by the autonomy guaranteed to the CCP labor movement at Canton by the compromise.

While Eugene Ch'en and others negotiated to settle the Hong Kong Strike, Ch'en Kung-po received complaints from those at odds with the strikers—both within the government and in the private sector. His ministry also heard accusations from landholding peasants "persecuted" by the expanding peasants' associations. When Minister Ch'en Kung-po ordered the organizations to "cease and desist," his order was ignored.[25] By June 1926 charges of embezzling and extorting fees from union members leveled by businessmen against the Strike Committee and their unions required that his ministry conduct an investigation.[26]

In an effort to bring the expanding structure of mass organizations into line with the KMT's plans for the Northern Expedition, the Workers and Peasants Ministry began to register all old and new unions and peasants' associations. Although it was hoped that this process would give the KMT a chance to withhold legitimacy from offenders, the process of registration and its enforcement swamped the ministry with new headaches.[27] While the anti-Communists pressed Ch'en to be more vigorous in restraining insubordinate unions, the CCP and its labor organizers accused him of misusing his authority.

By mid-June 1926, Ch'en Kung-po in frustration was discussing resigning from the Ministry of Peasants and Workers. As Ch'en grappled with the problems of regulating labor and ordering the strike pickets to fight provincial bandits instead of workers, newly unionized restaurant workers threatened to close all Canton eating places. As a mediator Minister Ch'en did manage to halt the union's use of *armed* pickets. At the same time, Ch'en faced interunion confrontations involving the vital Shih-ching Arsenal and the Canton-Kowloon Railroad.[28]

In late June, still another thorny labor problem emerged as the GLU worked to bring about a strike against the foreign-run Canton Customs Office. When organizers arrested the entire Chinese staff, Mayor Sun Fo of Canton had to face protesting foreign customs officials.[29] The failure of

Ch'en Kung-po to restrain the mass organizations stirred the anti-Communists and others to pressure for a new head for the ministry who would better serve the aims of the KMT. Caught in the cross fire, Ch'en Kung-po accepted an invitation to join the Northern Expedition as a member of the commander-in-chief's staff, which allowed him to resign from an impossible task.

CHAPTER 8

The Promotion of the Northern Expedition

How then did Chiang Kai-shek, the leader of the March 20 Coup and the prime mover of the Northern Expedition, relate to the mass organizations as he pressed the NRA to march north? In the Revolutionary Base, Chiang seems to have begun with a rather ambiguous political attitude toward the "masses," with whom he had limited experience. Like Sun, he wished that the lives of the Chinese peasants and workers would be uplifted. He believed that this would not take place under the exploitation of the warlords and their foreign collaborators. China's modernization, political unity, and social progress all required the reintegration of China as a nation under a strong government. To Chiang and other partisans, it had become obvious since 1911 that this reunification demanded military power, as had been the case during the founding of all prior regimes in China. As a military man, Chiang gave priority to military means that would defeat the several major warlords on the battlefield. During the victorious Eastern Expeditions of 1925, Chiang had been impressed by the effectiveness of mobilized peasants and workers. However, as Chiang observed the mass organizations come under CCP direction and pull away from what he considered the Party mission, he developed anxieties about their role.

Chiang observed at close quarters the growing Hong Kong Strike apparatus from June 1925 through the fall of 1926. Although the KMT had earlier created unions and peasant associations on its own, its efforts were of a small scale compared to the organizing of the masses by CCP allies in 1925. As military director of the successful Second Eastern Expedition,

Chiang saw that supportive union members and peasants had speeded the movement of his forces by carrying materiel and by serving where needed. At a crucial juncture, railroad workers had deprived Chiang's enemy of the use of the Canton-Kowloon line. Even after the March 20 Coup against their Communist leaders, Chiang retained an awareness of the military value of cooperative masses, and on May 1, 1926, he reaffirmed this in a speech to a joint session of the Second National Labor Congress and the Second Provincial Peasants' Congress. He acknowledged that the victory of the Party Army in Kwangtung had been won through a confederation of peasants, workers, and soldiers, so that ". . . from my [Chiang's] past experience I realize the benefit of the cooperation of peasants and workers with the revolutionary army." After an interval in which their paths had diverged, Chiang again hoped to draw the mass organizations back into this same kind of collaboration, but on a larger scale. Chiang reminded the assembly that the role of the soldiers of the NRA was most crucial in that they could quicken the overthrow of the warlords and the imperialists. He stressed that while the union of classes had already proven itself in Kwangtung, ". . . this must be a National Revolution,"[1] and suggested that his military leadership would provide the catalyst to galvanize these classes to fight for the reunion of China.

CCP interpretation had to place the earlier Eastern Expeditions in an ideologically correct framework so that "only after the Hong Kong-Kwangtung Strike was the Canton government able to consolidate power in Kwangtung and then have the power to carry on the Northern Expedition."[2] The Communist versions slight the *military* nature of the Eastern Expeditions and ignore the fact that the enforcement of the strike and the rapid expansion of the strike apparatus, including unions and peasants' associations, *followed* the military conquest of Kwangtung.

However valuable the strikers may have been as military auxiliaries in 1925, Chiang concluded that by 1926 they were a financial drain on the struggling Canton regime. Once again, Chiang urged the use of idle strikers on public projects such as road building or on the project to make Whampoa a deepwater port.[3] At the mid-April 1926 meeting of KMT leaders, the National Government Committee stated tactfully that it would give unemployed strikers "preference" when hiring workers for the Whampoa port project.[4] This moderate approach complied with the compromise worked out with the Russians, but the response from the Strike Committee was nominal and disappointing. To Chiang's May Day call for support from the workers and peasants in the coming Northern Expedition, the Strike Committee had countered with a campaign to extend the strike (which Chiang wanted settled) and to promote it through a union of all labor organizations favoring the strike and thus "strengthen the foundation of the National Government."[5]

As Chiang gained more authority at Canton he felt better able to press for the settlement of the strike and the commencement of the Northern Expedition. He had been chairman of the Military Council since April, and he could also count on Chairman T'an Yen-k'ai of the Political Council to promote the expedition. With rivals Wang Ching-wei and Hu Han-min gone from Canton, both the Left and Right KMT were weakened. During April, Chiang had been able to gather the backing he needed, although after the March 20 Coup he had faced considerable opposition *within* the KMT as well as from the Russian-CCP bloc. At the April 16 meeting of the KMT, the talk had even revolved around *abandonment* of the expedition in favor of consolidation of the Revolutionary Base[6]—the line later promoted by Borodin, chief military advisor Galen, and Ch'en Tu-hsiu.[7] Chiang felt confidant enough on May 11 to demand that the Party approve his plans to launch the expedition.[8] By May 17, the CEC had approved Chiang's compromise with the CCP and appointed him to the bipartisan board that was to oversee CCP-KMT relations. Thus secured in his authority, Chiang had the Military Council publish a manifesto openly attacking warlord Wu P'ei-fu and urging the masses to join together against him.[9]

Under Chiang's dominance the Military Council sent off the financial aid required to keep the new Kwangsi allies poised along the border with Hunan and ordered Fourth Army elements north to reinforce T'ang Sheng-chih in his rebellion against the clique of overlord Wu P'ei-fu.[10] By this time Chiang was promoted to *acting* commander-in-chief (C-in-C) of the NRA, with CEC-designated powers over *all* branches of the KMT's new military system, which then included seven "armies," the navy, air force, arsenals, and Political Departments (in conjunction with the CEC).[11]

As Chiang ordered the vanguard of the expedition into Hunan in May 1926, he again confronted the contradiction between KMT aims and those of the Strike Committee. In the absence of a railroad, moving the war materiel over the high passes into Hunan demanded the use of large numbers of human carriers. Chiang appealed to the Strike Committee to release unemployed strikers quartered in Canton—this time for carrier duty. Once again, the token response was slow. In the meantime, to fill the needs of the Fourth Army at the advance post of Shaokuan, Chiang's supply corps had to hire porters in the sparsely populated mountains. Ultimately, from over 60,000 strikers then in Kwangtung dependent on the Strike Committee, only 1,500 arrived in Shaokuan for paid carrier work.[12] At that rate the NRA had to continue to recruit the carriers near the front. Chiang's many new titles did not outweigh the influence of the Russian mission and its pet project, the Strike Committee.

An eight-point agenda passed by the CEC on May 31, 1926, revealed KMT concern over the Hong Kong Strike and other problems, some of which were related to the strike and Russian aid.

1. The National Government at Canton should end the official oil (Russian oil) and kerosene monopoly by June 15.
2. The Foreign Ministry and concerned agencies should begin negotiations to settle the Hong Kong-Kwangtung Strike.
3. In order to end banditry and piracy in Kwangtung within two months, the Military Council should appropriate C$500,000.
4. Create an arbitration board chaired by a member of the National Government and representing equally labor and management.

5. Prohibit the use of arms by civilian organizations in order to end rioting.
6. Investigate corruption in the government and severely punish the offenders.
7. Those spreading rumors, plotting, and organizing seditious political parties must be investigated and punished by court martial.
8. Plan and maintain programs for education, road construction, and harbor improvement.[13]

Soon after, on June 4, the CEC voted Chiang the title of commander-in-chief of the Northern Expedition with orders to launch an offensive as soon as possible.[14]

In accordance with CEC decisions, Canton's Foreign Ministry reopened negotiations with British Hong Kong over the strike. Foreign Minister Eugene Ch'en and the British side quickly dispatched their negotiators to Macao for talks.[15] The British and Canton agreed to begin with the question of the confiscation of contraband British goods from Hong Kong.[16]

While T.V. Soong participated in the negotiations, his Ministry of Finance sought new revenue outside the trade sector. Authorized by the CEC to end the unpopular oil monopoly (part of Russia's aid), Soong released the sale of oil to private retailers, but placed a high tax on oil products—especially the widely used kerosene. Backed by the sound fiscal reputation of Canton's Central Bank (also under his supervision), Soong issued C\$5 million in government bonds to provide quick capital. Since the Canton government had expanded its authority throughout Kwangtung it could utilize the main provincial railroads for revenue as well as communications—thus Soong increased the fares by 50 percent and placed a surtax on freight charges. On Kwangtung's rivers, the KMT navy helped enforce a new requirement for registration of the multitude of river craft, thus checking piracy as well as increasing revenue through a registration fee. Without the flag that came with inspection and registration, a vessel was suspected of involvement in piracy. The government chose to profit from popular fan-tan rather than ban it, and therefore taxed the gambling.[17] To reduce the strain on Canton's existing sources of revenue, the NRA's Supply Corps at the Hunan front made plans to sell Kwangtung salt once it had pushed into salt-hungry Hunan.[18] To cut Canton's expenditures for the Hong Kong strikers and regain commercial revenue lost through the trade boycott, Soong also argued for an end to the strike and boycott.

Affiliated with the strike organization were the many CCP-directed mass organizations that distracted those trying to launch the Northern Expedition. However, since Chiang still hoped that the organized masses would serve his troops, and since he was still dependent on Russian aid for weapons such as aircraft with Russian pilots, he could not afford himself the luxury of breaking up the United Front. While Chiang pressed for the settlement of the strike and the service of the strikers, at the same time he appeared to sympathize with the Left's social revolution when he preached looking to "the Russian Revolution as a model and example."[19] To counterweigh the CCP's role with the masses, a new non-Communist alliance was to gather in the older KMT unions, such as the Mechanics' Union and the KGLU, and the peasants' associations and merchants' groups. To inaugurate this more cooperative bloc, the KMT gathered a mass of 100,000 at the East Parade Ground on June 14, 1926. Half of the crowd were members of KMT-affiliated unions. A parade with lanterns and banners, and fireworks enlivened the demonstration. A new slogan "Support the National Government and the KMT" was emblazoned on the banners that flapped as the procession passed the National Government and KMT buildings.[20] Presiding over the mass meeting was a delegate from the Chamber of Commerce, symbolic of the role the merchants played in the KMT's all-class union. This new mass organ provided the KMT with needed influence upon various elements in Canton society. The alliance became a convenient sounding board for the KMT, which publicized actions taken by the Party in response to the petitions received from this mass alliance.

That Chiang could not elicit equal obedience from the Strike Committee was evidenced by its counterdemonstration four days later on June 18 in celebration of the Hong Kong Strike's first year. Strikers in propaganda units preached the continuance of the strike to the city people.[21] The affair was held at the East Park headquarters of the Strike Committee, which the CCP later recorded as "actually a revolutionary government" in itself.[22] A few days later on June 23, Chiang did join in a demonstration in memory of the Shameen "massacre," which sought to rekindle the emotions of 1925 with large gory photographs of the casualties, and a parade of simulated wounded in torn, bloody garments. To further stir up nationalistic zeal, Chiang shouted to the assemblage of 30,000 that if they united with the KMT in the National Revolution, they could not only settle the strike but regain Hong Kong and put an end to the unequal treaties, an appeal aimed not only at the masses but at the ubiquitous Russian advisors seated on the podium.[23] The Strike Committee prudently avoided forcing Chiang into open opposition, but rather tantalized him with prospects of cooperation. Within days after the June Shameen anniversary, the Strike Committee sent Chiang word that the crack, blue-shirted strike pickets, with a year's training and experience in political work, and other strikers would join the Northern Expedition *after* the strike was settled.[24] Upon persuasion, the Strike Committee consented to set up a subcommittee to aid the NRA Supply Corps in an immediate recruitment of carriers for the expedition.[25] A Communist historian later claimed that the Strike Committee sent north 3,000 strikers in "transportation units" to move the NRA over the Wuling Range into Hunan.[26] Three thousand strikers would have been less than 3 percent of the 120,000 strikers of Kwangtung and Hong Kong that the CCP claimed to control in 1926.[27]

The third point on the KMT's May 31 agenda was aimed against piracy and banditry within the Revolutionary Base. Since rebels and dissidents had traditionally been classified "bandits," their suppression had political significance. For this purpose Chiang called on Li Fu-lin's Fifth Army of the NRA since Li had many connections with provincials. Banditry in Kwangtung's uplands threatened the coming expedition in that the vital rail line to Shaokuan passed through territory infested with Kwangtung's notorious bandits. Dispersing the bandits would guarantee the transportation of valuable war materiel by train and would also weaken the argument for the CCP's arming of their peasants' associations into self-defense corps. The local self-defense militias that developed during the nineteenth century into the White Lotus and Taiping rebel armies had proven the dangers of allowing locals to form militias. In mid-1926, Chiang not only ordered various elements of the NRA to suppress unauthorized armed groups in Kwangtung, but also saw to it that trains en route north to Shaokuan were well guarded and the line patrolled.[28] At the line's Canton terminal, Chiang appointed Cantonese Li Chi-shen of the Fourth Army to collaborate with the garrison command and police in defense of the capital, as well as to act as Chiang's chief of staff in the C-in-C's headquarters.[29]

Five thousand of Li Chi-shen's troops made up the vanguard at the Kwangtung-Hunan border. Representing the Kwangtung contingent, Li's forces also acted to balance the Hunanese composition of T'an Yen-k'ai's Second Army and the Seventh Army of Kwangsi. Once the expedition moved through Hunan, Chiang would not be able to afford a powerful Hunanese entente. In the Military Council, Chiang further balanced T'an's influence with Chekiangese Chang Ching-chiang and T.V. Soong.[30]

Keeping the KMT and the Revolutionary Base together required much political skill because the Party did not monopolize the use of arms. Since the postcoup compromise had allowed the CCP to organize the peasants even to the point of arming them, as the spring proceeded, some rural parts of Kwangtung seemed to be on the verge of class struggle rather than class union. General Ho Ying-ch'in, Chiang's appointee as First Army First Division commander and head of the Ch'aochou branch of the military academy, was also the East River Party Committee chairman and he worried about the rising tensions in rural eastern Kwangtung. The expansive peasants' associations had been creating self-defense corps through which they pressured local landlords and big merchants. In eastern Kwangtung, the peasants' associations cooperated with the Strike Committee branch in Swatow in blocking the trade between local rice merchants and Hong Kong markets. In motion was also a revolution in the land rent system. One system promoted by the peasants' associations was to divide land produce so that the peasants would retain 60 percent, the landowners 20 percent, and the peasants' association 20 percent—an income that would give the associations great economic power with which to arm themselves. As the Communist combine of peasants' associations and strike pickets began to exercise authority in rural Kwantung, a flood of complaints of persecution poured into Ho Ying-ch'in's headquarters from the gentry. By early June 1926, General Ho, in response to the threat of strife in his districts, ordered troops into the countryside "to protect the people."[31]

As the Party's leader in East Kwangtung, Ho moved against what he considered to be instigating the disorder—the Communist peasant and worker organizations. He prohibited unions from trying outsiders in their courts, threatening the local rural officials with force, slandering and accusing falsely, and seizing arms from the old gentry-dominated rural militias (*min-t'uan*) for use in armed union demonstrations. A spokesman for Chiang, Ho criticized organizations that ". . . spread propaganda pamphlets, drove away *hsien* (district) officials . . . and overstepped their authority merely on the basis of their party membership."[32] Quite likely, the point in the KMT's May 21 agenda on "banditry" and "the use of arms by civilian organizations" referred indirectly to Communist mass organizations and their growing *rural* power, as well as their autonomy in Canton.

Thus, when Canton's declaration of war was issued against Wu P'ei-fu during the first week in July, it can be argued that Chiang was not a military dictator moving out from a secure Revolutionary Base. In fact he felt forced to gamble against the overwhelming superiority of his warlord adversaries, numerically and in firepower. Within the Revolutionary Base, Chiang faced banditry throughout the countryside and the escalating conflict between the peasants' associations with their self-defense corps and the rural establishment (portents of the coming year's events). Chiang and the KMT had not been able to force the Strike Committee and the Russian mission to accept a settlement of the Hong Kong Strike, so trade remained stymied by the armed pickets spread out along the heavily populated coast of Kwangtung. In Canton, the temporary "capital" of the KMT National Government, strife had become endemic between the unions of the Strike Committee and those that had predated the strike. Dominated by the Strike Committee, workers who had been unionized according to trades by the armed, blue-shirted, strike pickets confronted their employers violently, who in turn reacted vigorously. Although forbidden by the regime, even the postal service, vital railways, and arsenals indispensable to the expedition had been disrupted by walkouts, strikes, and disorder.[33]

Defensive about burgeoning rival CCP power, the KMT military was susceptible to "reactionary" leadership promoting a clean sweep of radicalism and Russian imperialism. Against those anxious forces on the right, Chiang had to use what moderates and Leftists he could gather. In the balance was the tenuous and ambiguous support of the CCP and Russian aid from Stalin. While contained in Kwangtung, the KMT could not afford to offend its generous Russian patrons. The compromise following the March 20 Coup, which Chiang catalyzed, was unstable and weakening. There were rumors of conspiracies and planned coups from March until the declaration of war against Wu. Then, the threat of a combined northern offensive against Kwangtung helped those in the Revolutionary Base to reunite. In late June and early July 1926, word arrived of the victories of Wu P'ei-fu's Hunan allies against the troops of rebel T'ang Sheng-chih with the NRA vanguard.[34]

Although the Russian strategists and the CCP had recently mouthed their support of the Northern Expedition, they were anxious about a campaign led by a military force outside their influence. Even as the KMT launched the expedition during the first week in July, and after the appointment of Chiang as Minister of Soldiers, C-in-C of the NRA, and chairman of the KMT Standing Committee, Ch'en Tu-hsiu could still criticize the rashness of the offensive. According to the CCP leader:

> . . . from the political circumstances within the National Government [at Canton], the scope of influence of the National Government, the fighting strength of the troops of the National Government, and the ideology of the revolution, it can be seen that the time for the Northern Expedition has not yet arrived. The true question at this time should be not about a Northern Expedition but how best to defend? How to defend against the *Southern* Expedition of Wu P'ei-fu? How to defend Kwangtung against ruination from the force of the anti-red armies? . . . Furthermore, at this time the words of the nation's masses are not "Rise up for the Northern Expedition" but "Support the Revolutionary Base in Kwangtung!" Trapped by a four-sided attack, the leaders of the National Government should stand together in maintaining the liberty and rights of the people. This is where the fighting Revolutionary Army differs from the warlords. [35]

The dangers that abounded in Kwangtung energized Chiang and the NRA. For him and the KMT, time appeared to be running out. The Party had suffered the successive frustrations of defeat and exile during three decades. Just five years prior, on the eve of an earlier northern expedition, Sun had been betrayed by factions within the KMT. In the meantime, regional overlords had become even stronger. Would the KMT lose its chance to unite China and implement its dreams? Outside the confines of Kwangtung's hilly border, Chiang saw chances for:

1. an entrance through the mountain passes into Hunan due to the defection of T'ang Sheng-chih;
2. an expansion of the KMT's military potential through a gathering in of defectors and sympathizers, such as T'ang and Russia's protegé Feng Yü-hsiang and his Kuominchün (National People's Army) in the northwest;
3. the capture of the arsenals and industrial resources of Wuhan and then those downstream at Nanking and Shanghai (site of China's largest arsenal and entrepôt of most of China's capital); and
4. the achievement of independence from Russian aid and Communist influence.

Furthermore, it was hoped that the expedition from Kwangtung, not only against warlord Wu, but also against foreign imperialism in the Yangtze valley, might spark the nationalism that Chiang counted on to unite the KMT and China. As Chiang told a group of propagandists leaving for the front from Whampoa: "Chinese have always been politically apathetic, but if there is aggression from foreigners they may fight for national survival."[36] The KMT rationale for the Northern Expedition can also be read from speeches and orders published in early July 1926.

On July 1, 1926, the KMT promulgated the Mobilization Order for the Northern Expedition as part of an anniversary celebration honoring the establishment of the National Government in 1925 at Canton. After ten of the Party's hierarchy swore loyalty to the principles of Sun Yat-sen, Chairman Chiang of the Military Council read the order:[37]

Our army keeps alive the will of the late generalissimo and hopes to carry out his revolutionary proposals. To protect the welfare of the people we must overthrow all warlords and wipe out reactionary power so that we may implement the Three People's Principles and complete the National Revolution. Now, gather we our armies, first to occupy Hunan, then Wuhan, and pressing further to join up with our ally the *Kuominchün* to unite China and restore our nation. Since the Fourth and Seventh Armies have already moved out, I order the Second, Third, Fifth, and Sixth Armies to move forward and mass together. . . .[38]

On July 4, a special meeting of the CEC explained that:

The hardships of the workers, peasants, merchants, and students and the suffering of all under the oppressive imperialists and warlords; the peace and unification of China called for by Sun Yat-sen; the gathering of the National Assembly ruined by Tuan Ch'i-jui; all demand the elimination of Wu P'ei-fu and completion of national unification.[39]

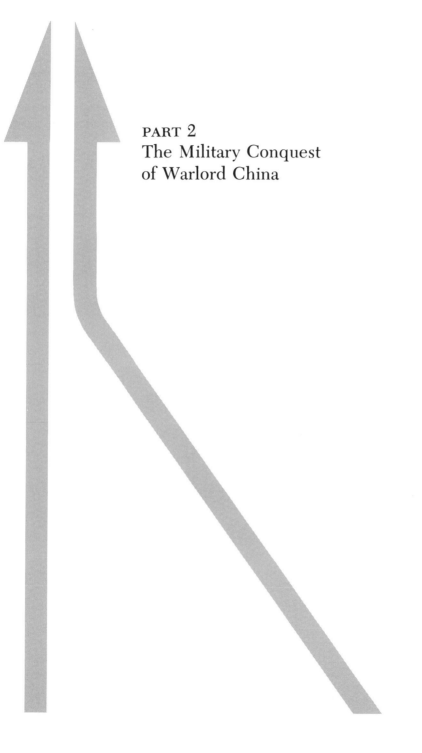

PART 2
The Military Conquest
of Warlord China

CHAPTER 9
The Launch into Hunan

Facing staggering odds, Canton's KMT launched what seemed to some
outsiders to be a romantic episode from a Chinese opera. On the verge of
disintegration with inadequate materiel and only tentative Russian aid, the
military campaign was a gamble. Chiang and his supporters had to count
more on the weakness of their enemies than on their own powers. The
expedition, warned against by the Russian experts,[1] could well have
proven to be another quixotic blunder, but it was victorious, at least in
military terms. The record of the NRA offensive, except for a lengthy army
chronology of the positioning of units, has been glossed over with a set of
orthodox clichés and anti-KMT rhetoric. The Northern Expedition set in
motion again centripetal forces that began to reunite China, this time as a
modern nation—a process that continues under the CCP. This wide-
ranging military campaign needs to be scrutinized in a chronological
framework. Ideology aside, there is evidence that there was more military
action involved than was admitted by those partisans who, in hoping for
political solutions to China's ills, wrote off the expedition as a tragedy.

Although such partisans described the expedition as an easy sweep
northward led by a vanguard wave of Communist propagandists whose
ideas knocked down warlord forces, there is more to be seen. The Communist propagandists only participated in the two-year campaign north
from mid-1926 until the split with the KMT in early 1927—at best a period
of nine months. I intended primarily to study the political techniques used
by these successful propagandists, but a closer look at the actual combat

could not be avoided. Part 2 will chronicle the military aspects of the expedition and Part 3 will focus on the political work.

Moving north, the campaign had both traditional and modern colorings. As with the founding of China's innumerable dynasties, the NRA moved out of a defensible provincial basin (Kwangtung) and conquered one regional rival after another and gathered military allies until China had again the semblance of a political entity. The consolidation from such a hegemony into a single, centralized state would remain still another phase in the rebuilding. In 1926, however, there was something more than the usual charismatic strong man at the head of his personal army. To be sure there were personal armies within the NRA confederation, but, in addition, at the core, there were the pooled modern talents of two political parties and the stirring vision of modern nationhood and progress. There was also a shared concern that the resulting political system should move *toward* democracy rather than revert to the ancient institution of imperial autocracy.

THE OPENING EPISODE—HUNAN

The first phase of the expedition, against the rich middle-Yangtze provinces of Hunan and Hupei under Wu P'ei-fu, began under less than propitious conditions. The route of the Northern Expedition into Hunan and Hupei, down the Yangtze, and then up the North China Plain toward Peking, followed that of the Taiping rebels who had also started in weakness. Then, Chiang's buildup in 1927 in the lower Yangtze was also reminiscent of Chu Yüan-hung's strategy preceding his capture of Peking as the first Ming emperor.

To enter Hunan, rather than count on its military power and authority, the KMT and Chiang were forced to consider heavily the realities of local politics. The situation in Hunan exemplified the inner workings of the Northern Expedition in other provinces. In 1926, before the Northern Expedition, Hunan—as with most of South and Central China—rankled under the domination of *northern* Chinese warlords—outsiders. Antagonisms festered between the native subordinates and these regional overlords, providing unstable political situations with which the KMT could deal. Although avowedly nationalistic, the KMT played upon and manipulated local and provincial ambitions where they could weaken an overlord or win an ally. The exploitation of local interests and provincialism, or self-rule, was one of the weapons in the diverse KMT arsenal, along with modern and traditional political techniques and a military machine that had been energized by nationalism. But, how did the NRA manage to penetrate the first, highly defensible mountain barrier to Hunan?

In Hunan, the opportunity presented for KMT intervention or invasion was a provincial power struggle. The Hunanese gentry had kept alive the desire for provincial autonomy as delineated by the Hunan Constitution on 1922. The governor, Chao Heng-t'i, was a native of Hunan; he was subordinate to the Shantung overlord, Wu P'ei-fu.[2] By 1926 a conflict emerged

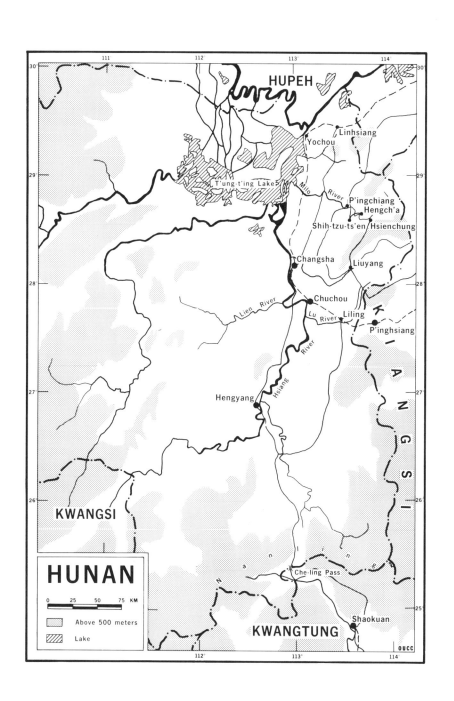

HUPEH

Linhsiang

Yochou

T'ung-t'ing Lake

Mlo River

P'ingchiang
Hengch'a

Shih-tzu-ts'en Hsienchung

Changsha

Liuyang

Chuchou

Lien River

Lu River Liling

P'inghsiang

K
I
A
N
G
S
I

Hengyang

Hsiang River

KWANGSI

N a n l i n g

Che-ling Pass

KWANGTUNG

Shaokuan

OUCC

HUNAN

0   25   50   75 KM

Above 500 meters

Lake

among the four Hunanese division commanders, and Governor Chao favored Yeh K'ai-hsin, commander of the strongest provincial force, the Third Hunan Division, when awarding patronage. Governor Chao sought to weaken the local power of the division commanders while centralizing his authority over the province. Thus, he used Yeh to check the power of T'ang Sheng-chih whose Fourth Division was the largest. With his troops, T'ang held a sizable subfief in southwestern Hunan. T'ang's defensiveness over Governor Chao's move to assume grass-roots power attracted the attention of neighboring Kwangtung. The promoters of the long-postponed Northern Expedition turned their attention toward Hunan.

Intervention in Hunanese provincial politics had required that the KMT utilize those of its members with personal connections there. The Party membership did include among those with personal ties in Hunan both civilian and military figures. As a national Party, the KMT enjoyed an advantage in that its membership transcended any single provincial or regional basis. Although some foreign observers misread the movement as a Cantonese affair, Party members working at Canton or at assignments elsewhere came from Central and South China predominantly, but also from North China. While the CCP may have had among its cadre men like Mao Tse-tung who worked with the *rural* masses of Hunan, the KMT had ties with those at the apex of Hunan's power structure.

At Canton was KMT member and leading proponent of the Northern Expedition T'an Yen-k'ai. T'an had been the first governor of Hunan elected by the Provincial Assembly after the Revolution of 1911 and had then become active in the movement for federalism and Hunan *self-rule*. Although forced into exile by northern military might, T'an maintained an interest in Hunan and held in Kwangtung a force of 15,000 Hunanese troops, renamed the Second Army of the NRA. His own personal ideology epitomized the KMT accomodation of provincialism and nationalism. Prior to 1926, T'an had already led one military campaign to retake Hunan for Sun Yat-sen. Back in late 1924, during Sun's final attempt to achieve a coalition with the northern powers, T'an had launched an ill-conceived and short-lived campaign, which was supposed to enhance Sun's bargaining position in Peking. A military commander in Kiangsi had forced T'an and his troops back into Kwangtung to await a future opportunity.[3] The failure of T'an's rather crude invasion may have taught the lesson of the importance of political as well as military preparations.

By the spring of 1926, Chiang and other promoters of military reunification of China thought that their plans to invade Hunan were progressing well and the gamble worth the risk.

Aside from ex-governor T'an Yen-k'ai, the KMT at Canton included other men who had been associated with T'ang Sheng-chih of Hunan. Liu Wen-tao and Ch'en Ming-shu had been classmates of T'ang at the Paoting Military Academy where in 1912 they had collaborated in a student reform movement. As recently as 1925, Liu had utilized this connection in Hunan to arrange with T'ang Sheng-chih for a propaganda tour of the province. Liu Wen-tao, by then a professor of political science with a French doctorate, toured China lecturing on the Three People's Principles of the KMT. T'ang had seen to it that Liu gained an audience with the officers and soldiers of not only his Fourth Hunan Division, but with other Hunan forces.[4] Incorporated into the KMT's NRA was the Seventh Army of Kwangsi militarist Pai Ch'ung-hsi, another schoolmate of T'ang. Elsewhere in Hunan, the KMT had connections with another Hunan division commander, Ho Yao-tsu, through KMT member Ch'eng Ch'ien, who was Hunanese and a classmate from Tokyo's Shikan Gakko, and commander of the NRA's Sixth Army—primarily a Hunanese force.[5] At the top of Hunan's military-political structure was Governor Chao Heng-t'i whom Chiang Kai-shek tried to win over as late as the week before the July 1926 launching of the expedition. Chiang approached him as a fellow member of the old "Ko-ming Tang" (Revolutionary Party) and pleaded by telegram that they should be reunited in a new national movement that would strengthen China against her enemies.[6] Thus, the leaders of the Northern Expedition could communicate with relative ease with the leaders of Hunan. If ambitious T'ang Sheng-chih in Hunan and others could be won over as military allies, the NRA could avoid a bloody struggle for the mountain passes guarding the Yangtze basin.

In southern Hunan, T'ang Sheng-chih, dominating the Hsiang valley with his 9,000-man division, derived provincial prestige from his father, an ex-Ch'ing mandarin, who continued on in the provincial office of Councillor of Domestic Affairs—one of the five highest councillors of the provincial *civil* administration. The real power of T'ang centered in his division, the largest provincial military unit. T'ang also had ties with many of China's warlords through Paoting, the alma mater of China's warlords.[7] From 1921 to 1926, T'ang Sheng-chih had carefully expanded his domain to include twenty-seven of Hunan's seventy-five tax-collection districts. However, in early 1926, Governor Chao ordered all four Hunan division commanders to remit the local taxes they gathered to the provincial capital at Changsha.[8] Obviously Chao's move to centralize provincial authority would conflict with the local interests of his subordinates. The loss of revenue from taxes would have made T'ang dependent on the provincial governor for support of his division, and therefore T'ang began to evaluate his own chances for provincial leadership. According to one estimate made within Hunan, at stake were the following sources of revenue: T'ang's twenty-seven tax districts in Hunan from which the land tax brought him a minimum of $800,000 monthly; the provincial lead and zinc mines at Shui-k'ou-shan worth $90,000 monthly; the "special tax" on opium collected in his districts, which brought him nearly $1 million monthly; and the monthly allocation from the provincial government of $240,000 for T'ang's Hunan Fourth Division.[9] The leadership in Canton responded to the signs of T'ang Sheng-chih's resistance to Governor Chao by approaching T'ang with the prospect of an alliance.

Official talks between the KMT and T'ang Sheng-chih had begun at least as early as February 1926. At that point T'ang may not have favored direct intervention from Canton. Regional militarists had learned that invited allies often exhibited rapacious appetites while within a host's domain and tended to stay on as unwelcomed guests. Since T'ang did control Hunan's largest, if not the best, division he chafed under Governor Chao and overlord Wu. Merely the threat of Canton's intervention might give T'ang bargaining power over Chao. T'ang also sought from the KMT the assurance that Hunanese T'an Yen-k'ai would not rush north to fill the vacant governorship once Chao was ousted. (In March 1926, T'ang also showed anxiety over the radicalism he observed in local KMT agents, which threatened his own local authority.[10]) By February 24, 1926, T'ang did accept Canton's offer of an alliance. When T'ang Sheng-chih moved his troops out against Governor Chao in February, Canton had not yet sent reinforcements, but overlord Wu was preoccupied in North China with Feng Yü-hsiang. Thus threatened, Chao fled the capital city of Changsha for safer territory to the north.[11] Significantly, as T'ang attacked Chao, he criticized the governor as a puppet of *northerner* Wu P'ei-fu and for ignoring the provincial constitution of 1922.[12] These were arguments of provincial autonomism, not nationalism. T'ang did *not* mention the tax districts, nor did the KMT. On the other hand, a barrage of nationalistic propaganda went out from Canton on February 25 and 26 against the northern warlords in general and against Wu P'ei-fu in particular, whose territories straddled the proposed route of the expedition.[13]

During February and March 1926, while Chiang struggled for the authority in the KMT to launch the Northern Expedition, T'ang's rebellion proceeded on his own resources. Still confident in early March, T'ang rebuffed the conciliatory offer of Governor Chao and marched across his province into northern Hunan.[14] In Canton at that time, the KMT's Commissioner of Foreign Affairs stated that no real support had reached T'ang Sheng-chih but the expedition to aid him would start out from Kwangtung in late April.[15] When T'ang captured Changsha in mid-March, a swell of gentry support from the Provincial Assembly encouraged him to accept the governorship. While his regiments overran Yochou on Hunan's northern border, T'ang postponed his acceptance until Canton would further clarify the nature of their alliance. But in March the tensions between KMT factions, partly over the launching of the Northern Expedition, made the future of the campaign insecure, indeed. The March 20 Coup expedited aid to T'ang in Hunan. Within days of the coup, on March 25, T'ang Sheng-chih had accepted from Hunan's Provincial Assembly a post equated with acting governor—that of Councillor of Domestic Affairs. With his new authority, T'ang proceeded to purge his opponents from the provincial administration, again arguing as a provincial autonomist that they had not been appointed in accordance with Hunan's constitution. T'ang then installed his own candidates.[16]

In late March 1926, Wu P'ei-fu responded to the threat against his hegemony in Hunan by threatening to return south with his Honanese troops. Although Wu's forces were still engaged in North China against Feng Yü-hsiang, T'ang paused since Canton's reinforcements still had not materialized. Aware of the defensiveness of Wu and his northern allies against the "radicalism" in the south, T'ang played down his connections with the KMT for a time and posed as a neutral provincialist. In Changsha, T'ang shut down a new "radical" KMT newspaper, *Ta Hunan jih-pao* [Greater Hunan daily] protected the vacant residence of Governor Chao against confiscation by KMT agents, and forbade partisans from committing any hostile acts against foreign consulates at Changsha.[17] When the northern alliance expelled Feng Yü-hsiang from the North China Plain in early April 1926, Wu had been freed to deal with the rebellion in Hunan. At that point Wu's threat was effective.[18] Since T'ang still stood alone, he recalled his regiments from northern Hunan, evacuated his forces from the provincial capital, and began to dig in defensively in his home valley.[19]

As with most of the overlords with provincial subordinates, Wu P'ei-fu understood the importance of conciliating provincial feelings. To rebuild his eroded authority in Hunan, Wu had tried the common device of appointing natives to manage a province for him. From the existing power structure of Hunan, Wu on May 5 named Hunan Third Division commander Yeh K'ai-hsin to be the acting military governor, and the commander of the First Division, Ho Yao-tsu, to be civil governor. However, Wu backed down when Hunanese gentry for self-rule in the Provincial Assembly cried out immediately that this was a flagrant disregard of the authority guaranteed them by the Hunan constitution.[20] Thus thwarted, Wu reverted to the use of armed power to pacify Hunan—the most common solution to political questions in twentieth-century China.

During May 1926, T'ang Sheng-chih had suffered defeat and had fallen back on the defensive against the Hunan allies of Wu P'ei-fu. It was from this threat that CCP leader Ch'en Tu-hsiu argued for defense of Kwangtung instead of an offensive campaign. Until the troops of the NRA climbed over the border mountains to reinforce T'ang's crumbling defenses in the Hsiang valley, there was little to inspire his faith in his future or that of the National Revolution. Thousands of troops of the NRA's Fourth and Seventh armies did begin to arrive during the latter weeks of May.[21] But even then the zealous troops of the only CCP commander, Yeh T'ing, were still outnumbered and stymied in southern Hunan.[22]

Not until June 2, did T'ang accept from Chiang Kai-shek the long-offered title of commander of the Eighth Army in the NRA—a final symbol of his incorporation into the National Revolution. Besides renumbering the military units that defected to the NRA, the larger unit commanders were raised in status and pay by redesignation of their units as the next larger size. Thus, T'ang moved up from a divisional command to an army command in the NRA, and his regimental commanders likewise became division commanders. This manner of promotion for a unit commander and his subordinate officers followed existing practices in warlord China and was used during the rest of the Northern Expedition. A few days after T'ang accepted his new status, the NRA forces in Hunan accepted T'ang Sheng-chih as front commander. It was not until July 9, 1926, when the offensive showed promise that the Northern Expedition was launched formally at Canton. T'ang's local authority was further enhanced and legitimized when the KMT's National Government notified him from Canton that it recognized his provincial preeminence. From his Hengyang stronghold, T'ang announced that in the name of the National Government he would head a provisional Hunan government as acting governor.[23] Thus blended in Hunan the aspirations of T'ang Sheng-chih and the national revolutionaries.

Behind the word storm of nationalistic propaganda that swirled around the KMT's reunification movement, the Party had been forced to hold out the lure of provincial autonomy and federalism. The launching of the Northern Expedition into Hunan was a marriage of convenience between the promoters of nationhood and the local power holders. Even among Chiang's major supporters in the promotion of the expedition had been one whose career incorporated the ideologies of provincial self-rule and national unification. T'an Yen-k'ai had developed his prior reputation in Hunan more as an advocate of provincial autonomy than as a nationalist.[24] In the Hunan of 1926, provincialists and federalists could concede that only a united China could withstand the avarice of foreign imperialists. With the KMT apparently ready to allow a significant degree of provincial self-rule, the defection of provinces to the National Revolution would also speed the removal of the hated northern warlords, as well as end the exploitation by the imperialists. In mid-1926, some observers named the expedition the "Anti-North Campaign."[25] As overlord of Hunan, Hupei, and Honan, Shantung warlord Wu P'ei-fu was the first target. While the KMT carefully dealt with provincial feelings, it also had fostered its image as the source of national leadership. In bestowing titles and statuses on provincial collaborators, Canton's National Government asserted that it had the highest authority in the republic since it had evolved out of the National Assembly and the national election of 1912.

In July 1926, when Fourth Army divisions under Chang Fa-kuei and Ch'en Ming-shu arrived at the front, the combat changed from defensive to offensive. At that point, Wu's main forces were still far off in North China and the Hunan allies on whom he relied were soon to be outnumbered by the KMT troops pouring in from Kwangtung.

It was in these circumstances that Wu's governor, Chao Heng-t'i, defended himself during July and August along the north banks of two rivers tributary to Hunan's major watercourse, the Hsiang. From late June to early July, the KMT prepared to ford the Lien River on the west of the Hsiang basin and the Lu River on the east. Down the Hsiang lay the provincial capital, Changsha. Poised along the Lu were two Fourth Army divisions and Yeh T'ing's Independent Regiment from Canton and a Hunanese regiment of T'ang Sheng-chih as chaperone. On the Lien gathered the Kwangsi troops of the Seventh Army with the remainder of T'ang Sheng-chih's Eighth Army. As the first major allied offensive began, T'ang had the status of general director of the Hunan front as well as acting provisional governor of Hunan. The presence of T'ang Sheng-chih and his troops helped the Hunanese to identify with the movement instead of resisting the Northern Expedition as another incursion of outside troops—this time a "Cantonese" invasion.

The breakthrough along the Lien-Lu line began first with the Seventh and Eighth armies on the left wing on July 5. By the tenth, the Fourth Army elements on the right flank had joined the enemy in a battle that took the NRA down the valley through Changsha.[26] In that eastern sector, Hunan bordered Kiangsi, a satrapy of Sun Ch'uan-fang, overlord of the lower Yangtze, where the NRA scrupulously avoided any provocation that would bring in Sun to aid Wu. For as long a period as possible, the KMT strategists wished to enjoy the advantage of taking on one adversary at a time.

The NRA also gained advantage from the flooding Yangtze, which backed water up the streams of northern Hunan and greatly slowed enemy communications from the north. With reinforcements from Wu's headquarters at Wuhan thus impeded, his subordinates in Hunan faced the threat of being trapped in a vulnerable, outnumbered position. On Wu's western flank, two Kweichow militarists watched ambiguously the tide of battle. Their presence endangered the western end of Wu's Hunan defenses. The poor growing season further strained the fouled communications in Hunan, since the defenders became unusually dependent on food from farther north at Wuhan, which even with the use of Wu's Yangtze navy could not be moved in adequate amounts to the southern front. Also complicating the feeding of Wu' forces was the passive resistance of Hunanese peasants who hid their produce from his supply masters.

The loss of the Lien-Lu line left Changsha defenseless, so that on July 11 the defeated troops merely retreated *through* the provincial capital to a more defensible line to the north. By mid-July, General Director of the Hunan Front T'ang accepted the fruits of victory as he collaborated in setting up the provisional Hunan administration.

With new units entering Hunan from Canton and Kwangsi, and with Hunanese joining the army,[27] the NRA gathered strength and began again to move north sporadically along the flooded lowland roads. The offensive ground along slowly from the capture of Changsha on July 11 until mid-August when the front had moved northward a mere fifty miles. Reinforcements and materiel for the NRA could be moved only half way from Canton by rail. Crossing the tortuous pass from Shaokuan, Kwangtung, into Hunan took more than a back-breaking week on foot. Soldiers had to march the distance as did the coolies hired to carry needed supplies and arms. This form of transportation limited the largest weapon used to small field cannon, which were carried by teams of carriers. In spite of the precautions followed by the sanitation teams of the NRA, cholera picked off the overheated, exhausted soldiers and civilians. Ch'en Kung-po, in his memoirs, tells of hundreds dying daily in one mountain town on the route north.[28] In August, both sides gathered their strength along the new front—the Mi-lo River. A Second Army advisor wrote in his letters that "Sometimes there are no provisions, my colleagues tear off some sort of grass, chew it and are full."[29]

The northern side could not counterattack without the full support of Wu P'ei-fu's main force, which was still supporting Chang Tso-lin's offensive in North China against Feng Yü-hsiang's Kuominchün. Casting about for aid,

Wu tried in vain to gain loans or aid from his former protégé Sun Ch'uan-fang, who was now a rival ruler in southeast China. The British refused Wu, as did the Japanese who considered Wu and the Yangtze to be within the British sphere.[30]

Despite floods and cholera, C-in-C Chiang was able to rendezvous at Hengyang with a considerable force in early August 1926.[31] By this time the commanders who gathered at Hengyang represented around 100,000 troops of the NRA *in Hunan.*[32] These numbers had swelled to include the troops of the Kweichow militarists, P'eng Han-chang and Wang T'ien-p'ei, who were attracted by the victory against the Lien-Lu line. The Kweichow force moved in West Hunan to clear out pockets of resisting soldiery.[33] In the expedition, warlord defectors tended to join the NRA when it was winning. With the aid of willing Hunanese coolies and auxiliaries, the NRA moved smoothly to set up the offensive against the line on the Mi-lo River. The peasantry, suffering from floods in the north and droughts to the south, were quite willing to work for pay for the NRA, both as carriers and army recruits, thus greatly increasing its mobility.[34] In contrast, Wu's Hunanese troops, low on ammunition and scrimping on short rations, went unpaid.[35] In NRA-controlled territory, the Hunanese peasants sold what produce they could spare, but in a year of natural calamities the Supply Corps had to rely heavily on rice carried north from Kwangtung.[36] The NRA's prudent policy of paying for services and goods instead of shanghai-ing coolies and confiscating food was a primary motivation for the cooperation of the peasantry.[37]

A final conference at Changsha on August 12 brought together Chiang's allied commanders and the Russian advisors headed by Galen. On the fifteenth, orders went out for the general attack on the Mi-lo line that would secure Hunan and carry the NRA into Hupei. The right wing was to be prepared to defend that eastern flank should Sun Ch'uan-fang come to Wu's aid from Kiangsi.[38] Across the northern horizon beckoned Wuhan with its Hanyang Arsenal, its commercial revenues and industry, and its gateway down the Yangtze. Chiang sent his generals off to battle with a spirited address:

> The importance of this fight is not only in that it will decide the fate of the warlords. But, whether or not the Chinese nation and race can restore their freedom and independence hangs in the balance. In other words, it is a struggle between the nation and the warlords, between the revolution and the anti-revolutionaries, between the Three People's Principles and imperialism. All are to be decided now in this time of battle . . . so as to restore independence and freedom to our Chinese race.[39]

The general plan was to break through the Mi-lo River line and quickly press north to take Wuhan. Speed and timing were vital in this gamble to gain the objective before either Wu's main force returned south or neighboring Sun Ch'uan-fang could enter the war to keep the revolutionaries from the Yangtze valley. Canton feared a combination of warlords forming against the thus far victorious "Red Army." From northern Hunan to

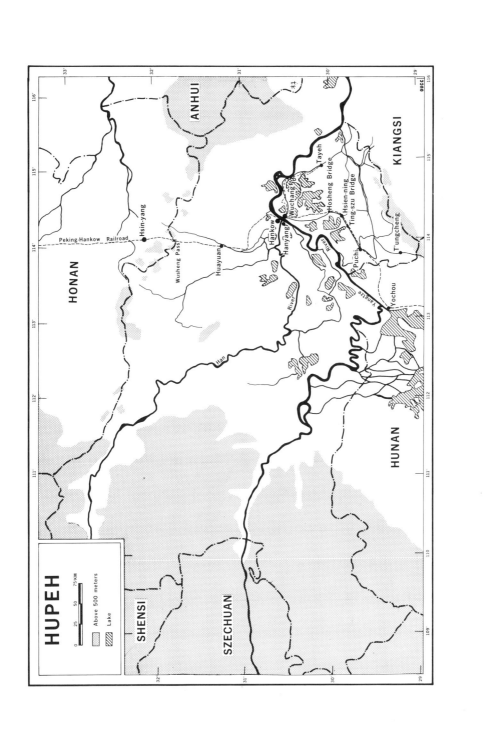

HUPEH

0 25 50 75/KM

▦ Above 500 meters
▨ Lake

SHENSI

SZECHUAN

HONAN

ANHUI

HUNAN

KIANGSI

Peking-Hankow Railroad

Hsin-yang

Wusheng Pass

Huayuan

Han River

Hankow
Hanyang
Wuchang
Tayeh
Hosheng Bridge
Hsien-ning
Ting-szu Bridge
Puchi
Yangtze
Yochou
T'ungcheng

Wuhan, the NRA attacked an enemy of about equal numerical strength. Sun Ch'uan-fang's potential to the east was much greater—probably double to what Chiang could muster.[40]

Thus, when the Fourth and Sixth army units crossed the Mi-lo River, the position of the NRA in North Hunan was precarious indeed. The crossing on August 17 did successfully flank the line and ease the downstream crossing of the left wing of the Seventh and Eighth armies. By August 19, Wu's troops had been forced up out of their trenches and resisted only sporadically as they retreated north from Hunan into southern Hupei.[41] The northern force split up during its two-day retreat, the western flank taking refuge in Wu's naval stronghold at Yüehchou, Hunan. The port was to have been heavily fortified, but its location at the point where the Tung-t'ing Lake meets the Yangtze allowed the backed-up floodwaters to cover much of the defenses.[42]

Continuing its speedy thrust, the NRA cut across Yüehchou's railroad link to Wuhan and surrounded the vulnerable enemy.[43] Wu had ordered the naval base held until he could detach himself from his Hopei operations and return to assume command himself. However, while Wu conferred at Paoting, Hopei, with Chang Tso-lin, his Hunan remnants embarked on naval vessels, river craft, and sampans and headed downstream for Wuhan.[44] With the fall of Yüehchou on August 22, 1926, Hunan was practically cleared of Wu's regular forces. His navy did continue to harass the NRA along the banks of the lake and the Yangtze, but was finally turned back by a mass of flaming rafts.[45] As the NRA pursued the retreating enemy, its way was eased by the cooperation of railroad workers on the line into Hupei. These workers helped by cutting rail and telegraph lines to obstruct the northern retreat from Yüehchou. Blocked in that manner, whole trainloads of troops and ammunition fell into the hands of the pursuing NRA.

The end of August had seen Chiang's well-timed gamble pay off. Although gravely threatened by potentially hostile forces in Kiangsi, the NRA had been able to face successfully just one warlord in Hunan. Its victory was not lost on the various warlords in surrounding provinces. As the Kweichow generals came over to the KMT after Changsha had been won, the Mi-lo victory influenced Sun Ch'uan-fang in Kiangsi. Some of his subordinates there began to reconsider their loyalty to him, while Sun's anxieties over the "Red" menace heightened.

In hindsight Sun could see that if he had intervened in Hunan during June or July the NRA could have been defeated, possibly prejudicing the course of the Northern Expedition and even the future of the Canton "Reds." If Kwangtung, the Revolutionary Base, had not fallen to a Sun-Wu invasion, the KMT might very well have either withered away in impotence or been supplanted by the contending CCP cadre. Chiang's role in decision-making would certainly have been curtailed, if not ended, by the stigma of defeat. However, success in Hunan proved Chiang's calculations and popularized the expedition and his leadership. Including the activity of the vanguard in May, the Hunan campaign had cost the revolutionaries in blood and hardships during four months of combat. In late August, with intelligence reports of the southward movement of Wu's reinforcements, Chiang ordered a bold strike against Wuhan while his luck held.[46]

THE BATTLE OF WUHAN

Attacking north toward the three-city complex were mainly regiments of the Fourth Army under Ch'en Ming-shu and Chang Fa-kuei. The retreat from the Mi-lo line from August 22 to 25 had allowed Wu's Hupei forces to fortify a highly defensible line behind which his mauled units from Hunan could recoup. The key Canton-Hankow railway followed a narrow land route between the Yangtze and upland ranges, and crossed several flood-swollen bridgeheads. To further narrow the land route to a few defensible bridge crossings, the northerners breached the nearby dikes of the Yangtze. Ting-szu Bridge (Ting-szu-ch'iao) was one such barricaded strongpoint.

There, barbed wire and machine guns along the northern riverbank confronted the vanguard of the NRA.[47] Its attack on August 26 only revealed the strength of the line. By that time both sides were being reinforced. Again the mobility of the NRA became decisive, greatly aided by local carriers and scouts who helped move the right wing upstream and then around the enemy's flank. When the Fourth Army thus threatened enemy rail communications to Wuhan, Wu's forces were vulnerable. Still made up mainly of the troops just defeated in Hunan, they were tired and also poorly coordinated. When assaults about the bridgehead joined with the flanking attack, the line disintegrated. During the night of August 26, the NRA stormed the defensive points one by one and by sunup the defenders were in flight. Again, some escaped by means of Wu's navy on the Yangtze; the rest tried to flee by train toward Wuhan.[48]

Ting-szu Bridge was taken, but heavy casualties limited the effective pursuit of the enemy to a vanguard. Once more, flooded lowlands slowed the advance. The top of the Yangtze dike was barred to troop movement by gunfire from Wu's river fleet. In addition to casualties suffered in battle, Wu's troops were furthered weakened by dwindling food supplies. Significantly, the opposite was the case with the NRA. In the environs of Ting-szu Bridge, following the evacuation of Wu's troops, a market sprang up and local people brought food to sell to hungry KMT troops as they passed.[49] By that time, word of the NRA's policy of paying for its needs must have preceded it. In sharp contrast stood the rapacious warlord forces, which often forced the peasantry to exchange goods for worthless printed scrip.

Immediately to the north, Hosheng Bridge lay fortified on a large scale athwart the route. On August 28, Hsien-ning, the local *hsien* seat, fell to the advancing NRA, but when the army reached Hosheng Bridge it found the defenses formidable and under Wu P'ei-fu's personal command. Returning south to his Hankow headquarters on August 25, Wu had received word of the loss of Ting-szu Bridge and had then proceeded to the front. Wu could not understand the defeat at the defensible bridgehead and blamed the cowardice of his subordinates. Upon his arrival at Hosheng, Wu gathered his officers as witnesses to the execution of the commanders of a brigade, a regiment, and six smaller units. On hand with him as he supervised his mercenaries was his Big Sword Corps, which functioned as on-the-spot executioners.[50] Wu hoped to soon change the defensive stance of his allies in Hupei—enlarged by a portion of his regulars returned from North China.

On August 29, Wu moved south against the NRA vanguard units of Li Tsung-jen's Seventh Army south of Hosheng Bridge. Wu's counterattack pressed on until slowed by the main units of the Fourth and Seventh armies arriving at the front. The NRA vanguard had been in dire straits and had withdrawn before Wu's thrust. In the predawn darkness of August 30, Wu attacked against what had become the NRA's line of defense south of the bridge. Probing for a weak point, Wu aimed for the sector dividing the Fourth and Seventh armies and pressed his offensive until the NRA managed to threaten him with a flanking movement. A well-coordinated barrage of artillery and rifle fire from the infantry took a heavy toll among Wu's attacking force.[51] To stiffen resistance, Wu's sword-wielding executioners served up the heads of several more timorous officers, but the northern attack broke up into a rout.[52] In attempting to gain the offensive, Wu lost the advantage of his superior defensive line along the river. When his troops fell back across the bridge, the Seventh Army flanked Wu upstream and took a small bridge, which threatened Wu's lifeline—the railway back to Wuhan. By noon of August 30, Wu's Hunan and Hupei troops were in a general retreat north.[53]

The defeat in Hunan and southern Hupei had been costly to Wu P'ei-fu both in men and materiel. During the retreat from Hunan, NRA flankers had cut off the vulnerable railway and captured three trains laden with troops and arms.[54] Within several days, Wu lost at the two bridgeheads more than 8,000 troops—over 1,000 killed, another 2,000 wounded, and 5,000 captured *along with their rifles*. Following this debacle Wu failed to regain the offensive and repeated his pleas to Sun Ch'uan-fang down the Yangtze for aid and reinforcement.

Calling another warlord into one's satrapy was fraught with danger. All Sun and Wu had in common was antipathy for the Canton Reds and a craving for territory in the Yangtze basin. Upon Wu's return to Central China, he had telegraphed Sun from Hankow requesting that Sun threaten the NRA's flank from Kiangsi, cut off its supply lines back to Kwangtung, and isolate it in Hunan.[55] In late August, Sun still dallied, ambiguous to outsiders and undecided as to where his best interests lay. In that invaluable interim, the NRA fortified its Kiangsi flank as best it could, tried to reassure Sun, and rushed its attack toward the prized Wuhan complex.

In full retreat Wu P'ei-fu breached dikes behind him to slow the enemy's approach to Wuchang, the provincial capital of Hupei on the south bank of the Yangtze. Leaving behind a garrison of 10,000 within the sturdy city walls, Wu ferried most of his force across to Hankow to avoid being trapped with his back to the unbridged Yangtze.[56] Across the Yangtze, Wu divided his troops further—one part holding the coveted Hanyang Arsenal and another defending the metropolis of Hankow, Wu's headquarters. By then, three of Wu's Honan divisions had arrived to reinforce his defense.

In close pursuit of the retreating troops, Ch'en Ming-shu's Fourth Army vanguard division took a high point overlooking Wuchang on August 31. As other Fourth Army units arrived during the next two days they filled in a circle around the city. On September 2, 1926, the NRA began frontal assaults to test the defenses, but lacking heavy siege cannon, and with inadequate communications, the attackers lost several thousand casualties before pulling back to more permanent siege works.[57]

More successful were the efforts against Wu's Hanyang Arsenal. Once Wu had withdrawn his river fleet downstream for patrol off Hankow, the NRA was able to cross to the north bank of the Yangtze upstream from Hanyang. By September 5, Hanyang was surrounded on land. Defending the Hanyang perimeter was the Hupei division of Liu Tso-lung, dug in on high points fortified with artillery battalions.[58] The advantage of this defense was lost to Wu from within. During what should have been a futile assault of the fortified heights by the NRA, Liu Tso-lung and his division defected and *joined* in the capture of Hanyang and its arsenal.[59]

With his arsenal gone, the vanguard of the NRA already sweeping north to threaten his rail link to Honan, and the support he awaited from Honan still en route, Wu decided to salvage what units he could for a last ditch defense in the border hills to the north between Hupei and Honan. By retreating up the railroad to Wusheng Pass, Wu hoped to hold out until more troops could move south from Honan. Once again the mobility of the NRA proved decisive in that Wu was deprived of the time he needed to dig in at the pass. After a succession of aborted stands, Wu lost the pass and fell farther back—into Honan.[60]

The walled city of Wuchang did not fall along with Hanyang and Hankow. This portion of Wu's forces did have the will to resist—for well over a month. Without siege guns and distracted by the threat from nearby Kiangsi, the NRA had to wait until hunger and lowered morale worked on the city's defenders. Wu had never imagined that the Red rabble from Canton would take Hunan and then Hupei so quickly, and so had not prepared the provincial capital for a long siege. Along with the 10,000-man garrison, hundreds of thousands of civilians were locked within the walls.[61] Inside were also the first foreigners in sizable numbers that the NRA encountered on the expedition.

Although most foreigners were across the river in the sanctuary of Hankow's foreign concessions, a group of missionaries, educators, and doctors remained at Wuchang. Within sight of the besieged city, a fleet of foreign gunboats gave grim reminder to the NRA of the threat of an international intervention. Arriving at the front near Wuchang, Chiang wired Foreign Minister Eugene Ch'en that he should inform the Hankow agents of the world powers that ". . . on the matter of protecting foreign nationals, I have already informed the armies to observe my prohibition against the military occupying or obstructing affairs in foreign-established churches, schools, and the like. . . ."[62] Apparently Chiang's personal surveillance of the matter proved effective, for there were no antiforeign incidents of significance at Wuhan.

Back in mid-August at the Changsha conference of NRA commanders, Chiang had called for the capture of the Wuhan complex within one week.[63] Although secret negotiations between Canton and Sun Ch'uan-fang had been in progress at least since February 1926,[64] Sun's leanings were unclear and intelligence reports claimed he was massing troops where his provinces of Kiangsi and Fukien bordered KMT territory.[65] Sun's excuse was that he was responding defensively to the NRA buildup in Hunan. One allegation was that Chiang and Sun had agreed that the NRA would take Changsha while Sun would be freed to concentrate against Chang Tso-lin in Shantung.[66] Earlier, Canton had apparently approached Sun with the prospect of a nonaggression pact, and the invitation to join the National Revolution upon Sun's submission to the National Government at Canton.[67]

However, Sun had been unable to reconcile his personal rule of his five "United Provinces" with the prospect of a lesser role under the KMT. In late August, Sun moved to answer Wu P'ei-fu's pleas for aid. Meeting then with his confederated provincial subordinates in Nanking, far downriver from besieged Wuchang, Sun ordered them to prepare a two-pronged attack from Kiangsi and Fukien west into KMT territory. Sun's potential force of 200,000 troops was mainly on paper since they were divided among provincial subordinates and difficult to assemble in concentrated numbers outside their home provinces.[68]

Chiang was aware of Sun's potential, and chose to gamble on another offensive. In the past, the NRA had done well by keeping on the offensive. The invasion of Kiangsi was by three routes over the north and central highlands, and over four passes converging on Kanchou, southern Kiangsi.[69] Quickly building up momentum, the well-coordinated attack rolled across the Kiangsi border on September 4. By this move, Chiang committed the NRA to a fight for the lower Yangtze.

CHAPTER 10

The Expedition Moves Eastward:
The Kiangsi Campaign

In northern Kiangsi, the attack moved up and over the passes and down the stream that washed the mountain flanks. Sun Ch'uan-fang's main forces were still en route to Kiangsi as the NRA quickly descended toward the rich lowland plain that slopes to Poyang Lake. The provincial capital, Nanchang, was immediately threatened. Farther south the major city of Kanchou fell after three days of attack, along with most of southern Kiangsi. Victory there was sped by the defection of Lai Shih-huang, whose Kiangsi Army Fourth Division had been deployed to defend against an attack from Kwangtung.[1] The fresh tide of offense was still in flow on September 19 when the center prong swept down on Nanchang, whose dazed defenders fled.[2] The sweep to Nanchang was to attract Sun's fresh troops pouring into northern Kiangsi from recently arrived Yangtze steamboats.

In the north near the Yangtze, the NRA offensive ground to a halt against the vanguard of Sun's reinforcements. Sun's new troops halted the invaders and hurled them back toward the Hupei border in a fierce three-day counterattack.[3] As the NRA frantically drew reinforcements from all possible sources, the besieging troops 100 miles away at Wuchang dropped to a skeleton force over a week's span from September 10 to 16.[4] Although the NRA had not yet met a decisive setback, its position in the Yangtze valley was obviously still quite vulnerable.

Sun Ch'uan-fang steamed from Nanking upriver to Kiukiang, Kiangsi, to personally direct the reinforcements that accompanied him. Landing on September 21, Sun cleared the lowland heart of the province, including

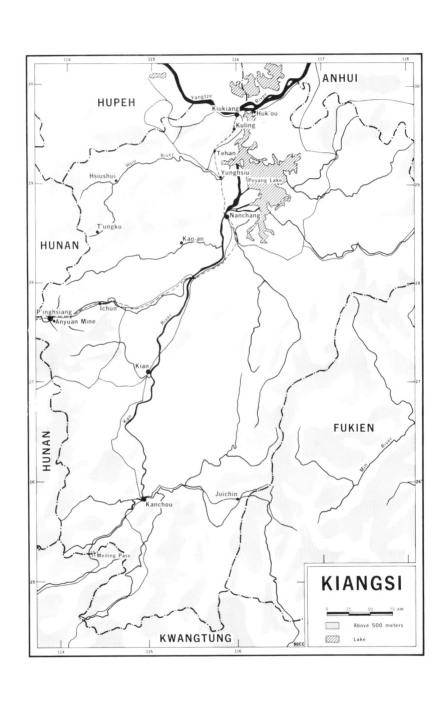

Nanchang, within days.[5] Having regained much territory in Kiangsi, Sun reasserted his authority by rounding up and executing hundreds of students, teachers, and KMT members suspected of collusion with the enemy. Radical students, male and female, were singled out by means of their *short* "Russian" haircuts, and dripping heads impaled on stakes in the public places of Nanchang and Kiukiang warned would-be sympathizers.[6] Sun recognized correctly the subversive influence of the students and their teachers—many of whom *were* actively supporting the revolutionary movement.

The latter half of September saw the fate of the expedition and even the Revolutionary Base truly hang in the balance. If Sun succeeded, the expeditionary forces would be isolated in Hunan and Hupei, unsupported by Kwangtung, which would also become less defensible. Wu could then regroup and join Sun for the kill in Hupei. From this calamitous prospect, Chiang considered his front and the base at Canton where the disorders of the unionists and peasants' associations still disrupted his logistical support. Putting his authority on the line, Chiang telegraphed to the Party government at Canton the order to *settle the Kwangtung-Hong Kong Strike, immediately!* In compliance, on September 23, Eugene Ch'en sent off a note to the British consul at Canton. Meetings with the recalcitrant Strike Committee followed, and then the government released announcements to the press of the departure of thousands of ex-strikers for duty with the NRA. Thus ended sixteen turbulent months of blockade and strike against Hong Kong and the British.[7]

At the Kiangsi front, the tempo of combat heightened throughout September. In several sectors the status of the NRA was grim indeed. In late September, there were reports that Chu P'ei-teh's Third Army had fallen back from central Kiangsi into Hunan.[8] Even Wang Po-ling's First Division of the prestigious First Army retreated, badly mauled, across the mountains.[9] (This jibes with Wang's dismissal and deportation to Shanghai.[10]) Sun tried to coordinate his counteroffensive with Wu P'ei-fu's besieged enclave at Wuchang by an ingenious landing on Lake Tayeh inland from the Yangtze dikes east of Wuchang. The landing on September 25 initially forced the Fourth Army back toward Wuhan,[11] and along the entire front the situation from mid-September through all of October was one of desperate defensive measures and reverses.

Sun's position was not entirely secure: his five-province army was even more loosely welded than was the NRA and the loyalty of subordinates in his five provinces of Kiangsu, Anhui, Kiangsi, Chekiang, and Fukien was questionable. A Peiyang Academy man from Shantung, Sun had little appeal for the southern gentry he was forced to acknowledge as administrators. Their fellow provincials continually nagged him with peace proposals and plans for provincial autonomy under his federation.[12]

From his precarious position during the ebb of NRA fortune, Chiang managed to negotiate with Sun. Earlier in September, Sun had offered not to press his offensive into Hunan in exchange for peace between Canton and his five United Provinces. With Sun's counterattack in gear, Chiang telegraphed him that the KMT had no wish to enlarge the war and that, if Sun withdrew his reinforcements from Kiangsi, the NRA would withdraw from the Kiangsi territories it still held.[13] Sun countered with an offer to halt his offensive at the Hunan border if Chiang would withdraw all NRA forces from Kiangsi.[14] Sun's bargaining position seemed firm but his counteroffensive had reached its high tide in late September.

In early October, the NRA began to hold its positions and then fight back. By October 5, Sun's thrust toward Wuchang had been foiled and his units reembarked on Yangtze steamers that took them back to Kiangsi.[15] There, a stiffening NRA fought Sun's troops back down to the lowlands where lay the Yangtze port of Kiukiang and the arterial railway south to Nanchang.[16] On October 3, the NRA severed communications via that railway at Tehan.[17] Sun countered with a fierce charge that retook the railroad town and threatened to flank the Seventh Army, which was holding that sector.[18] On the seventh, a combined force of KMT armies futilely stormed a fortified hill that dominated the railway at Yanghsiu. Sun's inner lines held and by the end of the day's combat had forced the NRA hurriedly back up into the mountains.[19]

To the south at Nanchang, the conflict raged back and forth in mid-October with the capital won and lost several times. Pouring in reinforcements, both sides staked all in their efforts to hold the rich core of Kiangsi.

Republic Day, October 10, held a good omen for the KMT at Wuchang. With hope ebbing after Sun's relief column failed and in desperate need of food, key units of Sun's force defending the besieged city quietly opened the gates to the city walls and allowed the NRA to take the city that day.[20] When the NRA had earlier negotiated the evacuation of the sick, the old, and the infants from Wuchang's garrison, nearly 100 had been stampeded to death in the rush to leave. Unable to rally support, Wu impotently bided his time in Honan.

During the latter half of October, the pitch of combat lowered—the NRA licked its wounds and Sun looked to a threatening political situation to his rear. Causing him anxieties over his control of the lucrative, "golden" city of Shanghai was a rebellion that threatened to erupt throughout the lower Yangtze region. In Shanghai, from early October on, various Chekiang dissidents had met in the sanctuary of the foreign concessions to discuss with Shanghai coconspirators the secession of Chekiang from Sun's United Provinces.[21]

THE CHEKIANG REBELLION WITHIN SUN'S UNITED PROVINCES

During the preceding month, these Chekiang elements had pestered Sun by telegram to block from entry into the United Provinces "aid" from the Manchurian and Shantung generals.[22] Heading the All-Chekiang Association (Ch'üan Che Kung-hui) was Ch'u Fu-ch'eng who had ties with the provincial supporters of fellow Chekiangese Chiang Kai-shek. Coordinating their movement with the NRA attack going on before Nanchang, the association telegrammed Sun on October 15. They demanded that the Chekiang units fighting for Sun in Kiangsi be returned to duties in their home province and that Chekiang be allowed to rule itself. But did these Chekiang dissidents represent nationalistic aspirations? Within this movement for provincial autonomy, articulate gentry presented ideas ranging from traditional provincialism and the mistrust of Southern Chinese for Northern Chinese to the more modern nationalistic and social concerns of the Kuomintang.[23] From Canton, Chiang's supporters backed the rebellion of Hsia Ch'ao, Sun's civil governor of Chekiang and the prime intermediary between overlord Sun and Hsia's fellow provincials.

In Chekiang, provincial loyalties had been strong during the late Ch'ing when local gentry became notoriously resistant to the dictates of Manchu Peking. During the warlord era, three leading commanders of Chekiang military had become quite adept at conceding suzerain power to a succession of outside regional overlords while consolidating their own local autonomy. Their superiors, mainly northern militarists, had been forced to conciliate Chekiang independence movements, which erupted sporadically in 1916, 1917, 1922, 1924, 1925, and 1926. The Chekiangese, a microcosm of the Chinese, were badly divided by topography and local economy, and failed to unite effectively against the oppressive northerners. Wealthy and influential merchants of Ningpo felt stronger kinship with the expatriate magnates of Shanghai than with the rural gentry of the hinterland. The key leaders of Chekiang's provincial forces, likewise, represented differences in background and perspective. Hsia Ch'ao, Chou Feng-ch'i, and Ch'en Yi were the Chekiang commanders whose defections to the National Revolutionary Army were so crucial to the conquest of that province and to warlord Sun Ch'uan-fang's loss of the lower Yangtze valley.

All three had gained political influence in the province through their military power, derived from the modern military training they had received during the final decade of the Ch'ing. Although from different parts of Chekiang, Hsia Ch'ao and his protégé Chou Feng-ch'i had common school ties from the province's military academy, the Chekiang Wu-pei Hsüeh-t'ang, and were close associates—both important ties in traditional terms.[24] From there they had moved into military posts under a succession of military governors and had become identified with a clique of Chekiang officers called the Kung-huo Tang,[25] and with a smaller faction, the Shih Hsiung-ti (Ten Brothers).[26] In 1916 and again in 1919, Hsia had also used the national influence of the Anfu clique to rise above his local rivals to become chief of the Provincial Police, a key post in Chekiang's hierarchy.[27] Needing natives to act as middlemen, successive Anfu *tuchüns* (military governors) had allowed Hsia considerable local power and the expansion of his police force. In this manner Hsia's personal force had grown from several thousand to over 5,000 by 1925.[28] Hsia had helped Chou Feng-ch'i gain a brigade command in one of Chekiang's three divisions, and both were in a position by 1924 to bargain with Sun Ch'uan-fang. Under their Anfu ruler from Shantung, Lu Yung-hsiang, the issue of provincial independence had been used as a means to increase Lu's popularity in 1921, 1922, and 1924. The flurry of interest in 1921 resulted in the drafting of the Chekiang Constitution—a political form holding almost mystical power for

Western-trained Chinese. In that same year, Sun Yat-sen at Canton, powerless but ambitious, promoted provincial rebellions in Kwangsi, Yunnan, Kweichow, Szechwan, and Hunan that would remove oppressive overlords and open the way for cooperation in a federal republic under Sun.[29]

By 1924 the outsiders in the top ranks of the provincial hierarchy caused Hsia Ch'ao, Chou Feng-ch'i, and Ch'en Yi to feel politically frustrated. When a struggle erupted between their Anfu overlord and the Chihli Tüchun in neighboring Kiangsu, they saw a chance for change. From his vantage point in Fukien, another Chihli military governor, Sun Ch'uan-fang, saw an opportunity in the Chekiang-Kiangsu War for him to move into Chekiang on the pretext of aiding his Chihli brother in Kiangsu. By this circuitous process, typical of the warlord era, Sun Ch'uang-fang marched his Shantung troops into Chekiang after gaining the defection of the dissident Chekiang commanders guarding the border. Conspiring with Sun against their Anfu superior were chief of the Chekiang Provincial Police Hsia Ch'ao, and Brigade Commander Chou Feng-ch'i, joined by Brigade Commander Ch'en Yi.[30] Easing Ch'en's relationship with Sun was their common background at Tokyo's Army Officers' Academy, the Shikan Gakko. The three Chekiang officers profited well from Sun's venture, which saw him add not only Chekiang to his domain but expand his interests into the lush lower Yangtze valley.

By the autumn of 1925, Sun had manipulated provincial feelings in the southeastern provinces of Chekiang, Kiangsu, Anhui, and Kiangsi to the extent that he was able to lead a military confederation to halt and throw back an invasion by the hated northern mercenaries of the Manchurian faction. For their support in these victorious campaigns of 1924 and 1925, Sun promoted his Chekiang subordinates: Hsia became Chekiang's civil governor as well as head of provincial police, Chou advanced from brigade to divisional commander of Chekiang's Third Division, and Ch'en Yi moved up to command Chekiang's First Division. Having set up the United Provinces with Nanking as his capital, Sun Ch'uan-fang then transferred Chou and his division there to stand garrison duty under his surveillance, and moved Ch'en Yi's division to guard Kiangsu's northern march at Hsüchou. In this manner, while apparently granting a degree of autonomy to Chekiang, Sun also removed Chekiang's largest provincial military units from their home base. Given the prevailing standards of warlord politics, the Chekiang commanders had been well treated. With his Chihli faction in power during 1924, Sun had the Peking Government legitimize the promotions for his new Chekiang lieutenants.

Although Sun's relationships with the Chekiang commanders were based on nothing firmer than the rewards that came with their new titles, the arrangements were mutually supportive. When a provincial independence movement broke out at Ningpo in October 1924, the rebellion was against Sun's new provincial administration as much as it was against Sun. Therefore, Sun held Hangchow with his troops while he dispatched his Chekiang lieutenants to suppress the Ningpo rebels.[31]

However, by October 1925, Civil Governor Hsia Ch'ao was disgruntled with Sun's supervision and, when Sun moved victoriously to Nanking, Hsia assumed that Sun would turn Chekiang over to him. Thinking that Sun was safely distracted by the management of his United Provinces, Hsia and a new independence movement engineered a declaration of autonomy and another constitution,[32] and sent out a call for Chekiang's two divisions to return home. Sun responded by sending troops to squelch the bid for provincial autonomy and installed his own man from Shantung, Lu Hsiang-t'ing, as the military governor.[33] Showing remarkable resiliency, Hsia conceded to Sun's superior military power and actually extended his welcome to Sun's new military governor when Lu arrived in Hangchow.

Hsia's interests had remained those of provincial autonomy. His recalcitrance toward Sun as an "outsider" (*wai-sheng-jen*) was matched by his obstructionist efforts against Westerners trying to exploit Chekiang through their prior Unequal Treaties. His reputation with foreigners was of being "notoriously backward in recognizing foreigners' rights," which made it ". . . practically impossible for any foreigner to conduct business in Chekiang according to the treaties."[34]

For Sun Ch'uan-fang, the year 1926, in which Chiang Kai-shek launched the Northern Expedition, was not a good one in which to win over the independence-minded Chekiangese. In the province, depressed economically by a poor harvest in 1925 followed by floods and drought, Sun had to compete with the Chekiang commanders for revenue.[35] After over a year of effort to consolidate his influence in Chekiang, Sun did not enjoy a solid base of support from either the local gentry or from his provincial middleman, Civil Governor Hsia Ch'ao. It was in this unsettled situation that Canton's KMT leadership became interested.

Even before the Northern Expedition invaded Sun's territory in Kiangsi, Chiang Kai-shek had attempted to negotiate with Sun as a Shikan Gakko classmate and to open communications with other subordinates.[36] Although the KMT had an active party branch at Hangchow and many distinguished provincial members, Chiang could also negotiate through his spokesmen as a fellow Chekiang provincial and as a fellow graduate with Hsia and Chou Feng-ch'i of the Chekiang Military Academy, and as a classmate of Ch'en Yi at the Shikan Gakko.[37] The KMT also utilized the friendship between Party member Ma Hsu-lün and Civil Governor Hsia Ch'ao. Ma was a native who had become involved nationally in the Party and in the Peking Government as a Minister of Education. In approaching Hsia on the possibilities of joining the National Revolution, Ma played on the dissatisfaction that he knew Hsia felt toward the predominance in Chekiang of Shantung military men.[38] Outwardly Hsia remained neutral toward the National Revolution and told an interviewer that he opposed *any* outside rule over Chekiang—be it northern or southern.[39]

But, Hsia Ch'ao could see by October the spectacular progress made by the NRA through Hunan and Hupei, which presented him with yet another incentive to defect from Sun. To the winner would go the rewards. Apparently the KMT agents offered Hsia a place in a future KMT-influenced provincial regime if he would cooperate in a conspiracy to weaken Sun's rear area and thus decide the bloody battle then raging over Kiangsi. His new title under the KMT would be the equivalent of the military governorship that he had coveted for so long—the chairmanship of the Provincial Military Committee. At Canton, a special KMT congress met in mid-October 1926 to approve the sort of division of authority between nation and province that had already been promised Hsia and T'ang Sheng-chih of Hunan.[40] Rather than risk the resistance of the provincial autonomists leading provincial forces in defending their homes, the KMT felt constrained to attract their support through compromise. Therefore, the KMT appealed more to Hsia's strong feelings of provincialism than to the abstract national goals of the KMT. It was reported at that time that Hsia had only been outside Chekiang twice, on recent trips to Sun's Nanking headquarters where he bargained for autonomy.[41] Hsia could identify with anti-imperialism (or antiforeignism), and trusted Chiang Kai-shek, the NRA's commander-in-chief, as a fellow provincial and as a military man trained at his alma mater, the Chekiang Military Academy.

During the hard-fought battle for Kiangsi occurred some of the heaviest fighting of the civil war era, and it was in that context that Hsia Ch'ao defected. Before Hsia's coup, he had appealed to Chou Feng-ch'i at the Kiukiang sector of the battlefront to bring his Third Chekiang Division back to Chekiang, but Chou could not extract himself. Some of his units were at Sun's Nanking headquarters as hostages, and furthermore the way back to Chekiang would be through hostile territory commanded by Sun. Some have claimed that Chou predicted defeat for Sun in Kiangsi and thus had urged Hsia to break away.[42] Chou was also pressed to cease fighting and return to Chekiang by the All-Chekiang Association, which passed through Kiangsi.[43] On October 14, Chou's reserves at Nanking did attempt to flee, but were surrounded and disarmed.[44] Only a few small units managed to return through Chekiang's western mountains on the pretext of a cross-country exercise.[45]

At Hsüchou, northern Kiangsu, Ch'en Yi with his division refused to aid Hsia against Sun, perhaps under a threat from the nearby anti-Red Manchurians in Shantung.[46] But Ch'en was also ambitious for status in his home province and may have felt that his rival there, Civil Governor Hsia, could offer him nothing more than a position *beneath* Hsia.[47] The point is that with the other two Chekiang militarists either unwilling or unable to support him, Hsia's mid-October rebellion was a gamble. Hsia hoped that with the element of surprise he might not only take Chekiang, but capture Shanghai as well.

However, on October 16 when Hsia, as he had before, declared the independence of Chekiang and boarded his troops on the train to Shanghai, his plans had already reached Sun—possibly via an intercepted telegram from Hsia to Chou.[48] Another allegation has been that Ch'en Yi leaked Hsia's request for aid as a means of eliminating Ch'en's most powerful provincial rival.[49] Approaching Shanghai, Hsia's unseasoned armed police found the track blocked and had to march toward prepared defenses. After only a brief skirmish on October 17, at Shanghai's western suburbs, the Chekiang rebels withdrew back to Chiahsing in Chekiang. In the meantime, the promoters of autonomy gathered in Hangchow.

On October 18, 1926, at a KMT-style mass meeting, the political activists at Hangchow publicized Chekiang's independence from Sun and pledged support to Canton's National Government.[50] A new slate of provincial officials gathered around Hsia Ch'ao who accepted from the KMT the titles of provisional chairman of the Provincial Government Committee and commander of the Eighteenth Army in the NRA—Canton's redesignation of Hsia's provincial force.[51] As the northern officials departed in haste, Hsia and his government appointed native heads to eight departments and certified new *hsien* leaders.[52] But, once again, the bravado of independence was untenable.

Forewarned, Sun transferred loyal troops from Nanking by rail to the Chekiang border. By the morning of October 20, his well-trained northerners were rolling across the boundary and pounding the flimsy defenses Hsia had thrown up at Chiahsing. Both had railroad cannon, but Hsia's fire was ineffective. Governor Hsia managed to escape with a few guards, but left behind a 6,000-man force that was untrained and hopelessly outmatched. By evening Sun's men had crushed the Chekiang independence movement and rounded up hundreds of Chekiang soldiers whom they machine-gunned in the moonlight.[53] Hsia Ch'ao was tracked down in his motor car and seized. To further dramatize the lesson to any subordinates who might be contemplating treason, Sun had Hsia shot in the street and decapitated, and ordered his severed head delivered to Nanking as a grisly reminder of Sun's justice.[54]

THE BATTLE FOR KIANGSI RENEWED

Chiang, hoping to remain on the offensive, had all uncommitted troops thrown into the Kiangsi sector. Included were the fourth class of officers graduated in October from Whampoa Academy and rushed north to lead new recruits from Hunan and Hupei.[55] The revitalized NRA began to crack Sun's rather demoralized defense and to move forward. First Sun's southern line sagged under the assault of the Second Army and the Fourteenth, a unit that had defected from Sun early in the Kiangsi campaign. By October 27, Sun's units from southern Kiangsi were in retreat north through Nanchang.[56]

As the campaign entered November, the NRA gathered along the Hsiu valley for a push against the Kiukiang-Nanchang line defending the railway. Reinforced by the Fourth Army's Tenth Division under Ch'en Mingshu, the Seventh Army again swept down on the lowland defenses at Tehan. When the line crumpled there, the NRA cut the arterial rail line, which isolated Sun's troops south along Poyang Lake. The capture of the ports of Kiukiang and Huk'ou on the Yangtze further strangled the provincial capital of Nanchang. By November 9, Nanchang had fallen and Sun's troops were in general retreat down the Yangtze valley.[57] As the momentum of the NRA offensive swept Sun's remnants from Kiangsi, Chiang again sent his agent to offer Sun a role in the revolution and the coming unification of China.[58]

In the Kiangsi campaign, both sides had thrown their best troops into the intense two-month battle; the casualties were among the highest incurred in the Northern Expedition. According to official KMT records, the final week's push to take the Kiukiang-Nanchang Railroad cost the NRA 20,000 casualties and the enemy 40,000.[59] The longer preceding period of bitterly contested setbacks for the NRA may have cost it another 100,000. Victory for the NRA had also meant the capture of large amounts of needed arms and ammunition, which greatly expanded its fighting potential. At Nanchang alone, although the NRA suffered nearly 4,000 casualties, it took 15,000 prisoners and 20,000 rifles—enough to arm an army corps.[60] The victory had been won despite the lack of heavy artillery, and thereafter other warlords would face a larger, better-armed, and battle-hardened enemy.

CHAPTER 11

The Coastal Campaign or East Route

Earlier, as the summer of 1926 had begun and Canton launched the expedition by way of Hunan, the First Army under General Ho Ying-ch'in gathered along Kwangtung's border with Fukien. As one of Sun Ch'uan-fang's United Provinces, Fukien posed a danger in the event Sun entered the war. Ho concentrated his troops at Swatow on orders to either defend the border or, if feasible, invade Fukien. In September, once the fighting began in Kiangsi, the First Army and Sun's Fukien allies engaged in skirmishes along the border. Although Sun then ordered his Fukien subordinate, Chou Ying-jen, to attack Kwangtung, Chou stalled until late September.[1]

When Chou did attack Swatow, Ho blocked the offensive with a well-prepared defense line along the rugged coastal terrain, although his force was outnumbered.[2] The tardiness of Chou Ying-jen's offensive characterized the poor coordination among elements of Sun Ch'uan-fang's military machine—a weakness not lost to the NRA. In another tactical blunder, Sun's navy, operating off Fukien simultaneously with Chou's attack, did not even bombard the port of Swatow.[3] In fact the admiral was quietly negotiating with the KMT on the possibility of his defection (see chapter 30).

In late September, Ho's First Army answered the Fukien threat. The well-timed defection of two of Chou Ying-jen's brigade commanders across the Kwangtung border provided General Ho with vital intelligence on troop placements and defenses.[4] The NRA offensive from Kwangtung into

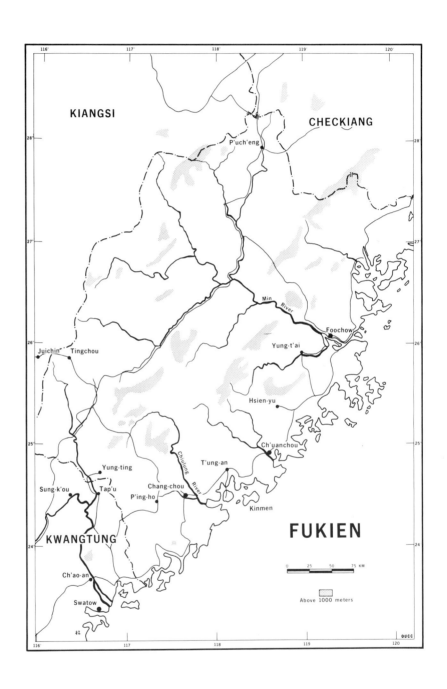

KIANGSI

CHECKIANG

P'uch'eng

Min River

Foochow

Juichin Tingchou

Yung-t'ai

Hsien-yu

Ch'uanchou

Yung-ting

Chiulung River

T'ung-an

Sung-k'ou   Tap'u

Chang-chou

P'ing-ho

Kinmen

KWANGTUNG

FUKIEN

Ch'ao-an

0   25   50   75 KM

Swatow

Above 1000 meters

OUCC

Fukien also served to threaten Sun's southern flank. The coastal road led to Shanghai. On October 9, 1926, to distract a Fukien force penetrating Kwangtung near Sung-k'ou, Ho moved his troops across the Fukien border to take Yungting, an action that was accomplished the following day. Although Chou held Sung-k'ou from October 9 to 13, Ho's counterattack had so threatened his rear lines of communication that he retreated northeast back into Fukien.[5]

During the rest of October, the First Army infiltrated the lightly defended hills of back-country Fukien. There the political workers, some of whom were Hakkas, contacted the local militias (*min-t'uan*). Chafing under the exploitative rule of Sun and Chou Ying-jen, the local people, including Hakkas, looked with hope toward the invading NRA. The good reputation of the nearby Revolutionary Base and the NRA had preceded the invading army, which eased the collaboration with local people. The *min-t'uan* contribution to the taking of Fukien was considerable, for they numbered over 10,000 provincials who knew well all the shortcuts and possible hiding places in the rugged uplands.[6] The NRA warmly accepted these Fukienese as additions to their group; the Fukienese comprised three divisions, one independent brigade, and three regiments.[7] With this Fukienese help, the NRA quickly forced Chou down out of the hills. The last fortified high point, Tingchou, fell before a joint attack of the Fukienese elements and the Fourteenth Army, which had arrived recently from Juichin, Kiangsi.[8] As he pulled back, Chou Ying-jen lost 500 rifles and machine guns, five cannon, and ammunition, all of which helped to arm the new NRA elements. In the unfamiliar mountain heights, Chou's northern troops in their straw footwear were ill-suited to defend themselves against the hit-and-run tactics of the *min-t'uan*. In the valleys, his communications were too easily severed.[9]

Along the coast, Chou's efforts also failed. Not only had his attack aimed at the ports of Ch'ao-an or Swatow been halted, but by October 14 Chou had been pushed back to Changchou well inside Fukien. The NRA pressed its offensive both along the coast and down the valleys from the interior so that Chou's defense of Changchou crumbled on November 8.[10] Digging in farther up the coast at T'ung-an, Chou held out there until October 20, whereafter the NRA maintained the momentum of attack and took Chüanchou the next day, and then Hsienyu and Yangtai on the twenty-sixth. Thus, from late September until December, Ho Ying-ch'in pressed along the southern, most populated, sector of the Fukien coast until the only holdout was the walled provincial capital, Foochow, across the broad Min River.

The defensibility of the city was subverted from within its beleaguered walls. The morale of Chou's subordinates wavered and vanished as Chou's pleas to Sun Ch'uan-fang for reinforcements went unanswered. Ousted from the portions of Kiangsi adjacent to Fukien and preoccupied with reconsolidating his authority in Chekiang, Sun was without means of easy access to Fukien.[11] Chou and his subordinates in Fukien had to defend themselves as best they could. Some key commanders chose another alternative—the Fukien navy and its marine brigade not only defected but joined in the shelling of Chou's troops as they retreated into Foochow along the Min River banks.[12] Likewise, the commander of Foochow's garrison, Li Sheng-chün, opened the city gates to the NRA, leaving Chou without a sanctuary.[13]

Thus, the thorny problem of capturing a city containing a foreign concession was solved when Foochow surrendered without a struggle on December 9, 1926. Trapped in the city, the dumbfounded Fukien governor exclaimed as he was arrested: "I don't understand what has happened! Our forces and weapons were superior but you have captured me!"[14] With less than 2,000 troops left of his original 60,000, Chou and his remnants limped quickly toward the Chekiang border.[15] Part of the credit for the smoothness of the Fukien campaign rightfully belongs to the First Army's Political Department. Their effective dealings with the leaders of Fukien's *min-t'uan* brought invaluable local support. Had the invasion from Kwangtung elicited hostility and resistance, the numerically superior forces of Chou Ying-jen might not only have defended Fukien but pressed over the border into the Revolutionary Base.

REGROUPING THE REVOLUTIONARY MOVEMENT

From mid-November through the end of 1926, *both* the national revolutionaries and their opponents paused to take stock and consolidate. Chiang had carried his offensive well down the Yangtze but tensions within the movement stirred the desire to slow down and regroup. Sun Ch'uan-fang had already received again the offer of peaceful inclusion in the National Revolution—a prospect for which he had little understanding or optimism. With Kiangsi and much of Fukien lost, Sun turned instead, however reluctantly, to the military governors of North China for aid. His fellow warlords had been fighting amongst themselves for years and had in common only the desire to preserve their holdings plus a new anxiety over the National Revolution. They had all come to wish the destruction of the "Red Army" from Kwangtung. However, calling in a fellow warlord often allowed him his foot in the door and the opportunity to grab what he could. Thus, on November 8, 1926, Sun Ch'uan-fang, with foreboding and in desperation, boarded the train in Nanking bound for Tientsin far to the north.

At Tientsin, Sun met with the generals of the Peiyang Clique, Chang Tso-lin of Manchuria and Chang Tsung-ch'ang of Shantung. They reviewed the earlier fate of Wu P'ei-fu against the NRA in Hunan and Hupei, and Sun painfully reported on his failures in Kiangsi and Fukien. Finally the northern warlords had to admit to the strange powers of the NRA against numerically superior troops and firepower. Not even the northerners' control of the railroads seemed to throw the balance in their favor. They decided to pool their resources to quarantine the Red disease in the south. Despite the improbable nature of the bedfellows, Sun agreed grimly to the alliance as his mind raced back over the roster of his "allied subordinates" in the United Provinces. Plagued by defection in Kiangsi and

Fukien, Sun could not afford feelings of insecurity over his control in Chekiang or the rich Yangtze delta.

With regard to Wu P'ei-fu, the first of their kind to suffer at the hands of the NRA, the Tientsin conferees decided to do what they could to reinforce him in Honan so that he might strike back toward Wuhan. They agreed also that if Wu refused their aid, their intervention might be necessary to protect North China from invasion through Honan.

To reinforce Sun in the southeast, northern troops would be sent, but their expenses would demand payment.[16] Chang Tsung-ch'ang looked covetously southward from impoverished Shantung and envied the wealth accrued by his fellow Shantungese at Shanghai, glittering on the southern horizon. Sun managed to hold Chang Tsung-ch'ang down to a guarantee of C$500,000 in silver collected from Chekiang and Anhui taxes in return for reinforcement with Chang's Shantung troops.[17]

On November 24, while Sun's forces in Fukien reeled under the NRA attack, the Tientsin conference agreements began to bear fruit. Chang Tsung-ch'ang's Shantung units rolled south across Sun's province of Anhui on board the Tientsin-P'u-k'ou Railroad bound for the Yangtze delta.[18] The 60,000 troops included crack White Russian units and armored train artillery. Within a week's time they came to represent part of a new combined warlord force—the Ankuochün (National Pacification Army).[19] The idea of engaging in war to achieve peace had been traditional among conquering founders of dynasties striving to unify a war-torn China. Chang Tso-lin "accepted" the authority of commander-in-chief, and on December 1 appointed Sun Ch'uan-fang and Chang Tsung-ch'ang his deputy commanders with headquarters in the P'u-k'ou-Nanking area. The new C-in-C promised to save China—familiar cry—from the "Red menace."[20] At his disposal was a numerically impressive force of half a million troops.

Sun's portion, however, was the weakest link with significant elements from southeastern China opposed to collaborating with the northern troops. In Sun's territory, the movement for provincial self-rule still undermined his security. Arriving Shantung units found a cool reception among the local people, stemming in part from their reputation of being among the most rapacious of all Chinese soldiery (certainly a distinguishing notoriety). The KMT and CCP capitalized on the misgivings of the delta peoples and promoted a movement to block the entry of the northerners. The movement especially captured the enthusiasm of Kiangsu and Shanghai merchants, as well as gentry and students, when the newcomers tactlessly tried to force the natives to accept the Shantung bank notes of Chang Tsung-ch'ang.[21] Sun's response to this organized subversion was immediate and direct. He executed conspicuous KMT workers in Shanghai and elsewhere, so that overt opposition failed to materialize except in Chekiang. Sun's authority there was too tenuous to seek out the disloyal. In fact, defected subordinates Ch'en Yi and Chou Feng-ch'i supported with their troops Chekiang leaders who declared themselves independent of Sun's United Provinces.

Although Sun had been weakened, NRA C-in-C Chiang did not feel secure enough to follow up the advantage of the Kiangsi victory. At his Nanchang headquarters in Kiangsi, Chiang watched with anxiety the problems within the revolutionary ranks. Borne out was his earlier warning that Sun Yat-sen's northern expedition of 1921 had been defeated not at the Shaokuan front but to the rear in Canton. Back in July 1926, Commander Chiang had postponed his movement to the northern front, hoping to see an end to the divisive Hong Kong Strike. When later in September Chiang had demanded an end to the strike, he had still been frustrated because strike supporters managed to salvage the powerful strike organization to lead an expanded national voluntary boycott of British goods in the newly liberated territory.

By November the news reaching the front was again that of strikes and disorders in Canton. Strikes occurred on the arterial Canton-Hankow Railroad in Kwangtung and spread into Hunan. At the revolutionary capital, the Cantonese workers at the Shih-ching and the mortar arsenals struck, and the CCP agitated the seamen and other unions to join the strike.[22] Even outside the Government House in Canton, excited workers stormed about demanding higher wages. The level of turbulence in the Revolutionary Base perplexed the KMT military at the front but delighted "counter-revolutionaries" such as the Western merchants of Shanghai. On Chiang's order, the head of the NRA's Political Departments, Teng Yen-ta (Tse-sheng), traveled back from the front in late November to observe and reconcile the fractious elements if possible. In December, a temporary lull vanished in an outbreak of strikes and disorders in which armed pickets closed up rice shops and the banks.[23]

From the reports that reached him at the front, Chiang feared that the war materiel Canton did produce was now endangered. In his December 8 speech, Chiang pointed out the regrettable enervation that resulted from conflict *within* the revolutionary movement.[24] Following his speech, Chiang acted: he appointed garrison commander Ch'ien Ta-chün to act concurrently as Canton's police chief with the task of pacifying the city. Meeting with Chiang at Kuling, Kiangsi members of the KMT Central Political Council passed an order restraining labor violence and prohibiting strikes in Canton against strategic activities, such as communications, banks, and the supply of food and other "vital necessities."[25]

The tri-city area of Wuhan, once the NRA had arrived with its Political Department organizers and auxiliaries from the Hong Kong Strike, also became the scene of an even more disruptive labor movement. Echoing the experience at Canton, the unionizers pulled the workers out on strikes for higher wages and better working conditions. After this the strikers became dependent on the newly formed unions. With strikes and frequent work stoppages for union demonstrations, by late 1926 Wuhan's production was in decline.[26] KMT leaders became increasingly apprehensive as they saw unfolding a replay of Canton's troubles. When the news of plans for a general strike of Wuhan on December 3 reached Chiang Kai-shek, he moved to intervene. Besides protesting against the imperialist employers of the three cities, the general strike was intended to bring pressure for higher pay and improved working conditions. Chiang quickly called together at Nanchang various KMT cadre and Borodin, who with other leaders had just arrived from Canton.[27]

The group discussed Chiang's proposal to "regulate" the labor movement and the movement of the National Government north to Wuhan from Canton.[28] From Wuhan the united response of employers heightened the tension when the Chamber of Commerce gathered 10,000 demonstrators opposed to union pressure who threatened a general lockout unless the unions lowered their demands. Borodin recommended that the CCP cooperate in restraining the union disorders. Political Department personnel proposed disbanding 1,000 armed pickets who were operating in Wuhan in the manner of the Hong Kong Strike pickets of Canton.[29] Especially at Hankow, the union violence stirred in Chiang's imagination the spectre of foreign marines swarming ashore from the large fleet of gunboats anchored in the Yangtze to protect the concerns of their nationals.[30]

The radicalism stimulated a reaction within the KMT Right. In an effort to defuse the polarization of the Right, the Party appointed many of these dissidents to the new government at Wuhan.[31] In a move complementary to this effort, Mme. Sun Yat-sen (supposedly a Leftist) pleaded for the release of Wu T'ieh-ch'eng, the anti-CCP casualty of the postcoup compromises of April and May.[32] Thus, that winter, the KMT responded to its internal strains with a combination of repression and compromise. Sun Ch'uan-fang also had to act to hold his conglomerate empire together.

THE EXPEDITION ENTERS CHEKIANG

Despite the failure of Governor Hsia Ch'ao's rebellion and the presence of Sun's troops in Chekiang, the provincial autonomy movement of October retained its following even if no uprising materialized.

During late October 1926, Sun's forces moved through Chekiang and again attempted to create a regime that would harmonize arbitrary force with some conciliation of provincial feelings. Chou Feng-ch'i gained his transfer back to Chekiang, his division being so ineffective in defense of Kiangsi. Sun retained hope that, within his remaining provinces, his provincial lieutenants might prove the best defenders of their home areas. His own propaganda corps spread the word that the Cantonese army was bestial in its treatment of civilians and aimed at breaking up the family system. To further placate the Chekiang autonomists, Sun brought Ch'en Yi and his division back to Hangchow and by October 31 installed him as the successor to Civil Governor Hsia Ch'ao.[33] At the same time Sun kept his own personal retainer, Lu Hsiang-t'ing, Chekiang's military governor. In Shanghai, en route back to Chekiang, Chou Feng-ch'i showed his flexibility when he declared that Sun had ordered him to defend his home province against the southern invaders.[34] Upon his arrival at Hangchow, Chou stated that he did *not* sympathize with the National Revolution, and that rumors of his desertion in Kiangsi were given the lie by the fact that it had been Chiang who had fallen back before him. At a welcoming reception on November 25, Chou echoed his executed mentor, Hsia Ch'ao, when he said that while he would sacrifice anything for Chekiang, ". . . neither the Northern Army nor the Southern Army were his friends and that any who invaded Chekiang automatically became his enemy . . . ."[35]

Although Sun claimed to be promoting provincial self-defense, he frightened many southeastern provincials when he consented in November to combine with Chang Tso-lin. Sun accepted Manchurian reinforcements as part of a massive military conglomerate of warlords against the NRA. Although inclusion in the Ankuochün may have enhanced Sun's military position, it also lost him the credibility with provincials he needed. As for the issue of provincial autonomy, he did not appear to be as flexible as the KMT.

Expanding its peace movement against Sun Ch'uan-fang, the KMT integrated the All-Chekiang Association with the Affiliated Association of Kiangsu, Chekiang, and Anhui—the provinces remaining under Sun. KMT members from Chekiang included Ts'ai Yüan-p'ei and C.T. Wang, the drafter of Chekiang's autonomous constitution of 1921. To bring peace to the southeast, the association called for self-rule for the provinces. They proposed, from within the sanctuary of the Shanghai settlement, a federal system within which provincials would handle their own affairs while the national assembly would manage larger concerns.[36] In early December 1926, within Chekiang, the provincial military met with proponents of self-rule and considered means of implementing Chekiang's constitution. At the same time, the association continued a steady dialogue with both Sun's Nanking headquarters and the NRA, camped just over the border in Kiangsi.

Gambling that provincialism would defend Chekiang against the southern Reds, Sun decided to remove one pretext for the NRA invasion. He ordered Civil Governor Ch'en Yi to declare Chekiang independent, a move calculated to offset the NRA claim that Chekiang was under oppressive northern rule.[37] Chiang had stated that the NRA would not enter a Chekiang that had broken with Sun, if there remained no northern troops.[38] Sun had already publicly vowed to the Ankuochün that he would defend to his last man his remaining territory against the NRA.[39] Rumors that the support of northern reinforcements pouring into Kiangsu and Anhui would require new tax levies in Chekiang further prejudiced Chekiangese against Sun.[40]

Once again, a group claiming to represent all of Chekiang met in Shanghai's foreign settlement to create an independent provincial regime. Convening on December 8, the body set about electing a Provincial Government Committee—a form favored by the KMT. Among the nominees were seasoned provincial autonomists, some of whom had led the Ningpo Rebellion in 1924. (The Ningpo Rebellion of September and October 1924 had been an attempt by local gentry and their military allies to set up their own local self-rule, independent of northern overlords at Hangchow.) Highest in status was KMT Party member and ex-Chekiang governor Chiang Tsung-kuei, who had led the abortive Ningpo venture

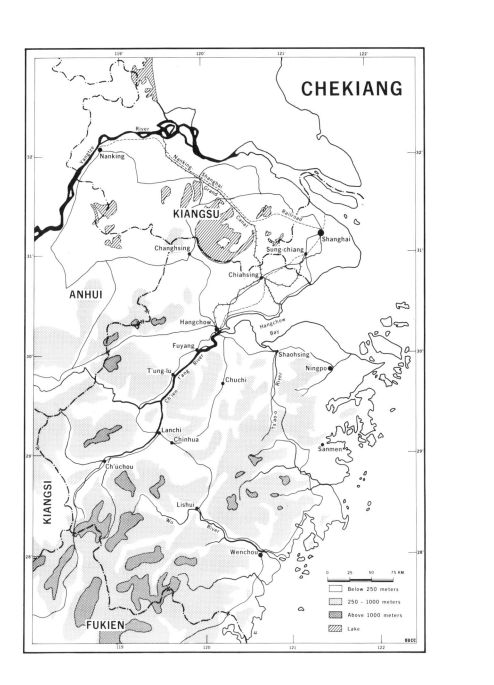

CHEKIANG

KIANGSU

ANHUI

KIANGSI

FUKIEN

Yangtze   River
Nanking
Nanking   Shanghai
Grand
Canal   Railroad
Changhsing   Sung-chiang   Shanghai
Chiahsing
Hangchow   Hangchow   Bay
Fuyang   Shaohsing   Ningpo
T'ung-lu   Chuchi
Chien-t'ang   River
Lanchi   Chinhua
Ch'uchou   Sanmen
Lishui
Wu   River   Ts'ao-o   River
Wenchou

0   25   50   75 KM

Below 250 meters
250 - 1000 meters
Above 1000 meters
Lake

OUCC

and who most recently had acted as intermediary between fellow class-mates from the Shikan Gakko, Chiang Kai-shek and Sun Ch'uan-fang.[41] Also elected to the nine-man committee were Civil Governor Ch'en Yi, still ambitious with regard to the National Revolution, and Chou Feng-ch'i, whose troops manned the key western mountain passes by which Chekiang could be defended. Also significant was the participation of Party member Ch'u Fu-ch'eng, veteran of Ningpo, proponent of a federalism that would bring together de facto provincial leaders in a national commission,[42] and member of the All-Chekiang Association and the Affiliated Association of Kiangsu, Chekiang, and Anhui. Canton's agent, Ma Hsu-lün, also a native, worked behind the scenes to bring together the diverse provincial elements against Sun.

On December 11, during the Shanghai conference, Chou Feng-ch'i declared his defection to the National Revolution and thereby added to the momentum of the break with Sun. With his field headquarters at Ch'ü-chou astride the western passes, Chou gained promotion first to commander of the Twenty-sixth Army in the NRA (his old Chekiang division) and then to field commander for the ensuing operations in Chekiang.[43] Kuomintang agents continued their efforts to win over Civil Governor Ch'en Yi. The Provincial Assembly chairman and the head of the Hangchow Chamber of Commerce each decided in favor of the KMT version of provincial autonomy and pressed Governor Ch'en to make a similar commitment.[44] Ch'en and his spokesmen traveled between Hangchow and Nanking seeking some settlement, but Sun adamantly refused to remove his troops from their station within the Chekiang border at Chiahsing because Chou had already joined the NRA and its vanguard had been reported to be within the province.[45]

On December 17, Ch'en Yi accepted from Chiang Kai-shek the NRA designation of his division as the Nineteenth Army and the promise of a worthy post in the new Chekiang administration.[46] Then, on the Nineteenth, the Shanghai convention announced that Chekiang was independent of Sun's United Provinces, and that it was an autonomous province, which would: 1) implement self-government for Chekiang with provincial personnel; 2) oppose militarists who might seek to carve out their own "autonomous" areas; 3) make public the provincial government affairs; 4) subordinate the Chekiang military to the Provincial Government; 5) provide for the civil freedoms of assembly, press, organization, and speech; and 6) abolish all unconstitutional taxes. According to the Shanghai press, this declaration was delivered to both Sun Ch'uan-fang and Chiang Kai-shek.[47]

This latest effort toward autonomy lacked the unified support of gentry and military; the support of the military was particularly necessary in the absence of NRA reinforcements. The collaborators were former provincial rivals and antagonists, and many of its civilian leaders postponed returning to Chekiang from Shanghai in fear of Sun's retaliation. Among the nine electees, seven had military training. Four were Shikan Gakko classmates, while two were graduates of the Chekiang Military Academy. Chou

Feng-ch'i for one did not stay to defend Hangchow, but withdrew swiftly to the safety of his highland retreat at Ch'ü-chou. Still preoccupied with the takeover of Fukien and Kiangsi, the NRA did not commit more than a vanguard in support.

Sun gathered his four best divisions at the Chekiang border. Gaining the agreement of his Ankuochün allies and subordinates in Kiangsu and Anhui to guard his flank, Sun acted with resolution and hurled his forces into Chekiang's fertile lowlands. In a fast march, a tactic for which Sun was rightfully famous, Sun's field commander, Meng Ch'ao-yüeh, forced the Chekiang divisions out of the valleys and nearly to the Kiangsi border. Maintaining the offensive throughout January 1927, Sun seemed to have succeeded again in gaining Chekiang by force. Within the first day of the attack, Governor Ch'en Yi was captured and replaced by Sun's loyal followers.[48]

When Meng Ch'ao-yüeh's pursuit reached the upland, it halted apprehensively, allowing the Twenty-sixth Army and the few NRA units that reinforced it to maintain an enclave at the head of a valley on the Fukien border.[49] There at Ch'ü-chou the rebel force dug in, providing the NRA with a gateway into Chekiang from Fukien.

Another wing of Sun's pacification force sought out the remnants of rebel Ch'en Yi's Nineteenth Army, eastward along Hangchow Bay's south shore. At the Ts'ao-o River, the pursuers met the Chekiang rebels who, short of bullets, were forced to fall back until they were decisively defeated at Chuchi. From there the remaining rebels fled through the southwestern hills until they met up with the other force holding out at Ch'ü-chou. When Sun's forces again moved toward Ch'ü-chou in mid-January, the KMT's Chekiang operation had not been going at all well.

Included in Sun's offensive were remnants of the Fukien troops of defeated Chou Ying-jen. Sun's troops had pushed to within ten miles of the rebel stronghold at Ch'ü-chou when the rebel towns Lanchi and Chinhua fell on January 10.[50] At this point General Ho over the border in Fukien had to either concede the loss of his easy entry to Chekiang or rush in massive reinforcements.

Mobility again gave the NRA an advantage as First Army units rushed over the border hills to besieged Ch'ü-chou before Sun's offensive came within cannon range. On January 20, Pai Ch'ung-hsi took over direction of the NRA's various allied forces, and by the twenty-ninth he had launched a counterattack down out of the highlands.[51] Under the guidance of locals familiar with the terrain, the NRA marched down tributary valleys leading into the broad Ch'ient'ang plain where the provincial capital, Hangchow, could be seen in the distance. The opponents were now more nearly equal, and, when they engaged at Lanchi and Chinhua on January 29, a bloody battle raged. When the smoke of battle cleared on February 1, the tide of military power in Chekiang had turned. In their defeat at Lanchi-Chinhua, Sun's forces lost vital leadership—killed were the commanding officers of a brigade, regiment, and three battalions, as well as 2,000 soldiers. The NRA captured a haul of weapons, including three precious large cannon.[52] The battle decided the campaign in Chekiang so that Sun's side never regained the highlands or the offensive.

Pai Ch'ung-hsi, military director of the campaign for the NRA, divided his strength into two prongs aimed at Hangchow. When Meng Ch'ao-yüeh attempted to fight back up the main valley, the NRA stood fast, flanked the counterattack, and by February 11 at T'unglu sent Meng in flight down the valley.[53] Meng then tried to hold Fuyang, fortifying his line with artillery and reinforcements, but failed.

Defeat undermined the morale of the northern side to the point where Chou Ying-jen lost control of the Fukien units. Apparently mercenaries did not stand up well, unless victorious. As retreating soldiers panicked and broke ranks, the civilians, from Fuyang down to Hangchow, packed up and fled toward Shanghai. Their towns were looted and battered as the defeated soldiers sought to steal enough to pay their way home, to North China for most of them.[54]

When the battle at T'unglu went against Sun's forces, they began to pull back out of all inland garrisons and coastal sectors toward Hangchow. Hangchow at least offered the security of the rail line back to Shanghai and the north. In one sector, as the NRA pincers closed on Hangchow, it caught one body of 8,000 troops waiting to be ferried from the east bank of the Ch'ient'ang over to Hangchow on the west bank.[55]

Sun Ch'uan-fang ordered more reinforcements into Chekiang, but they did not cooperate with field commander Meng Ch'ao-yüeh who had similarly not gained the cooperation of the Fukien units.[56] Thus, rather than risk another stand to hold the last northern corner of Chekiang at Hangchow, Meng ordered his 20,000 troops into a general retreat into Kiangsu—one of Sun's last two provinces. Boarding trains jammed with troops, General Meng Ch'ao-yüeh and Sun's civil governor of Chekiang left dejectedly for Shanghai on February 17, 1927.[57]

Even the retreat out of Chekiang was plagued from within. Meng could not easily keep discipline among his dejected troops. By the time they had rolled the fifty some miles to Chiahsing in cold cattle cars, many had become mutinous. As the train halted there, the town elders pleaded with Meng to keep his men on board and pass through peacefully. Meng would not risk the confrontation with his troops, so numbers of them scrambled off the train into the town, bent on helping themselves to its resources, human and material. Meng, trying his best to stay ahead of the advancing NRA, reboarded his train and resumed his passage to Shanghai. What he left behind in Chiahsing illumines one of the basic differences between the National Revolutionary Army and the more traditional personal armies of the warlords.

Armed northern soldiers broke down the barricades quickly nailed up by the terrified shopkeepers, ransacked the interiors, and made off with whatever valuables they could carry. The pillage of Chiahsing was by no means unique. Entering the looted cities, the NRA was in marked contrast disciplined and well-behaved, which made an indelible impression on the Chinese townsmen. The pragmatic Chinese tend to weigh actions more heavily than propaganda. In Chiahsing, where only a few of the town dignitaries had *pro forma* seen Sun's officials off as they withdrew, when the NRA vanguard marched in, a greatly relieved welcoming crowd waved flags in greeting.[58]

By February 23, the NRA had cleared Chekiang of Sun's allies—most of whom had withdrawn behind a defense line west of Shanghai. That line centered on the Hangchow-Shanghai rail line at Sungchiang. With Hsia Ch'ao dead and Ch'en Yi held by Sun, Chou Feng-ch'i emerged as the Chekiang militarist most valuable to the National Revolution. From his command of the Chekiang front, Chou quickly advanced to the chairmanship of Chekiang's Military Committee and membership in the Chekiang Government Committee.[59]

CHAPTER 12
The Taking of Shanghai

In preparation for the attack on Shanghai, the East Route Command, under General Ho Ying-ch'in, assembled opposite the Kiangsu border at Chiahsing. In the consolidation of KMT authority in Chekiang, Party member Ts'ai Yüan-p'ei, of the provincial KMT branch, and Chou Feng-ch'i began to set up a new government for the province, while the NRA leadership mapped out its strategy for taking the rich Yangtze delta nearby.

Chiang Kai-shek was reluctant to attack Shanghai directly. There was, of course, the large civilian population in the sprawling metropolis to consider. But, as de facto head of the Party's National Government as well as C-in-C of the NRA, Chiang feared, with good cause, a full-scale foreign intervention at Shanghai. The world powers had their largest concessions and investments at Shanghai, as well as the largest concentration of their nationals, and they had reacted defensively to the KMT's antiforeign propaganda. By February 1927, there had been enough antiforeign incidents to panic those foreigners enjoying the good life in Shanghai's profitable but vulnerable concessions. Just the month before, at Hankow and Kiukiang, infuriated Chinese mobs spurred by agitators from within KMT ranks had overrun the British concessions. Only by turning over a part of the authority of the concessions did the British avoid a bloodbath and the surge of xenophobia that would have followed. Foreign residents in the Yangtze valley evacuated in large numbers to Shanghai, where they helped circulate a daily fare of atrocity tales.

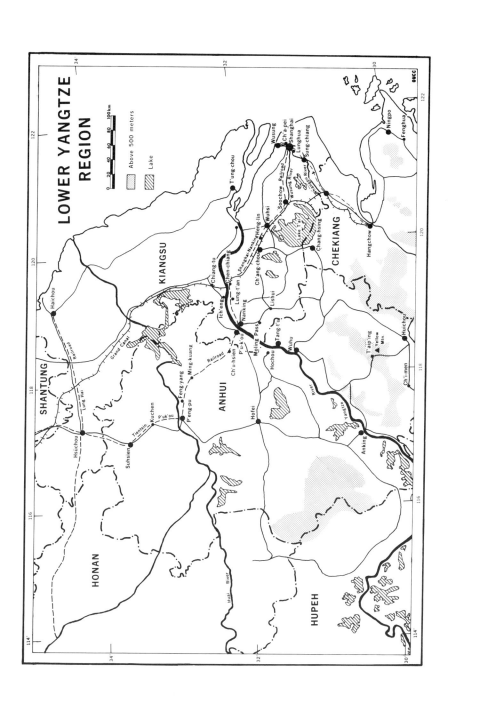

LOWER YANGTZE REGION

Above 500 meters

Lake

0 20 40 60 80 100 km

SHANTUNG

HONAN

KIANGSU

ANHUI

CHEKIANG

HUPEH

Haichou

Hsüchou

Suhsien

Kuchen

P'uk'ou

Feng-yang

P'eng-pu

Ming-kuang

Ch'u-hsien

Hofei

Hochow

Wuhu

T'ai-ping

Yellow Mtn.

Ch'i-men

Anking

Chiang-tu

Chen-chiang

Tch'eng

Lung-t'an

Nanking

Fang-t'u

Moling Pass

Lishui

T'ung-chou

Wuhsi

Meng-Heng-lin

Ch'ang-chou

Wusung

Ch'a-pei

Shanghai

Lunghua

Sung-chiang

Soochow

Chang-hsing

Hangchow

Huichou

Ningpo

Fenghua

Lake T'ai

Grand Canal

Lung Hai Railroad

Tientsin

Shanghai-Nanking Railroad

Soochow Railroad

Wusung River

Huangpu River

Yangtze River

Huai River

The consensus of the foreign powers involved at Shanghai was not to pull out without a fight. Comparisons of the contemporary situation with the Boxer Rebellion were rife. Military reinforcements poured in from all the nations who had invested in the Yangtze region, and corps of local trained volunteers patrolled and drilled in the streets. As befitted their influence in the region, the command of the defense of Shanghai's foreign quarters went to the British. Commander Duncan, headquartered in the Richard Hotel, coordinated a truly international force of nearly 10,000 troops, mainly crack marines, plus those on board the numerous warships that steamed anxiously in the vicinity. By agreement with Sun Ch'uan-fang, Duncan fortified the defense perimeter and expanded it outside the concessions to include certain defensible points. Rumors spread that the British were requesting their own government and those of the United States and Japan to commit themselves to full-scale war with the "Cantonese" should they attack the concessions.[1]

Sun Ch'uan-fang, as his position worsened, had solicited outside support for his regime—both from other warlords and from the foreign powers. As early as November 1926, Sun had stirred up the foreign community by warning that he was unable to "guarantee safety" against the radical, antiforeign activities of the Reds in Shanghai.[2] The concessions, themselves, had long been sanctuaries for Chinese revolutionaries and political exiles. There, anti-Manchu operators had enjoyed their own relatively sheltered bases "outside the wall," just as earlier barbarian conquerors had built up their strength beyond the Chinese pale. Concession authorities had been hard pressed enough keeping track of their own foreign flotsam and jetsam to bother with the Chinese. Policing Chinese who traveled incognito and mixed with the daily influx of Chinese workers was a security force's nightmare. In early January 1927, Sun collaborated with the International Adminstrative Office in rounding up and executing the revolutionary agents who infiltrated Shanghai and the concessions. On the evening of January 10, inspection teams made up of foreign volunteers patrolled the streets and alleys of the concessions identifying and searching passersby. Suspected revolutionaries ended up back in the police stations of Sun's Chinese city. The concessions further cooperated by prohibiting Chinese political activities and meetings—in order to "maintain order."[3] By late February, when the NRA began massing across the nearby border of Chekiang, Sun announced that he and the Japanese and British authorities of Shanghai were cooperating in checking disorders caused by Chinese labor unions and subversives. The announcement was followed by a police roundup of union activists and press members sympathetic to the revolution.[4]

Thus, as Chiang approached Shanghai, there was a definite risk there of massive retaliation from the foreign powers, who seemed to be aligned with Sun in a commitment against the National Revolution. An intervention that might have opened a new front, in addition to the one against Sun and a potential one against the northern warlords, was to be avoided. Rather than risk a military confrontation with the Shanghai concessions, Chiang chose subterfuge.

At the Sungchiang front near Shanghai, the NRA East Route Command appeared to be poised in readiness for an attack. Up the Yangtze, the other half of the NRA offensive pressed toward Nanking. Were Nanking with its ferries linking it to the Tsin-P'u (Tientsin-P'u-k'ou) Railroad to fall, Sun would be in danger of isolation on the south bank of the Yangtze, cut off from the rail line that supplied him with troops and materiel from North China. Within Shanghai, the KMT could call on the unions of the KMT and CCP and on other partisan organizations to elevate the level of disorders to the point where the city would not be worth Sun's defense. The abortive, poorly organized "First Uprising" of October had at least provided experience.

On February 19, as Sun pulled his defeated forces out of Chekiang and awaited further Shantung reinforcements promised by Chang Tsung-ch'ang, the Second Uprising began in Shanghai to capitalize on his vulnerability. Since November 1926, the supposedly allied CCP and KMT in Shanghai had been gathering in union recruits and strengthening their unions' authority over members. Although the numbers of modern factory workers in China constituted an infinitesimal portion of the Chinese millions, most of them were concentrated around the factories of Shanghai. Numbering several hundred thousand, they did present a considerable potential within the city. Following the November conference that committed the new Ankuochün to the lower Yangtze, the Shanghai unions found an issue to use along with the economic goals most popular with the workers. The unions attacked Sun's bringing in of Shantung mercenaries and his and the northern warlords' connections with foreign imperialism, and they also preached the need in Shanghai for local self-government.[5] From late 1926 through January 1927, the unions, particularly the CCP-directed ones, organized their memberships to work against Sun Ch'uan-fang and imperialism.

In February, the anti-Sun movement in Shanghai became more radical. The National General Labor Union (GLU) of the CCP engineered assassinations to terrorize both Chinese and foreign industrialists.[6] To bring the workers of Shanghai more under its influence, as well as to distract Sun's defense efforts, the GLU organized a political strike that, like the Hong Kong Strike, would include enough economic incentives to captivate the proletariat. The general strike in Shanghai was called for February 19, and was to include the foreign concessions' factories and services.

The strike declaration promulgated by the GLU included five general political demands and twelve economic demands. One aim of the strike was to seize power through the use of the masses, even from an armed regime like Sun's. By directing large crowds of workers against Sun's police stations and garrison posts, it was thought the GLU could seize enough weapons to arm a workers' corps.[7] The experience of the Hong Kong Strike organization had already proven the value of arming workers. But, the response of the Shanghai regime differed from that of the KMT in Canton.

Sun Ch'uan-fang's garrison commander in Shanghai responded vigorously and without delay. Broadsword-carrying executioners and troops marched quickly through Shanghai, striking terror as they beheaded on sight anyone apparently involved in the general strike or the subversion against Sun. The sight of gory heads impaled on the lamp posts at street corners must have had a highly dramatic effect. This Chinese-style punishment, for which Sun had already become notorious in Kiangsi, involved public display as a teaching device. Of the estimated 100,000 to 350,000 workers striking,[8] the "head count" of those who fell before the broadswords was at least 100,[9] and may have run as high as 500 considering that many were seized in secret.[10] Although the GLU cadre among the strikers continued to attack police stations, the general strike lost its momentum on the third day.[11] Meanwhile, Shanghai workers held a mass trial and execution of at least one police "running dog." When the new garrison commander, Pi Shu-ch'eng, arrived as part of the reinforcements from Sun's Shantung allies, the GLU conceded the futility of further bloodletting and ordered those still on strike back to work.[12] The Second Shanghai Uprising thus ended without achieving its goals.

An aspect of the Second Uprising showed, however, the continuing weakness of disunity within even Sun's military machine. By this time, Sun's Shanghai navy had apparently been subverted and acted suspiciously. On February 22, as the GLU led sorties against the Shanghai police, shells from the warships *Chien-wei* and *Chien-k'ang* fell about the famous Kiangnan Arsenal. Blaming junior officers for the bombardment, Sun merely gave Admiral Yang Shu-chuang a demerit.[13] Sun was reluctant to act against his conglomerate subordinates for fear of further straining already weakened relationships. Actually, Yang Shu-chuang was merely awaiting the right moment to go to the aid of the NRA, as will be seen later. Although the bombardment failed to knock out the arsenal, a fire that began mysteriously on February 28 touched off forty crates of artillery shells and burned out a section.[14]

Although the Second Shanghai Uprising contributed little to prying Sun and his Shantung allies loose from the rich port, the NRA strategy of entrapment moved on. From Hangchow, Chekiang units began to shift toward the Sungchiang front and Lake T'ai; while from Kiangsi, the NRA, in March, moved downriver toward Nanking, the southern terminal of the northern rail line from Tientsin. Besides the signs of troop movements, the NRA strategy was even described in the Chinese press—possibly to drive home to Sun's regime the threat of their impending isolation.[15] However, even as the NRA's Sixth and Seventh armies moved along the Kiangsi-Anhui border and the Eastern Route Command poised itself near Shanghai, political disunity to the rear threatened the prospects for victory.

STRAINS WITHIN THE REVOLUTIONARY CAMP

In December, at the Nanchang conference, Chiang and Borodin had apparently tried to smooth again the strains that showed in the facade of the National Revolution. Borodin had agreed to curtail union disorders that interfered with war efforts, in order to preserve the valuable CCP-KMT alliance. However, within the newly conquered territory, which contained great industrial potential, the economy was increasingly disrupted by strikes and labor violence. Although this situation was dangerous to the Northern Expedition, from the Communist point of view it held great promise for organizing the proletariat of China's greatest industrial complex. As the CCP-Russian bloc and their KMT followers grew in power at Wuhan, they also became less willing to cooperate with Chiang. To them, Chiang was less dependent on Russian aid and thus less under their influence since he left Kwangtung, and a more tractable KMT military figure would better serve their interests. This desire to see Chiang eclipsed coincided with, and promoted, the endemic centrifugal forces within the KMT. As part of the anti-Chiang movement, its engineers recolored Chiang's political image from that of being a part of the Red KMT Left and isolated him in the KMT Right. By December 1926, at the latest, the anti-Chiang movement had begun to influence the progress of the Northern Expedition.

At that point, C-in-C Chiang found it necessary to wire the Wuhan administration three times for funds needed to pay the disgruntled Seventh Army soldiers arrears in their wages.[16] That administration was mainly a newly created Joint Council of Party and Government instigated by Borodin and generally pliable to his suggestions. One of the leaders was Hsü Ch'ien, Minister of Justice and representative of Feng Yü-hsiang, whose desire to see continued Russian aid to Feng allowed Borodin valuable leverage.

According to such widely divergent observers as Wang Ching-wei's followers, the CCP, and Chiang's supporters, the new Joint Council at Wuhan during January and February 1927 became quite responsive to Russian "advice." By early February, CCP branches were instructed to attack Chiang with orally delivered, *unwritten* rumors linking him with warlords and Japanese imperialists—a betrayer of the Three People's Principles.[17] To replace Chiang in the KMT hierarchy, Hsü Ch'ien, Eighth Army Commander T'ang Sheng-chih, and Wang Ching-wei (still abroad) were considered. The Communist movement in KMT territory was progressing so well that few wished to prejudice it by risking open strife with the KMT. Borodin and CCP leaders like Mao Tse-tung were encouraged by the growth of mass potential in the countryside and in military units around Wuhan. As the Northern Expedition had moved through Hunan, membership in CCP-influenced peasants' associations there had shot up so fast that the CCP cadre was strained to retain supervision (see chapter 22). So also had been the case with the peasants' associations of Hupei and the unions of Wuhan. While highly elating to the Communists, the antiland-lord efforts of the rural organizations stirred reactionary responses among the NRA officers who were also needed on Wuhan's side.

The Hunanese commander of the Second Army (composed mainly of Hunanese) warned at a KMT meeting of the rising danger of internal divisiveness as members, neglectful of the war, had become sidetracked by ". . . ideas . . . not indicated in Sun Yat-sen's instructions," and warned that they should ". . . not belittle the enemy." Defending Chiang's central authority as C-in-C, T'an Yen-k'ai pointed out that "our enemies are now uniting together and gathering to attack us. We should concentrate the power of the Party and obey its orders strictly regardless of our own opinions."[18]

Seeing his authority as C-in-C endangered, Chiang launched his own counterattack against his enemies within the ranks of the revolution. He claimed that the CCP strategy and those who followed it threatened the all-class union of the KMT. On February 19 he urged a KMT audience to look to ". . . the doctrines of Sun Yat-sen and nothing else."[19]

The anti-Chiang movement was evident at Wuhan, where a few days later on February 24, a crowd of 50,000 was assembled at the Party headquarters parade ground. Speakers fired salvos at the C-in-C, at those who had come to power after the anti-Communist coup of March 1926, and at the reorganization that launched the expedition. Decrying the Northern Expedition, the opening speaker said, "All we have seen is military power, but no Party power; individual will but not Party will. . . . Old degenerate counterrevolutionaries have caused these pathetic facts of the Party. That is why we must . . . knock down the feudal influences." After several chanted choruses of "Down with the Old and Degenerate!" another orator went on that "a few individuals could not do the work. . . . Now the old, rotten feudal thinking members manipulate the KMT, we must therefore knock them down." They replied with "Down with Chang Ching-chiang" (the CEC chairman elected after the March 20 Coup) and "Oppose the Military Dictatorship." The next speaker blasted "personal dictatorship" as the Party's greatest problem. The head of the NRA's Political Departments, Teng Yen-ta, advised that "democratic centralization was the way to achieve the ideals of the Three People's Principles, but now our leadership has been occupied by the old, ignorant, and the incompetent . . . ," and "we must overthrow personal dictatorship . . . and bring the military under control. . . ."[20]

The very next day Chiang refuted the charges as being made by those who wanted power for themselves, and singled out Hsü Ch'ien who had made himself chairman of the new Joint Council without Party authorization (see Appendix). His speech underlined what Sun Yat-sen had seen as the political weakness of the Chinese—the tendency to divide fractiously without a consensus. Having concluded that Borodin was directing the attack on him, Chiang telegraphed Moscow on February 26 requesting that Borodin be ordered back to Russia.[21] At a Party meeting on February 27, Chiang observed that, in the newly occupied territory, while the people saw the KMT members and their NRA, they heard the propaganda of the Communists. As Chiang became more concerned about an impending disintegration of the Party, he came to feel that Wang Ching-wei had the potential to pull it together again.[22]

By March the strategy of the Russian mission focused on replacing Chiang with General T'ang Sheng-chih, the Hunanese defector who commanded the Eighth Army. According to a secret Soviet report of March 5, T'ang would be more dependent on Russian aid and had decided to cooperate in gathering an anti-Chiang group among the generals. A new alliance would depend on the support of units from Chang Fa-kuei's corps, Ch'en Ming-shu's Eleventh Army, Chu P'ei-teh's Third Army, and the Ninth and Tenth armies.[23] According to the report, T'ang had successfully turned Li Tsung-jen against Chiang, a defection which may have sprung from Chiang's inability to obtain funds from Wuhan to pay Li's Seventh Army.

Within the National Revolutionary movement, the disintegrating centrifuge accelerated as the events of spring 1927 became increasingly muddied by shifting personal loyalties and political machinations. Relevent here is the effect of those divisions on the offensive capability of the NRA. Excepting the East Route operation through Fukien and Chekiang, the NRA progress north from Wuhan and downriver from Kiangsi lost its momentum. Chiang managed to hold the support of the East Route corps and his armies on the Kiangsi-Anhui border, but they halted their offensive. In southern Honan where the NRA force nearest Wuhan faced Wu P'ei-fu, there was only the ringing of rhetoric from October 1926 to May 1927. Party infighting as much as the winter's chill slowed the expedition.

Downriver from Wuhan's wordstorm, Chiang somehow maintained his authority and discipline among the many corps. The lower Yangtze was his home territory and Chiang's confidence was increased and his financial resources replenished through the support of local Party branches and merchants who sided with him. The resumption of the offensive began with the defection of a key force of Sun Ch'uan-fang's in Anhui. Ch'en T'iao-yüan, classmate of Sun from Tokyo's Shikan Gakko and the C-in-C of Sun's Anhui forces, had become disenchanted with his superior and the United Provinces, especially upon experiencing the defeat in Kiangsi. Ch'en's lack of enthusiasm had been noted even in the press. On December 5, 1926, Ch'en secretly dispatched a representative, Fan Shao-kai, to discuss the possibilities of joining the National Revolution. At the same time, Sun maintained his hope of holding together his front in Anhui through promoting his subordinates. Sun appointed Ch'en to the post of director of defenses for the province on December 21 despite his apparent ambivalence.[24] Throughout January 1927, the arrangement seemed to be in effect, but in February the situation became fluid.

On February 20, one of Ch'en T'iao-yüan's divisions under Liu Pao-t'i defected to the NRA at the strategic pass of Ch'imen, gateway through a 5,000-foot-high range into Anhui.[25] With this mountainous side door to Anhui in the hands of the NRA, the province was quite vulnerable. Of greater significance was the fact that these mountains were the last natural barrier behind which Sun could defend the lower Yangtze—including, of course, Shanghai. Within two weeks, Ch'en T'iao-yüan bent before the inevitable and committed himself to the National Revolution.

He proved his defection by turning over his defense sector athwart the Yangtze on March 2, and by bringing with him the mixed brigade of his subordinate Wang P'u and remnants of the Hunan Army under Yeh K'ai-hsin. The NRA under Chiang then moved over Yellow Mountain and down to take Taiping, Anhui, the next day. Practically unopposed, the

NRA marched rapidly toward Nanking through Anhui along several routes. By March 17, the Seventeenth Division of Ch'eng Ch'ien's Sixth Army had sped to Wuhu 200 miles downstream the quickest way possible—by river steamers. Nanking was but a mere seventy some miles off.[26]

On the north bank of the Yangtze, an NRA spearhead pressed quickly in the direction of the soft midsection of the north-to-south railway. In mid-March, the NRA captured the city of Hofei, a crossroads in northern Anhui, leaving less than 100 miles of low hills to the railway to be taken. As the allegiance of Sun's Shanghai navy became suspect, he became increasingly dependent on the arterial Tsin-P'u Railroad since he could not be assured an avenue of escape to the north by sea. Thus, by mid-March, the NRA strategy of threatening Sun with being trapped in the Yangtze delta at Shanghai was proceeding in a most effective way.

The southern part of the strategy saw the NRA offensive moving out of Chekiang into the delta region. One pincer pressed north along the west shore of Lake T'ai aiming to intersect the Shanghai-Nanking Railroad at Ch'angchou.[27] Although the force did make a diversionary feint eastward toward Soochow, the heaviest concentration of troops was along the lake from Changhsing north. When this attack began on March 6, 1927, the Sixth Army on the Yangtze in Anhui cooperated by attacking Wuhu.

At Wuhu, the taut nerves of the foreign community in the river port snapped when antiforeign disorders broke out—NRA political workers rallied a crowd of civilians and soldiers who mobbed the foreigners' clubhouse and the Maritime Customs Office, where it terrorized the foreign staff. Following this, nearly all the foreigners fled downriver to Shanghai by ship, carrying with them new tales of antiforeignism.[28] Apparently the tradition in China of turning over conquered towns to the lusts of the victorious troops was in some sectors transformed into antiforeign acts. The nationalistic element in the revolution, which promised to right the wrongs committed by the foreigners, also plucked the chronic raw nerves of China's xenophobia. Although Confucian social mores frustrated aggressive behavior within Chinese society, this hostility could still be unleashed against those "foreign devils" outside the pale.

To the south, the Eastern Route Command slowed as the enemy bombarded it with heavier artillery and as enemy reinforcements continued to arrive from Shantung during the second week of March.[29] As the several spearheads pressed toward the rail link with the north, Shanghai's defensibility became more precarious so that northern defense measures began to shift in emphasis from holding golden Shanghai to defending the Nanking area with its circle of rugged hills and the southern terminal of the Tsin-P'u Railroad across the river. By mid-March, indeed, some forces were being evacuated from Shanghai toward Nanking positions.[30]

The breakthrough for the Eastern Route force came on March 15 on the hills overlooking Lake T'ai when units succeeded in flanking enemy artillery placements. With that blockade eliminated by March 16, the NRA pincer pressed west against Lishui, a mere forty miles from Nanking.[31] Around the east shore of the lake, the NRA was still effectively blocked by the superior artillery of the Shantung elements. However, this sector of the lower delta was rapidly losing its value for Sun. Mid-March reinforcements who arrived at Ch'angchou on the Nanking-Shanghai Railroad were turned back for reassignment around Nanking.

From Wuhu, the NRA moved out around the enemy's riverside defense line causing Tangt'u to be flanked and captured on March 17 at the same time the East Route force ground on into hilly ridges within fifty miles from Nanking where Sun had been headquartered.[32] On the eighteenth, far to the north of the Yangtze, the Seventh Army captured Hofei with its routes leading to the coveted railway.

With the diminishing defensibility of the delta area, the decision of the Shantung commander, Chang Tsung-ch'ang, was predictable. He ordered the general withdrawal of his forces from the Shanghai perimeter to better defense positions north of the Yangtze. With that, on March 19 Shanghai's defenses began to crumple at the Sungchiang front and Pi Shu-ch'eng's troops there retreated into the city toward the railroad station—but did not proceed to Nanking as ordered.[33]

According to foreign and Chinese press reports that followed, Pi Shu-ch'eng was awaiting the best circumstances for his defection to the NRA. He had apparently negotiated the turning over of Shanghai with a leading local KMT figure, Niu Yung-chien.[34] This, along with the military strategy of the NRA of isolating Sun in South China, was a move toward the desired end of capturing Shanghai without either a bloody battle or gunfire that might provoke foreign intervention. When Sun's order to evacuate Shanghai came down, although Pi Shu-ch'eng ignored it, there were other units there that were not a part of the arrangement with the KMT. Among them, a crack White Russian artillery continued to defend its position from an armored train as it retreated from Sungchiang back into the city.[35] The NRA managed to flank the railroad artillery on March 20 with the assistance of another defection, that of the waterway police. Since the delta around Shanghai was a crosshatch of canals, the defection and assistance of the local waterway police greatly eased the mobility of the attacking NRA.[36] As it rapidly penetrated the front outside Shanghai from a multitude of routes, the northern line disintegrated all along the Nanking-Shanghai railway retreat route. Simultaneously, the city of Soochow and the sector from Ch'angchou to Henglin fell to the NRA.[37] No aid came to Sun from the sea where, the preceding week, his admiral, Yang Shu-chuang, had steamed the fleet upriver and joined with the revolutionaries' river fleet.[38] Yang's defection had been in the mill since August 1926, but he had timed his jointure with the NRA to coordinate with the Shanghai campaign. Thus, up to March 21, 1926, the planned bloodless occupation of Shanghai and avoidance of a coordinated foreign defense proceeded smoothly.

However, on March 20, the Shanghai branch of CCP's General Labor Union met and noted the entry of NRA units to Shanghai's southwestern suburbs. The CCP's interests in Shanghai did not coincide with those of the incoming NRA Eastern Route Command under Chiang's domination. For the CCP, a tantalizing opportunity was presented as most of the northern defenders awaited to surrender while the NRA massed outside the city—thus creating a virtual vacuum of power. By moving quickly, the masses of the GLU could take unawares the northern soldiers and Shanghai police, who would be easily disarmed. The weapons thus gathered could arm GLU pickets who could then move to control the city for the CCP. In order to gather as many workers as possible, the GLU called another general strike, to commence the next day, March 21. On that day armed pickets attacked Pi Shu-ch'eng's troops, the remnants of Sun's elements, and the Shanghai police stations.[39]

This action gained for the GLU several police stations (which allowed control of the surrounding city districts) and considerable stores of weapons. Fighting between GLU members and police and resisting Shantung soldiers spread throughout the city. The northern soldiers fled in confusion through the city toward the railroad station and the coast, looting as they ran.[40] Shells were lobbed from the armored train at attackers. As the conflict between workers and soldiers raged, fires flared up in the heavily populated areas. In the northern suburb of Ch'apei, the workers' quarter near the train station, flames destroyed nearly 3,000 dwellings.[41] The workers were the expendables in this struggle of the CCP to take the city.

By the evening of March 22, Pai Ch'ung-hsi's NRA units had moved in and occupied Shanghai. However, the general strike and its disruptions *continued* until after General Pai ordered the GLU to call it off on March 24. During the four-day strike, according to some estimates, 322 Chinese were killed and 2,000 wounded.[42] The evidence does not substantiate the romanticized version originating with the Communists, especially the Trotskyites, that the valiant proletariat proudly turned over their hard-won city to the NRA, which then betrayed their trust. By that time, the CCP and Chiang's faction of the KMT had become polarized to where there was *no* trust to be lost.

As the NRA occupied and consolidated its authority in Shanghai, its spokesmen there—Chiang, Ho Ying-ch'in, and Pai Ch'ung-hsi—promulgated declarations to quiet the taut nerves of the foreign community with its frightened refugees and international sentinels on alert along a barbed-wire perimeter. Real and exaggerated tales of antiforeign atrocities inland had rekindled the embers of terror smoldering since the Boxer massacres. The NRA notices gave assurance that:

> The purpose of the military operations of the Northern Expedition is to establish a nation governed by the people and to get rid of the warlords. Our army occupied Hunan, Kiangsi, Hupeh, Fukien, Chekiang, Anhui, and other provinces and the unification of the entire nation will be accomplished soon. The Party Army's success is the victory of the people. . . . In accordance with international morality we shall guard the lives and property of foreigners. We have occupied Shanghai by more than force. We request that consuls inform your nationals to carry on your activities as usual and order the marines not to misunderstand our motives and not to carry out means to obstruct our revolutionary cause.[43]

Within a matter of days, the antiforeign actions that followed the capture of Nanking required a repetition of the assurances.

The last dispirited northern rear guard crossed over the Yangtze to the safer north bank, making the rail terminal at P'u-k'ou the southern outpost of the Ankuochün. The NRA vanguard entered Nanking on March 24 with elements of the Sixth Army and two affiliated units, one of which had just defected to the NRA in Anhui. The truth about what actually happened in the Nanking Incident has yet to be documented.

Chiang's faction of the KMT charged the head of the Sixth Army's Political Department, CCP member Lin Tsu-han, with masterminding the attacks on foreigners. Such action could have provoked the foreign powers to attack Chiang, thus diverting him from completing the expedition and weakening his power vis-à-vis the CCP at Wuhan. Rather than controlling a united China hostile to communism and Russia, he would at least be neutralized fighting the British imperialists in their sphere of influence on the lower Yangtze. Thus, elements in the Sixth Army stirred the latent xenophobia among the soldiery and the masses at Nanking. However, the foreigners who lived through the Nanking Incident generally agreed that the attacks were not made by civilian mobs, but by calculating southern soldiers. Whatever the motivations, what happened at Nanking signified a grave breach of military discipline if the promulgations of the C-in-C's headquarters are to be given credence.

For Chiang Kai-shek to have permitted the attacks was inconsistent with his long-standing strategy to avoid provoking a foreign intervention. By the time the Nanking refugees disembarked at Shanghai, there were over 25,000 foreign army and naval personnel defending the concessions—with the promise of more standing by. [44] Considering the success of the strategy that had unfolded so successfully in Kiangsu, the antiforeign acts seem superfluous to Chiang's designs. Had Chiang been a part to a demonstration of Chinese mass power against the foreign imperialists, he would not afterward have negated the allegation so adamantly. Most relevant to the expedition is the interpretation of the Nanking Incident as a symptom of the *internal* disunity in the National Revolution, which was itself such an inclusive movement that it was interpreted differently by its allied components.

CHAPTER 13
The Party Divided

One of the murkiest chapters in the history of KMT politics must be the origins and development of the internal divisions that culminated in the split within the Party. The strains in the Party could be traced all the way back to its origins, and were obvious the preceding year at the time of the March 20 Coup, which only centralized—temporarily—power in the hands of one faction but did not eliminate the dissidents. Regardless of who led the Nanking Incident, it definitely coincided with the decline of that centralized authority that the C-in-C had marshalled to launch the Northern Expedition. Earlier, on January 3, 1927, elements of the KMT at Wuhan had triggered the mob action that had gained a return of authority over the British concessions at Hankow and Kiukiang to the Chinese. The Party had reached no agreement on the immediate recovery of foreign concessions. There were a multitude of other political and philosophic questions on which the CCP and many of its KMT allies disagreed wholeheartedly. The Western Hills faction had already bolted from the United Front with the CCP and its Russian patrons. March 1927 saw the long frustrated tensions between Chiang's faction and its antagonists at Wuhan rise toward a climax.

Between March 7 and 17, Wuhan's Joint Council, already openly defiant of Chiang's power, first convened a plenary session and then what it called a CEC meeting. These gatherings represented mainly the interests of the KMT Left and its CCP allies. It is significant that the CCP histories term that spring of 1927 the "Communist Period of the Wuhan Government."

The sessions met in the highly charged atmosphere of Hankow where anti-Chiang posters and slogans welcomed the participants.[1]

The KMT Left and the CCP coalesced and proposed resolutions strengthening the CCP's representation in the National Government by the appointment of its members Su Ch'ao-cheng and T'an P'ing-shan as ministers; the promotion of the CCP's peasant and labor organs; and the dispatch of three representatives to the Third Communist International to discuss what China's role was to be in the world revolution.

Wuhan's CEC gathered political authority at the expense of the office of the C-in-C and those who supported him. Thus it voted to take direct control of military funds, which had been managed by Minister of Finance T.V. Soong (considered a supporter of Chiang). In order to gain influence in more of the army corps of the NRA, Wuhan strengthened the existing ideal of Party control over its army through Party Representatives whose rankings would parallel the military chain of command. The CEC appointed a recruiting committee to gather *suitable* Party Representatives. Wuhan especially hoped to place their representatives in the many newly defected army corps—many members of which had developed ties already with the C-in-C who had been a party to their defections.

The growth of the NRA was dramatic and a cause for concern among the enemies of its C-in-C. From the eight "armies" that had participated in launching the expedition in July 1926, the NRA had expanded to include forty by March 1927. Wuhan's fiscal and political control over the corps in the NRA would greatly undermine Chiang's authority. The faction at Wuhan hoped that the newly incorporated armies would submit, therefore, to its Joint Council, Standing Committee, and Military Council—as, according to its interpretation, should Chiang. Chiang's power to strike back within Wuhan's sphere was further curtailed when the regime there ordered the censorship of anti-Communist criticism.

The centralized power that Chiang had fought to achieve at Canton during the spring of 1926, Wuhan's CEC divided up among its own various executive committees. In theory, the Military Council became the chief recipient. Of the leading members, Wang Ching-wei and Chiang were absent so that Hsü Ch'ien and Teng Yen-ta made the decisions. Since both were highly responsive to Russian-CCP strategy, that was the prime source of direction at Wuhan. Wuhan sought to neutralize Chiang by abolishing the posts that he held—thus apparently stripping him of legitimized authority and status. Chiang's Ministry of the Military (or Soldiers) was displaced by Wuhan's Military Council. Wuhan also whittled down the functions of the C-in-C's headquarters as it took away the authority to allocate the output of arsenals to the various armies and gave that also to the Military Council. The direction of military education through the various academies and schools was removed from Chiang's supervision, depriving him of the source of a loyal junior officer corps. Appointments, promotions, and dismissals of division and army commanders were to emanate from the Military Council, that is, from Hsü Ch'ien and Teng Yen-ta.[2] When Wuhan's Military Council relieved Ch'en Ming-shu, a Chiang supporter, and replaced him with Moscow's new star, T'ang Sheng-chih,[3] it became obvious that those who owed their commands to Chiang had little security and would either have to switch their allegiance to Wuhan or chance riding out the storm with Chiang.

As Wuhan legislated away Chiang's authority, the coordinated unity of action that had been one NRA advantage over Wu and Sun began to disintegrate. Once again the centrifugal forces in China seemed about to predominate. Without a high degree of coordination, the NRA found it difficult to confront the numerically superior warlord forces of the Ankuochün. In March 1927, Wuhan decreed the nullification of all regulations that Chiang's headquarters had ordered. Although the C-in-C was to retain his authority over troops at the front, the controlling faction at Wuhan claimed control over all other troops. Obviously, units within the NRA confederation felt the contradicting pulls of the opposing factions as the Party centrifuge accelerated. Within the Party, the attack on Chiang and the confusion over what had happened at Shanghai and Nanking ripped off the thin scab that had formed during 1926 over the wounds of members of the KMT-CCP United Front. To many within the KMT, the attack on Chiang seemed to be a CCP maneuver to assume leadership of the National Revolution.

As to the expedition in Kiangsu, the momentum of the delta victories carried the pursuing NRA across the Yangtze. Although the wide, unbridged lower Yangtze was a defensible moat, crossing was eased by the recently defected Shanghai navy, which had become part of the National Revolutionary Navy. On the other side, the timely defection of the brigade of Chang Chung-li simplified the landing (see chapter 30). Those elements that had already been operating north of the Yangtze (the Third, Seventh, and Tenth armies) pressed farther north out of recently captured Hofei and took P'engpu in early April 1927.[4] As Anhui's capital, the bridgehead over the Huai River, and a railroad supply depot for the Shantung Army of Chang Tsung-ch'ang, the capture of P'engpu could have opened the offensive into North China. However, the momentum of attack ground to a halt as confusion and insecurity over the direction of the expedition and its logistical support grew behind NRA lines.

To counter the Communist-dominated faction at Wuhan, Chiang appealed to the Center and Right of the KMT. Even before the capture of Shanghai, an anti-Communist group including Wu Chih-hui, Niu Yung-chien, and Yang Chüan of the KMT's Shanghai headquarters had begun to study and discuss the evidence of subversion of KMT authority by the CCP. On March 6, these men questioned CCP leader Ch'en Tu-hsiu and his Shanghai labor expert, Lo Yi-nung, as to the intentions of the CCP. Ch'en's placatory reply probably echoed an earlier thought of Stalin. Ch'en said that since communizing China would take at least twenty more years, the CCP would continue to need the cooperation of the KMT.[5] When the CCP sponsored an attack on the building holding the Western Hills headquarters in the French concession, KMT nerves were further irritated, as they were by a demonstration held on the Nanking Road against the KMT Right.[6] Chiang profited from the ensuing anti-Communist reaction among the large KMT following at Shanghai. When the NRA did take Shanghai, Chiang wrote to members at Wuhan whom he considered independent of CCP influence and invited them to Shanghai. On March 24, Chiang addressed the following letter to T'an Yen-k'ai at KMT headquarters in Wuhan:

> Please forward this letter to the National Government. Shanghai and Nanking have been occupied and there is much work to be done here. I hope committee member T'an and Ministers Sun [Fo] and Soong and Ch'en [Eugene] will come to Shanghai to handle affairs here so I can devote my attention to military matters.[7]

Chiang neglected to mention the insubordination within his ranks that had precipitated the Nanking Incident to which he was rushing that day. We can see that Chiang did not try to supplant the civilian Party apparatus with his own military following, but rather tried to re-form a coalition away from CCP-Russian influence. Apparently the recipients of Chiang's appeal already had misgivings about Borodin and the CCP at Wuhan, following the recent Joint Council decisions that increased CCP representation within the National Government and deprived Wang Ching-wei of his chairmanship, and including as well the actions taken toward Chiang.[8]

As March came to an end, the split within the KMT, between Communist-allied Wuhan and those supporting Chiang at Shanghai, was all but formalized. Both Wuhan and Shanghai used the press as a weapon, each attacking and censoring the other. From Wuhan, Borodin lambasted the "reactionaries" of Shanghai. At Shanghai, the Party's Central Control Committee, which predated Wuhan's new organs, met under Ts'ai Yüan-p'ei to discuss how to put an end to the Communist influence emanating from Wuhan. Ts'ai, a famous intellectual, has been deleted by CCP historians from that phase of history. At Wuhan, the Joint Council moved against more of Chiang's men as it dismissed the officers of the branch headquarters of the C-in-C there, turning over those functions to Wuhan's Military Council. Shanghai's Control Committee retaliated against an organ in Shanghai that still followed Wuhan's dictates, the local branch of the Political Department, which it ordered placed under surveillance.[9] The contest lapped over into Kiangsi as the Joint Council decreed the KMT headquarters there disbanded and its members confined as "counterrevolutionaries."[10] Working through the Shanghai branch GLU, the CCP promoted the creation of a "provisional municipal government," which began making political appointments in the city as a kind of workers' soviet. Wu Chih-hui spoke for the Control Committee and Chiang when he declared the GLU's new body to be an enemy of the KMT and not to be recognized by Party members or the army.[11]

Occurrences in early April reveal the escalation of tensions within the United Front to physical violence. In Shanghai, the CCP used its labor organ, the GLU, to undermine Chiang's regime. In response Chiang placed the city on a curfew and declared at a press conference that he would "suppress all irregular movements."[12] It became known that Chiang had invited a group of KMT civil and military leaders from Canton to Shanghai where they discussed measures suitable for dealing with the CCP threat in the two cities.[13] Shanghai received news that Wuhan's merchants were being seized and held for ransom by radical unions and that they were then driven from their establishments.[14] In Shanghai, anti-Communist and neutral workers complained that they were being persecuted and beaten by members of the CCP unions. Using the KMT unions as a nucleus, the KMT gathered non-Communist workers and created a labor organization to displace the GLU—the National Labor Union (Ch'uan-kuo Kung-hui Lien-ho-hui)—with a local branch in Shanghai.[15] Labor continued to be the chief political weapon, as the GLU branches in Shanghai and Hangchow launched a general strike as leverage to force the ousting of Chiang. The KMT unions responded by burning the headquarters of the GLU branches in both Hangchow and Ningpo.[16]

The factional struggle polarized provincial party leadership as the violence rose. Wuhan's precipitate attack on some provincial headquarters forced some people into Chiang's camp in self-defense. In attacking its opponents in Canton, Wuhan's Joint Council declared the election of Canton's branch executive committee to be illegal, and on this basis ordered it disbanded for reorganization. The response in Canton was to arrest the Investigative Agent from Wuhan, refuse Wuhan's orders, and close the provincial border against possible attack from Hunan.[17]

Chiang became increasingly concerned about the halted Northern Expedition and the danger of a warlord resurgence. He still hoped that he could convince key KMT leaders to turn from the CCP, provided he could isolate them from its influence. For this purpose, Chiang and his associate chairman Chang Ching-chiang in early March had dispatched a friend of Wang Ching-wei to seek him out and persuade him to return to China. Chang Ching-chiang also wrote Wang, a fellow Party cadre member since before the 1911 revolution, warning him of the threat of a CCP take-over and of China's need for his return from Europe.[18] When Wang did arrive, via Moscow and Vladivostok, in Shanghai by steamer, Chiang was prompted to wire his confused generals on April 1 that:

> Comrade Wang has returned and I have had a serious conference with him about the Party and the country. From now on he will be responsible for the Party as well as political affairs. I will devote my attention to military operations. The military and civil administration, finance and diplomacy will all be under Wang and be consolidated in the central government. My armies and I will obey unanimously. Military authority and operation orders, however, I will direct as before. Wang has indicated that he thinks there should be no intra-Party conflict until the military operation has been completed and that everyone should support the C-in-C until a discussion of the matters involved can be held.[19]

Chiang's optimism about his talks with Wang during the first week in April was premature. Although Wang did apparently feel the need for reunification of the Party, he distrusted his old rival and felt vulnerable without the pro-Communist faction of the KMT about him. He and that faction had risen during 1925 and 1926 partly through their identification with the Communist alliance and with Russian aid. Thus, when Borodin telegraphed Wang from Wuhan to come there quickly, Wang obeyed.[20] When Wang boarded a river steamer secretly, he left behind a public letter he had signed along with CCP leader, Ch'en Tu-hsiu, which argued that the CCP neither wanted to displace the KMT nor to create a proletarian dictatorship.[21]

Possibly Wang wished to see for himself the extent of CCP power at Wuhan. Apparently he did not yet know that the Joint Council had relieved him of his highest posts. According to his own later version, Wang had hoped to bring the Wuhan faction back to Nanking where the power struggle could be settled democratically (to his advantage). The Party plenary session that Wang promoted for April 15 would, he hoped, reunite the KMT. However, Wang claimed that when he arrived in Wuhan he found the NRA in Hupei about to resume its offensive in Honan. He concluded that if an all-KMT gathering at Nanking decided to purge the CCP this would endanger the Honan campaign in which CCP members were attached to many units, and so he squelched the Party meeting.[22]

In the second week of April, clashes between CCP and KMT affiliates became more violent. Interunion fights broke out in Canton, and in Chenchiang, Kiangsu, riots between unions left 150 dead and wounded.[23] The military side of the Shanghai regime became involved when the Shanghai garrison troops had to be brought in to quell attacks by the armed pickets of the GLU. Chiang had ordered the GLU to either disband the 5,000 armed pickets or be regarded as a "conspiratorial organization . . . not to be permitted to exist."[24] On April 6, Chiang used troops to raid and close down the Shanghai branch of the Political Department, headed by CCP member Kuo Mo-jo and under surveillance since the capture of the city.[25]

That same day, Peking's ruler, Chang Tso-lin, raided the Soviet Embassy at Peking, and Shanghai's concession police and those of Tientsin raided the Soviet consulates. The raids must have been coordinated; the evidence gathered in the raid found its way to the KMT at Shanghai. Although the documentation of subversion of the KMT helped to precipitate the ensuing "Party Purification," the rising level of physical violence and acrimonious charges made an open conflict between the CCP and its enemies within the KMT inevitable. As for Chiang, although the entire CCP may not have sought his overthrow, the cadre at Shanghai who controlled tens of thousands of union members did hope to use that power to topple Chiang and Shanghai's KMT rule. Chiang's displacement was a matter of timing for the CCP, since even Stalin, who promoted the United Front in a nationalist revolution, had pronounced in early April that in the future when Chiang was no longer valuable he would be discarded like a "squeezed out lemon."[26] Who would betray whom first?

Shanghai's Control Committee met from April 1 to 5, and pressed Chiang to use his power as C-in-C of the KMT armies to "nip the uprising in the bud." On April 10, 1927, the Committee formalized its position by requesting Shanghai's CEC to act to suppress the CCP conspirators before they could act. This request also represented Canton's cadre, who had earlier met with Chiang and the Control Committee. They were Fifth Army Commander Li Chi-shen, Ch'en Shu-jen who spoke for Canton's garrison commander, and Ch'ien Ta-chün whose division already defended Kwangtung's borders against the KMT Left and the CCP from Hunan. Representing the Kwangsi leadership were Huang Shao-hsiung, Li Tsung-jen, and Pai Ch'ung-hsi, who met with Chiang and KMT leaders at the Lunghua Garrison Command.[27] Circulating at these meetings were reports on CCP activities in Hunan, Hupei, Kiangsi, Chekiang, Anhui, and Shanghai. The consensus was that the CCP was well on the road to seizing the leadership of the National Revolution and suppressing the KMT's role.[28] Thus, although Communist histories have painted Chiang in autocratic impetuosity liquidating the CCP at Shanghai, he did in fact represent a considerable faction of the KMT.* Harold Isaacs also points out the meetings Chiang had with representatives of twenty-nine merchant associations. Some of the KMT support came from the long-frustrated Western Hills faction, which had been calling for the purge of the CCP for nearly two years, as had been also Tu Yüeh-sheng and his Green Society or "gang" (a traditional secret society of local workers) of the lower Yangtze.

The Party Purification was not a bolt out of the blue striking the defenseless CCP and its unions unaware. The Chinese and Western press corps had covered the anti-Communist demands in the KMT during the first two weeks of April, and a warning reached the leader of the GLU's 5,000 armed pickets on April 11 that military action against them was imminent. Therefore, the pickets were put on the alert at strongholds in Ch'apei, Woosung, Putung, and South Shanghai.[29]

The Party Purification begun in Shanghai and Canton has parallels with the breakup of the United Front during the Second Sino-Japanese War. In both cases, while fighting a war, Chiang decided that the rival within his ranks was more dangerous than the external enemy. At both times the question of internal unity (the centrifugal forces) precluded the continuation of external combat. On April 12, 1927, when the NRA at Shanghai moved to "solve" the CCP problem, the purge was not launched from a position of security. In fact the atmosphere there was that of desperation—of having their backs up against the wall.

DIVIDED WE FALL

Although the NRA had pursued Sun's retreat across the Yangtze after the capture of Nanking in March, the offensive was plagued by the uncertainties of the political system that supported it. After the capture of P'engpu in

---

*When Wang Ching-wei arrived in Shanghai, T. V. Soong, who had come from Wuhan, met him at the steamer and took him to the Soong house where they met with Chiang, Wu Chih-hui, Li Shih-tseng, and Chang Ching-chiang. Other participants in the Shanghai meetings over the CCP question included Po Wen-wei, Ku Ying-fen, Kan Nai-kuang, and two-thirds of the old Control Committee, who had gathered there under Ts'ai Yüan-p'ei.

early April, the momentum of victory in Anhui and Kiangsu fizzled out. The Ankuochün licked its wounds in Shantung and, as its position consolidated and the pressure from the NRA slacked off, it began to push south along the Tientsin-P'u-k'ou Railroad. While the Shanghai KMT sat in judgment on the CCP conspiracy, the Ankuochün counteroffensive began in northern Kiangsu on April 3. The NRA lacked spirit and logistical support.[30] Its resistance was so lackluster and ineffective that the succession of defeats in April 1927 have been omitted from the official military histories of the expedition. From April 3 to 11, the NRA fell back 100 miles through Kiangsu and Anhui until it dejectedly made its way back across the Yangtze.[31] This was certainly the NRA's lowest ebb since the desperate fighting in Kiangsi the preceding autumn. This time the larger, more conglomerate NRA could not be pulled together; its C-in-C's attention had been distracted and his authority nullified by the Wuhan faction the month before. These defeats further weakened Chiang's position.

CHIANG'S POTENTIAL AT SHANGHAI

As a base of operations, Shanghai held certain advantages over Wuhan that enabled the KMT in Shanghai to win out in the intra-Party struggle and against the CCP. Although the Shanghai faction comprised mostly outspoken anti-Communists—dramatically so after the April 12 purge—the door remained open to all "pure" KMT members regardless of their beliefs (provided they did not openly work against Chiang). Numbers of even the KMT Left had become disillusioned with the ambitious CCP and its foreign patrons. To some, the dictatorship at Wuhan could be envisioned as Borodin standing behind Hsü Ch'ien. Thus, Shanghai and then Nanking became havens for the dissidents of Wuhan. What did Shanghai have to offer them, and other potential allies?

Shanghai's tangible assets outweighed those of Wuhan—partly due to the economic breakdown upriver that had ensued from radical labor disruptions. In union with its Canton supporters, Shanghai had a more reliable fiscal base. Shanghai was a repository of Chinese capital, and its tax revenues were far higher and had been undisturbed by the violent confiscations and terrorism that was crippling Wuhan's economy. Wuhan's total annual revenues from affiliated provinces had shrunk, despite more efficient collection methods, to only one-fourth those brought in from Shanghai's territories—C$200 million from Kwangtung, Fukien, Chekiang, and the prosperous delta.[32] At Canton the Central Bank continued to hold the bulk of the KMT's hard currency—the largest Chinese silver reserves by 1927—and chose to underwrite Shanghai rather than Wuhan. Wuhan's branch of the Central Bank found itself printing a devaluing paper money. Finance Minister T.V. Soong had moved to Wuhan from Canton, but once there he felt increasingly frustrated with the emphasis given politics and ideology over his expertise. When Soong's own car was menaced by a politicized crowd on the Hankow bund, he packed his bags for the familiar surroundings of newly conquered Shanghai, his home town.[33]

Chiang and his supporters had managed to gain the confidence of the financial and commercial leaders of the great port city, who seemed to have no better alternative. The KMT's Three People's Principles and the ideal of the all-class union in a national movement had long appealed to Shanghai's capitalists and was successful in eliciting their continuing financial support. Chiang reaffirmed these attractive principles and de-radicalized the KMT through Party Purification, thus guaranteeing against a reoccurrence of Wuhan's apparent class struggle and confiscations. Chiang called for arbitration between workers and management and spoke of goodwill and *harmony*.[34] Chiang's own origins near Ningpo, Chekiang, coincided with those of an important segment of Shanghai's commercial element, which eased his communication. However, chafed by daily contact with foreign arrogance and inequality, the Chinese of the treaty ports like Shanghai were the mainspring of Chinese nationalism and Chiang also had to address those feelings.

There have been speculations that Chiang tried to deal with the Japanese upon entry into Shanghai—apparently he did see Chinese representatives of Japanese firms and on March 28 did call on the Japanese consul.[35] There was, of course, the need to soothe the offended sensibilities of the Japanese—and other foreign powers—after what the foreigners called the "anti-foreign outrages at Nanking." The massed military presence of the powers could not be ignored after the Japanese and English presented their formal protests on March 26.[36] Chiang felt constrained to repeat his guarantee that he would be responsible for protecting foreign lives and property, and to differentiate his policy from that of the radicals at Wuhan,[37] *but* at the same time he could not offend the inflamed nationalistic feelings among his supporters. The Japanese intervention in Shantung later in June was a decision made by the Japanese cabinet in late May; it turned Chiang's eastern flank and helped push his troops back south again. Since the Japanese decision was made in May, it would seem to preclude Chiang's having made a deal with them in March or April.

During press interviews in late March, Chiang calmed the foreign powers, but firmly stated that an "objective of the national revolution is to seek international equality. . . . If a nation treats China fairly, China will return friendship."[38] In an interview with a German agency, Chiang supported Shanghai's Foreign Minister who had called for the withdrawal of foreign troops and a return of the foreign concessions. But, Chiang stated that lacking the means to conquer the concessions militarily, he would leave that to the peaceful means of the Chinese politicians.[39] Later, while conceding that he was investigating the responsibility for the Nanking Incident, he parried that ". . . as long as foreign troops and warships undertake to protest . . . we will not be responsible. . . . Incidents are unavoidable in a revolution."[40]*

---

*Mao Tse-tung had the same awareness of the violence of political change in China, but he stated it more poetically: "A revolution is not the same as inviting people to dinner, or writing an essay, or painting a picture, or doing fancy needlework; it cannot be anything so restrained and magnanimous. A revolution is an uprising, an act of violence. . . ."

That the powers could not be trifled with was evidenced a few days later at Hankow when GLU workers rioted against the Japanese concession. With their affinity for "direct action," the Japanese commander there immediately had several hundred marines landed, armed another hundred Japanese nationals, and trained the guns of the Japanese cruisers out on the Yangtze toward the Chinese bund.[41] Using machine guns to halt the mob, the Japanese marines killed over ten Chinese and wounded another ten, according to KMT accounts.[42] The threat of a Japanese intervention continued to distract Wuhan until an uneasy settlement was reached on April 27.[43] This provocation of the Japanese presaged the policy of the CCP's November Plenum of 1927—"Attack the Foreigners" (*Ta wai-kuo-jen*).[44]

In Shanghai, Chiang stuck prudently to the use of rhetoric against the powers. When he called for the powers to negotiate the return of the concessions, he still denied them a tangible pretext for military intervention. His strategy brought a tacit acceptance of the KMT regime, which contributed to the increasing potential at Shanghai. Where the Wuhan KMT found themselves hampered by large-scale unemployment, a disrupted economy, dwindling revenue, political tensions, and the hostility of the powers, Shanghai began to see developing fiscal and economic stability, financial resources, and a degree of internal political consensus over the Communist question.

As Wuhan's chief mentor, Borodin saw the regime weakening and advised a cooling off of labor radicalism and the peasants' movement in order to begin reconstructing the economy.[45] If Wuhan's affiliated armies were to defend the regime and launch a military campaign into Honan, its units would need more tangible support than exhortations and slogans.

Thus despite the weakness of Shanghai's military position in April as the NRA's solidarity crumbled, there was more potential for power there than Wuhan could muster. It became necessary, however, for KMT civilians to face up to their dependence on the Party's military arm. Following the Party Purification, the Shanghai KMT established the "permanent" National Government capital at Nanking, in accordance with the wishes of Sun Yat-sen. But even as Hu Han-min and Ts'ai Yüan-p'ei presided at opening ceremonies, the threatened bombardment of Chang Tsung-ch'ang's artillery boomed ominously across the Yangtze and hammered at Nanking's waterfront.[46] The Party announced resolutions to put down the *chün-fa* (warlords) and to "knock down all evidence of imperialism," thereby committing itself anew to the Northern Expedition. Following the ceremony, a more crucial meeting commenced, a meeting composed of the generals who had allied themselves with Nanking and the leadership of Chiang. They coordinated plans for the renewal of the offensive and considered the possibilities of being attacked from Wuhan.

In April it was difficult for Nanking and Wuhan to set priorities on which opponent to deal with first—the rival faction or the northern warlords. Within the divided KMT, each side nullified the authority of the other, claiming to represent the will of the Party. Having already downgraded the powers of the C-in-C, Wuhan dismissed Chiang from the post and canceled his Party membership. This was mainly a gesture, since both Wuhan and Nanking temporarily turned their attention toward the warlords. In late April, Wuhan began to concentrate its NRA units for an offensive into Honan.[47] Combat in this sector, centering on the Peking-Hankow Railroad, had lapsed for seven months following the capture of Hupei in the fall of 1926.

CHAPTER 14

Taking the Expedition into North China

After the extensive losses sustained during the general retreat from northern Kiangsu and Anhui in April, Nanking's troops began to move again on May 10, 1927, after a month of fruitless negotiation with Sun Ch'uan-fang while Ankuochün artillery daily bombarded the NRA on the south bank.[1] Made up of First and Sixth army regiments and the corps of recently defected Ch'en T'iao-yüan and Ho Yao-tsu, the new offensive crossed the Yangtze into Anhui and invaded Hochou. On May 16, Li Tsung-jen led a force composed of his own Seventh Army and the corps of Wang T'ienp'ei, Wang P'u, and Yeh K'ai-hsin out of the bridgehead he had been holding in western Anhui. The attackers marched to retake Hofei.

With the Ankuochün thus pressured in the Anhui sector, Chiang unleashed a coordinated four-pronged crossing downriver in Kiangsu during the next week. Against Ich'eng, Yangchou, Ching-chiang, and T'ungchou, Ho Ying-ch'in led the Fourteenth, Seventeenth, and Twenty-sixth divisions of his First Army. By that time in Anhui, Li Tsung-jen had taken P'engpu followed by Suhsien on May 28, after which the beleaguered Ankuochün general, Chang Tsung-ch'ang, withdrew his 15,000 men into Shantung.[2]

In Kiangsu, the NRA pressed against Sun Ch'uan-fang's sector via the Grand Canal and coastal roads. On June 9, Ho Ying-ch'in's troops captured Haichou, the coastal terminal for the east-west railway from Ch'engchou, Honan. That Lung-Hai Railroad opened the possibility of communication with Feng Yü-hsiang should he fight his way across Honan.

Although the Ankuochün continued to enjoy superiority in firepower due to its heavy artillery, in Kiangsu and Anhui it was outmaneuvered by the NRA with its greater mobility, which it used to flank, encircle, and threaten the railroad to the north—the umbilical cord of the Ankuochün. To this tactical advantage must be added the heavy pressure placed on the Ankuochün on its westernmost flank in Honan. There Wuhan's troops coordinated their attack with Feng Yü-hsiang's Kuominchün moving east out of Shensi. Somehow the divided elements of the National Revolution managed to call off their fratricide long enough to attack the warlords. The outcome was positive—but short-lived. Actually both factions were competing for the assistance of Feng Yü-hsiang's large Russian-trained and -equipped army.

Wuhan's Expedition in Honan

The Peking-Hankow Railroad cut through the mountains bordering Honan at Wusheng Pass where in early May Wuhan began to mass its troops. Although the campaign moved out from a rather shaky base, Wuhan wanted its troops to be the first in North China so that a show of strength could win over northern sympathizers and thus decide which faction would unite China. Nanking shared this motivation. At Wuhan, the GLU continued to lead anti-British and anti-Japanese riots and strikes, which kept the foreign warships anchored in mid-stream with their guns trained on the NRA's arsenal, warehouses, and rail terminals. Despite Eugene Ch'en's diplomacy, the foreign powers refused to either leave or disarm their establishments in Hankow.[3] In fact British diplomats were in the process of severing their strained relations with Wuhan in favor of negotiations with Nanking's Foreign Minister, C.C. Wu.[4] The ideological purity of Wuhan's social revolution was apparently bogging down in an economic morass that crippled its armies.

The commencement of Wuhan's Honan campaign coincided with a timely defection of a portion of Wu P'ei-fu's army across the mountains in Honan. These defectors were gathered in by T'ang Sheng-chih (Wuhan's C-in-C), who then moved against Wu near Chumatien and defeated him decisively in the first major battle of the campaign.[5]

Proceeding north, this combined force met the lines of Chang Hsüeh-liang, the "Young Marshall" and son of the Manchurian C-in-C of the Ankuochün, Chang Tso-lin. The center of the northern line was the town of Hsi-p'ing, Honan, where the Peking-Hankow Railroad crossed a defensible river. The Wuhan force pushed Chang back after a three-day assault forced him to withdraw north to Yench'eng on May 15. Again Chang counted on a river fortified with his artillery to hold against the NRA. This time the northern line held during a week's heavy frontal attack aimed at crossing the Sha River. Not until a paralleling NRA route moved north downstream from Yench'eng, threatening Chang's flank and the railroad to the rear, did the Ankuochün line crumble and withdraw.

Of even greater threat to this rail link to North China was the offensive launched out of the Shensi "land within the passes" by Feng Yü-hsiang.

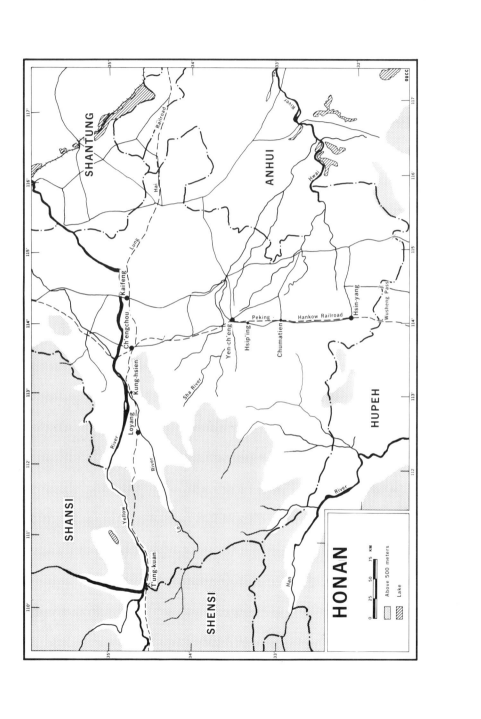

SHANTUNG

ANHUI

SHANSI

SHENSI

HUPEH

Railroad

Hai

Lung

Kaifeng

Ch'engchou

Kung-hsien

Loyang

River

River

Yellow

River

Tung-kuan

Sha River

Lo River

Han River

Yen-ch'eng

Hsip'ing

Chumatien

Peking

Hankow Railroad

Hsin-yang

Wusheng Pass

River

Hwai

River

HONAN

0   25   50   75 KM

Above 500 meters

Lake

110° 111° 112° 113° 114° 115° 116° 117°

32° 33° 34° 35°

Starting from the ancient Wei River valley, periodically used as a "revolutionary base" in Chinese history, Feng moved his Kuominchün out through T'ung-kuan Pass on May 6 and captured Kuanyint'ang, the mountain gateway to Loyang, by the twelfth.[6] When Loyang fell on May 28, Feng was less than seventy miles from Ch'engchou, the Peking-Hankow Railroad bridgehead on the Yellow River. Chang Hsüeh-liang responded to this threatened isolation south of the Yellow River without rail communications to his rear by withdrawing north. North of the Yellow River, his rail supply line would be shortened appreciably and he would be able to consolidate a defense against one front instead of two.

Racing east across northern Honan with his cavalry vanguard unopposed, Feng Yü-hsiang beat Wuhan's NRA to Ch'engchou and Kaifeng on the Yellow River by the end of May.[7] Feng then straddled the Lung-Hai Railroad. Since Hsüchou, Kiangsu, had fallen simultaneously to Chiang's NRA, the two potential allies were in direct rail communication—as was Feng with Wuhan via the Peking-Hankow line. Thus, Feng received ardent offers from Wuhan and Nanking, both of which would require his aid were they to control North China.

Feng's existing alliance with Russia and his KMT ties made his inclusion in the revolutionary ranks natural, but he had to choose a faction that could satisfy his own interests. Not only did Feng need to weigh the relative advantages of each side's offerings, but also whether the entire revolutionary movement would outlive its suicidal internal division.

Apparently Feng had become anxious over the disorders evident in Wuhan's economy and society—especially the confiscation of land by the CCP's peasants' associations in Hunan. With its greater resources, Nanking had more tangible incentives to offer than Wuhan: a promise of C$2 million monthly for maintenance of the Kuominchün plus military aid, and Feng's chairmanship over the new provisional government of Honan to which Nanking would send Yü Yu-jen as cochairman.[8] Yü was Feng's fellow provincial. Despite Feng's capture of Honan's Kung-hsien Arsenal in the Lo valley (which served him, significantly, as his headquarters), his poor industrial foundation in Shensi forced him to depend on outside military aid. Aid from Russia arrived by a long, circuitous, and vulnerable overland route from the north. For several days, Feng had to be concerned over the probable forfeiture of Russian aid were he to join with anti-Communist Nanking. However, once Wuhan, too, broke with the Communists in early June, Feng's decision-making clarified. By June 20, 1927, Feng Yü-hsiang had decided to join with Nanking (see chapter 29). The decision frustrated Wuhan's hopes of moving through Honan into North China, but greatly strengthened Nanking's northern offensive.

Nanking's Campaign into Shantung

During June, Chiang's portion of the NRA pressed into southern Shantung. Taking Liangch'engchen in late June, the coastal wing reached to within sixty miles of the great port of Tsingtao out on the Shantung peninsula.[9] Japan still considered Shantung within its sphere of national interests. The Japanese with whom Chiang had discussed relations in late March and early April represented the Katō government and Shidehara's conciliatory diplomacy—both under attack from Japanese military elements as being too "soft" on disruptive Chinese radicalism and nationalism. These proponents of direct action in meeting Sino-Japanese problems used the antiforeign outrages at Wuhan, Kiukiang, and Nanking as ammunition for their argument. To them the Chinese Nationalists would not be the ones to bring order to China and cooperate with Japan's interests.

When Prime Minister Katō Kōme died and a new government was appointed, the military element found their opportunity to influence policy on China. The new Prime Minister, General Tanaka Giichi, took up his duties on April 20, 1927, after the talks with Chiang. By the end of May, Tanaka's cabinet, under pressure from the Japanese Kwantung Army, decided to reinforce Japan's holdings in Shantung—Tsingtao and its tie with the hinterland, the railroad to Tsinan.[10] A Kwantung Army mission numbering 2,000 crack soldiers steamed quickly from Liaotung, arriving at Tsingtao on June 1. For the purpose of protecting Japanese nationals, the Japanese continued to reinforce their lines in Shantung during June.[11] The Tanaka government claimed there were 20,000 Japanese nationals in Tsingtao, 2,000 at Tsinan, and another 800 strung out along the railroad. All would be imperiled by the advance of the antiforeign revolutionaries. By early July 1927, at least 6,000 superbly equipped and trained Kwantung Army troops were on standby in Shantung.[12]

The disadvantages of the Kwantung Army's style of diplomacy became apparent from the Chinese response. As they learned of the Japanese troop movement, political activists formed committees and gathered mass support for huge demonstrations in Shanghai and other cities to protest the violation of China's territorial sovereignty. The KMT strategists found the issue an effective means of rallying support, and called for an anti-Japanese boycott.[13] The feelings against the Japanese move were of such immediate intensity that even Chang Tso-lin, whom the revolutionaries called a "running dog" of the Japanese imperialists, was affected by public opinion. Having also become infected with nationalism, although he may have solicited Japanese aid earlier in his career, Chang formally protested the Japanese influx in Shantung in early June rather than risk the further taint of being labeled a Japanophile. Chang Tso-lin protested directly to the Japanese ambassador in Peking, but the diplomatic corps had little sway over the Kwantung Army.[14] One rationale offered by the Japanese was that during the NRA advance onto the Shantung peninsula, units from Sun Ch'uan-fang's army had defected and damaged the Japanese railway.[15] However, the military presence of the Kwantung Army did help the Ankuochün block NRA entry into Shantung. In the long run, the Japanese intervention of 1927 helped the national revolutionaries—especially Chiang. It was in that emotional period that Chiang and Feng Yü-hsiang met in June to discuss collaboration. Chiang then could present himself as the leading Chinese defender against Japanese imperialism. Wuhan was

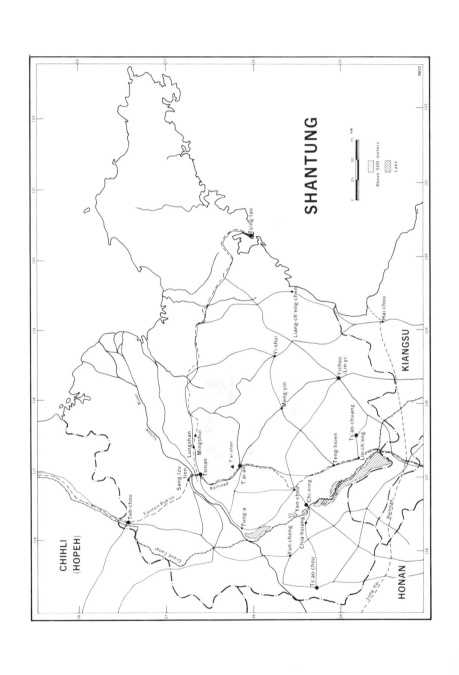

SHANTUNG

CHIHLI
(HOPEH)

KIANGSU

HONAN

Teh-chou
Tientsin Puk ou
Sang-tzu-tien
Yellow
Grand Canal
Lungshan
Mingshui
Tsinan
Railroad
T'ai-shan
Tung-a
Yen-chou
Chi-ning
Yun-cheng
Chia-hsiang
Ts'ao-chou
Lung Hai
Railroad
Teng-hsien
Ts'ao-chuang
Lin-ch'eng
Yichou
(Lin-yi)
Meng-yin
Yi-shui
Liang-ch'eng-cheng
Hai-chou
Tsingtao

0 25 50 75 KM
Above 500 meters
Lake

overshadowed. A decade later, Mao Tse-tung was to capitalize on a similar position during the Second Sino-Japanese War.

The revolutionary camp that received the ground swell of popular support against the Japanese was still suffering more from internal dissension than from the external threat. Even when facing a "barbarian" challenge, the Chinese have always experienced great difficulty in closing their own ranks against invaders. The attempt to achieve ultimate, preeminent power among Chinese as primary to defending China seems to have been a common response in premodern history, of Chiang in 1927 and during the 1930s, and then of Mao Tse-tung in the "Fu-t'ien Incident" or purge of his ranks in 1930/31, in Mao's "rectification" of the CCP cadre from 1942-1944, in the repression of opposition during the Korean War, and in the *Hsia-fang* transfer of millions of urban students and intellectuals during the confrontation with the USSR during 1969 and 1970.

THE THREAT OF COMBAT WITHIN THE REVOLUTIONARY MOVEMENT

When it became apparent to Wuhan in mid-June 1927 that it would not have the cooperation of Feng Yü-hsiang in taking North China, Wang Ching-wei ordered the forces under T'ang Sheng-chih, which had been badly mauled by Ankuochün heavy artillery, recalled to Hupei. Back near Wuhan, those troops could recoup and consolidate the power of the regime in Hunan, Hupei, and Kiangsi. Even within the KMT Left there was the danger of disintegration.

As the confiscation of large landholdings in the surrounding countryside went on under CCP promotion, the class struggle threatened the holdings of the families of the NRA officers, who began to question the direction of Wuhan's revolutionary movement. The officers and troops of the NRA staged in May an anti-Communist purge at Changsha, Hunan. Following shortly in mid-May was the defection from Wuhan of Hsia Tou-yin, who, joined by pro-Nanking Szechwan forces under Yang Shen, moved on Wuhan with the intent to force out the CCP and its followers.[16] The attack failed, but it did show up the need for a strong loyal force to defend Wuhan as *the* capital of the National Revolution.

With the bulk of their troops concentrated about Wuhan, Wang Ching-wei and his fellow leaders evaluated the opponents: (1) Feng Yü-hsiang was occupied with the Ankuochün in Honan. (2) The Kwangtung forces of the KMT Right would not likely chance a long, difficult attack over the passes into Hunan. (3) Along the Szechwan border, Wuhan's troops sufficed to guard against Yang Shen. The most vulnerable sector along Wuhan's periphery was the broad Yangtze approach up from Anhui. Thus, the fraternal conflict with Nanking bulked largest in the view of Wuhan's military leaders at least—a view shared by the CCP and Russians after Shanghai's purge. Again can be seen the craving of Chinese leadership for absolute unity within a movement before opposing outsiders. In 1932, after Japanese aggression at Shanghai, Chiang could state: ". . . it would be necessary to effect internal pacification before we could successfully resist external aggression."[17]

Having recuperated from the campaign in Honan by early July 1927, T'ang Sheng-chih moved his troops out of Wuhan through Kiukiang, Kiangsi, to face Nanking's units near Anking, Anhui, on the Yangtze—less than 200 miles from Nanking. Responding defensively, Nanking on July 13 ordered back from the Shantung front units of Li Tsung-jen's Seventh Army and the corps of Ho Yao-tsu and Yeh K'ai-hsin.[18] As Wuhan's civilian regime disintegrated, its military commander, T'ang Sheng-chih, rose as a regional power hostile to the authority Nanking sought to gain. By late June, T'ang held the titles of Hunan's provincial governor and military head. His presence downriver in July caused Nanking's vulnerable western flank to bristle.[19] Dug in at Anking, T'ang consolidated his hold on the mid-Yangtze and posed a threat to the city of Nanking.

When Chiang moved NRA units from the northern line to check T'ang, the Ankuochün seized the opportunity. In Shantung, the northern side began to regain its lost territories on July 5 and 6 as the NRA lost in quick succession Tenghsien, Linch'eng, and Ts'aochüang along the Grand Canal route, and the Tientsin-P'u-k'ou Railroad.[20]

Although Ankuochün C-in-C Chang Tso-lin had lost Honan in June, one advantage he had gained was a shortened front, which allowed him to concentrate his armies, while Nanking's NRA had to string its units out along two fronts. Although the NRA managed to recapture and hold Linch'eng from July 10 to 19, its lines began to crumble under Ankuochün heavy artillery bombardments and the enemy's fresh reinforcements. On July 23, the Ankuochün crushed the Tenth Army at the strategic crossroad city of Hsüchou, and the Tenth Army fell back into Anhui. Although Chiang got Feng Yü-hsiang to cooperate with Yen Hsi-shan in pushing against the Ankuochün's flank in Hopei, neither that harassment nor Chiang's counterattack against Hsüchou halted the northern offensive.[21]

When Sun threw his 50,000 troops against the NRA line it crumbled. Rolling south into his old United Provinces, Sun took P'engpu on August 9, 1927, as the NRA retreated toward Nanking. In defeat, Chiang's authority lessened in the eyes of Li Tsung-jen and the generals of the Kwangsi clique. However, as the crisis heightened against the Ankuochün, relations between Nanking and Wuhan's KMT became more pliable.

WUHAN BREAKS WITH THE CCP

During the spring of 1927, the dislocated economy and tension-torn society caused alarm among the KMT of Wuhan. Although the CCP claimed it was cooperating with the KMT Left in regulating the activism of the CCP's unions and peasants' associations, by June disillusionment among KMT members had deepened regarding true cooperation with the CCP. Such luminaries as Wang Ching-wei, Sun Fo, General T'ang Sheng-chih, and even Hsü Ch'ien had come to feel impotent before the CCP with its new ministers in Wuhan's National Government and the power of its mass organizations so in evidence everywhere.[22] According to Wang Ching-wei, when Comintern representative M.N. Roy showed him Stalin's telegram calling for an armed Communist take-over of the National

Revolution, the KMT was even expected to "actually join the CCP."[23] The indiscreet disclosure further provoked the Wuhan KMT, which was already experiencing strong feelings of reaction. In June, the Wuhan KMT began to plot against the CCP in a move that led to their official split, publicized on July 15 long after the series of anti-Communist actions by military units in May. This lag in time was mainly due to Wang Ching-wei's hopes of maintaining the United Front until after Wuhan's troops had neutralized Chiang. Thus, by mid-July, *both* the so-called Right and Left KMT factions had turned against the CCP-Russian bloc. Chiang in defeat felt the need for a Party reunion. Believing that he stood in the way of the rapprochement, he announced his retirement as C-in-C of the NRA.

THE NORTHERN COUNTERATTACK

This announcement came on August 12, 1927, just as NRA elements sped to safety on the south bank of the Yangtze[24] after strong points to the north had fallen like dominoes before the Ankuochün artillery. The last rear guard escaped to the south bank on August 19. The KMT's NRA had been decisively defeated and routed—an occurrence enough to shake even a stable regime.

Facing the Nanking government was the old problem of Chinese politics—factionalism. Even the onslaught of the Ankuochün into KMT territory did not halt the divisions. The Nanking regime had been a coalition of KMT members who had agreed on purging the CCP, but whose union now disintegrated over the continuance of support to Chiang—the defeated C-in-C. Within the military, the Kwangsi clique of Li Tsung-jen and Pai Ch'ung-hsi were openly opposed to Chiang's policies; while Ho Ying-ch'in and others were ambivalent. The divisiveness spread among civilian politicians, so that when Chiang "retired" to Shanghai, following him went an entourage of such improbables as Hu Han-min, Ts'ai Yüan-p'ei, Chang Ching-chiang, Wu Chih-hui, and Li Shih-tseng.[25] To them, the alternative of some *other* general at the helm was not attractive. The exodus did not achieve the recalling of Chiang and the others to Nanking. After a short rest at his family home at Fenghua, Chekiang, near Ningpo, Chiang steamed for Japan where he discussed futilely with Prime Minister Tanaka Giichi the matter of reorganizing the KMT's National Revolution, and visited acquaintances he had met before 1911 and during Sun's later exile.[26] Chiang's exile in Japan lasted from September 28 to November 10,[27] during which time he managed to gain at least the approval of mother Soong to take daughter Soong Mei-ling as his second wife (the marriage took place back in Shanghai on December 1, 1927).

The situation of the KMT at Nanking was desperate indeed in August. Its seasoned C-in-C was in retirement, but this had not brought the Wuhan faction downstream in reconciliation—instead T'ang's troops prowled hostilely above Nanking. With the artillery shells of the Ankuochün pounding Nanking's waterfront, KMT fortunes had reached another low ebb. But Sun Yat-sen and his Party had seen many setbacks, and although the KMT had again lost the rich lowlands of Anhui and Kiangsu north of the Yangtze, the NRA leaders began to pull back together. In this "do-or-die" situation, the Kwangsi generals, along with First Army Commander Ho Ying-ch'in, defended the south bank with the blessings of Chiang who had ordered the defense of the Nanking government before his departure for Japan.[28]

Besides Chiang's resignation, the Nanking KMT signaled its desire for reconciliation with praise of Wuhan for its treatment of the CCP threat in July. Nanking called for a plenary session, which would include all the CEC members authorized in the spring of 1926 in Canton, regardless of their current affiliation.[29] After the initial gathering of representatives on August 24, 1927, discussion and negotiation between the two camps became routine.

However, the military situation deteriorated further as Feng Yü-hsiang suffered setbacks on the Ankuochün's Honan flank, which allowed a resurgence of northern military might into the Yangtze. While the KMT politicians met to work out their *modus vivendi*, Sun Ch'uan-fang's artillery pounded NRA positions along the south bank until the Nanking shore was a smoldering ruin. The bombardment on August 25 by Sun was to soften up NRA defenses so that he could move to regain his lost provinces. While Ankuochün leader Chang Tso-lin had favored a containment of the national revolutionaries in an enclave until the KMT further disintegrated, Sun could not pass up the opportunity of regaining golden Shanghai while the KMT was in disarray.[30] His existing share of poverty-plagued Shantung was little consolation.

As Sun's bombardment reached a crescendo during the night of August 25, he dispatched several landing parties toward the Yangtze's south bank. Some acted as diversionary movements for the main force of two regiments, which landed at 3 A.M. the morning of August 26 near the town of Lung-t'an, a station on the Shanghai-Nanking Railroad (see map of lower Yangtze, chapter 12). Having secured a landing zone, the vanguard quickly pressed inland while Sun rushed thousands of troops across the river on all manner of commandeered river craft. Since the NRA had to spread its numbers thinly to cover the entire lower Yangtze, Sun's vanguard was able to make a penetration quickly in the wide sector defended by Li Tsung-jen's Seventh Army. Northern troops in civilian dress spread out to cut telegraph and rail lines and to prepare a perimeter around the riverside hilltops.

On the twenty-sixth, the Yangtze near Lung-t'an swarmed with river craft that landed Sun's units at three adjacent beachheads, from which the troops massed around the Lung-t'an station. As the first day of combat drew to an end, Li Tsung-jen's troops began to consolidate and were able to resist more effectively so that they drove Sun's forces off most of the hilltops and away from the Shanghai-Nanking Railroad.[31] This initial fight cost the NRA 800 casualties but brought in 3,000 captured enemy troops who had been cut off from their comrades along with their field guns and weapons. Thus ended the first day of what became the "Gettysburg" of the National Revolution.

On August 27, Sun continued to boat troops across the wide Yangtze onto the Lung-t'an beachhead. Reinforced, Sun's attackers again captured the railroad station, thus bisecting the key line. Among them was one of the Ankuochün's crack White Russian units gleaned from the flotsam of the Russian Revolution that still drifted about Manchuria and the port cities of China. Hurrying troops in from both Nanking and Shanghai, the NRA also reinforced its defenses,[32] which grew rapidly to meet the Ankuochün challenge and still managed to contain some 30,000 attackers within a perimeter of several square miles enclosing the landing zone and the Lung-t'an station. As the NRA concentrated all available local troops in the battle area, it sent out communiqués calling for the disintegrated NRA confederation to pull together and to apply pressure to the Ankuochün's flanks.

As the battle of Lung-t'an raged on during August 28, Feng Yü-hsiang in eastern Honan responded by attacking into Shantung where he threatened Ts'aochou. The rally of the KMT-affiliated corps revealed the power of the revolutionary military system, *when* the parts worked in concert—which is what Sun had gambled against. The following table shows the proliferated and diverse National Revolutionary Army that gathered to defend Nanking, and the significance of the many units who defected from their warlords.

On August 30, T'an Yen-k'ai wired Wang Ching-wei and T'ang Sheng-chih from Nanking and asked them to support their revolutionary brethren by moving troops into Anhui from Wuhan territory. Apparently with Chiang offstage, the feelings of Wuhan leaders toward the KMT faction downstream had softened. Launching an offensive toward Hofei, Anhui, the Wuhan NRA sought to flank the Ankuochün's Tientsin-P'u-k'ou Railroad. Farther north, Feng's diversionary tactics took Ts'aochou—a mere seventy miles from the same railway.[33] From the direction of Shanghai, Ho Ying-ch'in's First Army divisions converged on the eastern sector of Sun Ch'uan-fang's beachhead.

By August 30, the coordinated effort against Sun's attack across the Yangtze began to tell. Drawing reinforcements from as far away as Hangchow, Chekiang, the NRA began to tighten its noose around Sun's beachhead. Bringing its gunboats, the *Ch'u-ch'ien* and the *Ch'u-t'ung*, into play, the NRA was able to prevent Sun from shipping more reinforcements across to the south bank.[34] In this action these elements of the defected Shanghai navy of Yang Shu-chuang proved their value. Fighting its way through the enemy perimeter, the Seventh Army took the Lung-t'an station for the second time, against desperate resistance, early in the evening of August 30.[35]

During the night, Sun's subordinates gathered nearly 40,000 troops in the river mists for a predawn counterattack. The counterattack began with the northern troops fighting with their backs up against the river and little possibility of evacuation because of the presence of the NRA's river fleet. Their hope was that they could recapture a defensible circle of hills from which they could await Ankuochün aid. Their assault and the NRA defense were equally stubborn—the NRA leaders realized that the fall of Nanking

Allied Revolutionary Army Units, Combined under Nanking's Military Council, Defending the Lower Yangtze during the Attack on Lung-t'an

Commander	Army Designation	Station
First Route under Ho Ying-ch'in		
Ho Ying-ch'in	units of First Army	Lung-t'an to Shanghai
Wang T'ien-p'ei	Tenth Army	*
Lai Shih-huang	Fourteenth Army	*
Ts'ao Wan-hsün	Seventeenth Army	*
Yang Hsiao	Eighteenth Army	*
Chou Feng-ch'i	Twenty-sixth Army	*
Second Route under Pai Ch'ung-hsi		
Wang P'u	Twenty-seventh Army	*
Po Wen-wei	Thirty-third Army	*
Ch'en T'iao-yüan	Thirty-seventh Army	*
Hsia Tou-yin	New Tenth Army	*
Ma Hsiang-pin	New Eleventh Army	*
Wang Chin-t'ao	Independent Division	*
Yen Teh-chi	Independent Division	*
Third Route under Li Tsung-jen		
Hsia Wei	Seventh Army	Nanking to Lung-t'an
Liu Tso-lung	Nineteenth Army (orig. Fifteenth Army)	*
Ho Yao-tsu	Fortieth Army	*
Yeh K'ai-hsin	Forty-fourth Army	*
Revolutionary Army Naval Units on Yangtze under Yang Shu-chuang		
Ch'en Li-liang	First Unit	*
Ch'en Shao-k'uan	Second Unit	*
Ch'en Hsun-yung	Third Unit	*

SOURCE: The information is based upon the KMT account that appears in *N. Exp.*, vol. 3, p. 853, Table 62.

*Units that joined the Revolutionary Army after the July 1926 launching of the Northern Expedition, both defected units and local forces reorganized under the NRA.

would probably mean the loss of the delta. The NRA would be reduced to holing up in the mountainous regions farther south, but without the revenue from Shanghai and its surrounding wealthy provinces the chances of retaining the support of the many defected corps might be slim, for they could not even be fed. During the fierce struggle on August 31, as the First Army, which was defending the railway station, reeled under fire, Ho Ying-ch'in ran along the line brandishing his pistol and shouted that if the enemy overran them now, he would turn the pistol on himself. When the momentum of Sun's attack did finally slow, Sun saw crushed along the Yangtze bank nearly his entire army as well as his dream of retaking Shanghai and his United Provinces. Having thrown the bulk of his 40,000 troops against the front at Lung-t'an, Sun found his escape route blockaded, his flanks surrounded, and his river craft at the bottom of the Yangtze. Although he and his guards managed to escape, Sun had to leave most of his army behind.

Estimates of Sun's troop strength had run from 40,000 to 70,000, and when the NRA tallied up its gains at midday August 31, it had accepted: the surrender of 30,000 troops, including ten commanders of brigades, regiments, and divisions; thirty pieces of artillery; and 35,000 rifles. Over 10,000 of Sun's troops died in the six-day conflict. A mere several thousand escaped with Sun to rejoin his small rear guard of less than 10,000 on the north bank. Where he had fielded eleven divisions and six brigades, there remained only three divisions and several brigades.[36]

The NRA victory was hard won. Although the KMT did not report its losses in detail, it declared them to be between 8,000 and 10,000 dead and wounded. Included among the casualties were 500, or nearly one-half, of the Whampoa Academy's Fifth Class, graduated just the year before in July 1926.[37] The battle marked decisively the high tide of warlord resurgence in the Northern Expedition. It is the battle most cited by the KMT victors (while the CCP glorifies the 1926 victories in rural Hunan). That the badly fractionated KMT had been able to pull itself together at all was amazing, but its coordination of such stiff large-scale resistance to the enemy was an extraordinary feat. The reunification however was a tenuous one because the diverse revolutionaries had responded out of desperation.

The centralizing effect of the KMT organization was equal to the powerful centrifugal forces of provincialism and militant factionalism, *only* when subjected to hard outside stress. The divisions experienced at Canton during the March 20 Coup, the KMT-CCP squabbles over the mass movements, the Wuhan-Shanghai split, and the purges of the CCP were only a preview of the factious divisions of the 1930s, which took place under the shadow of invasion from Japan. Chinese nationalism in the 1920s was still too weak to provide the adhesive needed to keep China integrated. Apparently, it would take the stronger centripetal powers of the CCP's "democratic centralism," the ideological magic of promising land to the farming masses, and galvanizing doses of xenophobia to force the Chinese into a single nation. Often during the twenties it seemed that the development of a modern elite group in the twentieth century had only exacerbated centrifugal potentials in such a large, intersected land mass.

Following Sun Ch'uan-fang's failure to storm the delta, his decimated remnants dragged themselves along roads heading north and onto the trains bound for Shantung. Had the NRA been secure in a stable base and better able to concentrate firepower in pursuit of the retreating Shantung troops, it might have taken the North China Plain up to the Yellow River. A vanguard did cross gallantly at P'u-k'ou, but paused when the atmosphere at Nanking changed from relief to anxiety when in-fighting returned midst the revolutionaries. On September 2, 1927, Li Tsung-jen and Ho Ying-ch'in reigned in their troops, who were eager to cross the Yangtze. They awaited the arrival at Nanking of the KMT's diverse "leaders," providing a ring of military presence around a city wary once more of attack from upstream.

A group from Wuhan—Wang Ching-wei, Ku Meng-yü, Hsü Ch'ien, Ch'en Kung-po, and Ho Hsiang-ning (Mme. Liao Chung-k'ai)—joined at Shanghai with Sun Fo, T'an Yen-k'ai, and other delegates. Meanwhile, Chang Tso-lin's Po Hai fleet provided them with a constant reminder of the need for unity by its bombardment of Shanghai's Woosung docks. Shells damaged the coastal batteries and an Ankuochün small aircraft taking off from a gunboat bombed Shanghai. With the resumption on September 7 of reunion talks at Shanghai, the NRA gingerly began to recross the Yangtze, anxious over the political compromises in process behind them. Landing at four points on the north bank, the NRA offensive divided into three columns: the Right followed the route between the Grand Canal and the Yellow Sea, the Center marched north along the railway, and the Left remained stationary in Anhui facing not the Ankuochün, but T'ang Sheng-chih's 25,000 troops from Wuhan. [38] In early September the various KMT delegates managed to put together the usual temporary coalition, this one later known as the "September Government."

The September Government and the Northern Expedition

By September 14, 1927, the reconciliation talks in Shanghai had progressed far enough that the delegates decided that the group should be expanded into a plenary session for a KMT Fourth National Assembly at Nanking. The promoters of the new coalition were the Kwangsi generals Li Tsung-jen and Pai Ch'ung-hsi and the Wuhan moderates Sun Fo and T'an Yen-k'ai. With allied troops in the vicinity of Nanking, Li and Pai had leverage to use against the other civilians. Wang Ching-wei was hundreds of miles from his military confederate T'ang Sheng-chih, and, thus, had refused to recognize a "hostile" territory like Nanking as the National Government's seat. Sputtering that Sun Fo and T'an Yen-k'ai had "betrayed" the Wuhan faction and refusing to follow the others to Nanking, Wang Ching-wei left Shanghai on September 13 for Kiangsi.

At Nanking on September 15, thirteen KMT members representing the CEC, the Control Committee, and the Military Council met as a body to create a coalition of KMT members. By September 19, the gathering had completed the necessary compromises to achieve the formation of a new government to express: faith in the Three People's Principles, obedience to KMT authority, opposition to CCP interference, and the resolve to complete the Northern Expedition and the unification of China.[1] The credo was to be broad enough to encompass as many "pure" KMT members as possible, but the September Government excluded the two most able to lead—Wang Ching-wei with his flair for attracting civilian support, and Chiang, representative of the symbiosis between the Party and its vital military components. By September 1927, the stimuli of the Northern Expedition and the antiforeign activity had swelled the heterogeneous ranks of the KMT to several million members. Although the Party's membership has not been made public, the CCP claims that the KMT grew from 500,000 in mid-1926 at the launching of the expedition to 5 million by its completion, ". . . due to the activists among the masses entering the revolutionary movement."[2] Allowing for possible exaggeration of rhetoric, it still indicates a tremendous period of growth for the KMT and the ensuing problems of Party discipline and interrelations.

The September Government faced a multitude of hostile forces, three of which were: (1) T'ang Sheng-chih up the Yangtze valley, (2) the Ankuochün of North China, and (3) CCP insurgents. Under the guise of moving troops into Kiangsi to confront Chiang, the CCP had managed to maneuver sympathetic units of Wuhan's NRA to Nanchang, where they staged a coup in early August with the aim of taking over Kiangsi as a revolutionary base of their own. Although the Nanchang Uprising lasted only from August 1 to 4, it marked the beginning of an autumn of armed uprisings in Kiangsi, Fukien, and Kwangtung. Upon failure at Nanchang, the CCP's Central Committee resolved to maintain its existence through "underground" operations and future armed uprisings. The means would be to: centralize CCP authority, tighten discipline and "absolute obedience," carefully reexamine loyalty of membership, and continue its work through its influence over unions and peasants' associations.[3]

To suppress these insurgents, on August 10 before his retirement, Chiang had ordered Li Chi-shen to commence operations out of Kwangtung into the rebel areas of Hunan and Kiangsi. By August 12, Li's old subordinate, Chang Fa-kuei, had also begun an anti-insurgency campaign there. However, lack of security in the southern border hills was to remain a problem for Nanking.

Other challenges abounded for Nanking. Seeing no chance for his rising through the Nanking regime, T'ang Sheng-chih had resisted inclusion in the September Government and had even broken with most of the Wuhan KMT. His opportunism bade ominously of the reliability of defected warlords. By August 21, 1927, T'ang had pushed the Nanking-affiliated forces of Wang P'u and Hsia Tou-yin out of Anking, Anhui, and from there he moved downriver along the south bank to invest Wuhu on September 6. At that point, T'ang could boast control of Hupei, Hunan, Kiangsi, and the heart of Anhui, now that the Wuhan government had dissolved. Under his command were his old subordinates from before his defection in early 1926—Ho Ch'ien with his new Thirty-fifth Army on the Yangtze's north bank, and Liu Hsing and his Thirty-sixth Army on the south bank at Wuhu. T'ang was anathema even to his old associates of the KMT Left; some claimed he had colluded with Sun Ch'uan-fang during the desperate Lung-t'an campaign.[4] When Feng Yü-hsiang had been distracted by the Ankuochün in Honan, T'ang had used that to his advantage in early September by sending his troops into southern Honan over the Wusheng Pass.

On the NRA's western flank, T'ang's hostile presence prejudiced the expedition moving north, so that during September the advance north slowed to a crawl. With units shifting east to end T'ang's "rebellion," the NRA Center merely maintained a bridgehead at P'u-k'ou with its vanguard posted at Ch'uhsien, a mere twenty-five miles to the north.

Finally on October 15, the NRA began to move units up the banks of the Yangtze against T'ang. Those forces cooperating with Nanking included Li Tsung-jen and Ch'en T'iao-yüan on the north bank and Ch'eng Ch'ien's Sixth Army and Yeh K'ai-hsin's Forty-fourth Army on the south bank. Chu P'ei-teh with his Third Army threatened T'ang from the Hunan-Kiangsi border hills. From the south, Li Chi-shen poised his troops along the Kwangtung border, and in early November finally attacked into southern Hunan.[5] Completing the encirclement, from western Hupei Yang Shen again moved toward Wuhan. Although the main fighting against T'ang occurred along the Yangtze as the Nanking force moved upstream, a coordinated effort had, as usual, won the day. T'ang "retired" to Japan aboard a Yangtze steamer on November 12.[6] It was only after NRA allies secured the vulnerable western flank that they could resume in earnest their offensive against the Ankuochün in North China.

Since September, conditions at the bridgehead across the Yangtze had remained static, but once again the NRA moved north quickly over thirty miles, taking Mingkuang, Anhui, on November 9, then Fengyang on the fourteenth, and after two attacks captured Anhui's capital, P'engpu, on the sixteenth. Although the offensive centered on the Tientsin-P'u-k'ou Railroad, the NRA avoided frontal attacks on the line fortified by heavy railroad artillery, and instead, in tactics that it had perfected, swept around the enemy's flanks and threatened the enemy by moving toward its rail communications to the rear.[7] Even though the warlords were skilled in scouring the countryside for livestock, food, and coolies, the peasants were apparently well-schooled in the age-old practice of hiding their produce and vanishing (as did the Taoists) before the strength of the voracious soldiers. Thus, without the steady flow of supplies, especially ammunition, the northern units faced an inevitable withering upon the vine.

Sun Ch'uan-fang attempted to counterattack P'engpu so as to isolate the city from southern communication lines, but, upon failing, had to withdraw his exhausted soldiers north out of the strategic Huai River valley by means of the railroad. The NRA sped up the withdrawal of Sun's troops by continuing its flanking and circling maneuvers behind his front line. Thus, when Kuchen fell in November, Sun's Shantung troops once more found themselves in northernmost Kiangsu with their backs up against the rugged hills of their native province.

Poised in Shantung were the 150,000 troops of Chang Tsung-ch'ang. Although Sun and Chang were recent allies in the Ankuochün, since 1924 they had been contenders for the interstice between the Yellow River and the Yangtze—the traditional route of Chinese conquerors. Chang's native army, known as the Lu-chün (Shantung Army), would collaborate with Sun only when under attack by the revolutionaries. Sun could not easily coexist with Chang in Shantung, but had to reconquer at least Kiangsu. Sun needed more than the southern NRA to prod the northern allies to overlook their differences.

As in the preceding summer retreat of the NRA and then during the northern counterattack at Lung-t'an, Feng Yü-hsiang provided a distraction on the Ankuochün's flank in Honan. Promised vital arms and financial aid, Feng remained "loyal" and helpful to Nanking from his settlement with Chiang in June of 1927 through the completion of the expedition in 1928. The November and December campaign into North China was won through cooperation among the NRA's various elements.

Moving toward the Hsüchou, Kiangsu, sector under Ho Ying-ch'in's command were his First Army, the Ninth, Hsia Tou-yin's new Tenth Army, and Ho Yao-tsu's Fortieth Army. Forty miles to the west, Po Wen-wei's Thirty-third Army moved north to join with Feng in assaulting the western approaches of Hsüchou.[8] On December 12, the Ankuochün combine responded by counterattacking down the rail line from Hsüchou with Chang Tsung-ch'ang's 60,000 troops and 10,000 troops of Sun Ch'uan-fang. Although spearheaded by the armored train's firepower and the air support of a covey of aircraft flown by White Russians, Japanese, French, and Chinese pilots who strafed NRA positions, the counterattack ground to a halt on its second day, December 14. The NRA repulsed the Ankuochün and turned the wings of the movement so that with pressure from the west as well as the south, Hsüchou came under siege. When the city fell on December 16, Sun's whole front along the east-west Lung-Hai Railroad crumpled, forcing the Ankuochün to beat a fast retreat over the border hills into Shantung, where they dug in for the duration of the winter.

The cooperation exhibited in the autumn offensive belied the continuing divisions within the Nanking regime. The era of the Northern Expedition reveals as much the weakness of Chinese nationalism as it does its strength. The repetitious coming together and breaking apart of the KMT coalition as first one faction and then another won primacy, often with the support of military elements, seem almost as dismal as the vagaries of the warlord "opportunists." No sooner had Nanking's troops pacified the rebel T'ang Sheng-chih in the mid-Yangtze then another disgruntled element broke off. The September Government lacked stability since neither Wang Ching-wei nor Chiang had been neutralized. Both resented the new influence of the Kwangsi generals over Nanking. Bristling against the dominance of the upstart generals, members less than two years of the National Revolution, Wang Ching-wei had stomped away from the KMT reunion effort and eventually headed for the region in which he felt the most secure politically—his home province of Kwangtung. Although the generals in Canton had cooperated with Nanking in drawing the noose around T'ang Sheng-chih's base area, by October 1927 they fell under Wang's charisma as he built up his own base. To Kwangtung came a coterie of KMT civilians, who, with Wang, tried again to utilize the defensible province as a fortress from which to expand political power—this time to recapture the National Revolution.

In need of more support, Wang was politically "flexible" enough to consider Chiang Kai-shek's potential. After all, they had both been frustrated by the Kwangsi clique and had both suffered the pangs of political impotence. To rebuild his image, which had become tainted with Communism from 1925 on, Wang began a recantation of his prior alliance with the Russians and the CCP. On November 5, 1927, Wang published an open letter in Canton's Sun Yat-sen University daily newspaper.[9] He admitted that upon return from abroad in March, he had believed, in his naïveté, CCP leader Ch'en Tu-hsiu's protestations of CCP cooperation with the KMT, but said he now believed that Chiang had been correct. He had come to agree with Chiang's restraining of the CCP, both on March 20, 1926, at Canton, and during the following spring in Shanghai. The recantation was not lost on Chiang who was at that time communicating with Wang by telegraph.[10]

However, even the Kwangtung that Wang Ching-wei coveted as a base was not easily unified. Identifying more with the Nanking regime than with Wang were Li Chi-shen and elements of his Fourth Army and Huang Shao-hsiung with his Kwangsi troops. Colluding with Wang were Chang Fa-kuei and a portion of his corps that had fought the Communists in Kiangsi and then southward into Kwangtung, and Hsüeh Yueh's division, and Li Fu-lin's Fifth Army, all the leaders of which were rankled by the Kwangsi ascendancy. After Chiang had telegraphed Wang Ching-wei and Li Chi-shen on November 10 asking them to negotiate with him and T'an Yen-k'ai, who was representing Nanking, Wang decided to go to Shanghai.

The day following Wang and Li's departure on November 16 from Canton, Wang's general, Chang Fa-kuei, led a coup against Li Chi-shen's troops at Canton. Apparently Chang also hoped to catch Huang Shao-hsiung and his Kwangsi troops off guard and make them turn over their weapons and the Shih-ching Arsenal to a pro-Wang Ching-wei armed force. Chang's coup succeeded in taking Canton and a portion of Li Chi-shen's troops; but the rest and Huang Shao-hsiung's Kwangsi troops managed to escape north into the hills. While Wang conferred with Chiang and other KMT members during the rest of November, Chang Fa-kuei tried to consolidate his military supremacy around Canton. The continued existence of military rivals within Kwangtung was but one of Wang Ching-wei's problems in his home province. Chang Fa-kuei worked to eliminate the pervading influence of the CCP in Canton's mass organizations and placed the Russian consulate under surveillance since he knew from the KMT's past experiences that the Russians directed CCP activities. Chang Fa-kuei's anxieties over CCP subversion were well founded.

During November, the CCP also planned the seizure of Kwangtung as a new revolutionary base. Through the Canton consulate, Stalin sent in mid-November his order to step up armed activism in China. Beginning by strengthening control over union labor and peasants' associations, the CCP used the economic issue of the low standard of living of the masses, the need to overthrow the KMT, and the alternate advantages of the Soviet economic system to induce people to join in its efforts. Slogans of the propaganda campaign included:

Raise the Soldiers' Pay to 20 Silver Dollars!
Food for the Workers!
Land to the Tillers!
Knock Down the KMT and the Warlords!
Kill All the Country Bullies and the Evil Landlords!
Confiscate the Capitalists' Homes and Give Them
    to the Rebel Masses!
All Authority to the Workers, Peasants, and Soldiers![11]

This decision of the CCP was precipitated by Chang Fa-kuei's move to finally close down the venerable Hong Kong Strike Committee establishment. By late November, a "Red Defense Corps," including "Dare-to-die" units of disbanded Hong Kong Strike pickets and members of the Seamen's Union, trained and gathered arms under the direction of the CCP.

In December, just as Wang Ching-wei's prospects for a return to political eminence seemed within his grasp, events in Kwangtung turned against him. During the second week of December, after a rising crescendo of strikes including one by the Canton public utilities union, the CCP sprang their coup. Led by Chang T'ai-lei and Su Ch'ao-cheng, ex-leader of the Hong Kong Strike apparatus and ex-Minister of Labor at Wuhan, the Red Defense Corps moved into the Canton streets in the predawn hours of December 11, 1927. The activists first induced numbers of sympathizers within Chang Fa-kuei's army to join the uprising along with Communist workers. With the morning light, the "Dare-to-die" units and groups of workers completed their seizure of police stations including police rifles, machine guns, and armored cars. Captured city buses and trucks helped spread the rebels, who quickly took the KMT's government buildings, the Central Bank with its silver reserves, and the local barracks with more arms. To suppress resistance, the CCP executed ten "reactionary" officers and, during the street fighting, marked and set afire the homes of KMT cadre. Many of those who did not escape were executed.[12]* Hoping to combine the urban uprising with rural support, the CCP at Canton expected peasants' associations to seize power throughout Kwangtung. At Hailufeng where there had been Communist supervision for several years over the peasants' association, a peasants' soviet was set up exemplifying rural support. Rushing down from the hills of Kwangtung, remnants of the

---

*The CCP used burning cans of kerosene to give the impression of large fires in the night, which brought residents out from behind their locked doors where propagandists informed them that Canton had been taken over. The red-arm-banded cadre shouted that rewards of thirty silver dollars would go to those who would identify policemen and KMT members for execution. Houses to be burned were marked with a red slash, a circle meant an inhabitant was to be killed, a yellow mark meant the contents were to be confiscated, and a black mark guaranteed safety.

Red Army that had been fighting and retreating from the Nanchang Uprising entered Canton under Yeh T'ing's leadership.[13]

However bloody and victorious the take-over, it was short-lived. Outside Canton, Chang Fa-kuei, aided by Li Fu-lin (Fifth Army), river gunboats, and loyal Mechanics' Union personnel within the city, outmanned
and outgunned the participants in the uprising so that the red hammer and
sickle flags came down from the smoke-hazed Canton sky on December
14—after less than four days. The ensuing impassioned anti-Communist
bloodbath carried away even Russian collaborators from the consulate,
underlining Wang Ching-wei's protests in Shanghai that his KMT Left was
guiltless of the CCP coup. A "White Terror" at Canton spread to Wuhan
where it may have exceeded in thoroughness the April purge in
Shanghai.[14]

The reaction within the KMT against the violent CCP uprising changed
the course of the reconciliation talks going on in Shanghai. The day before
the uprising, December 10, Wang Ching-wei, at a KMT plenary session for
the Party's Fourth Congress scheduled for January, proposed that Chiang
be invited back to his post as commander-in-chief. The reaction added
more steam to the movement favoring Chiang's return to power. Chiang
maintained his anti-Communist stance; on December 13 he called for the
cessation of relations with Russia, which Nanking implemented on the
fourteenth by ordering closed all Russian consulates and agencies in KMT
territory, and the speedy return to Russia of all Soviet personnel.[15]

Although Wang Ching-wei had agreed earlier to Chiang's leadership of
the NRA while he himself led the Party government, the Canton Uprising
in Wang's own backyard further solidified suspicions of his laxity toward
the CCP—suspicions that were the legacy of his honeymoon with the CCP
at Wuhan during the past spring. Once again this tragicomic figure found
himself being hauled off the national stage just as the curtain was ready to
be raised. On December 17, 1927, Wang Ching-wei again boarded a
steamer, this time bound for France and a "rest cure." When his ship
stopped at Hong Kong, so near Canton, Wang did not even step ashore.[16]
Also departing China was an exodus of Russians, all of whom had left
Nanking's domain by December 24.

With Wang gone, the focus of Party attention narrowed on Chiang
Kai-shek. No other single figure remained who could begin to weld the
NRA confederacy into a cooperative force and who could claim to represent
the party of Sun Yat-sen. Although Chiang had risen in 1924 and 1925
through his identification with the so-called Left, his return in the winter of
1927 seemed dependent on the anti-Communist reaction within the KMT.
Chiang's union with the accomplished Soong family through his marriage
to Soong Mei-ling early in December, which was followed by her brother
T.V. Soong's return to Nanking from Wang Ching-wei's camp where he
had acted as Finance Minister, symbolized the support Chiang was to
receive from the modern elite of the port cities.

On December 20, General Ho Ying-ch'in telegraphed Nanking from the
northern front calling for an all-KMT assembly and Chiang's resumption of

his old duties as C-in-C.[17] Thereupon, the Shanghai branch of the KMT petitioned Chiang to take up his duties, a plea then repeated by all the various Nanking agencies. Finally on January 1, 1928, the National Government at Nanking invited Chiang by telegraph to first delineate the NRA's chain of command and then return to Nanking to hold all revolutionary powers.[18]

CHAPTER 16

Launching the Last Phase of the Expedition

As early as December while he awaited the customary invitations to accept power, Chiang again began setting in motion the expeditionary apparatus. In late December 1927 he dispatched Lu Ho-sheng into hostile North China as a secret agent empowered to persuade warlord leaders and their subordinates to defect from the Ankuochün. As was by then a common practice of Chinese revolutionaries, Lu was to make his base of operations in a foreign concession of a treaty port—this time Tientsin. Chiang also began promoting a new Central Military Academy at Nanking, from whose graduates he might replenish the badly thinned ranks of the officer corps. This kind of school, which created military specialists indoctrinated in KMT ideals, had, earlier at Canton, been a boon both to the Party and to Chiang, Whampoa's superintendent at that time. Once the new academy was created, Whampoa would become one of several preparatory schools.[1]

Party reconstruction moved apace in January of 1928. Once again the KMT went through the already familiar process of smoothing over the group's ruffled feathers and jerry-rigging patches over the widely publicized divisions. Accepting portfolios at the official ceremony at Nanking on January 4 were: Sun Fo who was named Minister of Construction after his participation in the Wuhan government, and T. V. Soong who resumed his place as Finance Minister after his adventure in Wang Ching-wei's Canton movement. The old Revolutionary Base of Kwangtung reverted to the control of Li Chi-shen and Huang Shao-hsiung, both true to Nanking in their fashion.

The Party quickly resumed operations on January 7 with proposals emanating from what was called the Standing Committee of the CEC. Beside setting up committees to work on Party Affairs, such as the pending Fourth Party Congress, the Standing Committee felt confident enough to censure several members of the KMT, including Wang Ching-wei. In telegrams to CEC and Central Control Committee members, the Standing Committee ordered them to return to Nanking for assignments without delay.

The CEC that met on February 7 reconstructed the Party organization by reshuffling the membership of the key councils. Restored was the Central Political Council, which included Hu Han-min, T'an Yen-k'ai, Chu P'ei-teh, C.C. Wu, Sun Fo, T.V. Soong, and Chiang, and to which were added Yi P'ei-chi and Yü Yu-jen. Yü was former dean of Shanghai University and Party Representative to Feng Yü-hsiang. The CEC appointed a new Standing Committee comprised of Chiang, T'an Yen-k'ai, Yü Yu-jen, Tai Chi-t'ao, and Ting 'Wei-fen. T'an Yen-k'ai became chairman of the National Government Committee. Chiang regained his chairmanship over the seventy-three-man Military Council with its high-ranking Standing Committee of Generals Li Tsung-jen, Li Chi-shen, Pai Ch'ung-hsi, Chu P'ei-teh, Ch'eng Ch'ien, Ho Ying-ch'in, T'an Yen-k'ai, Feng Yü-hsiang, Yen Hsi-shan, and Admiral Yang Shu-chuang.[2] Noteworthy there were the Kwangsi generals and the two defected northern warlords—Feng and Yen. The Party membership discussed in vain the prospects of electing a Fourth Party Congress—which Chiang declared must decide on the finalization of the break with Russia, on the return from Communist ideology to the Three People's Principles, and on whether these principles would be followed in the union and peasant movements so that no one class would be dominant.[3]

Along with reconstructing the new government went the process of centralizing its powers. Chiang began his effort by providing financial support to the conglomeration of armies vowing loyalty to Nanking. Earlier at Canton, the success of the Central Bank under T.V. Soong had attracted the support of generals and their troops concerned with practical realities. At Nanking, Soong worked to apply the methods proven in the Revolutionary Base to the financial problems of the larger National Government and its proliferated NRA. Revenue control was always an important phase of consolidation of power in China, and first to be examined were the provinces closest to Nanking's influence—Chiang's Chekiang and Soong's Kiangsu. Soong announced on January 7 that the revenue systems of those two provinces were to be organized so that his ministry would see a monthly revenue of over C$10 million to more than match the expenditures—a significant collection increase over the C$3 million per month realized up to then.[4] Soong was hamstrung in increasing his range of collection by the lack of direct control over politics outside the lower Yangtze—a problem never solved by the Nationalist government.

After January's feverish reconciliation and reconstruction, Chiang felt secure enough to turn from the mundane affairs of Nanking to the more romantic prospect of finishing the Northern Expedition. On February 9, 1928, Chiang took the members of his headquarters' general staff on board a train bound for the front near Hsüchou. There they inspected the preparations in process for the spring campaign. The lines had been relatively stationary since mid-December, in the midst of the bitter cold that prevailed out of frigid Mongolia. During the inspection, on February 11, the National Government wired C-in-C Chiang and the Military Councilmen an order to complete the plans for the final campaign to take North China.[5] The plans called for a quick, three-month campaign to sweep from north Kiangsu to Peking.

From Hsüchou, Chiang and his party traveled by the Lung-Hai Railroad to meet with Feng Yü-hsiang at his Kaifeng headquarters. On February 16, Chiang and Feng discussed their cooperation in the final campaign to take North China.[6] The meaning of national "unification" was rather ambiguous considering the existing nominal loyalties of Kwangtung, the southwestern provinces, and Hunan-Hupei. Even before the conquest of North China, Nanking's ties with its provinces were mindful of the ancient federations or the first Han emperor's control over his fief-holding generals. Provincialism would die hard after dominating China since the Taiping rebellion. But, given China's natural divisions, there was a tendency for prospective rulers to use any means to secure, however loosely, the provincial relationships to the hegemon, and then turn to the long struggle to centralize real power.

During February, Chiang had to prove that he did, indeed, represent *the* hope for pulling the disordered military camp back into an operable whole. In meetings with Feng and in correspondence with Yen Hsi-shan, Chiang had to allow these regional commanders considerable autonomy and status. Both controlled highly defensible bases: Feng ran Shensi, that ancient bastion "within the passes" from which so many dynasties had conquered China, and Yen held the mountain fortress of Shansi. If dissatisfaction with Nanking's treatment drove them into a temporary collaboration with the Ankuochün, they could frustrate the KMT take-over of North China. Even their neutrality would have greatly slowed the expedition. Nanking's compromise was typical: in return for nominal subordination to Nanking and cooperation in the expedition, Feng and Yen would gain material aid and the status of near equality with C-in-C Chiang. Status could never be ignored in Chinese political relationships, as in most other relationships for that matter. Where Chiang in 1926 and 1927 had headed an NRA of some forty army corps, in the new military structure he coordinated four Collective Armies of corresponding magnitude. (Collective Army will be abbreviated CA; Collective Armies CAs.)

The Collective Armies represented the real division of power in Central and North China. Guarding the lower Yangtze basin was the First Collective Army, including the forty army corps of the earlier NRA. Controlling Shensi, Honan, and parts of the near northwest was Feng's Second Collective Army. Holding pivotal Shansi overlooking the North China Plain was Yen Hsi-shan's Third Collective Army; and astride Kwangsi, Hunan, and

Hupei was the Fourth Collective Army of Li Tsung-jen (and the Kwangsi clique). Li had himself become entrenched after forcing out T'ang Sheng-chih. Although these four commands were relatively equal, Chiang and Nanking held the purse string, which made them suzerain. If Chiang could get these four commanders to synchronize their efforts in a massive assault on the North China Plain, a quick victory would be assured. On February 18, 1928, Nanking's Political Council settled on and announced Chiang's new title—C-in-C of all Northern Expeditionary forces of the Revolutionary Army. His associate Ho Ying-ch'in received the title of chief of staff for the four Collective Armies.[7]

Closely related to the restructuring of a satisfactory military system was the political power that emanated from the Collective Armies. The KMT had to fit these various military leaders in their regions into the Party apparatus and Party government so that status and political prestige would be assured to all—including the KMT. By 1928, the KMT was the largest single political force in China, and the only source left to confer national political legitimacy on Chinese leaders craving titles to match their real power. With his powers of coordination over the NRA, Chiang's influence among members of Nanking's hierarchy was such that he could gather the political status needed to support his military role. He did not want to be dependent on a covey of fractious politicians for the political support he needed as C-in-C—that much he had learned through his experience with the Wuhan government. On March 7, 1928, the Political Council appointed Chiang as its chairman.

The Political Council then divided up political authority among the other four commanders by region, with Li Chi-shen as chairman of the KMT branch in Canton, Li Tsung-jen chairman of the Wuhan branch, Feng Yü-hsiang over the Kaifeng branch, and Yen Hsi-shan over the T'aiyüan branch. Later appointments filled the branch committees with appointees both of Nanking and the respective branch chairmen. The Political Council also designated the provincial power holders as chairmen of their new KMT-style provincial government committees.[8] Rather than imposing its leadership on the various regions of China, all the KMT could attain was its legitimization of those power holders with which it could coexist. Since Chiang was to be preoccupied in coordinating the four CAs, he had T'an Yen-k'ai made acting chairman of the Political Council. In the spring of 1926, T'an had supported Chiang in the March 20 Coup against the CCP and in the launching of the expedition. Again in early 1928, Chiang and T'an cooperated in order to speed up the military reunification of China.

In northern Kiangsu in late March, the First CA gathered for the resumption of the expedition after the mid-winter halt. Paralleling the east-west Lung-Hai Railroad, it faced a rested and reinforced Ankuochün. Now Chang Tso-lin's troops coordinated with Sun Ch'uan-fang and Chang Tsung-ch'ang to the north in Shantung,[9] and again there was the threat posed by the Japanese. In a March 17 interview in the Party newspaper, Chiang had admitted that the Party had been considering the danger of another Japanese intervention in Shantung. Therefore, the "Foreign

Ministry had been delegated the authority to deal with the problem basing its policy on a spirit of equality." By preventing the intervention, the Foreign Ministry would be supporting the expedition, as would the rest of the National Government agencies. To this end on April 1, 1928, Chiang requested that the Political Council order the provinces of Kiangsi and Anhui to begin collection of a monthly quota of 7 million catties of rice to feed the armies.[10]

As First CA leaders gathered at the Hsüchou headquarters on April 1, 1928, to receive their final orders, Feng and Yen were already engaged against the Ankuochün—north of the Yellow River in Honan, along the Peking-Suiyüan Railroad, and in Shansi's mountains bordering the North China Plain. Another portion of Feng's Second CA was poised facing Shantung alongside Chiang's sector.

At the Hsüchou meeting were leaders of the new political branch of the NRA. Symbolizing the change of complexion of the NRA from 1926 to 1928 was the General Political Training Department directly under the C-in-C. Although the value of political work among the KMT's soldiers and with civilians could not be denied, the old Political Departments had been infiltrated by CCP members and followers. Heading the new political organ created at Chiang's suggestion on January 18 was Tai Chi-t'ao, a devout anti-Communist, Party ideologist, and allegedly an ex-Communist himself.[11] The Nanking KMT's view of the mass organizations had soured through its experiences in 1926 and 1927, and, thus, in April 1928, the Political Training Department's goal was turned inward and directed toward keeping NRA elements correctly indoctrinated and motivated.

Commencing with the required flourish, the Party CEC announced from Nanking on April 7 the launching of the Northern Expedition. At a ceremony Chiang pledged that:

> On this struggle depends whether the Party and nation will exist or die, whether principles will win out or fail, whether the people are to prosper or suffer, and whether our comrades flourish or fade. Comrades, from all our armies and people, be of one heart. Observe discipline strictly, follow orders, do not sacrifice wrongly, but do your best, stir up your spirit, and accomplish what is needed. We must swear to remove the Fengtien [Manchurian] and Shantung warlords, complete the national revolution, and implement the Three People's Principles. Do not hold back in your love of country and the salvation of the people. Never turn your backs on the hopes of the people, but rather satisfy the souls in heaven of the *Tsung-li* [Sun Yat-sen] and those soldiers who have already died.[12]

That oath and the order that commenced the general offensive went out to the commanders at the front by telegraph—certainly exemplifying the interrelationship of nationalism and the Industrial Age.

Once again, as the offensive gained momentum, the value of unity and cooperation was obvious. While the First CA rolled north into Shantung along the Tientsin-P'uk'ou Railroad, Feng's Second CA pressed in from the west. By the following week, on April 16, the First CA had progressed nearly fifty miles to Tenghsien, and the Second CA had moved toward the Yellow River taking Yünch'eng on April 13 and Chiahsing on the Grand Canal on the fifteenth. Seeing these pincers closing on the key city of Yenchou, Sun Ch'uan-fang hurled his forces against both fronts. Although he managed to push the First CA back nearly to the Lung-Hai Railroad, his western counterattack suffered during a flanking maneuver of the Second CA, which killed nearly 4,000 of Sun's force. Meanwhile, the First CA quickly recovered its poise and by April 18 had thrown Sun back before he could fortify his gain. Besides exhausting his forces in the two-front counterattack, Sun then found his vital rail link to the north threatened by the Second CA at Chining. As might be expected, Sun pulled back along the railroad toward Tsinan on April 21, rather than risk having to retreat on foot into the Shantung highlands.[13]

Receiving information of the failure of Sun's April 17 counterattack, Japanese Prime Minister Tanaka and his Kwantung Army advisors decided to reinforce the foreign business quarter of Tsinan, the provincial capital of Shantung.[14] Within two days, on April 19, Japanese marines were on the move by rail for Tsinan from Tsingtao. Some of these first Japanese units had landed as early as April 10, possibly without Tanaka's approval. Arriving at Tsinan on April 20, the 475-man Japanese vanguard was followed by over 4,000 troops who had landed at Tsingtao.[15] Had the Ankuochün generals invited the intervention of the Kwantung Army? In view of the surging anti-Japanese passions then loose in China, and the subsequent deleterious effect of that intervention on Ankuochün morale, an invitation seems less likely a statement of events than tacit acceptance. Certainly Chang Tso-lin was not the willing "running-dog" of the Japanese any more than Mao Tse-tung was later a puppet of the Russians. However, these allegations made good propaganda in a China where at least the xenophobic antiforeign element of nationalism was at high tide.

Sun Ch'uan-fang's second line of defense was strung along the mountainous backbone of the Shantung peninsula. To the north of that spine, Sun defended the railroad from Tsinan out along the peninsula to the port of Tsingtao. When First CA units dashed over the range and flanked the Tsingtao-Tsinan Railroad on April 27 at Lung-shan station, the Ankuochün lost control of Shantung's defense. After a two-day battle at Lung-shan, the First CA units of the Twenty-sixth Army and Ch'en T'iao-yüan cut off the Ankuochün's use of the rail line out along the peninsula. Again, employing overland mobility and speed, the NRA had successfully evaded the enemy's superior rail-borne artillery, and had threatened from the rear the loss of his rail communications.[16] The NRA moving west along the railroad would take the Yellow River rail bridge before arriving at Tsinan; thus, Ankuochün forces around the capital region faced the prospect of being isolated on the south bank of the river—a situation not different from Sun's dilemma at Shanghai preceding his retreat in March 1927. To prevent an Ankuochün retreat out onto the peninsula along the railroad, a battalion of engineers of the First CA sabotaged the line with explosives. In its rush to flee west, Sun's force defeated at Lung-shan left behind over thirty boxcars of food and ammunition, and 300 soldiers.[17]

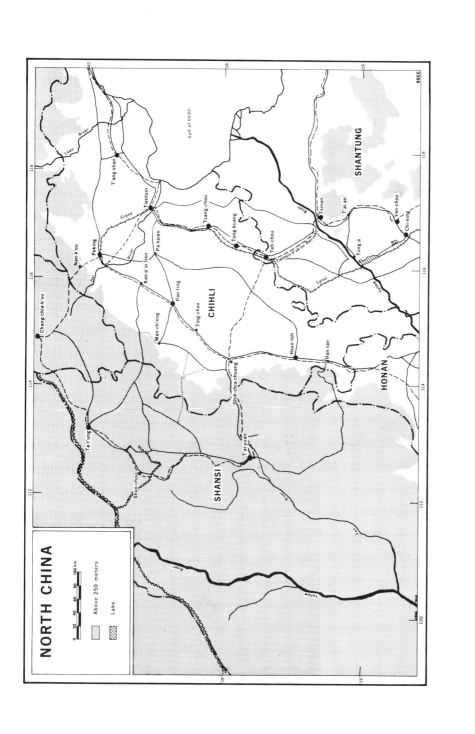

NORTH CHINA

0 20 40 60 80 100 km

Above 250 meters

Lake

SHANTUNG

CHIHLI

HONAN

SHANSI

Gulf of Chihli

Lüan River

T'ang-shan

Tientsin

Grand

Nan-k'ou

Peking

Chang-chia-k'ou

Kao-p'ai-tien

Pa-hsien

Tsang-chou

Tung-kuang

Teh-chou

Tientsin-P'uk'ou Railroad

Pao-ting

Man-ch'eng

Ting-chou

Hsun-teh

Shih-chia-chuang

Han-tan

Chi-nan

T'ai-an

Yen-chou

Chi-ning

Tung-a

Canal

Ta-t'ung

Shuo-chou

T'ai-yüan

Yellow River

OUCC

The First CA force that moved into Shantung along the Tientsin-P'u-k'ou line had avoided the main pass between T'ai-an and Tsinan. Instead it had moved up into the adjoining mountains where, from captured high points, NRA mountain artillery could fire down on the enemy's less-fortified high flanks.[18] Although weak in heavy firepower, the NRA continued to show greater initiative, mobility, and daring in its strategy of flanking the enemy's umbilical rail line.

Once the NRA blocked the Ankuochün from retreating by rail out onto the Shantung peninsula, the rail bridge across to the Yellow River's north bank remained the last avenue of escape. As Feng advanced along the south bank, which tightened the noose around Tsinan, the decision was made to evacuate the Ankuochün to the north bank. These units began to cross over the bridge on April 29, 1928; but as the general retreat sounded, order broke among the troops hurrying to escape across the bridge. Back in Tsinan, violence and looting erupted—characteristic of retreating Chinese troops. Defending the barricaded perimeter of the Japanese commercial and residential quarter, the tough Kwantung Army troops prepared themselves against any threat from the disorderly retreaters.

On April 30, 1928, the Chinese press reported a scuffle in Tsinan between Japanese and Chinese in which a Chinese had died of stab wounds.[19] Since NRA engineers had sabotaged the railroad to Tsingtao on April 28, they most likely had come into contact with Japanese patrols. Tensions mounted as Japanese reinforcements continued to land at Tsingtao and proceed to Tsinan. The idea spread among the Chinese that the Japanese had found another pretext to seize Shantung, as they had in 1914. Attuned to the public outcry swelling against the Japanese "invasion," which was linked to saving the Ankuochün from the NRA, Chang Tso-lin protested the action to Japan's ambassador in Peking. By this time there were at Tsinan over 3,000 crack Kwantung Army troops with heavy artillery guarding an alleged 2,000 Japanese civilians, and another 2,000 Japanese soldiers patrolling the rail link with Tsingtao.[20]

The first NRA element to enter Tsinan was a large plainclothes force, which filtered in without fanfare, in accordance with the usual procedure. To encourage civilian cooperation and to gather intelligence, this vanguard probably included propaganda units from the new Political Training Department.[21] Moving through Tsinan, on May 1 the vanguard secured the bridgehead on the north bank of the Yellow River after combat at Sang-tzu-tien.[22] Reported by telegraph was the eyewitness observation of a resident American missionary, who witnessed that "the Southerners have occupied Tsinanfu without trouble. The situation at present gives no cause for concern." After the Nanking Incident, foreigners were most anxious over the entry of the NRA. Disseminated by Reuters News Agency, this observation was apparently the last report out of Tsinan from nonofficial Japanese or KMT sources.[23] Following this release, the press reported that an official Japanese radio (presumably of the Kwantung Army) was the "sole source" of news from Tsinan. Foreign press coverage that followed originated from Tokyo news agencies.[24]

The First CA had approached Tsinan with apprehensions. The KMT's Foreign Minister and his negotiator at Shanghai had been in contact with Japanese counterparts since January 1928, at least. (Chiang may also have discussed the safety of Japanese nationals in the path of the expedition during his autumn stay in Japan.) On May 2, the second day of the NRA occupation, Chiang guaranteed that order would be maintained in Tsinan. However, on May 3, full-scale conflict erupted between the Japanese at their barricades and Chinese troops, which the Japanese press reported to be units of Feng Yü-hsiang.[25] The Japanese report was that undisciplined units or soldiers thereof had "run amok" robbing and massacring Japanese civilians.

Negotiations probably began immediately, but on May 4 the Japanese charged that their negotiator, Colonel Sasaki, was saved from being robbed and beaten to death only by the intervention of a staff officer from Chiang's headquarters, and that an agreement with Chiang to clear all Chinese soldiers from the commercial district had not yet been honored.[26] Thereupon, Major General Tatekawa Yoshiji of Japan's Peking mission declared that "it is necessary for Japan to chastise the lawless Chinese soldiers in order to maintain Japan's national and military prestige."[27] In light of the later claims of the Kwantung Army at the occasion of Chang Tso-lin's railroad "accident" the next month and then the Chinese "provocations" on September 18, 1931, there is a strong temptation to disregard the Kwantung Army version of the Tsinan Incident. During the first week of May, Japanese reinforcements continued to enter Tsinan along the railway, despite the destruction of a portion of it by the NRA. Apparently, on the night of May 3, a Japanese unit en route from Tsingtao came as far as possible by train and then in a fast night march crossed the last fifty miles to Tsinan.[28]

Understandably, the Chinese version of Tsinan differed, but antiimperialism had been a major ingredient welding diverse Chinese elements into a nationalistic whole. The abstract concept of imperialism may have become translated in the Chinese mentality as antiforeign feelings or xenophobia. Having not yet come into contact with the "foreign imperialists" before Tsinan, could Feng Yü-hsiang's soldiers have lost their restraint? The Japanese already considered Feng to be outspokenly hostile to them.[29] The Shanghai press quoted Feng as having asked permission at Tsinan to fight the Japanese ". . . to his last breath."[30] If indeed his troops did "run amok," the Kwantung Army officers were quite eager to accept any challenge.

C-in-C Chiang found his worst fears about to be realized at Tsinan. During 1926 and 1927, Chiang appears to have *spoken* loudly against the "imperialists" while actually avoiding any provocation that they could have used as a pretext for military intervention. Antiforeignism was mainly a convenient political tool. Chiang at Shanghai had quieted the foreigners there following the antiforeign murders at Nanking. Chiang was mainly interested in the reunification of China as basic to defending China against foreign threats, and thus concluded at Tsinan that the NRA must not allow the Japanese to distract or divert it from completing the expedition. On May 2, the day before hostilities commenced in earnest, Chiang had ordered the main force of the NRA to proceed *quickly* through Tsinan so that their presence would not present the Japanese with a pretext for hostilities.[31] Apparently on May 4, the second day of the incident, Chiang ordered all Chinese troops to cease returning the fire of the Japanese.[32]

Despite the distraction of the Japanese intervention, the Northern Expedition did continue north—probably faster than it might have otherwise. Once again the surge of "patriotism" that sprang from an encounter with foreigners acted as adrenalin in the Chinese body politic. Not only did the NRA soldiery feel an ideological boost, but the Ankuochün troops suffered a depression in their morale. Stirring their readers with gory pictures, tales of 3,000 Chinese killed, and untold soldiers and civilians wounded by the Japanese,[33] the Chinese press exemplified the role that the press in general can play in nation building. The civilians of North China responded with sympathy for the NRA, who had earlier been referred to as the "Southerners," and pondered the rumors of Ankuochün-Japanese collusion. Evidence that the Ankuochün suffered because of the Tsinan Incident can be seen in Chang Tso-lin's effort to disassociate himself in the public eye from the Japanese. Not only did he disavow the alleged collaboration, he urged that the KMT drop its quarrel with him and unite North and South in a struggle against Japan. On May 9, he issued a public telegram stating that ". . . in view of the situation I have ordered my troops to cease hostilities to save the country."[34] The situation then was, in some respects, similar to that less than a decade later when Mao urged Chiang to cease fighting the CCP and join in the resistance against the Japanese.

In the CCP attack on Chiang in early 1927, rumors had been spread of his involvement with the Japanese, and in May 1928 the device was again used by the CCP to criticize Chiang for not fighting the Japanese. In Hong Kong, British authorities kept check on a Communist campaign against Chiang led by the local branch GLU (outlawed in KMT territory), which accused Chiang of "uniting the nation only to surrender it to the Imperialists." This propaganda went on to say that having lost the support of the peasants and workers and having forgotten the spirit of the Hong Kong Strike, the KMT cooperated with the imperialists in killing Chinese. The slogans in the campaign were:

> Overthrow Chiang Kai-shek Who Has Betrayed Our Country and Killed Our People!
> Oppose the Five Demands of the Japanese Imperialists which Have Been Accepted by the KMT![35]

Thus, when the same device was used in the 1930s, it had already been tested during the previous decade, as had been many of the political means later perfected by the CCP. Actually, in China's vast body of historical literature, there are numerous precedents of rulers who had been too distracted by internal division to deal with the menace of the northern barbarians, or who, in going off to suppress the nomads, found themselves overthrown at home. The question of priority is still quite relevant with regard to internal unity over national defense.

Chiang chose the attainment of internal unification as more vital than concern with any foreign menace. China's vast spaces and teeming millions could prevent a sudden engulfment. (Perhaps the logic is not dissimilar to Mao's when he opted to give the Cultural Revolution precedence over a confrontation with Russia.) On May 1, 1928, when the NRA vanguard had secured the north bank of the Yellow River at Sang-tzu-tien, it halted its advance until the main body could catch up. To avoid Tsinan where the Japanese used their artillery to bombard NRA positions and the nearby approaches to the rail bridge, Chiang ordered his First CA to detour south of the city and march upstream to fording points rather than to risk movement by train through Tsinan.[36] The largest fording operation began at Tung-a.[37] Some foreign press observers were not aware of the maneuver and claimed that the Japanese had succeeded in blocking the First CA from its movement north.*

As the NRA regrouped on the north bank, the Ankuochün set up a new defense line from south of Tehchou to Hsün-teh. Although during the first week in May, Peking put out peace feelers, Wu Chih-hui declared for the KMT that, rather than combine with Chang Tso-lin and the Manchurian clique, "the Northern Expedition will be continued and completed in the shortest possible time."[38] Following the Japanese intervention and with the succession of NRA victories, the KMT at Nanking enjoyed unprecedented public support and could afford to drop the earlier practice of first seeking the defection of warlord leaders. It was only after the Peking campaign that Nanking once again turned to diplomacy to win over Chang Hsüeh-liang, the son of Chang Tso-lin, rather than fight its way past Shan-hai-kuan into the Manchurian basin, where the NRA could provoke massive Japanese intervention.

---

*George Sokolsky's press report seems to have gained wide currency and stated that the First CA "sits in Hsüchou and holds Feng's rear." The fact that Chiang and the First CA *headquarters* did remain in the Hsüchou-Tsinan sector until late in May probably confused the issue.

The Peking Campaign:
Completion of the Military Unification

In the second week of May 1928, the NRA began to move north out of its bridgehead on the north bank of the Yellow River. Despite having been deprived of the use of the Tientsin-P'u-k'ou Railroad and thereby being forced to make a sixty-mile march, Ch'en T'iao-yüan of the First CA* took Tehchou on May 13.[1] Having cleared northernmost Shantung of the Ankuochün, the First CA could now combine with Feng on the North China Plain in a common front facing Peking—still nearly 200 miles distant. In the northwest, Yen Hsi-shan's Third CA was in place to make up the left wing of the front, which arced around from the Yellow River all the way to the Great Wall near Peking.

THE SHANSI SECTOR

Yen's Third CA had been fighting the Ankuochün since early in April when Chang Tso-lin tried to take on Shansi before the NRA arrived in the north. In mid-April in the rugged Shansi mountains that overhung the railroad to T'aiyüan, Yen's capital, Chang's offensive had been blocked. In northernmost Shansi, Chang had pressed deeply inside the ancient Great Wall, taking first Ta-t'ung and then Shuochou. On May 8, Yen was finally able to mount a counteroffensive, which retook Shuochou and pushed

*The NRA sectors may already have merged since *Ta-shih chi* and James E. Sheridan, *Chinese Warlord, the Career of Feng Yü-hsiang* (Stanford: Stanford University Press, 1966), p. 238, concur that Tehchou fell to Feng's Second CA the prior day, May 12.

Chang's Ankuochün back out of northern Shansi. By May 25, the eastern point of the counterattack along the railroad connecting T'aiyüan with the North China Plain pushed the Ankuochün down out of the Shansi highlands. As Yen's Third CA descended to the plain, there were on that ancient battleground nearly one million troops—more than half of which sided with Nanking.

Down on the plain, Feng followed the Peking-Hankow Railroad while Yen's forces paralleled the route north through the highlands bordering Shansi. Both converged on Paoting, which they besieged. There, again, on the North China Plain was an example of what unified action could accomplish—however fleeting was that unity. In his attack from northernmost Shansi, Yen threatened the side gate to Peking and forced Chang Tso-lin to divide the Ankuochün defensive force. While the Ankuochün held on tenaciously at Paoting in the south, Chang-chia-k'ou, the strategic gateway of caravans and armies to Peking, fell to Yen on May 25, followed a day later by Nan-k'ou, the last mountain pass defending the route to Peking.[2] Yen's contribution was, thus, quite valuable and placed him first in line to enter Peking.

THE BATTLE FOR THE NORTH CHINA PLAIN

The joint operation by the three Collective Armies under KMT coordination had not moved north unopposed. In early April when the Ankuochün had attacked Yen in Shansi, it had also moved south against Feng Yü-hsiang's bridgehead along the Yellow River. Had this double offensive succeeded, the Northern Expedition might well have bogged down during the Tsinan episode with the Japanese. At that point the three components of the Ankuochün still numbered around one-half million troops and enjoyed the advantages of shortened rail communications. However, by mid-April, Feng's Second CA had halted the thrust south and not only had managed to hold onto the bridgehead, but had thrown the Ankuochün back. While south of the river, units of Feng's Second CA aided Chiang in his move against Tsinan, to the north, the Second CA main force took Han-tan, a station on the Peking-Hankow line, on April 17.

Hampering progress up the North China Plain was the effective bombardment of the long-range heavy artillery that the Ankuochün had had mounted on railroad cars. While the northern warlords continued to enjoy superiority of firepower, they also had become overdependent on their rail lines. As had happened successively earlier in the expedition, once the NRA was in position to threaten the enemy's arterial rail link rearward the northern commanders retreated to defend it. Thus, when Yen's Third CA broke out of the Shansi highlands and confronted the Ankuochün down on the plain at the rail crossroads of Shih-chia-chuang, Chang Tso-lin began to withdraw northward defensively. Following the Ankuochün retreat, Feng joined Yen in the siege of Shih-chia-chuang from the south. Compressed from two sides, that important rail and highway crossroads fell to the joint offensive on May 9.[3]

The final push to Peking saw great masses of troops converging on a diminishing field. While from the southeast the route was still nearly 200 miles long to the ancient imperial capital, Yen's outposts in the northwest could practically look down on Peking, a mere two day's march down through foothills. The southern sector was divided into three routes: with part of Yen's Third CA moving north through the Shansi border highlands, Feng's Second CA pressing up the Peking-Hankow Railroad, and the First CA centering on the Tientsin-P'u-k'ou Railroad. While the main force of the First CA had detoured around Tsinan, some units did stay behind as a guard force ringing the city.* There remained considerable anxiety among the NRA leaders over the Japanese intervention, since the Japanese were reinforcing Tientsin and Peking on the route ahead.[4]

In mid-May, the end of the Battle for Peking was not yet in sight. Throwing 200,000 troops against the south, Chang Tso-lin staged a desperate counterattack from May 17 to 25. When Chang concentrated on the gap between the First and Second CAs, the First CA crumpled and fell back to the south. The First CA managed to make a stand at Tungkuang, but could not regain the momentum of attack until late May. In the central sector the counterattack not only smashed Feng's siege of Paoting, it forced the Second CA back thirty miles south along the Peking-Hankow Railroad to Tingchou, where Ankuochün artillery kept Feng's troops immobilized. It was not until May 25, when the Ankuochün failed against Feng's flank east of the railway, that the northern tide began to ebb.[5]

The counterattack had stirred a feverish high pitch of cooperation among the Collective Armies. From Honan, Li Tsung-jen rushed his Fourth CA under Pai Ch'ung-hsi north on the Peking-Hankow Railroad to aid Feng in his hard-pressed sector. Yen's taking of Nan-k'ou far to the north contributed to the weakening of the Ankuochün southern push. Speeding by rail from sector to sector, Chiang Kai-shek catalyzed the diverse components with promises and coercion. Finally, on May 25, the NRA regained the momentum of attack.

Sending out cavalry units, Feng Yü-hsiang pressed quickly north between the two north-south rail lines to threaten Ankuochün communications.[6] In the hills bordering the plain, Yen Hsi-shan's units fought their way down to the flatland and took Manch'eng on May 27. From Peking, Chang Tso-lin saw: his several hundred thousand Manchurian troops among the Ankuochün, as well as his hold on the plain, endangered; growing pressure on the two railways, from the flank along Shansi's border and from behind; and that Yen's troops had reached almost to the Western Hills suburbs of Peking.

Thus, on May 30, Chang Tso-lin, head of the Ankuochün, began to consolidate his defense of what remained to him of the North China Plain.

---

*Chu P'ei-teh, supervising the guard force, avoided large-scale fighting with the Japanese, but was subjected to daily harassment from what had grown to be a division-sized Japanese force complete with aircraft that bombed Chinese units, which returned rifle fire against the reconnaisance flights. Quite likely, the intelligence gathered found its way to the Ankuochün at Peking. (*SCMP* [May 28, 1928], p. 10, and [May 31, 1928], p. 12. *N. Exp.*, vol. 4, p. 1283.)

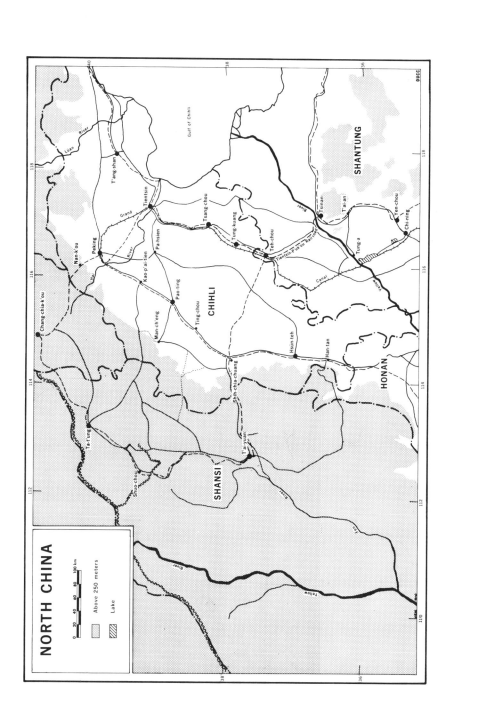

NORTH CHINA

0 20 40 60 80 100 km

Above 250 meters

Lake

CHIHLI

SHANTUNG

SHANSI

HONAN

Gulf of Chihli

Luan River

T'ang-shan

Tientsin

Grand

Peking

Nan-k'ou

Mai River

Kao-p'ai-tien

Pa-hsien

Pao-ting

Ting-chou

Man-ch'eng

Chang-chia-k'ou

Ta-t'ung

Shuo-chou

T'ai-yuan

Shih-chia-chuang

Hsun-teh

Han-tan

Tsang-chou

Tung-kuang

Teh-chou

Tsinan

Tai-an

Yen-chou

Chi-ning

Tung-a

Tientsin-Pukou Railway

Canal

Fen River

Yellow River

Luan River

when it did agree grudgingly to send strikers on the expedition, it organized only a few thousand for carrier duty under the Supply Corps of the expedition's headquarters. That was but a tiny fraction of its potential. Both the CCP and the Strike Committee at Canton saw that a transfer of disciplined proletarians (hard to come by in China) to KMT jurisdiction would leave the committee and the CCP separated from the base of its power. The CCP was certainly not about to devote the energies of its mass organizations to the success of the KMT's Northern Expedition, except where the CCP's social revolution could be furthered. [67]

CHAPTER 19

The Role of Organized Masses in the Military Campaign

Chiang's hopes of using the strike organization as an auxiliary of the NRA were not realized to a meaningful degree. As the expeditionary forces marched up and over the border mountains into Hunan, carriers became a primary consideration in logistics. Above Shaokuan, the northern terminal of the unfinished Canton to Hankow rail line, loomed high the Che-ling water gap in the Nanling range. A climb of a thousand-foot incline was necessary to get goods and people over the pass before they could descend into the broad Hsiang basin. In peacetime, this was accomplished by pack coolies and sedan chair carriers. Since Kwangtung was lacking in pack horses, the expedition's supplies would have to go over on the strong backs of thousands of coolies.

During the two months before the July 9 launching, Chiang, the C-in-C of the expedition, and his military aides sought carriers from all possible sources. The professional carriers who worked the pass could not possibly handle the unusual demands of the expedition. Even offering the peasants around Shaokuan the high daily wage of one Chinese dollar plus an additional sixty cents for the day's food did not entice the needed numbers. Chinese peasants had learned from long bitter experience to avoid dealings with armies. When the Central Executive Committee of the KMT convened on May 20, it tried to solve the problem by requesting the services of the strike organization's tens of thousands of striking workers. However, when the vanguard began to move north in May, the unit of strikers that accompanied it provided only token support, a mere 1,500.[1]

With rising labor costs in Kwangtung, the recruitment of carriers did not proceed smoothly. Chiang dickered with the Strike Committee, but, the press reported, the committee would only concede that *after* the British met their demands then the committee would dispatch 3,000 armed pickets and strikers to work for the NRA.[2] In the Canton area, the KMT assigned coolie recruiting to the police, who were hard pressed to fill their quotas for paid *volunteers*. When individual police officials fell back on the traditional means of simply seizing coolies, the Party was forced to punish them in order to maintain its credibility.[3]

The KMT worked hard to adhere to its motto "Don't Seize Coolies," which it tried to combine with fair payment and treatment of volunteers. Gradually peasants in the areas through which the expedition moved overcame their skepticism as they learned of the unusual policy and did volunteer to work for the NRA. The recruitment policy stood in sharp contrast to that traditionally employed by warlord armies.

Warlord recruiting meant sending patrols into the countryside to seize sturdy males whereever encountered. Shackled together in a line, the carriers were prodded along and handled like cattle.[4] For shelter, the coolies could count on little more than cattle cars, the dank holds of riverboats, or overcrowded, unsanitary bamboo sheds. After a long, hard day's haul, they had no blankets to cover their overheated bodies. For food, they could expect little more than a large communal pot of rice once a day. Barely staving off starvation, the stronger fought at the rice pot for handfuls. Unsupported by a modern supply system, the carriers for the warlords gradually lost their meager clothing and went uncovered and barefoot. When maneuvers took a unit off the roads and up mountain trails, the warlords used a group of ten coolies to carry a field cannon, followed by reserve coolies to replace those who dropped along the way. To speed up movement, the guards used whips and showed their skill by beating the coolies only enough to speed up their pace but not wound them mortally. Given the lack of a nutritious diet, the exhaustive pace, and the lack of sanitation, the carriers dropped from disease or exhaustion—whichever hit them first. They were left along the trail to be replaced by locally seized manpower, which was in plentiful supply in the overpopulated countryside. The problem was the rapidity with which the Chinese peasantry had learned to vanish upon learning of the approach of an army. According to an account of the fate of a group of several hundred Chekiang coolies seized by a subordinate of Sun Ch'uan-fang, over one hundred died during the three months of their forced labors through Chekiang and Kiangsu.[5]

Thus, the revolutionary recruiting policy of the NRA enjoyed a high repute, which undulated outward amongst the sea of peasants. Not only did this new movement profess to have the interests of *all* the people at heart, it proved to the pragmatic Chinese peasant that it could be a source of livelihood.

In Kwangtung the recruitment of carriers was not eased by the foot dragging of the CCP in its support of the Northern Expedition. When criticized by the public and even CCP members for this lack of involvement, Ch'en Tu-hsiu felt constrained to dispel the image. In a letter to Chiang published in the *Hsiang tao* in early June, Ch'en countered by saying that his comrades were ". . . not completely opposed to the Northern Expedition, but they merely mean that Kwangtung should gather its strength . . . and not lightly risk it in an attempt. . . . Our opinion differed on the matter of *when* the Northern Expedition should begin."[6] Failure of the NRA to win over Hunan could mean a rush of warlord forces into Kwangtung, which would suppress the flourishing CCP movement. However, as popular enthusiasm rose over the expedition, it had become necessary to exhibit nominal support. But as late as the week preceding the formal launching of the expedition, after the vanguard had long been fighting in Hunan, Ch'en Tu-hsiu seemed as obstructive as ever when he wrote in the *Hsiang tao* that Kwangtung should remain on the defensive, rather than promote an offensive.[7]

Then when the Central Committee of the CCP met from July 12 to 18, it concluded that "the southern National Government's military campaign is actually merely to block the attack of the anti-red army into Hunan and Kwangtung and not a genuine Northern Expedition carried out with revolutionary power."[8] Even after the victories in Hunan during the fall of 1926, the CCP Central's analysis set down its continued lack of enthusiasm for the KMT's Northern Expedition:

> Recently the greatest problem for the CCP has been the Northern Expedition. Thus, we have had many differing opinions on the question, such as those of comrades who oppose the action. They reasoned that quick results could not be achieved. If this attitude had prevailed it would have been bad for the Party. Although the Northern Expedition cannot succeed, it is an aid to the National Revolutionary Movement because the new warlords are closer to the revolutionary movement than the old warlords.[9]

Thus, as the expedition began to manifest some signs of succeeding, the Russians and the CCP let up in their resistance to it and began to shape a new strategy that would utilize the expedition for their purposes. The change first appeared in the attitude of the Strike Committee during the first week of July—just prior to the formal send-off of the expedition. Naming a subcommittee to work with the Supply Corps of the NRA, the Strike Committee agreed to help fill the need for carriers.[10] The first batch of 2,000 strikers boarded trains on July 5, bound for Shaokuan, followed by another 500 on the seventh. On July 8, 1,000 strikers marched to the Canton railway station from their East Park headquarters, accompanied by a KMT marching band.[11] At that point, as the expedition was officially acknowledged as having begun, the Strike Committee could also claim that 3,000 strikers were working as carriers in the expedition to the north.[12] That the effort made a significant contribution at that point can be seen in the termination of carrier recruitment by the Canton police.[13] Ex-Peasant-Labor Minister Ch'en Kung-po, who had just resigned from his burdensome post to move north with the NRA Political Department, reported that in crossing the border range over 80 percent of the carriers were strikers "who had no work in Canton."[14] From July on, the CCP and its Strike Committee claimed publicly to be staunch supporters of the Northern Expedition—eventually presenting the image through Communist writers of being the primary promoters and supporters of what they entitled the Great National Revolution.

However dramatic the aid of the strikers as carriers may have appeared in July 1926, their role thereafter is rather unclear. That most articulate observer of the expedition from Canton to Wuhan, Ch'en Kung-po, complained that the strikers had joined the campaign in a state of emotional excitement, but that once they trudged into the humid heat of the subtropical Kwangtung summer their spirits wilted considerably. The climb was a hard, hot one, and those making it reeled under attacks of cholera and other diseases. Due to the prior defection of T'ang Sheng-chih in southern Hunan, at least the climbers had only to fight the pull of gravity in ascending the pass. According to observer Ch'en, the Cantonese coolies, aware of the KMT's liberal recruitment policy and the avoidance of force, refused to carry supplies for the NRA much past the Kwangtung border.[15] According to another report, over 400 carriers had come down with various diseases during the climb,[16] and that may have contributed to the faintness of heart that returned large numbers of Cantonese strikers to their hometown by early August.[17] Then, too, the Strike Committee may have had in mind only a temporary transfer of strikers out of their authority. Once into Hunan, the NRA had to recruit Hunanese to carry its supplies.

THE NRA RECRUITS ITS OWN CARRIERS

The NRA's vanguard having preceded the main force into Hunan in May 1926, the Political Department workers already had valuable contacts with the local people by the end of July. They had especially sought out trade guilds and associations to help with procurement. The NRA's attractive recruitment policy quickly became common knowledge wherever the expedition proceeded. In Hunan the peasantry found it especially attractive because during the summer of 1926 they were plagued by a drought in the south of the province and by floods in the north. Thus, the normally acquisitive peasants flocked to receive the NRA's high pay and daily food ration. Whereas to the Hong Kong striker the per diem rate of C$1.60 was only slightly more than the strikers' daily stipend he could receive without working, to the Hunanese peasant the wage was well worth the effort.[18]

The most common initial contact made by the Political Department in its search for carriers was with the local *hsien-chang* (highest *hsien* official). Requested to publicize the NRA's need and the wages offered, the *hsien-chang* would act as the middleman in passing the request on to trade guilds or workers' associations—especially carrier associations—which would fill the quotas.[19] If the local *hsien-chang* had been one of Wu P'ei-fu's appointees and had fled with the appearance of the NRA, then the Political Department members had to contact the local peasantry or workers.

When Hunan came under the NRA's control, the NRA found the skeletal structure of the KMT-sponsored Union of Labor Associations (Kung-t'uan Lien-ho-hui), which Wu P'ei-fu's subordinates had suppressed. Like most warlords, Wu suppressed the modern workers' unions because he considered them subversive, but in Hunan the union's leaders and membership, although disbanded, were available for reorganization once the province came under the NRA. A letter from the Changsha *hsien-chang* to Chairman Kuo of the Hunan Union of Labor Associations provides some details:

> We have just received a telegrammed order from the General Director's Headquarters which says, "Our army has been victorious. Now a great deal of ammunition and military supplies have been carried here from Kwangtung and should be moved quickly to the front. To transport these things please gather as soon as possible at least a thousand carriers." The other army corps have already gathered over 10,000 for service at the front and now we have been ordered to gather more. It is very difficult. We think that the future of the revolution depends on the cooperation of the masses. After discussion, you have agreed to organize the transport teams as Chairman. Because we cannot afford a delay you should organize the transport teams within the next few days. Each team should include 100 carriers. For the time being organize twenty teams.[20]

This type of team was generally formed around a group of men with either their profession or locale in common, such as rickshaw workers, stevedores, night-soil carriers, or area peasants.[21] A report from Changsha claimed that the heavy demand for local coolies from the NRA had taken most transporters out of town and allowed those who remained to charge much higher than usual prices. Later in the fall of 1926, during Sun Ch'uan-fang's massive counterattack in Kiangsi, even such items as barbed wire for the defenses was borne in quantity by carriers from Shaokuan, Kwangtung, down to the rail line in Hunan.[22]

Various types of professional and social organizations were present in Hunan before the arrival of the NRA. CCP reports include all sorts of traditional secret societies and village defense groups. In some villages, young student activists, sons of local gentry, had returned home and attempted to organize peasants in their villages for education and political discussions on the Three Peoples' Principles, but their effectiveness can be questioned. Some had been sent by middleschool student unions, which had motivated and trained them; a few had been sent by the KMT (and CCP) to the Kwangtung Peasants' Movement Classes.[23] We have already observed that thirty-six Hunanese had been so enrolled from late March to September 1926.[24]

The effectiveness of such efforts prior to the occupation of Hunan by the NRA can be questioned. Wang Chien-min recalled that a group of peasants in his home village gathered to hear his political message and showed curiosity about the photograph of Sun Yat-sen that Wang displayed. He was questioned as to who "that foreigner in the picture was"—Sun's dress and moustache appeared foreign to the rural people, as many of his ideas must also have. To Wang the rural peasantry seemed apathetic to any but its own local interests such as the demands made by passing armies for produce and manpower and anxieties over being seized or robbed by the strangers. It was upon this attitude that the Political Department capitalized by using the attractive recruitment policy and respectful treatment, and by paying good prices for the produce purchased for the NRA. As the ways of the NRA became known, it moved into areas where, rather than finding that the peasants had fled into hiding, it found instead curious peasants lining the roads *selling* tea and rice gruel to the passing troops. [25] In some areas, peasants had also heard the Party propaganda promising that tax and rent burdens would be lightened by the NRA. It had been common in China's history for the founders of regimes to balance anew the rural economic system by redistributing or confiscating the land of those who had fallen fighting for the old regime, or who had been its rural middlemen.

Later CCP historians are quite insistent that organized peasants played a crucial role in the campaign through Hunan. There is little mention of large-scale, organized peasant support of the NRA outside CCP literature. The cases cited by the CCP writers were located entirely in that sector traversed by the Right Route of the Hunan operation. This portion of the NRA was composed of the Fourth Army's Tenth and Twelfth divisions plus Communist Yeh T'ing's Independent Regiment and moved north along the east side of the Hsiang River basin. [26]

Of the ten geographic points cited where peasants' associations or unions worked actively as guides, intelligence gatherers, saboteurs, snipers, or combatants, nine of the ten are located in that eastern sector. [27] Even these examples of peasant and worker support are not particularly large in scale; support is counted in terms of a few hundred workers or peasants. In one case, workers led by students spread across approximately ten miles of countryside on July 11 to harass selected enemy points from the rear by firing bird guns and throwing daggers, and then joined with Yeh T'ing's regiment to attack the front. [28] At the same time on the Canton-Hankow Railroad in Hunan, workers sabotaged the rails and electrical power lines of the enemy and gathered intelligence along the branch railroad between Chuchou and Liling (also in the eastern sector). [29] To the north between Yochou and Lin-hsiang, peasants reportedly damaged Wu P'ei-fu's rail supply line back to Hankow in early July. [30] The only mention in CCP sources of the apparently non-Communist battle sector, the Center and Left routes, was that of the failure of an attempted general strike at Changsha.

Because of its rail connections and its centrality as a hub of roads in Hunan, the provincial capital was the target of a large offensive. By early July, when the NRA was approaching Changsha, the KMT and CCP political agents with the Political Department had been working in Hunan for at least two months. Within Changsha there existed the nucleus of a workers' association, the Union of Labor Associations already mentioned. As the battlefront neared Changsha, the underground leadership of the union gathered 1,000 workers and planned to spearhead a general strike to harass enemy Yeh K'ai-hsin's rear. However, when the "union's" workers began their strike on July 8, 1926, Yeh's troops in the city far outnumbered the unarmed workers and their leaders and quickly suppressed the strike. Thus frustrated, the union provided no further support until the arrival of the NRA was imminent. On July 9, the union formed a "peace-maintenance corps" to protect the Changsha burghers from looting by the troops who might retreat back through the city en route north. Farther south the Lien River line of Yeh K'ai-hsin became untenable as a flying column of the Eighth Army threatened the rail line north of Changsha. By July 11, Yeh's troops were straggling through Changsha out of formation so that the units of the "peace-maintenance corps" were able to isolate and disarm batches of soldiers—some of whom were probably bent on looting. Upon Changsha's occupation by the Eighth Army, the union was ordered to turn over the captured weapons, a part of which the union leaders did give up. However, the CCP account claims that a portion of the weapons was retained and later used to arm a force of union pickets. Apparently, there was from the start a lack of real cooperation between some leaders of the organized workers and the NRA.[31]

The CCP interpretation could mean that either its cadre in the Right Route was more able to elicit "mass" support (even if limited to several hundred) or that with more CCP cadre in the eastern sector more stories that showed the power of the masses were recorded. The sector *west* of the Hsiang River, interestingly, is the broader, much more heavily populated area with more farm villages (including Mao Tse-tung's own home village), while the east sector, publicized for its mass organizations, is more rugged and sparsely populated.

The next campaign for which the CCP recorded organized civilian support was that of the Mi-lo River line, the last stand of Wu's forces in Hunan. Both sides had been gathering strength along the riverbanks since the fall of Changsha, a full month before. During the retreat toward the Mi-lo River, while a part of the northern force marched through Hsien-chung, a local KMT headquarters led the area's peasants in harassing the bands of stragglers. It was just such bands that usually strayed to loot small villages. According to the report, the organized peasants killed two enemy soldiers and captured, along with eight rifles, ten others who were executed the following day. At nearby Peichiang, peasants reportedly attacked and killed numbers of stragglers with their hoes. Later, during the fourth day of the Mi-lo offensive, a group of peasants are recorded as having guided an attack up a steep hill, thereby flanking the enemy's upland flank at Pai-shih-ling. These peasants were organized by a peasants' association, which claimed to have lost 20 of its men in the battle while killing 300 of the enemy near P'ing-chiang. Its contributions included providing intelligence about the enemy's defenses, carrying supplies, guiding units of the NRA across the Mi-lo River from Heng-ch'a to Shih-tzu-yen, and collaborating with the propaganda units of the Political Department.[32] The geographic points named as having provided organized civilian support to the Mi-lo offensive correspond again to the eastern or Right Route of the Fourth Army's Tenth and Twelfth divisions and Yeh T'ing's regiment.[33]

Of the NRA that pursued the enemy's retreat after Mi-lo, Li Tsung-jen's portion of the Left Route followed the rail route on which the bulk of the enemy withdrew and appeared at the perimeter of the port of Yochou on August 22. The city's outer line of defenses lay under flood water. With information from local peasants that the defenders' morale was poor, and with the guidance of natives in approaching an undefended way into the city, Li launched a successful attack from the rear.[34] Another pursuit route took the Eighth Army of T'ang Sheng-chih overland to cut the rail line ahead of the enemy. The success of this maneuver resulted in the capture of many of the retreating troops and was aided at Lin-hsiang by the action of a *hsien* official who gathered townspeople into a unit that fired on the retreating troops, thus further undermining their will to resist.[35]

The evidence published by the CCP publications does point up the ideologically correct view that the masses are all powerful—especially if organized and led by the Communist Party. However, there remain a number of questions unanswered as to the significance of organized civilian support. The NRA was operating in Hunan for nearly two months before the battles cited by the CCP as those in which the peasants helped took place. What of that two-month portion (about one-half) of the Hunan campaign? Although instances of peasant aid are described for the eastern sector of the front, what about the role of the masses in the larger western sector and in the operation as a whole? The cases of peasant and worker aid mention small groups of less than one hundred to no more than one thousand persons doing battle in sites on the periphery of major combat. Is this to be accepted as massive, organized support of a sustained nature? Even guerrilla warfare, if it is to be of an effective nature, involves more than an isolated action in a restricted area. If the civilian support to the Right Route as led by CCP cadre was crucially significant, then that sector should have moved northward more easily and quickly. Why then did that sector, until July, make much less headway than the western sector across the Hsiang valley? That western, more populous sector did have its share of battles and enemy activity.

Nearly all the reports of organized mass support for the expedition in Hunan originated with CCP sources, such as the *Hsiang tao* article of July, "Hunan during the Northern Expedition," by-lined by a partisan in the field, Ko T'eh. Another *Hsiang tao* report drew from September issues of the Canton *Kuo-min jih-pao*, a KMT organ then dominated by the Left, which promoted the CCP's organizing of the masses. Another account that found its way onto *Hsiang tao* pages was "Facts on the Direct Participation of the Hunan Peasants in the Battles of the Northern Expedition," which originated in the September 14 edition of the *Chan-shih chou-pao* published by the Secretariat of the Hunan CCP Central Committee at Changsha.[36]

The nonpartisan, or at least nonofficial, press of that time, both Chinese and Western, differed in their reports from those of the above partisan sources in the interpretation of civilian support. Outside of Party organs, the press described the support as being unorganized, mainly spontaneous, and passive in nature. According to these sources, Chinese civilians facilitated the movement of the Northern Expedition through Hunan by the sale to the NRA of goods and services, and through acts of cooperation such as providing information and guides. Rather than fleeing before the NRA, or hiding in terror, the "people" stayed to welcome the NRA. Could the NRA have conquered Hunan without the tacit acceptance of the provincial people?

The presence of civilian support in Hunan was only one of *several* factors that favored the NRA's progress. By late June, the NRA probably outnumbered the troops of Wu P'ei-fu's subordinates in Hunan. It was not until late August that reinforcements from Wu became significant. The matter of numbers of divisions and regiments is clouded by the unreliability of units living up to their theoretical complements. Neither side was particularly meticulous in that regard. According to units in the field, the NRA had numerical superiority in Hunan. In the official account, during the Changsha campaign the northern side had somewhat under five divisions in strength while the NRA attackers had seven divisions, two brigades, and three regiments.[37] During the Mi-lo offensive in August while the northern force still awaited Wu's reinforcements from Hopei-Hunan, the NRA's numerical superiority was increased by two brigades.[38]

By the time the NRA carried the expedition into southern Hupei in pursuit of the defeated forces of Wu, its victories and reputation had become common talk in the country and cities alike. Moving north along the Canton-Hankow Railroad, the NRA met its first major resistance at the highly defensible Ting-szu Bridge. In a battle considered to have been the most fiercely fought to that time, the NRA enjoyed the aid of the local people. August 26 was spent futilely attempting to cross the bridge and the stream. A flanking movement was called for, and, according to the *Hua-ch'iao jih-pao*, this was accomplished with the help of peasants from Hsien-ning who knew the terrain well enough to move through the hills quickly in the dark.[39] Volunteers for carrying supplies had been plentiful and they also may have acted as guides, although the official military account makes no mention of such civilian aid. In his account of the following evening, Ch'en Kung-po recalled his surprise that so shortly following the battle people were back in the town of Ting-szu Bridge with the market set up and lighted for business as the NRA soldiers passed through. Another observer, CCP member Kuo Mo-jo, noted the ease with which the NRA troops could approach the local people to purchase food and seek shelter, while those of Wu P'ei-fu were avoided as "aliens" and, if caught as stragglers out of ranks, were beaten by the natives as "thieves."[40]

As the NRA's supply lines back to Kwangtung lengthened, food became an important element in pressing the Northern Expedition. The instance of the night market that greeted the NRA at Ting-szu Bridge contrasts with reports that simultaneously Wu's forces were low on food. Of course partly accounting for Wu's shortage were the shortages brought on by drought and floods. Admittedly, the NRA Supply Corps still had to draw on rice produced in the adjacent upland valleys of Kwangtung to fill its appetite for over 100,000 catties of rice daily,[41] but it also lived off the land to a significant degree. The sale of local food to the NRA helped feed it, and also deprived the enemy of that much food. Since the warlord forces had a reputation of confiscating visible food, or forcing the exchange of food for worthless warlord military scrip, the NRA Political Department cadre could convince the local peasantry more easily to avoid commerce with the enemy.[42] This reinforced the traditional peasant practice of fleeing to the hills with their stores of rice when armies were passing through.

As a movement of the twentieth century, the Northern Expedition often moved by rail or faced an enemy that did. The NRA had moved from Canton to the Hunan border by rail. As it took Hunan territory it came into possession of rail lines, but would have had no rolling stock or equipment were it not for that acquired from the enemy. Sun Fo, who was then Minister of Communications, recalled that the railroad workers were helpful in acquiring these. Affiliated with a secret KMT union, the rail workers slowed or prevented the northern supply authorities from moving rolling stock or equipment. In some cases, key parts of equipment were hidden, in other cases the rolling stock was hidden so that it was unavailable to Wu's retreating forces. By the time Wu had withdrawn his forces to the Yangtze and faced the problem of either ferrying the rolling stock over the bridgeless river or destroying it, the NRA had come into possession of much of it.[43] When equipment could not be hidden, and word came that Wu's forces were about to withdraw by rail, the regular workers would scatter and vanish so that the enemy troops could not readily put the train together and operate it.[44] As the NRA moved through southern Hupei en route to the Wuhan complex, the Canton-Hankow Railroad had become quite valuable as a mobile advance headquarters and temporary hospital and as a means to move troops and supplies quickly. Although the cooperation of some of the railroad workers did diminish the use of the rails by the enemy, it did not deprive Wu's troops of rail communications entirely. Many workers who could not afford to lose their wages continued to work for Wu, and a few of his soldiers also managed to operate the trains themselves when pressed. Thus, as late as August 23, when Wu's troops were in retreat out of Hunan, many moved by rail; one such unit was ambushed and captured by an NRA vanguard.[45]

As Wu suffered defeat at the Wuhan cities, many of the railroad workers in Hankow fled into the French concession there rather than work to move Wu's troops by train up the rail line from Hankow into Honan. Farther north where the railroad traversed the countryside north of Huayüan, rail workers cooperated with the NRA by tearing up the rails. Apparently, Wu's engineers could not repair the damage in time, and he was forced to march his forces north to the next defense line in the border hills. However, as the Eighth Army pursued Wu, the workers repaired the damaged rails making possible a speedy follow-up so that Wu and his forces were caught at Wusheng Pass before they had prepared their defenses.[46] In less than two weeks the NRA pursued Wu over 100 miles from Hankow to the pass, which it quickly captured.

According to the *Hsiang tao*'s reading of the official press of Canton,

Hanyang Arsenal workers in Hunan responded to the approach of the NRA by leading a general strike, which began on August 1 and lasted until September 7, the day after Hanyang's occupation.[47] Since the output of arsenals was crucial to the civil war, a strike would have been damaging, as had been the strike at Canton's arsenal. Little evidence is available about the effectiveness of the strike at the Hanyang Arsenal, but at the time of its capture by the NRA a large stock of ammunition was reported to have been captured also.[48] Thus, the strike had either not completely shut down production, or the arsenal's reserves had remained for capture. On the day of the capture, there were still 150 workers at their labors, who were kept there until the following morning. Then, the new director of the arsenal appealed for a return to work, promising first a two-day holiday and then regular pay for their work under NRA authorities.[49] The arsenal was apparently assigned to Eighth Army Commander T'ang Sheng-chih, whose agents hoped to increase production to meet the needs of the expedition.

Of the three Wuhan cities with their industrial and commercial wealth, the arsenal, and the large concentration of proletariat, all of which had attracted the NRA, Hanyang and Hankow fell in quick succession as the NRA forced Wu to withdraw into Honan. However, at Wuchang, the walled provincial capital of Hupei, a sizable force held out under siege awaiting Wu's return or help from Sun Ch'uan-fang in Kiangsi.

The siege, lasting from September 7 until October 10, enclosed an urban population of 300,000, which included students and workers. Kuo Mo-jo with the Political Department and Ch'en Kung-po both participated in the siege and acted as its chroniclers. Both were greatly aware of the workers' movements, but neither mentions any support provided the NRA from *within* the city. They describe only the problems of military combat, Kuo decrying the lack of heavy machine guns, large siege cannon, and the "faulty intelligence reports." Within the city, CCP member Yü Hsi-tu, heading a *small* insurrection corps that Chang Kuo-t'ao had dispatched from Shanghai, reported their efforts at propagandizing to incite military defections and small-scale acts of sabotage by CCP and KMT cadre—not by organized masses.[50]

Later the *Kuowen chou-pao* published an extremely detailed daily diary of a minor bureaucrat within the city. It makes no mention of any civilian effort working against the defenders from within the walls, although the account describes all sorts of civilian affairs, contacts with the defending troops, mediation efforts by the Merchants' Association, and the evacuation of the women, the aged, and the infirm. The picture is one of the people accepting the situation passively, hoarding their rice until the threat of starvation loomed, and attempting to leave the city in droves during a short-term evacuation of civilians.

Although the students had already come under the influence of the KMT's Student Union Movement in which many CCP members operated, they and their schools were clamped under close military surveillance. There is no mention of student-led subversion or collaboration with the besiegers. Although the city's people feared the arbitrary rule of Wu's defenders, they were also upset by the bombing carried on by the NRA and by the Russian "advisors," which demolished civilian quarters and killed noncombatants.[51] Rather than guerilla activities or subversion, the primary determinant in the fall of Wuchang on October 10 was the hopelessness of defending a starving city.

The Western histories that mention the Northern Expedition relied heavily on the CCP's political pieces as the basis for generalizations on the National Revolution, and thus have assumed as correct a picture of organized proletariat and peasantry so subverting the warlords' operations that the NRA took cities that had been won by the masses.* On the basis of a variety of sources, that interpretation seems highly insecure. This does not seem to have been the case at Changsha, nor at Wuhan. Except for an economic strike at Hankow's British cigarette factories during May and June, which the *Hsiang tao* reported, there was little union activity *until after* the arrival of the NRA and its Political Department labor organizers.[52] Through Comintern news sources, Paris' *L'Humanité* of the French Communist Party reported that in Hunan and Hupei, "The workers began propagandizing *during* the arrival of the Cantonese. They organized meetings and distributed tracts explaining the goal of the KMT" (emphasis added).[53] Chang Kuo-t'ao, from his own experience at Wuhan from September 11, 1926, on, claimed that ". . . the peasant movement led by the CCP was only beginning . . ." and of the labor unions after Wu P'ei-fu's suppression that the ". . . only survivors were a few trade union secret groups led by the CCP."[54] The political fruits of these efforts were gathered, not before the arrival of the NRA, but during the fall and winter of 1926 and 1927, when Wuhan had become the center of Communist organizing of mass groups. That was the period referred to by CCP accounts later as Wuhan's Communist Period. The military campaign moved from Wuhan toward the Kiangsi border in September 1926.

---

*This would have to include Harold Isaacs' *The Tragedy of the Chinese Revolution*, whose gripping version inspired my research. See the general surveys by Ho Kan-chih, *A History of the Modern Chinese Revolution*, and Hu Ch'iao-mu, *Thirty Years of the Chinese Communist Party*.

CHAPTER 20

Civilian Aid in the Push Down the Yangtze

About the Kiangsi campaign, although there are a few accounts in KMT sources of organized civilian aid, the CCP remained silent. KMT accounts describe workers in the modern sector of the economy, for example, railroad and postal workers organized and removed from the traditional paternalistic pattern. These are the same sorts of workers that the KMT organized in Canton. As Chiang transferred troops by rail from northern Hupei toward Kiangsi, they had to pass the besieged city of Wuchang. Although the railroad workers were under considerable danger from shelling as their trains passed Wuchang, they continued to run the trains and greatly speeded the reinforcement of the Kiangsi front. At the border, the NRA had the cooperation of the local postmen who reportedly guided the troops from Hupei and Hunan across little-known passes and along paths at night. In this way the NRA avoided the most heavily fortified strong points around Ichün, Kao-an, Hsiu-shui, and T'ung-ku. Since the postmen's delivery routes enabled them to cover a considerable amount of territory, they also had valuable intelligence to pass on to the NRA. They contributed greatly to the mobility of the NRA as it made surprise night attacks through the border ranges as the offensive opened.[1] Once the NRA was inside Kiangsi, however, the worst of the campaign began. The battle for the lowlands west of Poyang Lake and the Kan River was perhaps the most severe and sustained test of the NRA in the expedition.

Apparently there was considerable sympathy for the KMT movement in the Kiangsi lowlands and urban centers of Nanchang and Kiukiang, centering around the middle schools and universities. The contributions have not been chronicled by the KMT in detail, but they did gain the attention of warlord Sun Ch'uan-fang at the time. Most likely the quick surprise attack that took Nanchang the first time was eased by the efforts of students. Many, encouraged by pro-KMT teachers, had left their homes to join the NRA. When NRA units entered Nanchang on September 19, they included many local young people. There was even a unit of young women in mixed uniforms who were recognized as students.[2]

When Sun retook Nanchang after it had been occupied by the NRA for one week, he was well aware of the role of the student community. There are greatly varying reports of students and civilians decapitated or shot for collusion with the enemy. From Peking a press release reported 400 students executed,[3] while word of 2,000 citizens executed for collaborating arrived in Hong Kong. One means of singling out radical students was to arrest those with short "Russian haircuts" or the short bobbed hair of the modern young woman.[4] At Kiukiang, to serve as a warning, the heads of "KMT spies" were impaled and displayed around the city.[5] The suppression came as Sun personally assumed command at Nanchang in early October 1926, and followed the "anti-Red" policies of the northern clique of warlords.[6] Again in late October, Sun punished university leaders for their role in the subversion. For promoting the recruitment of cadets for Whampoa Academy, the president of the First Normal University at Nanchang was executed, and two other heads of schools were killed for collusion with Chiang Kai-shek.[7]

Although *organized* peasant support in Kiangsi was even less evident than in Hunan, it can be assumed that the successful dealings with the peasants and civilians continued. When Kiukiang and Nanchang fell in early November, the NRA entered both cities amidst welcoming crowds. At least the populace did not hide behind locked doors in fear of the soldiers, and even showed hopes that new authorities would be interested in their welfare and support.

CIVILIANS AND THE FUKIEN CAMPAIGN

In October 1926, after a month of border skirmishes, the NRA pushed across the border mountains and invaded Fukien. By January 1927, the entire province was occupied. The organized support of the civilians was in greater evidence, but of a different nature. In Fukien under Sun Ch'uan-fang's subordinate General Chou Ying-jen, the often underpaid and underfed northern troops had not been kept under discipline. Their disorderly conduct and appetite for loot had inspired an increase of rural militia (*min-t'uan*) to guard localities against their forays. Working hard to reach these *min-t'uan*, the Political Department staff of General Ho Ying-ch'in's East Route Army made limited gains until the NRA proved its military potential in victory. Then their acceptance by the local people resembled the traditional awareness of the Mandate of Heaven that went to the winner. Political Department agents had preceded the army into Fukien where they worked around Changchou with little success in bringing about an uprising among the *min-t'uan*. In fact, when the NRA arrived in Nan-ching, a *hsien* only some twenty-five miles from Changchou, the populace was so poorly "prepared" that they hid indoors until political workers presenting the KMT program convinced them that they were safe. For that purpose, in some circumstances, KMT women cadre were sent to knock on doors, and, using the local dialect, to soothe the anxious residents—the reasoning being that the people would not fear women.[8]

Once the NRA had won its way into Fukien, the Political Department had greater success in gaining the cooperation of the *min-t'uan*. Recruited *min-t'uan* were at first included in the First Army's organizational structure, but by December 1926, had been separated into the new Third Route of the East Route Army and classified as two regular divisions, one independent brigade, and three independent regiments.[9] This *min-t'uan* cooperation and then integration into the NRA was crucial to the taking of Fukien's interior highlands. Whereas the NRA and its new auxiliaries knew the terrain well, the enemy soldiers were mainly peasants from the North China Plain who wore straw shoes and were unaccustomed and unsuited to mountain fighting. Furthermore, because they had alienated the Fukienese peasantry, the northerners also found it most difficult to live off the land.

In the cities of Fukien, the students were generally sympathetic to the National Revolution spreading out from Canton, but they did not contribute significantly until the suppressive surveillance of Chou Ying-jen's troops was removed with the troops' withdrawal. There was a report of an armed unit of students in Foochow, the province's largest city and the locus of a major concentration of students. As the city's defenses crumbled before the NRA offensive, the armed students seized government officials and reportedly shot the "spies" of the defeated regime.[10] Upon the entry of the NRA, the "radical" students freed student prisoners who joined in a welcoming assembly and then in organizing demonstrations against the Christian missions of Foochow.[11]

Although the cadre of the East Route Army Political Department had learned CCP political techniques at Whampoa, only a few were secretly CCP members and none openly. This was a result of the March coup, which had cleared CCP cadre out of the First Army, the core of the East Route Army. The political workers used some of their new techniques in recruiting workers and soldiers. Carriers were essential in Fukien's rugged terrain, uncrossed by railroads or decent roads, and lacking in pack animals. The Political Department used local leaders to handle the hiring of coolies.[12] The political workers used the tried practical means of attracting those with needed services and goods: liberal payment in silver and hard currency, and fair treatment. This overcame the peasants' distrust of payments from the military, which had been ofttimes worthless. Volunteering to carry for a distance of only sixty miles after which they were allowed to return home with their pay, the Fukienese made eager workers for the NRA. In the southern highlands, women of the Political Department persuaded the strong, hardworking Hakka women to carry supplies for the NRA.[13]

CHEKIANG CIVILIANS AND THE EAST ROUTE ARMY

Helping the NRA as it approached Chekiang late in 1926 was the Party-supported Chekiang autonomy movement, which provided military and political allies. During December in Ch'ü-chou, the western gateway to Chekiang held by allies of the NRA, Political Department workers stirred the people to support the National Revolution. The military made the district middle school at Ch'ü-chou its headquarters and Political Department workers persuaded the students to help in the revolution. KMT workers actively propagandized and lectured on the Three People's Principles and the goals of the revolution to civilians and the newly defected allied troops of Chekiang. Those to whom the propaganda seemed most relevant were the shopkeepers of the small city and the middle-school students. Since some of the students were from distant *hsien* in warlord territory, they were in a position to provide intelligence services to the KMT military. On the pretext of visiting relatives or friends, the students traveled out of Ch'ü-chou individually and then returned with information on topography, enemy troop movements, and other news of activities behind enemy lines.[14]

The Chekiang campaign was a part of the offensive that moved on Shanghai up the South China coast and down the Yangtze River. When Sun Ch'uan-fang began to withdraw his troops from northeastern Chekiang to better defend the lower Yangtze, his Chekiang forces suffered a deterioration in morale and discipline. Fuyang had been pillaged by northern looters and many Chekiangese had fled to Shanghai. A detailed account published on the passage of warlord and KMT armies through Chiahsing, Chekiang, in February 1927 provides a lively comparison of each side and its impact on the psychology of the people.

Chiahsing had heard by telephone from Hangchow that Sun's subordinate, Meng Ch'ao-yüeh, was retreating in defeat by rail toward Shanghai. "Knowing that soldiers in retreat will rob, rape, and any such thing . . . ," the local residents prepared by bolting their doors and hiding. At a small factory, the 100-man working force set about blocking the gates with sand so the northern soldiers could not break in. Although that was the evening of the Lantern Festival, inhabitants waited behind shuttered windows and bolted doors in darkness. At Hangchow, the retreating generals had levied a contribution from the guilds in return for an *orderly* retreat through the city, but Chiahsing was on its own. When a military train stopped at Chiahsing, a few local gentry observed protocol and came to the station to see off the provincial governor as he withdrew toward Shanghai with Meng's troops. Seeing the rear section of the train filled with unsupervised rank and file, the town elders implored General Meng to place officers in that section to keep order and prevent the soldiers from dropping off to loot the town. Meng refused and, as the train began to leave, the local people watched in horror as the rear section, uncoupled, stayed at the station as Meng went on. The northern soldiers quickly spread into the town.

As mercenaries, the northern troops hoped to make some profit from their profession, which was held in such low esteem. Since they often went unpaid, they looted upon arrival in a locale and then upon their departure. The soldiers often sent the loot and cash extracted from terrified townspeople home to their families in Shantung and North China by mail. At Chiahsing one such group of looters, seven armed northern soldiers, forced two night watchmen at gunpoint to act as their guides. Since the stores were shuttered and boarded up, the two "guides" were made to carry a large stone to one barricaded shop to batter down the door. The soldiers rifled the store for fifteen minutes and then left, carrying all they could in packs. In similar acts, over two-thirds of the stores of Chiahsing were looted that night, with considerable damage done to doors and walls. In the morning, the shopkeepers and workers emerged to repair the barricades since more northern troops were expected. Many changed their store signs by adding the word "small" to the title, hoping that the soldiers would not waste their time on small shops but move past to larger shops.

On the second night of the looting, February 19, the townspeople again hid behind doors locked and barred against the soldiers seeking entry. The pillage subsided temporarily, when a subordinate of Sun Ch'uan-fang arrived and beheaded two soldiers caught looting. People still feared coming out since trains loaded with Fukien Army soldiers were passing through en route to the new Sungchiang line outside Shanghai. Many troops had to wait their turn in Chiahsing as the trains shuttled the thousands of retreating troops out of Chekiang. Finally on Febraury 20, while retreating soldiers were still passing through, a telegram arrived from a Hangchow factory to its Chiahsing branch asking, "Has the 'People's Army' (*min-chün*) arrived safely?" Soon the train station personnel passed the word to the townspeople that the NRA would be arriving. The town shopkeepers, feeling greatly relieved, complied with the request of the town police that they put out white flags in welcome.

Assured that the northern force was gone, on February 21 the townspeople turned out to visit with each other and assess the damage from the pillage. After meeting, the *hsien*'s KMT headquarters sent members and supporters out to erect signs to:

Overthrow Imperialism
Tear Down the City Walls and Build Highways
Welcome the Revolutionary Army, the Salvation of our Country and Fellow
    Citizens
The Three People's Principles are the Ones to Save the Nation

Similar slogans had been raised during the abortive autonomy movement of Hsia Ch'ao in late 1926 but then had been quickly covered over at Sun Ch'uan-fang's orders.

On February 22, news spread that the revolutionary army would arrive at noon by train (which the NRA had captured). In spite of the cold

February wind, a large crowd gathered at the station; some waved white flags, others circulated handbills. Although in the past when armies had entered only the town gentry had appeared to extend the official greeting, this time nearly the whole town came out to see the much-discussed army of the KMT. The first train to arrive held the vanguard, of which the officers paused long enough to speak to the assemblage at the station. The next train contained units of the First Army's First Division. The narrative of the passage of the warlord forces and that of the NRA concluded:

> They were very friendly and their uniforms smart. They all seemed to be about 20 years old. Although they were short, they were strongly built, but not like the tall, strong soldiers of the North. When the townspeople asked them questions, they answered in a friendly manner. None stepping into the ranks of the soldiers was scolded.[15]

CHAPTER 21

The Proletariat in the Taking of Shanghai

Events at Shanghai during late 1926 and early 1927 have received the devoted attention of CCP historians. The Shanghai of this period held the greatest concentration of China's true proletariat and thus the greatest potential for revolution in Marxist terms. Thus, the capture of Shanghai has been portrayed as a classic demonstration of the power of the organized masses. This interpretation has been widely accepted by Western historians, but deserves reevaluation. The uprising that began there on March 21, 1927, preceding the NRA occupation, was not the first one linked to the Northern Expedition.

Both the KMT and the CCP had long been aware of Shanghai as fertile ground for organizing. The city contained hundreds of thousands of workers of the modern industrial type, and thousands of modern-educated students who had been exposed to nationalism—as had been the Shanghai merchants. The two modern parties hoped to organize the Shanghai workers as a source of power. From within the concessions, and in 1926 particularly the French concession, the KMT and CCP laid their plans and sometimes cooperated, sometimes contended.

The first "uprising" of a political nature came in October 1926, when Governor Hsia Ch'ao's Chekiang autonomy movement developed momentum. In Shanghai, the local representative of the KMT's Canton regime, Niu Yung-chien, agreed with Hsia that if conditions were right he would organize a force at Shanghai to divert Sun's efforts to reinforce Chekiang.[1] There were rumors that the KMT faction promoting Hsia's movement was the Western Hills group, bent on creating another revolutionary base in Chekiang away from the Communist influence at Canton.[2] However, the CCP (according to its own account), agreed to participate in the uprising.[3]

On October 16, Governor Hsia broke with Sun publicly, moving 3,000 troops to the Kiangsu border opposite Shanghai.[4] From there, Hsia could either defend against a move by Sun to retake Chekiang, or attack Sun's limited defenses around Shanghai. At that time Sun's *main* concern was the bitter struggle for Kiangsi, and the Chekiang rebellion was an exasperating harassment. For several days after the sixteenth, there were reports in Shanghai of Hsia's forces maneuvering nearby, even crossing the border a mere thirty-some miles away, but the activists in the city did not respond.[5] Apparently the uncertain potential of Hsia's forces and of the subversives in Shanghai slowed action from the KMT in Shanghai.[6]

To defend Shanghai for Sun Ch'uan-fang, his small garrison of 1,000 soldiers and 2,000 police tore up sections of the railroad from Hangchow, Chekiang, to Shanghai and awaited anxiously for reinforcements.[7] Hsia's attack was rebuffed, which perhaps explains why the uprising the press had predicted for the night of October 17, which reportedly had been planned by the KMT, did not take place.[8] Quite likely, the rebels had word of the imminent arrival of Sun's reinforcements, which indeed did enter on October 17 in the form of Li Pao-chang's brigade.[9] That day, after a minor skirmish near the western approach to Shanghai, Hsia's vanguard retired back into Chekiang.[10] By the twenty-second, Sun's Shanghai forces had gathered a full scale counterattack together, which quickly forced Hsia's rebels to withdraw into the Chekiang interior.

In what seems an illogically timed act, the CCP began to form an uprising *after* Hsia's retreat from the Shanghai vicinity. First the level of disruptions heightened.[11] Although KMT leader Niu Yung-chien had called off any attack on the enlarged garrison in view of Hsia's weakness, the CCP decided to go ahead, entirely depending on proletarian power. In the morning darkness of October 24, 1926, riding in on trucks, armed union pickets attacked branch police stations. At the West Gate police station, several hundred workers and students moved in with small arms and bombs. Having been prepared for the attack, the police held their posts and then forced the crowd to flee after seventeen of them had been wounded and one killed. The Shanghai garrison arrested five union activists and placed the city under martial law. At other points the attacks were feeble and even less effective.[12] At the Kiangnan Arsenal, alerted authorities had sent workers home the previous afternoon and then prepared its defense.[13] The pathetic result of the First Shanghai Uprising was merely an awareness among the revolutionaries that a small-scale armed attack within the city would not suffice.

Later, from February 19 to 24, 1927, as the NRA cleared the last of Sun's forces from nearby Chekiang, the Second Shanghai Uprising occurred. The Shanghai branch of the GLU planned the insurrection, and Lo Yi-nung, a "political genius" of the CCP Central Committee and Secretary for Kiangsu-Chekiang affairs, led the operation.[14] After deciding on February

17 to stage a general strike, on the nineteenth the GLU ordered *all* workers to begin the strike ". . . in order to wipe out the remaining power of the warlords and to show the power of the people's revolution. . . . When the strike begins, you should obey the commands of the GLU. If you have not received an order to return to work, you must not return."[15]

During the first three days, the GLU's strike efforts were aimed primarily at taking as many workers from their jobs as possible. On the second day, the CCP claimed there were 275,000 Shanghai workers on strike,[16] a figure exceeding the total membership then claimed by the GLU[17] (Foreign and Chinese press estimates ranged from 65,000 to 120,000.[18]) Although the leadership of the GLU had clearly political goals in mind for the general strike, in its strike declaration eight of the thirteen demands were economic.[19] This exemplified a problem the CCP faced in China: that the small proletariat, and the peasantry for that matter, were at an immature level of political awareness and had to be moved to action by economic incentives.

On February 22 (the fourth day) the uprising became an armed one with attacks being carried out against small branch police stations and garrison posts in order to capture more weapons to arm the workers. As the attack began against the Ch'apei police station, ten rounds were fired out in support from two ships of Sun's Shanghai fleet, which were manned by dissidents. The bombardment was aimed at Kiangnan Arsenal; although it failed to hit its mark, it did show the existence of dissension within Sun's ranks.[20]

The suppression of the uprising had begun dramatically the second day of the general strike, February 20, when Sun's garrison commander Li Pao-chang ordered broadsword-wielding execution squads into the streets of Shanghai. Relentlessly the suppression continued on the twenty-third in a large raid on Shanghai University where over sixty students were seized.[21] At Nanking on that day, Sun met with the Shantung warlord Chang Tsung-ch'ang, an associate in the Ankuochün, who agreed to relieve Sun's forces in the Shanghai-Woosung sector with a brigade of Shantung troops under Pi Shu-ch'eng. The tough, tall Shantungese were commonly used as police in China, and Sun hoped these Shantung troops would be sufficient to put down the Shanghai workers. Apparently the GLU leadership agreed, for when Pi Shu-ch'eng's brigade arrived in Shanghai the next day, the union ordered an abrupt end to the general strike.[22] The CCP blamed the failure of the Second Shanghai Uprising on the ". . . barbarous means used by Sun Ch'uan-fang in attacking and suppressing . . . , lack of sufficient coordination with the Northern Expeditionary Army, deficient preparation for an armed uprising, and insufficient efforts to cause the reactionary troops to waver."[23]

What did the Second Shanghai Uprising accomplish? Despite the declining military strength of Sun Ch'uan-fang in the southeast, the uprising failed to overthrow warlord rule in Shanghai even with the support of masses of workers and hundreds of armed pickets. It did provide a new host of martyrs; as many as 500 were killed and another 700 arrested, some of whom may have been executed. It also provided the lesson that a more effective move would have to combine a general strike, armed uprisings with the city, and ". . . sufficient coordination with the Northern Expeditionary Army." The GLU effort did attract large numbers of workers and may have increased its membership to 800,000 by April.[24]

Under more propitious circumstances, the Third Shanghai Uprising took place from March 21 through 23, 1927. Rather than attack Shanghai with its large fortified foreign community, the NRA under Chiang had decided to flank the northerners up the Yangtze so as to threaten their rail link with North China.[25] The wisdom of their decision was proven as the NRA threatened Nanking on March 20 and another pronged attack endangered the rail tie between that city and Shanghai out on the delta. By the time the uprising began, the Ankuochün south of the Yangtze was in the process of withdrawing back north of the river to avoid being trapped. On March 20, the Ankuochün defense lines between Shanghai and Nanking crumbled. Shanghai's garrison commander, Pi Shu-ch'eng, had been ordered to pull out of Shanghai, but he had decided to defect to the NRA. Thus, the uprising was not needed to aid the NRA in ending warlord resistance, but rather to implement CCP designs for the city.

The pattern of a general strike followed by armed attacks on military and police positions bear a marked resemblance to the union activities at Changsha, Hunan, the prior year. At Changsha, the Union of Labor Associations had led an unsuccessful general strike on July 8, 1926, and then used a "peace-maintenance corps" to take arms from northern soldiers as they retreated through the city (see chapter 18). A part of those captured weapons was later used to arm union pickets.[26] At Shanghai, the GLU seized the opportunity presented by the lack of resistance from the Shantung brigade, the absence of the NRA, and the presence of quantities of weapons with which to arm the CCP's proletariat. Both KMT and CCP accounts claim that the CCP hoped to set up a workers' soviet to run Shanghai once the northern authority was ended. On March 21, the GLU held rallies to gather popular support for a workers' government, and armed picket units with masses of workers as auxiliaries attacked district police stations. As each police station fell, the armed pickets would gather the defenders' arms and turn them over to the worker auxiliaries, so that the contingents of armed workers expanded rapidly. Even before the seizure of the station in the workers' quarter at Ch'apei, a thousand captured rifles had been passed out to workers.[27] The attacks by the workers allowed the venting of pent-up bitter feelings against the northerners who had ruled so harshly; the Chinese Red Cross had the unpleasant duty of gathering up numbers of decapitated northern soldiers who had resisted the workers.[28]

During the general strike and the uprising, the GLU branch at Shanghai reached its peak of power, complete with plenary sessions for the creation of the workers' soviets for the various city districts. Again the tallies of numbers of striking workers allied with the GLU leadership vary widely, but they do indicate that this general strike was much more effective than the one in February. Undoubtedly, the weakness of the warlord garrison encouraged the workers. The CCP estimates ran from 200,000 to 800,000 strikers, while the local Chinese press reported 160,000, still a considerable body of followers for the GLU.[29] The shutting down of the railroads, streetcars, telephones, electricity, and city waterworks did not seem to coincide with the needs of the NRA forces, which occupied the city on March 22. The strike continued for another two days despite the request for arbitration instead of strikes from the NRA's Shanghai commander, Pai Ch'ung-hsi. Finally General Pai ordered an end to the strike on March 24 and prohibited public service workers from striking in an attempt to return the city to its normal functioning.[30]

Since Pai issued proclamations guaranteeing the foreign community full protection and at the same time warned strikers not to "create any riots which will affect the NRA's progress," it would seem that Pai feared that the CCP hoped to provoke a foreign intervention as well as to take over the city.[31] If the Nanking Incident on March 24, 1927, was such a provocation by the CCP, the fears of Chiang's generals were real. A later CCP account claimed that the Third Shanghai Uprising "overthrew the reactionary control of the Peiyang warlords and set up a municipal government of Shanghai led by the workers."[32] The cost of this uprising was 320 dead, mainly civilians, 2,000 wounded civilians, and over 3,000 families homeless from the fires related to the combat.

A local case of workers supporting the NRA is that of the workers of the Shanghai-Nanking Railroad, including those who serviced the branch line to the port of Woosung. These workers had been involved in strikes at the Woosung maintenance yard, the general strike of Shanghai, and in scattered acts of sabotage to the tracks outside Shanghai and Chenchiang. However, the traffic of the Ankuochün continued to be heavy on the line. During the evacuation of the Ankuochün from the Yangtze's south bank, workers reportedly attempted to obstruct rail transportation by more sabotage. By removing key parts of locomotives, the workers forced numbers of the northern troops to retreat on foot.[33] But, in that instance, the worried NRA had been slow to move its forces north of the delta, and the effect of the sabotage was largely lost. With April's "Party Purification" campaign, the CCP leadership of mass organizations was disrupted, and thereafter reports of their contributions to the Northern Expedition are lacking.

However, by this time, the NRA's reputation based on its effective policy for dealing with civilians was secure. That fair dealings with the "people" paid off could be seen in efforts by Chang Tso-lin to emulate that policy. In March 1927, Chang had propaganda units operating, and began to show interest in gaining the cooperation of the peasantry. During his campaign to occupy Honan and then move south against Wuhan, Chang took pains to attract coolies through fair treatment and by forbidding looting and extortion of money and goods from civilians. The Ankuochün in Honan avoided quartering troops in homes or antagonizing the Honanese. According to reports by the Chinese press, when Chang had to ford troops and equipment across the Yellow River in March 1927, he successfully recruited the carriers and workers needed. Thereafter, the Honanese considered Chang's army to be more welcome than Wu P'ei-fu's.

The participants in the National Revolution themselves lost confidence in the role of the mass organizations in the movement. During the spring and summer months of 1927, KMT leaders were filled with doubt and indecision, first at Shanghai and then at Wuhan, because the KMT-CCP alliance and the resulting mass organizations had not been built on a firm foundation of common goals. What was good for the CCP and its organizations did not happen to coincide with what was needed for the KMT's national reunification. Never putting into practice its promise of submission to KMT authority, the CCP within the United Front diverged off on its own route. Not truly cooperating, the two parties had, at the same time, used each other and competed against each other. Such competition and mutual skepticism predated the Northern Expedition and the anti-Communist coup. Sun Yat-sen had doubts about the CCP-Russian bloc within the KMT but thought that the tiny Communist group could be checked by the sheer numbers of KMT members and even won over. Later, although the CCP and Russians played court effectively to the KMT Left, there were in mid-1926 still those in the Left who were concerned about the growing independence of the CCP's unions and peasants' associations. Even as NRA troops continually circulated through Canton and Kwangtung en route to and from the battlefronts of the expedition, the mass organizations in the Revolutionary Base ofttimes seemed to be contributing considerably less than they could have to the war effort. The controversy, as before the expedition began, swirled around the Hong Kong strike organization.

CHAPTER 22

The Organized Masses on the Home Front

The Hong Kong Strike Committee, staffed with CCP members, had been reluctant all along to align itself with the goals of the KMT. The CCP historians do not bear witness to this when they claim that the Hong Kong Strike ". . . supported the Canton National Government, strengthened the Kwangtung Revolutionary Base, and allowed the National Government to send its army on the Northern Expedition without a backward look as it proceeded forward."[1] This claim and other rhetoric was not reflected in fact and when Chiang, C-in-C of the Northern Expedition, had postponed his move to the front in July 1926, and futilely pressed for a settlement, he had become convinced that neither the strike nor the activities of the committee served any aims but those of the CCP. Other members of the regime had already been frustrated in their dealings with the Strike Committee. The Finance Minister, straining to manage the expenses of the war, had to feed tens of thousands of strikers. Unable to curtail the pickets' activities, the Canton police were ordered to accompany the strike pickets on their raids, arrests, and searches of private buildings. This approach also failed to restrain the strikers who complained that the police were often "unwilling to cooperate."[2] Nonstriking elements in Kwangtung hounded the Peasant-Labor Ministry, the Civilian Affairs Bureau, the Industrial Bureau, Municipal Bureau, and the police with petitions protesting the arbitrary activities of the pickets.[3]

With Russian support, the Strike Committee remained recalcitrant. While Chiang maneuvered for the settlement, the strikers demonstrated for a continued "hard struggle" with the Hong Kong British over the Shameen Massacre, and trumpeted their prior demands for payment of lost back wages.[4] While the NRA fought north through Hunan during the remainder of the summer of 1926, strikes, intralabor squabbles and clashes, and economic distruption continued to plague the Revolutionary Base (as also happened later at Wuhan).

In July, the union for the arsenal claimed that a ticket collector had struck an arsenal worker and called a strike, which spread by means of the GLU to include the railroad union. Arsenal production was hampered and railroad traffic disrupted for two weeks.[5] The Canton government responded with an unenforced prohibition of strikes in vital public services.

In early August, despite the arbitration of the Peasant-Labor Ministry, the Canton Postal Workers' Union called a strike to obtain demands for a 50 percent wage increase and for the right of the workers to appoint postal inspectors instead of the foreigners, who were now doing so. Su Ch'ao-cheng, concurrently chairman of both the Strike Committee and the CCP's GLU, publicly praised the strike as an opportunity for the Canton government to take over the postal administration from the "imperialists." Shanghai's Postal Workers' Union demonstrated in sympathy. However, to the chagrin of the Canton government, the strike closed down many of the postal services in the Canton headquarters and all branch offices for nine days.[6]

In August 1926, the powers of Su Ch'ao-cheng's unions in Canton seemed unassailable. The GLU "arrested" members of rival unions and confined them in the East Park headquarters. Killings and armed battles between rival unions in particular industries increased in frequency, such as the August 1 murder by one union of a rival union member, followed on August 2 and 3 by clashes between two unions of the oil shop workers in which four workers died.[7] On the fifth, after another scuffle, the KMT-affiliated KGLU gathered 60,000 workers to demonstrate and parade in protest of the wounding of their chairman and the murder of union members by rival unions. For nonpartisan unions, it became increasingly difficult to remain neutral.

By that time unions carried white flags if they were KMT affiliated and red flags if they were part of the CCP's GLU. The polarization provoked violence from the two sides, both of whom pressured the government with demands for favors. With a publicized membership of 170,000 and the claim that its membership topped its rival, the KGLU petitioned the government to bring the "renegades" at East Park to justice or face a strike.[8] Although the police prohibited the arming of union members, and seized firearms smuggled into Canton by rail, the clashes between unions continued and the resulting deaths mounted.[9]

While tension crackled in Canton within the union movement in August and September, *rural* Kwangtung saw a heightening of polarization and disorders. Word came in to Canton from government agents and guards that when they had gone out selling provincial bonds to finance the expedition, the peasants' associations had driven them out.[10] As the new peasants' associations began to organize their own antibandit corps that would give them armed power, the existing rural defense corps (*min-t'uan*) led by local gentry resisted this intrusion of rival political authority. When peasants' associations became tied in with the Strike Committee branches in rural Kwangtung, these areas also experienced the confiscation of goods and seizure of persons for boycott violations. The *min-t'uan* accused the new peasants' associations of being merely a new brand of rural bandit (*t'u-fei*) and of interfering in local government. Despite violent resistance in rural localities, membership in the Kwangtung Peasants' Association increased during the period from May through August 1926 by nearly 75,000.[11]

A rural reaction deepened through September, evident among the KMT-appointed *hsien-chang* (highest *hsien* officials) and probably tacitly approved by the Canton headquarters. Rural officials generally lined up against the rival political power of the peasants' associations in their districts. The CCP press reported that NRA garrisons stationed around the countryside fought in mid-1926 with peasants' associations at Chungshan and Hsün-teh, and at Kwan-ning the *min-t'uan* had joined with other "reactionaries" to curtail the local peasants' associations.[12] In early September, the British threatened to attack the strike pickets as pirates if their interference persisted.[13]

Thus, while the expedition moved north into Hupei and began a life-and-death combat with Sun Ch'uan-fang in Kiangsi, there *was* cause for those at the front to look back at the Revolutionary Base with apprehension. Kwangtung, the source of financial and logistical support, and fresh troops, was, itself, embroiled in social, political, and economic struggles.

In mid-September, hanging in the balance along the Kiangsi border were the fates of the expedition and the Revolutionary Base as Sun's troops pushed the NRA back into Hunan. Desperate for more support from Kwangtung, Chiang pressed the Canton government to end the fifteen-month-old Hong Kong-Kwangtung Strike. Once the Political Council approved a declaration on the "recovery of communications," Borodin and Su Ch'ao-chang backed down, but warned that the Strike Representatives' Assembly still had to be convinced.

To counter any further resistance of labor led by the strike organization, KMT leaders, especially Eugene Ch'en, set about rallying support for the National Government. On September 22, to explain the financial boost to the Northern Expedition that would result from resuming trade with Hong Kong and the British, Minister of Peasants and Workers Ch'en Shu-jen brought together 125 union representatives to hear arguments forwarded by Foreign Minister Eugene Ch'en. Again on September 25, Sun Fo, T.V. Soong, Eugene Ch'en, and others spoke to a "United Committee of Workers, Peasants, Merchants, and Students," a group exemplifying the KMT ideal of the all-class union. This committee proposed that the government guarantee the strikers work upon settlement of the strike, and requested that the strikers be brought together at a meeting where they could be informed as to why the strike should end, what the workers could hope for after a settlement, and what the major points for negotiation were.[14] Thirty thousand workers gathered for that explanation, but apparently the Strike Committee wielded too much power to be easily superceded.

Rather than chancing an upheaval among the thousands of organized and armed workers under the GLU, the Canton government chose to compromise. On September 30, when over 1,900 representatives met for a Hong Kong Strike Representatives' Assembly, Chairman Su Ch'ao-cheng announced that the strike policy had been modified, rather than terminated. Instead of the local blockade of commerce with Hong Kong, a new anti-British movement would be expanded throughout the territory that the NRA had newly conquered, and from there throughout the nation. Su Ch'ao-cheng also announced the material rewards accepted from the government in return for a peaceful end to the strike. The terms dealt with the strikers in three categories: (1) the Strike Committee hierarchy and its staff estimated to include 3,000 were to be offered posts in the government and the KMT, with the lesser staff members to have the option of assignment as propagandists with the NRA or of compensation with a C$100 Treasury Bond. (2) The more than 5,000 pickets were offered the opportunity of enlisting either with the NRA for duty in the north or in the local garrisons, or of receiving retirement compensation of C$100 Treasury Bonds. (3) The ordinary strikers who then numbered around 60,000 were offered employment on government projects or recommendations from the Labor-Peasant Ministry for jobs in the private sector. If unemployed, the strikers were to be compensated with C$100 Treasury Bonds plus temporary room and board until employed. For this settlement, the KMT authorized the Ministry of Finance to set aside C$2,000,000 for strikers' relief.[15]

The Strike Committee supported raising tariffs to support any unemployed strikers and the strike organization itself. The Committee's declaration stated that:

> . . . now that the power of the National Revolution has reached the Yangtze, it is time to change the methods we use against the imperialists. Our new policy is a change from a blockade to a boycott by the entire nation, from our own strike to a united national effort. It is now time to prepare for a new struggle. We trust this new policy highly. The rewards may be a hundred times greater than those of the past 15 months.[16]

Thus, although the Hong Kong-Kwangtung Strike was to end, the committee came out of the settlement with the prestige of presenting significant economic benefits for its members, and with expansive hope for the future. The terms asked by the Strike Committee presented a new problem for the government. Despite the financial burden placed on the Ministry of Finance by the new demands, Foreign Minister Ch'en went ahead with plans to resume trade by scheduling a reopening of communications with Hong Kong on October 1, followed by economic-diplomatic traffic as of October 10. The Strike Committee continued to threaten resistance if the government at Canton did not either get money from the British for the strikers or pay from Canton's coffers. When the demanded compensation to strikers was not delivered on the first of October, the Strike Committee began "secret" meetings to discuss ways in which the strike organization could continue the strike.[17] Before calling in the picket units scattered along the Kwangtung coast, the committee demanded that C$50,000 of the compensation for strikers be paid immediately.[18] When October 10 arrived, the Swatow branch of the Strike Committee and the local branch GLU refused to halt the enforcement of the boycott and threatened violence if the resumption of trade were forced.[19] On the thirteenth, the Strike Committee postponed disarming the many pickets who functioned to enforce the blockade and stike. Atlthough the NRA, engaged in a desperate battle in Kiangsi, called for 50,000 fresh troops, the Strike Committee postponed the commitment of its strikers.[20] In practice the Strike Committee continued to function much as it had before the strike settlement. Although the pickets were to have been disbanded, the committee replaced them with a group called the Inspection Corps, whose purpose it was, in theory, to encourage the voluntary continuance of the boycott against the British. However, the Inspection Corps went about eliciting pledges from merchants to uphold the boycott, checking for British or Hong Kong goods,[21] and pressuring passengers from traveling to Hong Kong.[22]

As late as November, the Strike Committee still had enough power to maintain its East Park headquarters and operations, where it still kept eighty Cantonese who were being punished for strikebreaking.[23] To restrain the Strike Committee from its activities, the Canton government again turned to its police. On November 15, the police department warned that any interference with loading or unloading of British ships or British goods would be suppressed. Since Septemeber 4, the British themselves had been landing marines from gunboats to clear pickets from the waterfront.[24] To dampen the smoldering frustration at the strikers' East Park headquarters, the government also announced that compensation to strikers as well as compensation to landlords for unpaid back rent due on buildings used by the Strike Committee would begin that day.[25] There again was the effort to maintain the elusive harmony of the all-class union.

That the decision to move the National Government out of Canton was related to the atmosphere of apparently polarized and unreconcilable labor struggle seems quite possible, but the leaders of the National Revolution also wanted to break down the image that clung to them of being a southern regime, and transferring to Wuhan would be a step in that direction. The week before the move to Wuhan saw a railroad strike, followed by another in the arsenal that succeeded in forcing out a KMT-affiliated union.[26]

Later in November 1926, the head of the General Political Department of the NRA flew back to Canton from the front. Teng Yen-ta had been asked by Chiang to encourage the leaders of Kwangtung province to float a provincial bond issue to contribute to the war effort and also to check with Kwangtung's military leader, Li Chi-shen, and others about the disorders among the union.[27] During Teng's fact-finding trip, he witnessed the power of the unions when they applied pressure on the government in a demonstration by several unions demanding the support of the Peasant-Labor Ministry for their needs. On November 25, to force compliance with their demands, a crowd of unionized workers slept on the premises of the Government House. Represented were armed pickets and thousands of members of the seamen's, cobblers', rice millers', tailors', street cleaners', and dispensary workers' unions. When the rice shop workers struck for higher wages, they were joined by a sympathy strike of rice millers, distillery, and dispensary workers. After the arrest of a seaman by a customs collector, the seamen's union struck.[28] The arsenal workers, who had recently come solely under a CCP union, requested the aid of the GLU in attacking the director of the Canton Arsenal.[29]

In early December, the National Government leaders recently arrived at Nanchang gathered to discuss with Chiang Kai-shek matters including the unions at the Revolutionary Base. Meanwhile, Canton bank employees and bus drivers called strikes, the telephone operators threatened to strike, and a bloody skirmish took place between rival silk workers' unions.[30] Kwangtung officials had toyed with solutions including labor's unification under government direction and increased employment of workers in government construction projects, as well as the use of force to bring the unions into orderly line. Within the group at the meetings at Nanchang and then Kuling, Borodin conceded that the union movement may have become unruly and needed direction.

The response at Nanchang involved the appointment of a new police chief and garrison commander by telegram from the C-in-C on December 7, 1926. Chiang had come about from his days as a Leftist in 1925 through his disenchantment with the CCP's mass "support" of unions and peasants' associations. In his post as leader of the Northern Expedition, an activity that strained the resources of the KMT, Chiang felt harassed by the mass organizations and had become more susceptible to counsel from anti-Communists such as Tai Chi-t'ao, reportedly an ex-Communist. They had first become acquainted as fellow lieutenants of Sun Yat-sen in Japan during their exile before the 1911 revolution.[31] As one of the leading KMT theoreticians by 1926, Tai warned Chiang that dependence on the mass organizations as a power base would only lead to disintegration of the all-class union, and that what China needed was social harmony. Creator of groups of anti-Communist agents in Canton and even Moscow, Tai had become a prime target of the CCP's anti-Right campaign, a force that Chiang was soon to feel.[32] On December 9, Canton authorities ordered the bank employees to end their strike and return to work, and prohibited any further strikes that would affect the public sector or the military supply system.[33]

ORGANIZING THE PROLETARIAT AT WUHAN

The industrial complex of Wuhan repeated the experience of Canton except on a larger scale. Under the warlords the labor movement there had been harshly restricted, although infant unions could secretly nurture their organizations and leadership within the sanctuary of the concessions.

Although the record of union development and strikes before the arrival of the NRA was negligible, within the first two months after Hanyang and Hankow had been taken, the CCP had set up an encompassing labor structure and enrolled tens of thousands of workers. By December 1926, patterned after the GLU at Canton, the CCP created a Hupei branch GLU as a leadership organ, which coordinated sixty unions that claimed 300,000 workers according to occupations and industries.[34]

Ex-Minister of Labor and Peasants Ch'en Kung-po reported that *after* the NRA occupied Hanyang and Hankow in September (while Wuchang was still under siege) the initial tactic used in organizing was to incite all the workers of a particular industry or trade to strike for *economic* benefits. Once off the job, the workers became dependent on the GLU, which provided them with guidance and workers' compensation. Thus under the GLU wing, the strikers were easily unionized. "Within the first month of our occupying Wuhan over 30 unions struck."[35] Again the CCP trained a corps of several thousand pickets, which backed the demands of the unions in the GLU. Comintern publicity, as reported by the French Communist press, was quite optimistic; a release in November, the third month of NRA occupation, reported that "labor unions have been organized under a structure similar to that of Soviets and are masters of the municipality."[36]

The pickets of the GLU functioned to add muscle both to union demands upon employers and to union demands upon workers. Collective participation in the strikes was rigidly enforced, a tactic that both strengthened the GLU's power in the economy and provided the CCP with a mass of "disciplined" proletariat. In November the GLU movement included strikes for higher wages by the Canton-Hankow Railroad workers of Hunan and Hupei and the Hupei Postal Union. While the foreign factories at Hankow were particularly hard pressed, the strikes hit the Chinese-controlled sector of the economy as well.[37]

The leaders of the "mass" movement looked to Wuhan as an ideal environment in which to build organizational strength and perfect technique. In late 1926, with Shanghai still firmly under warlord restraints, Wuhan was second in the concentration of modern industry and factory proletariat in China. Proletariat power was even more likely to blossom at Wuhan than in the smaller, more commerce-oriented Canton. Then, too, General T'ang Sheng-chih and his Eighth Army, whose presence weighed heavy in Hunan and Hupei, seemed to be more tractable to the plans of the CCP-KMT Left combine,[38] while, in Canton, General Li Chi-shen and the Canton police and garrison were leaning toward suppression of the autonomous power of the CCP's labor movement.[39] A CCP-dominated base in the heart of Central China would be in an excellent position to expand. CCP tacticians and cadre who moved to Wuhan from Shanghai and Canton during the fall of 1926 included both Liu Shao-ch'i and Li Li-san who came as representatives of the national GLU.[40] From Canton, the GLU chairman sent his trained cadre from the Strike Committee and followed later in person when the national GLU headquarters was transferred to Hankow.[41]

However, to many KMT members directing the Northern Expedition, what was not needed was a repeat of the disruption at Canton. In November, Kiangsi had finally fallen, but with the northern warlords coalesced into the new Ankuochün, the KMT could not afford conflict within its ranks. Ch'en Kung-po, associated with the KMT Left and then appointed head of the provincial finance department at Wuhan, wrote that:

> There was nothing then that influenced the order and finances of the rear more than the strikes. What the KMT needed there was stability, but what the CCP needed was strikes. . . . The base of the CCP at Wuhan at this first stage was very weak so that this tactic and strategy was necessary. Local order, stability, and sources of revenue—those were the affairs of the KMT, not the concerns of the CCP. Therefore, due to the needs of the CCP . . . Wuhan, in its depressed market and with its workers parading and petitioning all day, clearly manifested the disruption of order.[42]

The power of the CCP's mass organizations reached a peak during the winter and spring of 1927 at Wuhan with the addition of the unions and the peasants' associations in the newly conquered region of the mid-Yangtze. This was what the CCP later referred to as the Communist Period of the Wuhan government. With the success of unionization based on economic strikes, labor costs spiraled followed by prices in general as the supply of needed goods slumped due to the strikes. The loss of income in commerce, industry, and wages cut deeply into the Wuhan government's sources of revenue. Boycotts and strikes against "imperialist" factories, stores, and goods greatly decreased vital tariff revenue. Most unusual was that this regime, so engrossed in fighting a war, permitted such widespread strikes and economic dislocation at home.

The phase of the Northern Expedition in Wuhan's sphere, the campaign by the Fourth and Eighth armies against Wu P'ei-fu in northern Hupei, ground to a halt from October 1926 to April 1927—a period of six months. Although the CCP claimed that its organized masses pushed the Northern Expedition from within KMT territory and pulled it ahead of the NRA, this was not observable at Wuhan. Despite the rise of "mass power" at Wuhan, that sector of the expedition did not proceed north out of Hupei. Nor did this power, theoretically under the leadership of the KMT Left, enhance the Left's potential to dominate the National Revolution from Wuhan. Ultimately Wuhan's power to deal with Chiang and the northern warlords varied inversely with the level of CCP-led mass "support." By mid-1927 when Wuhan's KMT Left began its purge of the CCP (three months after the KMT Right had done so), its economic base had deteriorated and its military machine had suffered correspondingly.

Thus, the generalizations of Marxian-based polemicists and historians that the effects of the organized masses in the territory ahead of the NRA assured it victory and even did its fighting is open to reassessment. The leadership of the union and peasant movement did turn increasingly to the CCP, but those movements actually coincided with or *followed* the northward progress of the *military* campaign. How effective were the movements in hostile warlord territories?

CHAPTER 23

Mass Movements in Warlord Territories: Vanguard of the NRA?

If the KMT was permissive, initially, to the organization of workers and peasants, the warlord regimes were not. Except in the concessions of the nearby treaty ports, organizers faced harsh restrictions within warlord territories. An example would be the union movement and its strike on the Peking-Hankow Railroad in Honan under Wu P'ei-fu. On February 7, 1923, Wu's troops struck quickly in bloody raids on the union's meeting places in the province; thirty-nine workers were killed in the raids.[1] In Hunan, his subordinate Chao Heng-t'i disbanded the union movement with force, as had Chang Tso-lin to the north and Sun Ch'uan-fang in his five United Provinces. Also hampering unionization was the paternalism in employer-employee relations common to the large traditional sector of the economy, and even the smaller modern factories. Where industrial operations were on a small scale, it was fairly easy to keep check on factory workers. With vast unemployment, workers also feared losing their jobs to the swarms of peasants who came into the cities from the overpopulated countryside. Large-scale industrial operations with an alienated anonymous proletariat were still the exception. Outside the concessions in Shanghai and Wuhan, the military police knew the effective use of quick armed force to break up open union bravado. Suppression was bloody and common. As the Northern Expedition moved forward, how strong were the mass organizations that might have supported the NRA in the territory ahead?

Although there are popular accounts that credit unions and peasants' associations with defeating the northern warlords before the arrival of the NRA, even CCP accounts admit that in 1925 (the year of the Hong Kong-Kwangtung Strike) and 1926 (the year the expedition began) the labor movement in warlord territories *had declined.* In the areas under Chang Tso-lin, Wu P'ei-fu, Sun Ch'uan-fang, and Chang Tsung-ch'ang, the unions ". . . had practically broken down under the iron boot of the warlords. . . ."[2]

If the collaboration of the CCP (including mass organizations) and the KMT in the Northern Expedition terminated after the Wuhan purges, then the period of this support from the CCP's mass organizations would be from May 1926 to the summer of 1927. During that year the provinces taken by the NRA were Hunan, Hupei, Kiangsi, Fukien, Chekiang, Anhui, southern Kiangsu, and Honan; they thus constitute the *area* of possible support. CCP sources give an indication of the status of unions and peasants' associations in these provinces before and after their occupation by the NRA.

Most accessible to cadre from the Revolutionary Base would have been neighboring Hunan with a population of 25 million—mostly farmers. Before the NRA moved through from May to August 1926, there does seem to have been a sizable peasant element organized into associations. According to the CCP's "November Report of 1925," there were 1,367,000 peasants represented by peasants' associations in twenty-nine of the provinces *hsien.*[3] Three months after the province was occupied, when data was more accessible, a CCP report of November 1926 gave the total peasant membership in associations at 1,071,137 in fifty-four *hsien* and noted that during 1926 the membership had *increased* by 600,000 Hunanese peasants.[4]

By interpolation there would have been somewhere between 400,000 and 700,000 organized peasants in Hunan during the military campaign, and these would have been spread out over thirty to fifty *hsien*— -a membership comparable to the organized peasantry in Kwangtung. These organized peasants were the largest group of partisan peasants in any province under warlord control and their presence may relate to the predominance in the CCP press and histories of reported aid from these Hunanese peasants' associations. Of greater significance was the rate of growth *after* the occupation of Hunan: by January 1927 the membership had practically doubled to 2 million and then by April 1927 the January membership had more than doubled to 5 million.[5] Although the Northern Expedition may have seen organized peasants operating in the sector east of the Hsiang River in Hunan, "mass" power in Marxist terms does not become available until the organizers who were with the NRA advanced through Hunan. The record of small-scale peripheral support of associations during the expedition bears this out.

The union movement of Hunan was similar to the peasant movement but started from an even less impressive base. In May of 1926, a CCP report on the state of the labor movement in China notes that Hunan's union membership is "progressing," although it is less than Peking's with 10,000 members.[6] In Hunan's largest city, Changsha, the one thousand unionized workers failed to lead the general strike prior to the NRA's arrival in July. According to a later CCP account, there were, "when the Northern Expeditionary Army arrived," 60,000 union members located in five *hsien*.[7]

On September 5, 1926, one week after the NRA had cleared Hunan of Wu's forces, Hunan's provincial executive committee of the CCP congratulated the branch GLUs at Hunan and Changsha after their establishment on September 1 and noted that there were already 100,000 workers in seventy-six unions.[8] The membership then must have multiplied by ten in the two months after Changsha fell to the NRA. In another two months, by November, union membership had grown some 30 percent to 150,000.[9] Recruiting began to expand significantly from the organized base in November, and by December 20, 1926, when Mao Tse-tung addressed the Hunan Peasants and Workers' Representatives Assembly, he spoke to 175 union delegates representing 326,000 members (a doubling in one month).[10] Although this growth of CCP unions under KMT protection was impressive and indicated a total membership near to that of industrial Shanghai, the membership of the outlawed unions prior to the occupation was spread thin and by no means could have provided "mass support." That Hunan's workers and peasants made the going easier for the NRA is not supported by the chronology of the expedition. The Hunan campaign from May through August was *slower* than the ensuing Hupei campaign (August 28 to October 10) or the campaign in Kiangsi (September 4 to November 11) where the unions and peasants' associations were even less developed.[11]

Despite the presence of the industrial complex of Wuhan, there is less data available on the numbers of organized masses in Hupei preceding the arrival of the expedition. The strikes were minimal in Wuhan before the fall of Hanyang and Hankow in September 1926, but from then until December 1926 the organizers set up 200 unions in the Wuhan area.[12] The effects have been noted in chapter 21. Nearly four months after the expedition had entered Hupei, the provincial peasants' associations claimed a total membership of 100,000 members in twenty *hsien*—obviously a movement that had expanded from a very small base.[13] However, once the base was established the movement grew rapidly to include 800,000 peasants by March 1927 and 2 million by May 15.[14]

In Kiangsi where the expedition had been nearly thrown back during October 1926, the peasantry organized in associations was nominal—a mere 6,276 members spread out over 128 associations. Following the capture of Nanchang and the creation there of the Provincial Peasants' Association Office, recruiting proceeded, and, by the month's end, associations claimed over 40,000 members. By the following May, after six months, the peasants' office listed 82,617 members.[15] The minimal size of this movement sheds some light on the debacle the CCP faced in its Nanchang Uprising in August 1927, and does not indicate a source of mass support for the NRA. Although the KMT account credits organized support from the provincial postal workers, neither CCP nor KMT accounts indicate more than nominal union activity before the NRA took Kiangsi.

In KMT or CCP sources on union and peasant movements, there is much less mention of the other provinces through which the expedition progressed in late 1926 and the spring of 1927. At the January 1927 meeting, the CCP Central reported on the status of peasants' associations in various provinces, some of which were behind warlord lines.[16] The report states that in Anhui organizing the peasants was postponed until the province came under KMT authority. Chekiang's rulers had banned peasants' associations since 1921, but in March 1926 the KMT did set up a Peasants' Department for the province. By January 1927, when the NRA began to enter Chekiang, the movement was ". . . beginning to start in secret." Kiangsu also prohibited the associations, and a leader of one peasant group had been recently decapitated by military authorities; but, there also, the KMT established a Peasants' Department. However, the January report claims that *hsien*-level peasants' associations are not to be found and also that there was nothing known of any peasant organizing. This CCP report disclaims any influence on the largest secret society in Kiangsu, the Green Society (or Gang), which was so helpful to Chiang in carrying out the purge of the CCP in Shanghai four months later.

The Red Spears Secret Society of Honan, the CCP reported as being within the peasants' association framework since "the various leaders of peasants' associations have come from this kind of society." The CCP reported on the Red Spears' nonpayment of taxes, a practice promoted in the Peasants' Movement Class at Canton that had adjourned in October. However, in early May 1926 Wu P'ei-fu had quickly moved to squelch any such movement in his territory—he attacked directly the Red Spears' headquarters at Chihsien, reportedly "massacring" 5,000, burning twenty villages, and then executing another 2,000 Red Spear members.[17] Both nonpayment of rent and *taxes* were involved in Wu's suppression.

According to the CCP account, Wu P'ei-fu had also sought earlier to utilize the armed strength of the Red Spears, which claimed to be able to mobilize 300,000 peasant fighters. He had attracted their support in early 1926 to fight Feng Yü-hsiang's Kuominchün by offering the Red Spears an end to a number of taxes. After defeating the Kuominchün, Wu apparently had second thoughts about abolishing the taxes and instead tried to liquidate the Red Spears.[18] After Wu's direct action against them had decimated their leadership, the Red Spears did not surface to participate in any action against Wu in the expedition. However, to the east in Hupei, the NRA gained assistance from the Red Spears through their attacks on Chang Tso-lin and Chang Tsung-ch'ang in the summer of 1927.[19] Thus, *both* of the modern political parties sought to utilize Chinese secret societies during the Northern Expedition—a strategy that placed them in the mainstream of Chinese "revolutionary" practice since most dynastic founders made use of this source of power against the existing regime. The CCP's January report of 1927 does not state whether it includes the Red Spears in its estimate of Peasants' Association membership at 145,000 for Honan.

For Fukien, there are no sure figures on peasants' associations, although the peasantry organized in the *min-t'uan* have already been noted. The union movement in Fukien was prohibited by Sun Ch'uan-fang and his subordinate there, and neither the CCP nor the KMT makes mention of any underground modern workers' union. Of course, in Fukien as elsewhere in China then, workers and artisans were organized into guilds but apparently behind warlord lines these were not politicized. Su Ch'aocheng's GLU at Canton claimed to have a branch operating at Foochow, perhaps secretly or in the foreign concession, but there are no reports of any union activities against the warlord regime there. What radical behavior was reported took place *after* the NRA had taken Foochow in December 1926, when workers turned on missionaries and ex-officials from Sun's regime.

Outside of the few large industrial centers in China, the workers or proletariat available as "mass support" were simply not present. Where numbers did organize to better their bargaining position, or to press for a reform, they faced bloody suppression by the warlords' police and troops. In Kwangtung where the CCP did unionize considerable numbers of workers, their aims did not generally harmonize with the immediate needs of the Northern Expedition. This divergence in direction can be analyzed in the CCP's most detailed work on the proletariat during the period: *The Workers' Movement during the First Period of the National Revolutionary War*. Of the sixty-three pieces reproduced from contemporary press and partisan reports, only two deal with the support of organized workers for the expedition *at the front*. One of these two relates the contributions of the Hong Kong Strike organization and the other the aid of Hunanese union members. The largest category of articles comprises thirty pieces focusing on the creation of new unions and their growth in areas occupied by the NRA—in other words, with workers' activities behind friendly lines. None deals with the organized masses rising up against warlord power within firmly held warlord territory.

In reality, what was most significant to the CCP was this growth of mass organizations *within* KMT territories as a result of the expedition. Behind the United Front with the KMT, the CCP not only nurtured and then controlled the new, proliferating mass organizations, but it also recruited from them, and from the student unions, new membership for the CCP itself. A Commnunist history written in the fall of 1926 after the occupation of Hunan and Hupei states:

> In 1926 the status of the CCP changed. In the past we had been merely a society that had studied doctrine and had no practical application. We studied, and now participate in practical work. . . . The aim of the CCP now is to gain power among the working masses and to become close to the peasants. . . . The CCP movement is developing day by day, without ceasing.[20]

Figures on total CCP membership at the start of the expedition in July 1926 are rather inconsistent, but are close to 30,000 members.[21] From its establishment in 1921 until 1925, the membership edged toward 1,000. In 1925, with the effective Hong Kong Strike, membership shot quickly to 30,000 from the start of the strike to the launching of the expedition.[22] Most of the new members came from within the Revolutionary Base and Hong Kong. From 30,000 in July 1926, this total nearly doubled to 57,000 members by April 1927 when the KMT split with the CCP began. KMT researchers claim CCP membership at the start of the expedition to have been closer to 7,000 than 30,000, but they support the CCP claim for the spring of 1927 with a figure of 57,900 CCP members.[23]

If, as the CCP claims, their mass organizations were crucial to the expedition, what of the progress of the NRA northward once it was purged of the CCP and its organizations? Did, in fact, the NRA proceed more quickly with or without the mass organizations created by the CCP? May 1926 to April 1927, the period during which the CCP claim their masses supported the expedition, was about nine months; the expedition went on without these organizations for another fourteen months—May 1927 to June 1928. Part of this latter period was consumed with intraparty conflict during the second half of 1927.

So far as the speed with which the NRA fought its way north during the CCP period is concerned, the campaign took Hunan, Hupei, Kiangsi, Anhui, Fukien, Chekiang, southern Kiangsu, and Honan in ten months. After the anti-Communist purge, the NRA took northern Kiangsu in three-and-one-half months and then Shangtung, Hopei, northern Shansi, Suiyuan, and Chahar in less than five months during the spring and summer of 1928 for a total of eight-and-one-half months without the Communist mass organizations. The final combined military offensive during the spring of 1928 from northern Kiangsu, Honan, and Shansi on to the North China Plain saw the fastest moving action of the civil war. Even the Japanese intervention in Shantung did not slow, significantly, the schedule for the taking of Peking. During this final military phase of the unification campaign, many KMT civilians bemoaned the greatly weakened condition of the Political Department since its purge of CCP cadre. However, the NRA's Collective Armies continued north into what had long been hostile territory, far from either the Revolutionary Base or the new capital at Nanking, without being slowed noticeably by difficulties either within its ranks or in relations with the populace along the way. Thus, the organized masses in China must have been something *less* than the primary force behind the success of the Northern Expedition.

The Northern Expedition held lessons for both the CCP and the KMT on the subject of "mass organizations." The CCP's cadre, which was to be the source of its hierarchy in the decades ahead, all developed techniques and gained experience in political organization and leadership. Mao Tse-tung who established the Peasants' Movement Class and the KMT's Depart-ment of Peasants and Labor is an example. The effectiveness of anti-Japanese nationalism and the need for economic incentives were all proven during the expedition. From the organized masses, the CCP recruited a wide following and its cadre, but it learned during the anti-Communist purges and then during the series of uprisings from mid- to late 1927, all of which failed spectacularly, that the control of organized masses was not enough. In 1927 both the few proletariat and the innumerable peasantry were generally too apathetic to any but their own economic concerns to devote themselves to a political movement. Therefore, the CCP cadre—especially Mao Tse-tung—learned that a successful political movement in China required its own military arm. Even armed with Marxism, political power in China apparently had to grow out of the barrel of a gun. The lessons learned by the KMT differed as to mass organizations in that the KMT came to fear unions and peasants' associations as uncontrollable, disruptive forces whose narrow interests upset the national harmony of the all-class union. The workers and peasants had to be included in the revolution in some way, but could not be trusted to guide it.

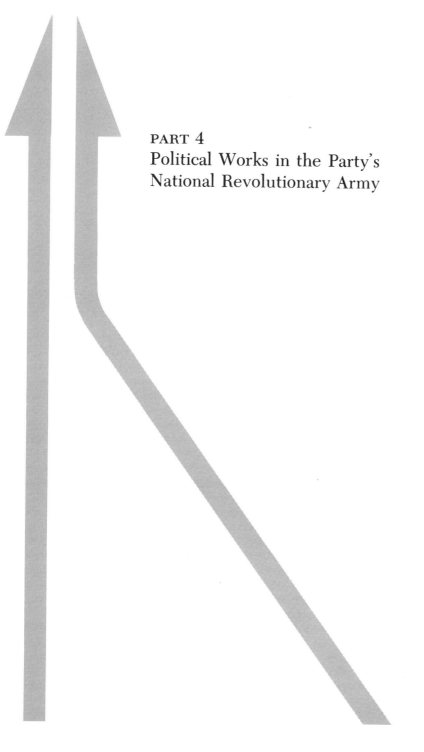

PART 4
Political Works in the Party's
National Revolutionary Army

CHAPTER 24

Politics within the Military System

The NRA proved to be far superior to its military opponents in its fighting spirit and political awareness, which were closely related. Besides the army's aggressiveness in combat, initially against staggering odds, the NRA was a great political asset. Strengthening the NRA's morale and its psychological "backbone" was the political training, the work of the Political Department, which was headed by Party Representatives, of each army corps. The political work within the military system and the Party Representatives were meant to keep the military an arm of the Party. The function and form of the Political Departments emulated the system of political commissars within Russia's Red Army. Visiting Russia with a KMT mission in the fall of 1923, Chiang admired the concept among other useful political techniques. When he returned to Canton where the KMT was struggling to create an army, first to protect itself and then to conquer the warlords of China, Chiang observed, "If the army is not to become a warlord's army, it must first of all become the Party's army."[1] To build an army that exemplified KMT ideals and responded to the Party rather than to a personal leader as did the more traditional armies of its opponents, the KMT began by providing the necessary training at its academy at Whampoa. Significantly Whampoa's official title was the Central Military and Political Academy and the original Student Army learned as much political technique as it did military science.

The first cadets to receive political training studied under Whampoa's Political Department in May 1924. At that time Liao Chung-k'ai was appointed Party Representative, and the official head of the department, Tai Chi-t'ao, received his title on May 10, 1924, followed on May 13 by the appointments of such luminaries as Wang Ching-wei, Hu Han-min, and Hsiao Yüan-ch'ung as instructors in political subjects—indicating the importance of this aspect of cadet training to the KMT.[2] The academy's first class matriculated from May through November, while its superintendent, Chiang, rose to dominate all aspects of Whampoa.[3] He and high-ranking Party leaders gave a series of political talks to indoctrinate the cadets organized into a student military unit called the Model Regiment or the Student Army—the precursor of the NRA's First Army.

The topics of these lectures contribute to an understanding of the early political orientation of the Whampoa cadets. The most significant titles are the following:

In Order to be a Member of the Revolutionary Party One Must First Understand the Value of Human Life.
Military Life as a Foundation for Spiritual Unification.
Humanity and Self-restraint are the Most Important Virtues for Military Men.
Soldiers Should Follow Discipline and Unite in Identifying the Existence of the Party as Their Own Life.
Why Party Soldiers Must Build Esprit de Corps and Character.
Hygiene Is a Most Crucial Element in a Military Organization.
The Nature and Source of Pay and the Concept of a Military Man Being Paid.
Soldiers, Members, and Officials of the Party Should Obey Its Orders Absolutely and Not Just Do as They Please.
Party Members Must Not Harbor an Attitude of Doubt and Criticism toward the Three People's Principles.
The Ways of the Revolutionary Party Should Eliminate Bad Chinese Ways.
In the Vital Relationship between Members and the Party, Members Should Acknowledge Party above Individuals.
Discipline in Conflict, Revolutionary Spirit, and the Value of Dying Are All Basic Principles Shared by Party and Army.
The Principle of National Salvation through Unification.
The Need for the Military and Its Status in the World.
The Understanding of Principles and Responsibilities Is Vital to Party Members.
The Nature of the Individual and the Nature of the Masses.

To inspire the cadets, Borodin and another member of the Russian mission exhorted them on "The Spirit Required of a Revolutionary Party" and "The Story of the Russian Revolution and the Red Army."[4]

Prominent Party spokesmen alternated in presenting lectures in the regular political course. Hu Han-min spoke on the Three People's Principles, Wang Ching-wei on Party history, and Tai Chi-t'ao on politics and economics. Since Tai performed many other official duties, as did most of the KMT cadre, he headed the Political Department only in a nominal way. Hsiao Yüan-ch'ung acted as the first department head until his resignation from the staff as a member of the Western Hills faction; Chou En-lai then took over.[5] After Wang Ching-wei succeeded Liao Chung-k'ai as Party

Representative at Whampoa, the instruction came to emphasize more socialistic elements. With Wang's approval, Chou En-lai sought to influence the cadets through use of reference books on socialism, communism, and Marxism. To accommodate the needs of the proliferating NRA, the Political Department expanded during the summer of 1925 to provide a system of political representatives. While Chou En-lai acted as Political Department head at the front during the Eastern Expeditions, another CCP member, Pao Hui-seng, headed departmental activities at Whampoa.[6] The honeymoon period of KMT-CCP collaboration in the Eastern Expeditions ended in late 1925 as Whampoa cadets and faculty became polarized over whether the Three People's Principles or Communist ideology would take precedence. Ultimately the question involved which of the two parties would lead.

The March 20, 1926, anti-Communist coup saw the ousting of Chou En-lai from his preeminence in the Political Department and the reorientation of political training about the primacy of Sun Yat-sen and his principles. The leaders of the coup also removed known CCP members from the other Political Departments, with closest attention given to the First Army. By May, the Whampoa academy periodical, *Ko-ming hua-pao* [Revolutionary pictorial] stressed the principle of the union of all revolutionary classes, and in its cartoons violently attacked Russian imperialism as being no different from other Western varieties.[7]

Although successfully ousted from the First Army, CCP members managed to hold on in the Political Departments of other army corps in the NRA. Their exclusion was prevented by the compromises achieved in April and May of 1926. What Chiang and his supporters did do was to subordinate the office of Party Representatives to the military commanders as a way of downgrading the remaining CCPs. Wang Ching-wei did have Teng Yen-ta appointed as head of the General Political Department over other Political Departments in the NRA. Teng strongly sympathized with the Communist cause—some have identified him as a CCP puppet. At the least he was responsive to direction from the Russian mission.[8] Certainly the Political Departments were the logical place in the military system for reinfiltration of CCP members. The following are known to have been active: Li Fu-chün in the Second Army Political Department, Teng Yen-ta and CCP members in the division-level Political Departments of the Fourth Army, Lin Tsu-han in the Sixth Army, cadre in division level of the Eighth Army, CCP members in Comrade Ho Lung's division of the Ninth Army, and alleged CCP members in the Fifteenth Army Political Department. Of greater relevance to this study is the function of the NRA's political arm with its troops and with the populace through which the troops marched.

The political indoctrination of the KMT's military machine was one of the tasks of the Political Department personnel trained at Whampoa. The cadets were trained to perform as either military commanders or the Party's political agents—the purveyors of revolutionary spirit. In an era when Chinese mercenaries generally stopped battles to eat their meals or to rest, the fighting spirit that the political workers inculcated was a definite advantage. The spirit involved rigid discipline, reflected in the Joint Responsibility Law of January 1925, which made the unauthorized retreat from battle by either a commanding officer or or his subordinates a capital crime. However, the fighting spirit of the NRA was related more to a belief in the morality of the revolution and troop morale than to fear of this law.

SEEING TO THE WELFARE AND MORALE OF THE NRA SOLDIERY

One of the functions of the political workers was to make certain that the Supply Corps and various army corps' commanders fed their troops well, clothed them suitably, and paid them regularly. The resulting physical well-being of the NRA was in stark contrast to the usual condition of Chinese forces and improved NRA soldiers' morale, as well as helped the army recruit from among the ubiquitous poor and hungry young men in China at that time. Besides regular food, during battles or as a reward for special duty, extra rations were issued. Kuo Mo-jo, then deputy chief of the General Political Department,* recalled the siege of Wuchang when the "Dare-to-Die" groups that tried to scale the city walls received cash bonuses for their efforts.[9] These were some of the means that helped the acquisitive Chinese identify with the NRA as an avenue of opportunity for themselves as well as for the "nation."

The hope of advancement in status within the ranks further promoted morale. Promotion based on merit and combat ability was quick— especially in the early periods of army growth between 1923 and 1926.[10] This policy was also influential in attracting defections since defecting commanders and their subordinate officers were often elevated in rank to the next strata. Promotion within the military system became more meaningful as the status of the soldiers and officers became higher in the eyes of the civilian society. Thus, the NRA also incorporated another of China's traditional social motivations—status orientation.

Giving NRA soldiers a new social status and pride in their role were the teachings that the Chinese people needed the soldiers' skills if the national revolution was to succeed. The soldier was one of the basic elements in the all-class union, which also included farmers, workers, merchants, and students (or intelligentsia). Through indoctrination, the soldiers and officers of the NRA came to identify their own well-being and futures with the national goals of the KMT. Besides study, catechisms, and lectures, the Political Department used culture to indoctrinate. The stage performances of its Blood Flower Drama Association promoted ideas and bolstered morale. The drama troop included a popular Cantonese dancing beauty and its members were recruited through the KMT's Women's Movement. Chiang, Mme. Sun Yat-sen, and other luminaries donated costumes for the shows and attended performances. The shows organized by the Political

---

*The central body that operated out of the C-in-C's headquarters, overseeing and directing the Political Departments in the army corps and other branches of the military.

Departments were often opened to the local public as well as to NRA members so that the exposure to the entertainment and ideology was made as wide as possible. Developed at Whampoa, the political use of drama was introduced into the activities of the various Political Departments.

INDOCTRINATION WITHIN THE NRA

Political workers sought the most simple means possible to indoctrinate the enlisted soldiers. Since most of them were illiterate and unaccustomed to dealing in abstract terms, the propagandists had to learn the language and interests of the troops. From army corps down through division to battalion level, the CEC of the KMT assigned Party Representatives and their Political Departments to teach the principles of the Party and the standards of military behavior.

With the policy of recruiting on a nation-wide basis, the NRA had to deal with the problem of communications in a polyglot body. There in microcosm was a major problem facing the Chinese nation. NRA political workers taught and used Kuo-yü (literally, national language or Peking dialect) with their troops. This program, too, began at Whampoa and spread among the army corps. Whampoa's instruction was carried on in Kuo-yü, although the primarily southern cadre seldom attained the purity of Pekingese pronunciation and when speaking with local citizens had to use the dialects. Similarly, the cadets came into contact with a "national" cuisine as the army cooks attempted to please as many palates as was possible. In the army corps, neither Kuo-yü nor the cuisine needed to be as universal, since the units were usually composed of troops from the same province, sharing the same dialect and culture.

The cadets and troops were also fed a steady diet of nationalism and idealism in the indoctrination. For example, all were ordered to memorize the following ten requirements for the success of the revolution and the building of a stong army dedicated to the national society:

1. Do not fear death.
2. Do not covet wealth.
3. Be willing to work hard.
4. Take pride in a good reputation.
5. Accept discipline and have a firm faith in the Three People's Principles.
6. Be willing to relinquish personal opinions.
7. Love the common people.
8. Be devoted to duty.
9. Be one in spirit.
10. Stick with your assignments until completed.

The enlisted men studied a catechism incorporating these ideals and were quizzed on them by their officers. The nationalistic element in the following is obvious:

Why must there be a revolution?   To save the nation and people.
Why should there be a national revolution?   Because we feel oppressed by the foreigners.

What are the principles with which to save the people?   The Three People's
  Principles.
Can we actually put them into practice?   We must do our best.
What is the symbol of our principles?   The Party flag.
With what have we paid for this flag?   With the lives of our martyrs.
Can you forget the violence of our betrayers?   No, we must consider them a
  national disgrace.
Do you know your enemies?   Yes, my enemies are the traitors and the
  foreign powers.
How can your humiliation be avenged?   Only in the hard struggle of the
  revolution.

One of the Whampoa cadets' catechisms manifested both Communist and
socialist elements of Sun Yat-sen's principle of the People's Livelihood:

Will the beating of all the military forces in China complete the revolution?   No, not until all corrupt officials, country bullies, and gentry are
  wiped out and the Three People's Principles realized.
As soon as we gain power, can we begin to regulate capital and equalize the
  ownership of land?   Only after we have the support of the peasant and
  worker masses can we regulate the wealth of the capitalists and equalize the
  property of the landlords.
What is the Third International?   It is a proletarian organization that aims to
  knock down the agencies of international capitalism.[11]

Carrying on political indoctrination of the enlisted men were not only
political workers, but also the cadets of Whampoa who were in training for
political as well as military functions. Observed by an experienced Political
Department worker, the cadets practiced their political techniques on the
troops and civilians.[12] During their careers, the graduates of Whampoa
were often transferred from military duty to political work,[13] and many
later were quite active in Party work. As the need for troops expanded from
1926 on, commanding officers of military units also joined in indoctrination
efforts. As the expedition proceeded north, another training duty of the
Political Department came to be the indoctrination of new troops, including recruits, prisoners, and defectors.

THE ORGANIZATIONAL STRUCTURE OF THE POLITICAL DEPARTMENTS

Since the NRA was created as the KMT's Party Army, there was considerable attention given by the Party to maintaining its control over NRA
activity. In theory this was to be accomplished by the appointment of Party
Representatives, who were concurrently heads of the Political Department. These Party Representatives were to consider the interests of the
KMT as being preeminent and to take orders from the Party as the ultimate
authority. At the highest level of the NRA as a military confederation was
the General Political Department, which functioned in the C-in-C's headquarters.

During the Northern Expedition until the Party split, Teng Yen-ta
(Tse-sheng) headed the General Political Department. A Kwangtung man

who had gained some reputation in the Revolution of 1911, Teng had studied military engineering at the Paoting Academy. From 1919 to 1923, Teng had worked in his native province for the military governor, Ch'en Chiung-ming, until the attack on Sun Yat-sen in 1923 when Teng transferred his loyalty to Sun and became a commanding officer in a brigade of the Kwangtung Army under Li Chi-shen. From his post in Li's Training Department, Teng was sent to Germany in 1924 to study military education. While in Germany and France he may have studied Marxism as well since he was close in sympathies to the Communists. As a returned student, Teng came back to the Whampoa Academy where he headed the Department of Training; later he headed Whampoa's branch academy at Ch'aochou. Most likely, Teng was an element in the compromise that followed Chiang's anti-CCP coup in 1926. Teng was not purged but seems to have been "kicked upstairs" to become head of the General Political Department of the NRA and later to act as political boss in Hupei to balance T'ang Sheng-chih.[14] Teng's Deputy Head in the General Political Department was CCP member Kuo Mo-jo, who as a literary figure specialized in NRA propaganda. Chief Soviet Advisor to the General Political Department was Teruni, probably assigned because he and Teng both knew German. Of course, Borodin oversaw his advisors and was highly influential with Teng at Wuhan.

Within each army corps, and in each of its divisions, regiments, and battalions, there was to be a Party Representative heading a Political Department. On the upper levels of the structure (the corps, division, and regiment), the Political Departments were served by secretaries who helped to administer three sections within the Political Department of the unit. These were the Propaganda, Administration, and Party Affairs sections. The Propaganda Section also had three branches, of which one gathered and published information and news for its unit; another wrote propaganda and disseminated it; and a third branch produced art for large painted posters, pamphlet illustrations, and signs.

The Administration Section's work expanded as the Political Departments increased to handle all sorts of civilian affairs in occupied territories. Besides a secretariat, this section handled all "general affairs," documents, and records. A Political Department was required by the Party to submit periodic personnel reports and data on its unit to the department above it, a craving for bureaucratic records that was not new to the Chinese.

The Party Affairs Section also had three branches, one of which organized army personnel and civilians in new areas into social and vocational groups. This provided the impetus for the organization of unions and peasants' associations in most cases. A second branch managed social activities, recreation, and welfare of the troops in the unit. A third branch, keeping watch on the unit's military command and local political conditions, acted as the military-political intelligence agency for the Party and also produced statistical reports on the unit upon request from the Party.[15]

The Political Departments' efforts to build a high moral reputation for the army apparently had a positive response in terms of the NRA's internal esprit de corps. As General Ho Ying-ch'in explained, the soldiers were taught to feel pride in their function, and they tried hard to live up to their good reputation because it gave them a status that Chinese society had not awarded to soldiers previously.[16] The reputation also elicited a valuable response from the civilian populace with which the NRA had to deal.

Joining the Army and the People

NRA political work also sought to relate the army to the "people"—the civilians in the territory through which the army moved. Sun Yat-sen had been a civilian political figure, but had been forced to acknowledge the need for military power in order to unify China. However, Sun made the point that the KMT must differ from its opponents by ". . . joining . . . the army and the people."[1] With the National Revolution's high principles and an army whose proven exemplary behavior proved its respect for the people, the campaign to unify China would receive wide support and defeat the warlords.

Indoctrinated in the ideal of his close relationship to the people, the soldier was taught that what harmed the people would ultimately harm him. Two of the NRA's key slogans were "Do Not Seize Workers" and "Do Not Live in the People's Houses." Rather than be parasites of the citizenry, the soldiers were to treat the people well and to pay them fairly for all goods and services obtained. Songs, as well as slogans, reminded the troops about the relationship between the army and the people. At Whampoa the cadets learned a song written in 1858 for Tseng Kuo-fan's soldiers in Kiangsi during their fight against the Taiping rebels.[2]

The song, *Ai-min ko* [Song of love for the people], is of interest as a source of the political ideas used by the NRA and its leaders, and gives an instance in which the KMT and CCP in their political technique do relate to the heritage of traditional China. Mao Tse-tung's later ideal of the army among the people like a fish in water evolved in part from his experience with the NRA and his respect for a heroic fellow Hunanese, Tseng Kuo-fan, a respect shared with fellow nationalist Chiang Kai-shek.[3] The song seems so relevant to the NRA and contemporary China that it is translated here in full.

Ai-min ko

Soldiers, listen carefully, loving the people is most important.
The robbers oppress the people; only we can save them.
They suffer from the thieves; all officers and soldiers must right this wrong.

Don't be lazy when making camp; don't take people's doors and boards; don't pull down their homes for a few bricks and tiles.
Don't ruin growing rice by tramping through the paddies.
Don't strike at the people's chickens and ducks, or borrow their pots and bowls.
Don't seize them to dig your trenches, nor make an inn of their homes.

When a wall is razed don't block the road, and when felling trees don't fell those on graves.
When drawing water don't take it from ponds with fish.
No matter what the argument is, concede to the people, and behave well when out on the street.

Set up camp every night, but don't go into the towns and take over the shops, nor use the houses in country villages.
Don't make an uproar over trifles, nor shove people aside if they don't make way.
If you have no money to pay, don't eat the vegetables along the road or drink the tea.

Of even greater importance, don't force them to work as coolies.
When one man is kidnapped to carry for you, his home will be torn by wailing.
A mother's eyes will be swollen from crying for her son, and a wife's tears will be used up for her husband.
Among them the local police extort their money, threatening that, if they don't send their quotas of men, then they must send money.
Their donkeys and pigs are also taken, the fowl fly, and the dogs run away, and even the fish in the ponds die of fright.

Discipline also must be strictly observed, so that soldiers do not roam freely from the camp, since once out of the camp they learn evil and always cause the civilians trouble.
Either they cheat money from the wealthy, or dally with the women of the poor families.
They get local rascals to join them in their plans, buy wine, get drunk, and then want to fight with civilians or take their anger out on the shopkeepers.

What a pity the people are beaten and bleed, and yet they dare not speak out.
Fearing the anger of the soldiers they pay them money and ask their pardon.

If you want the people to live in peace, the troops must be under discipline so
    that the soldiers do not go out, nor the sailors go ashore as they please.

At home you were good men and having become soldiers you are still men.
Military men are basically different from bandits; we are humans while they act
    as beasts.
Soldiers don't steal but the bandits do; Soldiers don't ravish but the bandits do.
If soldiers rape and steal, then they are of the same mind as the bandits, and then
    share the same, evil reputation.
If that is the case, your angered superiors will not pay your salaries.
When the people hear, they will be disgusted and not sell you their rice and salt.

An army that loves the people will be welcomed everywhere; an army that
    disturbs the people will be hated everywhere.
My soldiers have been with me a long time, and for many years have enjoyed a
    good reputation.
Now the people are worse off then ever, so please observe carefully my soldiers.
Soldiers and the people are like one family, so never take advantage of them.
If we sing the song of love for the people every day; heaven, earth, and man will
    be at peace.

The high reputation of most of the NRA elements in the Northern
Expedition testifies that many must have tried to live up to the ideals
inculcated by the army's political workers, who must have been effective in
their jobs. The political work of the NRA also had an impact on the Chinese
civilian population. It affected civilians in territory occupied by the NRA
and those under enemy control. In seeking through various forms of
propaganda to reach the people behind enemy lines, one aim of the NRA
was to turn the people actively or passively (as was most common) against
the warlord regimes. Another response hoped for was that the people
would come to relate their own needs to the goals of the KMT.

Propagandizing by the Vanguard

Contrary to some Western interpretations, there was not a mass wave of
propagandists preceding the NRA. However, as the Northern Expedition
began, there were small propaganda units and some individuals preceding
the armies that infiltrated parts of Hunan and Fukien. In hostile territory,
they made contact with local KMT members or sympathizers; sometimes
secret KMT branch headquarters were available. Both the KMT and the
CCP were close to the revolutionary tradition in China of using secret
societies as agents of subversion. The KMT had to operate in secrecy
outside its own territory since all the northern military regimes united in
opposing Communism and considered the KMT at Canton tainted "Red"
and under Russian influence. In mid-1926, Chiang and the NRA were
known as the Red General and the Red Army. Seeking outside aid in
spreading propaganda, the agents of the NRA and the Party found middle
school students to be the most responsive of all to the KMT and to the call of
nationalism and socialism.

Chinese students at that time seethed with frustrations as they were herded into overcrowded classrooms and primitive dormitories in schools whose operating funds went to feed the rapacious appetites of military authorities. Teachers went unpaid and provincial school faculties were understaffed. This was not at all acceptable in a society that revered its literate intellectuals. After graduation, students found further disappointment awaiting them in an economy that would normally only absorb a handful of the modern educated and that was slowed in its modernizing by civil strife and lack of political direction. The KMT ideology and its operation in Kwangtung gave rise to hope among many unemployed students who ultimately went south to join the National Revolution. These students were also available to cooperate with NRA Political Department propagandists when they arrived.

The Party cadre sometimes called upon students to organize parades protesting warlord practices and imperialism; the parades also served to disseminate slogans and catchwords useful to the KMT. In 1926, prior to the arrival of the expedition, provincial middle school students in Wuchang, Hupei, frequently left their classrooms to march in political parades. The common people were always curious about processions and tended to respect the students as their superiors. Although the warlord authorities generally ignored these parades as childish nonsense, the parades did spread propaganda and forged a link between students and the revolutionary movement. Those who committed themselves to the dangers of marching generally began to identify themselves with the revolution. The Student Unions of the middle schools and universities, usually organized and infiltrated by KMT sympathizers, led in organizing most of the parades.[4] In 1925 and early 1926, the Wuchang Student Union was led by a CCP member, Yün Tai-ying, who had been trained in Shanghai and sent back to his hometown to work in the student union.[5] Both the KMT and the CCP tried to utilize local talent if possible.

Spreading propaganda was difficult since severe punishments were meted out to those caught even reading KMT literature. Therefore, much of the propaganda was spread orally—a practice valuable in reaching the illiterate majority.[6] Some was spread by means of leaflets passed by students or propagandists who impersonated workers in order to move about inconspicuously. Posing as delivery men, agents could infiltrate even military camps and headquarters where they dropped their bills unnoticed.

Some of the student parades and demonstrations were called for more than propagandizing. On March 18, 1926, Peking students led by the head of Peking's KMT headquarters, Ting Wei-fen, and by Lu Yu-yü paraded against the Peking National Government. The occasion was Peking's concession to Japanese demands that international shipping not be examined by Feng Yü-hsiang's agents at Taku, an agreement that would allow shipments of Japanese aid to Peking Government authorities and to Chang Tso-lin in North China. The demonstration organizers hoped to provoke a response from the authorities that could be used to tie the Peking Government and Chang Tso-lin to their Japanese patrons. Because of his opposition to the agreement, Feng Yü-hsiang was then patronized by the Russians, the CCP, and the KMT. During the demonstration a guard force of the Peking Government obliged with a fusillade that killed between thirty and forty of the student marchers. This suppression was used to great advantage as propaganda with the intellectuals and students.[7]

The propagandists who preceded the NRA into southeastern China often emphasized the material benefits that would accrue should the new army be victorious. In addition to the benefits from the NRA's exemplary conduct and the policy of nonseizure of coolies, the Party and its army wanted to elevate the livelihoods of the people. Considering the level of political awareness and literacy on the countryside, appealing to the acquisitive nature of the Chinese peasantry seemed most practical (as it did in the 1960s and 1970s to the "revisionist" promoters of "economism"). One technique agents used in gaining the attention of the local countrymen was to enter a village eating place, order a large banquet, and invite in passersby. During the meal the agent would tell villagers of the victories being won by the NRA (always a good omen), of its concern for the well-being of the people, and of the employment of carriers and workers. After revealing his connection with the NRA, the propagandist would pay generously for the meal with *silver dollars* and tell his guests that these were what the army used to pay for carriers and food. The word would spread quickly and often upon arrival at a town or village an NRA unit would find a group of peasants or workers assembled ready for work and with a market for the sale of food and tea.[8]

As they entered Hunan during the summer of 1926, the political workers could take advantage of local calamity. Due to a combination of drought in the southern Hsiang valley and flood in the north around the lake, there were numbers of peasants unable to produce the usual food crops and desperate for ways to supplement their incomes. Since the NRA did pay well, the recruiting of carriers was simplified. So many went off as carriers that by mid-September in Changsha those who had not joined with the NRA as carriers or soldiers were able to demand exceptionally high prices for their services.[9] Apparently, starting with Canton, wherever the KMT movement expanded the cost of labor rose.

Another means of spreading revolutionary propaganda ahead of the NRA was through sympathetic coverage in the press—a natural ally of modern nationalism. Some of the newspapers in the north were secretly under KMT or CCP direction,[10] and on other newspapers, individual staff writers or editors—some Party members, some sympathizers—saw to it that the progress of the expedition and KMT movements received optimum coverage. According to a report from Peking University in November 1926, the students crowded reading rooms to read the newspapers that reported the progress of the Northern Expedition and the NRA, which was described as "brave . . . and well disciplined."[11]

Long a sanctuary for revolutionaries, like the region outside the Great Wall for the nomad conquerors, the treaty port concessions allowed the

Chinese newspapers considerably more freedom to transmit revolutionary points of view and to criticize warlord regimes.[12] Newspapers were a highly effective means of disseminating propaganda in urban areas. Concentrated in cities were students and other literates who were likely to have been exposed to concepts of nationalism through the modern public schools and mission schools. Especially in the ports, these elites were more aware of China's weakness vis-à-vis the "imperialists" and therefore susceptible to the KMT's propaganda about warlord greed and the oppression suffered by China at the hands of their imperialist cohorts. The vocabulary and issues were relevant.

In the countryside, the pragmatic Chinese were stirred to hate the warlords or favor the approaching NRA according to the effect of the antagonists on their livelihoods. Slogans such as "Don't Seize Coolies" and "Don't Live in the People's Homes" helped to separate the idealistic NRA from the rapacious warlord forces. The effectiveness of propaganda calling for the lowering of rent to 25 percent of the harvest or the equalization of land is more difficult to evaluate. On the one hand, the interest of tenant farmers in the area ahead of the army could be aroused, but on the other hand most of the farmers owned some land and might share with the gentry grave misgivings. In 1927 the landholders did effectively block the plans of the CCP for a take-over. Even in the late 1940s, Mao was still troubled by the sorting out of small peasants, middle peasants, and big peasant-landlords. Since so many of the NRA officer cadre were from landholding families, the KMT could not afford to lose the support of the gentry by promising radical land reform.

As the NRA was fast approaching Chiahsing, Chekiang, its local Party headquarters directed members to paste posters on walls around the town with slogans to "Knock Down Imperialism," "Welcome the Revolutionary Army Which Will Save Our Country and Our Fellow Citizens," "The Three People's Principles Are the Ones to Save the Nation," and "Tear Down City Walls and Construct Highways."[13] The local KMT and agents of the vanguard did spread widely the word of the pending arrival, the good reputation of the NRA, and their victories against the hated Shantung troops of Sun Ch'uan-fang. This "spreading the good news" must account in part for the large turnout of people to welcome the NRA there and elsewhere en route.

Another type of propaganda that was reminiscent of the military theoretician Sun Tzu was the use of the false rumor transmitted by the propagandists for the NRA. In one of its manifestations, agents would instigate cooperative civilians to spread the word that a large body of the NRA had been seen moving toward a particular sector of the front. The enemy commanders would pick up this information and transfer their troops to reinforce the threatened sector. Then, the NRA would glean intelligence from the civilians indicating the weakest sector in the enemy's line, which the NRA would then attack. This strategem was quite effective in the Fukien and Chekiang campaigns of the East Route Army, where rugged hills and valleys cut up the front line.[14] In the Kiangsi campaign late in 1926 and again in the Peking campaign in May of 1928, the NRA and a sympathetic press spread the rumors that the enemy leaders had lost hope. In Kiangsi the rumor used was that Sun Ch'uan-fang and his generals had sent their families back to Shanghai to avoid capture. In May 1928, it was that Chang Tso-lin's family and those of his subordinates had been sent back to Manchuria from Peking due to the hopelessness of defending Hopei.

Another function of propaganda was to ease the way for vital dealings between the NRA Supply Corps and the local people. This mundane aspect of political work done behind enemy lines arranged in advance for goods and services that the NRA would need upon arrival. As noted earlier, the propaganda quieted the anxieties of the peasants that they would be seized for work or that their goods would be confiscated by replacing these with guarantees of personal safety and assurances that providing food and drink for the NRA would be highly profitable. In the process, NRA agents lined up local people who had intimate knowledge of local topography to act as guides, and gathered civilian observations on the enemy's strength and placement. As the NRA approached, the agents were often ordered to stimulate interest among the local men in joining the NRA.

Recruiting took into account groups as well as individuals. In Fukien before the NRA invaded, a KMT front organization, the Hsin-min t'ung-chih she [The society of comrades of new Fukien], coordinated efforts for the NRA. (Quite probably the KMT with its pre-1911 history of Triad connections used secret societies as well.) The New Fukien Society men were able to meet with leaders of the rural *min-t'uan* and gain their sympathy for the KMT cause.[15] Quite possibly *min-t'uan* fought with the warlords behind their lines in Fukien; at least it is known that they definitely joined in battle with the NRA as it arrived. Apparently, part of Ho Ying-ch'in's offensive in October 1926 counted on winning a decisive victory early in the Fukien campaign in order to attract *min-t'uan* support. The practical Chinese peasantry was much more impressed by deeds and success than by ideology. If, as Chang Kuo-t'ao claimed, the *min-t'uan* were promoted by landed gentry, then this, too, would have checked the NRA Political Departments from advocating radical land reforms.[16]

The political workers ahead of the NRA also functioned as gatherers of political as well as military intelligence. In particular, the NRA's Political Departments wanted to determine whether the local officials, such as the *hsien-chang*, were respected for their ability and popular with the people. If the officials were acceptable, the KMT agents encouraged these men to stay on at their posts rather than flee with the enemy army. On the other hand if they were unpopular, perhaps from their greed or incompetence, or had fled, the political workers looked for qualified local men to eventually take the positions. For this purpose, the agents inquired after persons who were widely respected, not corrupt, and *sympathetic* to the KMT movement. Later upon the creation of provisional and then regular provincial and *hsien* governments, these men would be appointed as the new administrators—acceptable to the natives but dependent on the KMT for their authority in the absence of elections.[17]

The number of Political Department personnel and Party agents involved in propaganda work behind enemy lines can be only roughly estimated until the KMT's own records are available. A widely circulated guess of George Sokolsky in 1927 was that "at one time, it was estimated that as many as 40,000 strike pickets had marched in the van of the Nationalist Army from Canton to the Yangtze Valley."[18] But his report from Shanghai seems to be the result of confusion or it reflects the long distance from its source. When a body of Hong Kong Strike picket-trained propagandists moved north from Canton, a Western news agency may have equated this group for the entire Hong Kong organization—around 40,000 during the Hunan-Hupei Campaign. Closer to the source, Canton's *Chung-hua min-pao*, reporting on the "propagandists" for the expedition, published an organizational table in which five large groups of 180 each, or a total of 900 propagandists, were assigned to work in enemy territory ahead of the NRA as it moved north.[19] Considering the length of the front line and the territory ahead of the NRA, this would have meant several hundred Political Department workers in any one province under attack. In 1928, during the second phase of the expedition, the official table of organization for propagandists in the Political Training Department stated that there were 1,200 workers in the propaganda section.[20]

Most likely, the total number of KMT personnel moving into enemy territory *ahead* of the NRA numbered no more than one or two thousand, and even if the entire number of propagandists working for the Political Department had preceded the army, they would have numbered no more than several thousand. It is reasonable to estimate that by 1927, 6,000 cadre had been trained at Whampoa in political work. To this could be added 2,000 strike pickets. Since many of these potential political workers functioned *within* NRA units and since Political Departments left *behind* numbers of their workers as provisional civil administrators, this meant that those remaining to propagandize ahead of the armies were spread exceedingly thin along a front over 1,000 miles long in late 1926.

Thus, there was good reason for the Party to insist that the army build and maintain a good reputation in its dealings with the civilians. Since one of the greatest Chinese pastimes is passing on worldly stories about people and their politics, word about the NRA went out from the people themselves who had seen it in action, spreading ahead quickly and greatly encouraging civilian cooperation. All the military men and political workers cited here agreed that the exemplary *conduct* of the army impressed the "people" more than any ideological content in the propaganda. The Chinese people are perhaps unusually skeptical of abstract rhetoric isolated from deeds—as pointed out by Confucius and other Chinese thinkers. It was mainly the reputation of the NRA that preceded it into warlord territory.

CHAPTER 26

The NRA's Relations with Civilians in KMT Territories

As the NRA occupied an area, its Political Department cadre joined with any local KMT members available in full-time work with civilians. The absence of civilian rebellion behind the advancing NRA indicates that the work of dealing with civilians must have been effective. The cadre reinforced earlier propaganda that the people had received as to the possible benefits to be derived from the NRA and the Party it represented. When entering a remote area isolated from news of the outside, the political workers had to overcome the traditional fear of conquering soldiers.

In Fukien, as noted in chapter 20, where communication within the hilly province was still primitive, women cadre in the propaganda groups proved their effectiveness in breaking down fears about the army. The women would rap on barred village doors and in the local dialect would urge the people not to be afraid but to come out and see for themselves what kind of an army was passing through.[1] The sound of a woman's voice speaking the local dialect was quite effective in quelling fears.

The most common device used after the NRA entered a town was a "Soldiers and Civilians Joint Welcoming Meeting" held in the open air by the Political Department. To gather a crowd, political workers would spread throughout the town persuading town leaders and bystanders to attend the meeting. There a political worker would explain briefly and simply that the KMT and its army were not the radical beasts pictured in the warlord propaganda, that they did not share wives nor rape local women, nor did they demand money. The political workers would repeat the slogans "Do Not Seize Coolies" and "Do Not Live in the People's Houses," to impress upon the audience that the NRA would provide for their safety. Other cadre would sing folk songs and new revolutionary anthems to enliven the meeting. Finally, a speaker or a sympathetic town leader would urge the people to join in the work of the National Revolution by volunteering for carrier or guide work and by selling to the army the commodities it needed.[2] Althuough in some cases coolies were sufficiently touched by the appeals that they volunteered to carry for the NRA in return only for their food, more commonly porters came to work for the attractive wages. This type of meeting was perfected and used throughout the expedition.

Another popular means of propagandizing already mentioned was the parade and mass demonstration. Sometimes a parade was used to drum up interest in the "Soldiers and Civilians Joint Welcoming Meeting." Political workers joined by local Party members, students, and other sympathizers would march through the newly taken town or city to an open spot where a propaganda team would address the marchers and the spectators who had followed. The parade utilized visual and oral means of spreading ideology. Marchers carried colorful banners and signs with simple slogans and pictorial symbols of revolutionary ideology. Chanting slogans in unison, the marchers must have interested the illiterate masses and excitable students who followed the procession. The parade took advantage of the natural curiosity manifested in a society where religious and family processions had been traditional. The impact of such a parade on a quiet rural town must have been electrifying.

Street corner speeches were another means of attracting an audience used by propaganda teams of men or women. All but the speaker would dress as civilians and pose as an audience. When passersby and neighborhood people saw the beginnings of a crowd, their curiosity impelled them toward the propaganda team.[3] The cadets at Whampoa had practiced this procedure in the surrounding countryside and it shows in the new literate elite a willingness to descend from their status roles to communicate with the lower classes. This new attitude had been evident at least as early as the beginnings of the May 4 Movement when Chinese students had come down into the streets to evangelize on the national humiliation.

The artists of the Political Department's propaganda section were busiest when their military unit entered new territory. In that phase all sorts of picture posters and signs with slogans had to be painted and displayed. After painting the pictorial message and big character mottoes on large pieces of cloth, the political workers hung them with ropes, bedecking the walls along busy thoroughfares. Popular were gory posters that displayed graphically the bestial acts of warlords and imperialists.[4] The artists, trained in Western techniques of caricature and socialist realism, were so effective that Western observers mistook their artwork as "obviously" the handiwork of Russians.[5]

To maintain the reputation of the NRA as the expedition progressed, the Political Department workers continued the indoctrination program wherever encampment might be, reviewing the standards of behavior and principles of nationalism. Besides constant reminders to the troops on their behavior, the political workers took pains to remedy the results of any soldier's forgetfulness by settling complaints from civilians of thievery and misconduct from NRA soldiers. The political worker paid the civilian plaintiffs well for their losses and usually explained that the offending soldiers had been ordered out before they had been able to pay and that the political worker had been sent in their stead.

THE FUNCTION OF THE NRA's POLITICAL DEPARTMENTS IN CIVIL AFFAIRS

As military units moved ahead, their political departments assigned members to remain behind to coordinate Party affairs and arrange for the procurement of goods and services in the area. In the territory immediately behind the advancing front, one of the most important missions was to set in motion again the functions of local government so that public order would be maintained. In this effort, the political intelligence gathered by the advance agents or local KMT members helped decide whether to use existing local leadership or to appoint new persons more suitable to the Party and the local populace. Since many of the higher officials were the appointees of the warlord clique or had been in collusion with it, they often withdrew along with the warlord army. If there was no "qualified" local *hsien* or town leader, the highest Political Department authority in the battle sector appointed a political worker to remain behind to establish a provisional local government.[6] In those circumstances, the Political Departments behind the NRA lines increased their influence and expanded their political authority to the greatest degree. However, the proliferation of functions greatly strained the Political Departments, which had to work hard to make up for the shortage of trained cadre. On the local level, it was easier to select local people—either with Party connections or with a local reputation useful to the NRA.

Since the CCP retained members in some of the Political Departments, the administration of civil affairs provided them with excellent opportunities to make contact with the masses. In Hunan and Hupei through which the Fourth Army fought, its Political Department members were most numerous and developed power through the new local governments they dealt with. Since CCP members dominated the Political Departments of the Fourth Army, they were especially active in the lower levels of governing and in the Party headquarters of Hunan and Hupei.[7] It was there that CCP cadre were most able to find the right people with which to begin new mass organizations. These opportunities for the CCP were denied in the East Route sector under Ho Ying-ch'in. Ho's First Army had been purged of CCP members in March 1926, and the corps fighting along the south coast was practically devoid of CCP influence.

In September 1926, as the Political Departments expanded their functions and authority, their structures were modified by the creation of a Secretariat Branch. The Secretariat specialized in the many new civil functions, which included managing local Party headquarters, acting as judges in local courts, censoring news, organizing education, overseeing tax collecting agencies, and supervising tax police and regular police.[8] Recruiting carriers for the NRA paved the way for the organizing of unions around the transport teams and, from there, unions for the other occupations represented by the coolies. In Hunan and Hupei, in particular, unions sprang up in the wake of the NRA.

ARMY BUSINESS WITH CIVILIANS

A good example of the kind of dealings that the NRA had with local civilians would be that of the carriers already mentioned. These were attracted by the reputation for good treatment and pay in silver dollars, as well as the promise of a *local* haul of generally fifty to sixty miles. Permanent transportation teams probably accompanied the NRA for longer distances because the rural people preferred to stay within their home territory.[9] Most likely one local transportation team relayed supplies to another. This was indispensable service given the rugged terrain of South and Central China and the lack of railroads and usable roads, and the scarcity of pack horses. Also a political asset was the goodwill generated among the tens of thousands of employed rural laborers and their families. They were the judges and propagators of the NRA's reputation.

Women carriers, such as the Hakka women who worked as porters in Fukien, were a starting place for various rural women's movements furthered by the Party. The women political workers were also able to gather women and girl students to serve in medical teams that cared for NRA wounded. Here again, it was the shortage of competent cadre that restricted the expansion of Party activities among the myriad rural villages.

Political workers aided the NRA Supply Corps in the procurement of all sorts of materiel from the local people. Kuo Mo-jo related that the propaganda branch of the Fourth Army Political Department had to forage around the environs of Wuchang to buy rope and ladders to scale the city walls during an attack.[10] According to Kuo, purchases were made using "certificates of payment" there, which indicated considerable faith in the NRA on the part of the civilians who accepted them, and also that the Supply Corps must have run low on silver dollars. When setting up a local military headquarters, the political workers were the agents who borrowed or bought the furniture or had it built.[11] These business dealings all gave the propagandists an entrée with the civilians. At least *some* civilians would initially respond positively to the NRA as their potential customers.

CHAPTER 27

Problems Facing the Political Department

Since the military phase of the national revolution had to be followed by a political phase, the Political Departments that initiated that effort faced a seemingly elephantine task because the political role was so expandable. The young political workers were eager to change all of China, but their numbers were not up to the demands. Military unification had to precede the construction of the new China; therefore, the political work did not have first priority as the expedition lengthened. A succession of obstacles confronted the ambitious cadre.

POLITICAL INTEGRATION OF NEW UNITS

As the NRA enlarged its field of operations into Hupei, Kiangsi, and Fukien, the C-in-C called for the recruitment of new soldiers to replace casualties and to expand forces to cover the widening front. Some troops came into the NRA as individual volunteers, others as entire units. Incorporated by units, the NRA in Fukien gathered the *min-t'uan* under the leadership of the KMT advance agents who had arranged for their collaboration. Thus, in December 1926, after moving ahead of the NRA's East Route Forces, Kao Yi, who had worked through the comrades of the New Fukien Society, became the commanding officer of the First Independent Brigade of the East Route Forces composed of *min-t'uans*.[1]

Units that joined or defected to the NRA intact had to accept its Political Department system and, in theory, had to receive an assigned Party Representative. According to one political worker, many of the commanders of these units had already heard impressive tales about the Political Departments, to the point where commanding officers requested immediately upon joining the NRA that they be given a sign plate of the Political Department for their headquarters, more or less as a talisman to ensure "revolutionary strength."[2]

The political workers assigned by the General Political Department to new units had to set up Political Departments and begin indoctrinating and retraining the troops in Party ideology and standards. In the case of new troops recruited individually, this work had to be undertaken before they could be assigned to units already in combat. In the Kiangsi campaign, Whampoa cadets of the Fourth Class were rushed through graduation, sent north, and assigned to train and lead new troops recruited in Hupei and Kiangsi.[3] In November 1926, Chiang ordered the General Political Department to set up a program in Kiangsi to retrain over 30,000 prisoners taken that month in battle with Sun Ch'uan-fang.[4] Since the NRA attracted the defection of over thirty large units, which became army corps, the work of indoctrinating these also became practically overwhelming. In some cases, the Party Representatives were only *nominally* appointed by the KMT—being individuals already tied to the commanding officers.

Obviously with the passage of time during the fall of 1926, the personnel of the Political Departments had to assume more duties and they became more and more pressed to carry out all their functions effectively. Apparently the impetus of esprit de corps of the NRA and its reputation, which had developed at Canton and in the early days of the expedition, moved on despite the overburdened Political Departments, which had branched out into civil administration by the fall of 1926. Once experiencing the elevation in social status, or "face," which association with the NRA afforded, its soldiers were eager to live up to the reputation.

THE POLITICAL DEPARTMENTS IN THE CROSS FIRE OF THE PARTY SPLIT

During the early months of 1927, relations between the KMT and the CCP, and between proponents of the United Front and its enemies, became increasingly polarized. Anxiety among KMT members grew over the part of the NRA most under CCP influence—the General Political Department and its subordinate departments in the KMT military system. The political and economic turmoil behind the front lines and the campaign against C-in-C Chiang Kai-shek, to many, seemed to emanate from the NRA's political apparatus where known CCP members were highly visible. Teng Yen-ta, at the apex of the General Political Department and a KMT Leftist and CCP "fellow traveler," had been in a position to bring in more CCP members to head the subordinate branches. These included Kuo Mo-jo, Li Fu-chün, Lin Tsu-han, Mao Tse-tung, and Chou En-lai, among many.[5] Mao and Chou specialized in political warfare for the General Political Department, which in late 1926 created two branch offices, one to function under Lin Tsu-han at Nanking, and the other under Kuo Mo-jo at Shanghai.[6]

By the time the KMT at Shanghai and the East Route Force moved to purge the Communists from their ranks, they were well entrenched at all levels of many Political Departments. In April 1927, Shanghai's KMT headquarters nullified the authority of the Political Departments in its sector and ended the functions of Party Representatives. These posts continued on only in the Wuhan sector and there for a mere matter of months.

As the split disrupted the Party from April to August 1927, so also disintegrated the Political Department system. The new regime at Nanking removed known CCP members from its armies, but, although highly suspect, the remnant organization did continue under Wu Chih-hui's surveillance, with Ch'en Ming-shu and Liu Wen-tao as deputy chiefs. The burden of work, however, fell on the shoulders of Wu's secretary in the General Political Department, Tao Yeh-kung, secretly a CCP member.[7] As the KMT at Wuhan broke with the CCP in July, Teng Yen-ta and Kuo Mo-jo and other CCP members fell from power in the Political Departments there. With many of the ranking political workers being ousted, the shortage of replacements, and the lingering taint of Communist influence, first its funds were cut back[8] and then the new director of the East Route Forces, Pai Ch'ung-hsi, disbanded the General Political Department and its subordinate branches in the army corps on August 22, 1927.[9]

THE REENTRY OF POLITICAL WORK IN THE NRA

Chiang Kai-shek, one of the initial proponents of a political arm of the military, continued to press for a body to indoctrinate troops and to help link the NRA with the people. In January 1928, after Chiang had resumed his duties of C-in-C of the expedition, he ordered the reestablishment of a political branch of the NRA. This time it was to be under the direct control of the KMT's Military Council, which was, in theory, under the Party's Central Executive Committee. Executive, administrative, and budget control all centered in the Military Council chaired by C-in-C Chiang; thus, in practice, the Political Training Department was a function of Chiang's military headquarters. This reorganization avoided the ambiguity of direction from the Party and its army. The NRA was then less under Party control than it had been in theory earlier, except through the person of the C-in-C.

The new Political Training Department was headed by KMT theorist and firm anti-Communist Tai Chi-t'ao, with Ho Szu-yüan and Fang Chueh-hui his working deputies. Since the office of Party Representative had been discontinued, the Political Training Department lacked the direct lines with the Party Central Headquarters, but the mission and functions remained that of the old Political Departments.

Its organization differed from that of the Political Department system in that the earlier form had four sections: propaganda, administration, Party affairs, and secretariat. The new Political Training Department dropped the Party affairs sections, maintained the propaganda and secretariat sections, and added three new branches. The new branches were organization, the military history committee, and the staff of the *Kuo-min ko-ming chün jih-pao* [NRA Daily Newspaper].[10] Although the new structure fit under the C-in-C's headquarters, it was no longer included within the organization of the army corps, but it did have subdivisions attached to NRA units. Although the Collective Armies of Feng Yü-hsiang, Yen Hsi-shan, and Li Tsung-jen did have political organs, the First CA of Nanking alone had the political subdivisions of its Political Training Department attached to work with subordinate military units.

As the second phase of the Northern Expedition began in April 1928, the primary work of the Political Training Department was propagandizing. The department was to organize 1,200 cadre into a Propaganda Regiment subdivided into three corps of four divisions each. Over the Propaganda Regiment, Chiang appointed a graduate of Whampoa's Second Class. Each of the four divisions was to contain five twenty-man sections. The various units were to be available for assignment with military units at the front or wherever needed. The political workers were, therefore, much less identified with individual military units and more strongly influenced by C-in-C Chiang Kai-shek.

A continuing problem was that of manning the full complement of political workers. The Party was low on specialists in propaganda work who spoke the Mandarin of North China. One division of 100 propagandists was known to leave in early April with the Political Training Department that accompanied the Third Army. At the beginning of the expedition's second phase, the propagandists in the regiment probably numbered around 400, which meant a scaling down of propagandizing. Expansion was limited by the relatively small numbers of graduates from the Party Affairs School and the newly affiliated Hangchow Military Academy.[11]

As the expedition resumed in 1928, the propaganda included most of the earlier nationalistic rhetoric, but soft-pedaled vitriolic attacks on the foreign powers. In keeping with the reaction against Marxism, slogans avoided inciting class conflict in favor of the all-class union. The nationalistic slogans included:

> The Northern Expedition to Unify All China!
> To Establish the Nation, Complete the Expedition!
> Support the National Government!
> The National Revolutionary Army Is the People's Army!
> The Northern Expedition Will Obtain National Freedom!
> Abolish the Unequal Treaties!

Another target of the propaganda was the combine of warlords who controlled the North, the Ankuochün. This linked the warlords with local suffering and foreign imperialists. Thus, the KMT used the catchwords:

> Knock Down the Manchurian and Shantung Warlord Tools of the Imperialists!
> Knock Down the Manchurian and Shantung Warlords Who Destroy the Nation, Distress the People, and Block the Revolution!

In Shantung the KMT propaganda linked Chang Tsung-ch'ang both with the bandits who were bleeding the people (Chang had risen as a "bandit") and with the Japanese who desired Shantung as a sphere of influence.

The Northern Expedition Will Relieve the Suffering of the People!
The Northern Expedition Lessens the Burdens of the People!

This message was particularly effective in Shantung of 1928, where the rural residents faced starvation in areas ravaged by bandit forces who set fire to villages after looting them. To stir the reputedly phlegmatic northerners, other slogans exhorted:

People of the North Rise Up and Aid the Revolutionary Party!
People of the North Rise Up and Take Part in the National Revolution!
Awakened Manchurian Soldiers Join Us!

The partisan nature of the KMT's second phase of the expedition was evident in slogans such as:

The Kuomintang Should Unify China!
The Three People's Principles Are the Ones to Save the Nation and People!
The Revolutionary Army Fights for the Three People's Principles!
Fulfill the Late Dr. Sun Yat-sen's Will by Achieving the Revolution!

Since the KMT had reacted violently to the CCP threat, there was also in 1928 anti-Communist propaganda: "Exterminate the House-burning, Murderous CCP!" This warned against the revolution taking the wrong path and reflected the narrowing of the revolutionary spectrum with the end of the United Front. The part of the NRA that had been the sanctuary of CCP influence in the military and the convenient channel to reach the masses spearheaded *anti*-CCP investigation and espionage within the NRA and in its occupied territories.[12] Thus, the shrunken political arm of the NRA was burdened with the heavy duty of censoring its own ranks for hidden subversion in addition to its task of trying to subvert the enemy.

EFFORTS TO ACQUIRE THE AID OF SECRET SOCIETIES

Just as Wuhan and the CCP had earlier wished, the KMT in 1928 hoped that the Political Training Department could persuade the Red Spears Secret Society and others to fight against the warlords. The Green Society in Kiangsu had been quite valuable in supporting the anti-Communist purge the preceding year. However, the hundreds of thousands of Red Spears in North China who fought against Chang Tso-lin, Chang Tsung-ch'ang, and Sun Ch'uan-fang did so to defend their members against bandits—a term in China that can designate any militant opponent who levies taxes or exactions from the peasantry. In June 1927, the NRA successfully gained support from the Red Spears who attacked behind warlord lines in Shantung and Honan while the NRA attacked southern Shantung.[13] In April 1928, another large guerilla force of peasants operated in northern Shantung, attacking points on the Tientsin-P'u-k'ou Railroad in order to harass Chang Tso-lin and Chang Tsung-ch'ang—but attack-

ing in coordination with Yen Hsi-shan's combat in Shansi rather than with
Nanking's First CA.[14] Despite the lack of public information about collusion, it seems likely that some connection was made between the NRA and
secret societies, since the KMT had originated as a modified secret society
and many of its members, including Sun Yat-sen, had been affiliated with
other secret societies, such as the Triads and the Red and Green societies of
South and Southeast China. The KMT in Southeast Asia continued to enjoy
its ties with local Triad branches. Nonetheless, in North China it would
seem that the relative autonomy that the Red Spears enjoyed and their
own vested interests pulled them away from nationalistic pleas and efforts
to integrate the Red Spears in the NRA.

THE POLITICAL TRAINING DEPARTMENT AND
THE JAPANESE INTERVENTION

The threat in early May of a Japanese intervention in Shantung posed
new problems assigned to the Political Training Department. Chiang and
his staff adopted a policy of playing down the conflict and of negotiating a
settlement so that the Northern Expedition would not be waylaid. After
the decision, the department was ordered to modify the anti-imperialist
tone in its propaganda, and also explain to the NRA the value of patience
with Japan's provocations. Around May 5, Chiang ordered:

> . . . for the sake of foreign relations and the avoidance of a conflict and
> misunderstanding with the Japanese army, none of the Political Training De-
> partments are to post any slogans around Tsinan. The necessary corrections will
> be made in the work of propaganda.[15]

Such a policy was unpopular in an army indoctrinated to despise the
imperialists and among the growing ranks of zealous Chinese
"nationalists." When Feng Yü-hsiang, C-in-C of the Second CA, met with
Chiang near Tsinan on May 5, it was rumored that he favored an immediate
declaration of war against Japan. The press had also reported that the initial
clash with the Japanese at Tsinan had involved a vanguard unit of Feng's
troops operating in western Shantung. At their meeting, Chiang convinced
Feng that they must not divide their resources and divert their mission
from clearing North China of the warlords.[16]

The same week, Chang Tso-lin in Peking responded to the Tsinan
conflict by calling for a cease-fire.[17] Although it was in Chang's best
interests to halt the expedition before it moved on Peking, he most likely
shared the pangs of nationalism over the Japanese invasion. If anything,
Chang had *used* the Japanese rather than followed them, and his assassination at their hands less than a month later does work against his image as a
"running dog" of the Japanese imperialists. Chang had extended feelers
toward Nanking over the prospect of a joint operation against Japan,[18] but
within a week high-ranking KMT official Wu Chih-hui replied for the
Nanking regime that there would be no truce with the Ankuochün and that
the expedition would be completed in the shortest possible time.[19] Simultaneously, Chiang ordered the armies to move north across the Yellow

River by different routes. During the 1930s, Chiang similarly resisted allying with his Chinese political rival (the CCP) against the common Japanese threat. To Chiang the centrifugal forces that were constantly working to disintegrate China were the major threat.

Chiang's stance was difficult given the fervor of public feelings in favor of an immediate union of Chinese forces against Japan. Leading this war-hawk movement were numbers of Chinese students. A student corps of over 4,000 formed at Shanghai stated in its platform that "blood and iron are the only methods of obtaining diplomatic victories, of saving the Chinese race, of crushing imperialistic violence, and of saving the oppressed races of the Far East.[20] The CCP operating in Hong Kong and the treaty port concessions blasted Chiang for surrendering China to Japanese imperialism (see chapter 16) and pricked the exposed nationalistic nerve endings of the Chinese public, which the KMT had stimulated. Here is an early instance of the strong nationalistic bent of the Chinese Communists that outlived the influence of the Comintern. Nationalism was to be as valuable a political tool for Chinese and Asian Communists as the ideology of class struggle. Investigation in mid-1928 by Nanking of the propaganda work of the Political Training Department studied the explosive pitch of anti-Japanese feeling evident among political workers—long trained and motivated by anti-imperialistic ideology.

THE POLITICAL FUNCTIONS OF THE NRA IN 1928

The political techniques used in the NRA and in its dealings with civilians were modifications of those used before 1928, enhanced by a sophistication made possible by Nanking's increased financial resources. Each army corps' political unit printed a newspaper and other political materials with printing presses that accompanied the armies at the front. The First CA headquarters and Nanking's official presses also published periodicals and materials shipped to the front. In 1928 KMT aircraft increased the usage of propaganda leaflet drops, which till then had been used on a smaller scale, such as during the 1926 siege of Wuchang. However, because of the shortage of political workers in relation to the wide range of assignments, the Soldiers and Civilians Joint Welcoming Meetings could only be held in the larger towns of North China.

In 1928 the political work still included dealings with the civilian populace in the name of the NRA. Because the whole idea of organizing the masses had come under suspicion, the Political Training Department generally worked through *existing* civilian groups. As the expedition was about to resume on April 9 at the staging area of Hsüchou, across the Kiangsu border from the enemy lines in Shantung, the department gathered a joint meeting of various local groups to coordinate the servicing of the First CA. It is likely that the Hsüchou Peasants' Association represented at this meeting had been created by the KMT after Hsüchou's capture late in 1927, since a January 1927 report of the CCP indicated that the organization of Kiangsu's peasants had not yet begun.[21] Also included in a Hsüchou People's Volunteer Committee were representatives of the

Hsüchou Merchants' Association, the local police bureau, the local KMT headquarters, and *hsien* government, and the C-in-C headquarters and its Political Training Department. Its primary concern was to coordinate the recruitment of local carriers. This committee system made the department much less central to civilian affairs than it had been during the campaigns of 1926 and 1927.

In 1928 the carriers were recruited as in the earlier campaigns. North of the Yellow River, the NRA complained that its advance slowed at times due to the transportation problems.[22] In part this was due to the Japanese intersection of the Tientsin-P'u-k'ou Railroad at Tsinan, but it also may have been related to the failure of the Political Training Department to recruit carriers. The department criticized the seizure in some areas of peasants to provide carrier service.[23] This had been the case in the opening days of the expedition in 1926 and might indicate that in both cases the NRA's policy of recruiting volunteers at good pay was not uniform throughout. The political workers blamed the malpractice on the lowering discipline in the vastly proliferated NRA and on the emergency needs of the time.

In the first phase of the expedition, civilians had been gathered into medical teams to serve the wounded of the NRA—some had been groups of women students led by women's movement cadre. This work went on in 1928 near the front where *hsien* committees, such as the one at Hsüchou, organized civilian medical units for the front and in facilities behind the lines. Composing these units were Red Cross volunteers and the personnel from local "hospitals," including the common private clinics that mixed modern notions of medicine with traditional practices. Political workers coordinated the medical teams and maintained a Medical Unit at the C-in-C headquarters that provided overall supervision.[24] The committees in the expedition that linked the KMT apparatus with the populace presaged the continuing efforts of the Nanking republic and then the People's Republic of China to bring central authority down to the local level.

Besides dealing with civilian carriers and medical volunteers, the political workers continued to act as purchasing agents for the NRA. Department cadre were responsible for the chests of silver dollars that accompanied the NRA by train or on foot as it moved through new territory.[25] The first peasants who screwed up their courage and came to sell to the NRA as it moved in were rewarded with "lavish" prices. In North China, the illiterate rural people had not heard of the NRA's good reputation, but instead had been exposed to the anti-KMT propaganda that circulated there during the previous three years. Sun Ch'uan-fang's propaganda agency published anti-KMT materials and prepared news releases adverse to the revolutionary movement.[26] Chang Tsung-ch'ang's Shantung Army had propaganda posters critical of the NRA printed up on weatherproof tin sheets, which were nailed to walls and posts.[27] Within the Ankuochün elements of Chang Tso-lin and Chang Tsung-ch'ang, smartly uniformed propaganda corps worked with the civilians near the front.[28] Most northern propaganda portrayed the KMT movement as a Communist one that aimed to wipe out all Chinese culture and cherished traditions. Besides stealing the land from the people and confiscating their businesses, the propaganda pointed out that even wives were to be shared.[29] As the northern peasants came to sell to the newly arrived NRA, they observed and questioned the truth of warlord allegations. Their curiosity gave the political workers in charge of purchasing the opportunity to deny enemy propaganda and to acquaint the peasants with KMT ideology.

THE WANING OF NRA POLITICAL FUNCTIONS

The controversy over anti-Japanese propaganda in May 1928 brought the Political Training Department under fire from critics in the NRA, the Party, and the government. The expansion of the NRA into a conglomerate mass of around 1 million troops strained Nanking's resources since it had yet to exploit the revenues of the provinces within its sphere.[30] As the strain heightened, the political arm of the NRA became a casualty of economy measures, with cutbacks in funds and, in May, the disbanding of the Propaganda Regiment. The primary remaining function of the political workers shifted to providing relief for the distressed people of North China. Since in both Shantung and Hopei numbers of peasants were homeless and without proper food, the Political Training Department created and directed a Hopei-Shantung Refugee Aid Committee, which absorbed most of the cadre the rest of May.

On May 31, 1928, the order came down from Chiang that the Political Training Department units assigned to military units below the division level were to be disbanded. Those with divisions and army corps would be trimmed in proportion to the newly pared budgets allotted them.[31] In June as the expedition captured Peking, Nanking called back all political workers for investigation, after which 3,000 were reorganized.[32]

With the military reunification completed, the KMT began to phase out those functions of the Political Training Department that involved the public. Work with civilians was transferred to local and special Party headquarters. Political work with KMT troops continued, but in the decades thereafter turned inward to the problems of ideological indoctrination, troop welfare, and political surveillance. In the early 1926 phase of the expedition, the political branch of the NRA had been very influential and powerful as it indoctrinated the expanding armies and acted as public relations agent for the NRA in the civilian sea through which the NRA moved. The KMT institutionalized a revolutionary esprit de corps and standards of military discipline and behavior in the Political Department. The energy and high motivation among the young political workers were contagious. They spread first among the NRA soldiers and then, through successful contacts, affected the Chinese people. The empathy that the people generally came to feel for the National Revolutionary Army gave the army better mobility in its attacks, security in its logistics support, and pride in its reputation. Without the political workers, the NRA might never have overcome its image of being a Cantonese army. Considering the lack of affection felt by the Chinese for the troops from other provinces, the NRA might have faced a longer, more uncertain war without its political program. Unfortunately for the KMT, the program of indoctrinating the defected warlord forces was less successful. However, as with the military of other developing countries, the NRA and especially its political workers acted as agents of modernization among the premodern peasants.

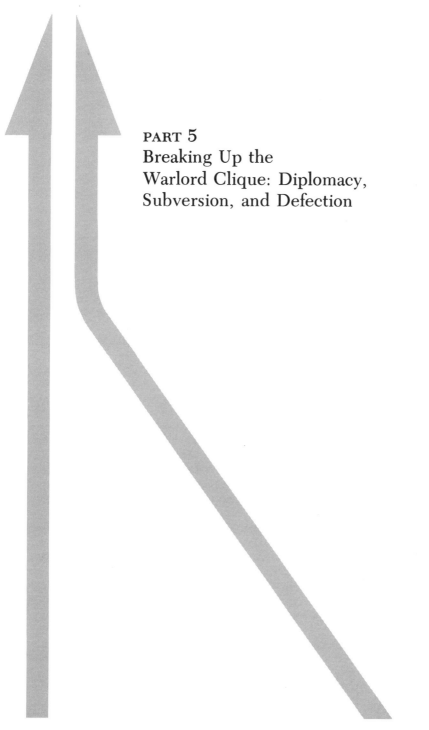

PART 5
Breaking Up the
Warlord Clique: Diplomacy,
Subversion, and Defection

CHAPTER 28

Political Offensive against Warlords

Had the KMT in the Revolutionary Base declared war on all the outside warlords and provoked their counteroffensive, the national revolutionary movement would have been overwhelmed by forces superior in numbers and firepower. When the expedition began in 1926, the entire conglomerate of the NRA approached 100,000 troops; a total of the warlord forces would have been nearly 1 million. Using practical Chinese reasoning, in the manner of Sun Tzu, the advocate of economical wars, the regime at Canton carefully conserved and consolidated their resources, and carefully considered the *weaknesses* of their opponents. Since the warlords feared each other more than the infant movement in Canton, the revolutionary diplomats sought to divide them, isolate one from another, and offer incentives for noninvolvement in or even collusion with the expedition. As in earlier dynasty founding, the revolutionaries were quite eclectic in their taste for allies—those who were not openly fighting against them were potentially for them. Initially, Canton singled out one warlord for attack (Wu P'ei-fu), promoted a rebellion within his camp, used this rebel (T'ang Sheng-chih) as an entrée to Hunan, and all the while spoke peace with the other warlords, inviting their inclusion in the *national* revolution.

In February 1926, when the KMT in Canton began publicizing nationally its hopes of opening a military offensive to reunite China, a national revolutionary movement, its manifesto denounced Wu, but carefully avoided mention of Sun Ch'uan-fang in his neighboring United Provinces.[1]

DIPLOMACY WITH THE RULER OF THE FIVE UNITED
PROVINCES, SUN CH'UAN-FANG

With his five provinces, two of which pressed rocky shoulders against
Kwangtung's borders, and three of which milled China's rice to finance a
large military machine, Sun Ch'uan-fang was not a power to take lightly. As
early as December 29, 1925, at Swatow, just across the border from Sun's
Fukien, and again on February 3, 1926, at Canton, the revolutionary
capital, Chiang and Wang Ching-wei met with representatives of Sun
Ch'uan-fang to discuss the future of their relations.[2] The details of their
"secret" agreement are not public, but involved a *quid-pro-quo* arrangement where Canton would not attack the United Provinces and Sun would
not come to Wu P'ei-fu's aid if Canton attacked Hunan.[3] Sun may also have
been invited to cooperate with the national revolutionary movement,
which, however, would have meant some lessening of Sun's power over the
fruits of earlier-won victories.[4] The agreement, as precarious as it must
have been, did begin to isolate Wu in his Central China enclave. When the
KMT brought Kwangsi under the National Government of Canton in
February 1926, Wu was becoming boxed into Hunan with only access to
the north.

While Canton's envoys met with Sun, efforts continued in March 1926 to
entice T'ang Sheng-chih and his Hunanese force away from Wu's clique.[5]
In a deal typical of those offered by the KMT, Canton probably offered
T'ang what he later received: promotion from division commander under
Wu to Eighth Army Commander under the NRA and at least chairmanship
of the *provisional* Hunan government and chairmanship of the KMT's
Hunan headquarters. The same arrangement had drawn Li Tsung-jen and
Huang Shao-hsiung of Kwangsi into the revolutionary fold. Should T'ang's
revolt succeed with NRA assistance, T'ang would move up in status in
Hunan to what amounted to acting civil-military governor of the province.
This would place him above fellow Hunanese division commander Yeh
K'ai-hsin, then contending with T'ang for military preeminence in Hunan.

To keep Sun Ch'uan-fang neutralized, Canton's agents continued to talk
with him. Frequently representing the KMT was the son of its beatified
leader.[6] Sun Fo's name carried the prestige of his father, Sun Yat-sen, and
helped to guarantee Canton's sincerity. When Sun Fo left Canton for
Shanghai and Nanking on March 4, 1926, it is likely that he met with
overlord Sun Ch'uan-fang.[7] Most of these diplomatic contacts with warlords related to the promotion of the Northern Expedition, Chiang
Kai-shek's goal in early 1926. The success of the anti-Communist coup
elevated Chiang and his plans for the expedition, so that when Sun Fo again
traveled to Shanghai in mid-April, it was on the *publicized* mission of
forming a better relationship with Sun Ch'uan-fang that might draw him
into the unification of China.[8] By July, Chinese newspapers were publishing reports of a "secret agreement of non-aggression between Kwangtung
and Fukien."[9]

Once the NRA invaded Hunan, Sun Ch'uan-fang began to have second thoughts about the wisdom of neutrality. Although his interests may have seemed closer to Wu's, Sun also relished waiting while the NRA weakened Wu's strength in Central China. By mid-July, Wu wired a request to Sun for support against the NRA offensive in Hunan, and Sun watched for the point when Wu would be worn down and yet the NRA would have to fight on two fronts. Then Sun stood a chance of taking all. By early August, Sun began reinforcing the Kiangsi border with Hunan.[10] Aware of his vulnerability, Chiang ordered his chief-of-staff on August 6 to send a telegram to Sun's Kiangsi governor stating that:

> The aim of our armies is to overthrow Wu P'ei-fu, but not to start a conflict with Kiangsi and break our friendly relationship. I have heard from Nanking that Sun has sent troops to Kiangsi and don't know if the actual idea is to attack Kwangtung or for another purpose. If he wants to maintain the friendship, he should make this clear in order to avoid a misunderstanding.[11]

Sun replied by telegram that he had reinforced Kiangsi for its defense, but he warned Chiang that he should get rid of the Russians and radicals in his camp or "we will consider you a 'red' and *will* attack."[12] Chiang's telegram on August 12 stalled by advising that Sun should be aware of the tide of revolution and not aid Wu in his continued disturbance of the nation with prolonged war.[13] In other words, Sun should be ready to reach an accommodation with the winning side. The psychology of victory in China was such that the NRA had to win victories during the opening months of the expedition if the people and warlords were to view the National Revolution as having enough power to succeed—the sanction of the Mandate of Heaven.

In August 1926, the dialog between Chiang and Sun Ch'uan-fang escalated, with messages clarifying and amplifying their respective positions, but both were merely bidding for time. In early August, KMT agents feverishly attempted to subvert Sun's subordinates in Kiangsi. By August 10, a defection settlement with Fang Pen-jen saw his secret appointment as the KMT's provisional governor of Kiangsi and the commanding officer of what would be called the Eleventh Army of the NRA, a settlement that Fang accepted on August 20.[14] In southern Kiangsi, the KMT worked on another subordinate who controlled Sun's key defense sector there. By August 23, Chiang had offered to call Lai Shih-huang's division the Fourteenth Army of the NRA under Lai's command upon his joining the revolution.[15] On the twenty-sixth, Lai secretly accepted his command from the NRA and proceeded to turn over valuable information on the defenses of Kiangsi.

To secure the NRA's mountainous *western* flank, similar offers had been made: The Kweichow troops of warlords Peng Han-chang and Wang T'ien-p'ei had become the Ninth and Tenth Armies.[16] (One of their regimental commanders was Ho Lung, destined to become a famous leader of the CCP's Red Army.) These Kweichow troops were readied to rush eastward through Hunan toward the Kiangsi border. Also on the western flank, the KMT had neutralized a group of Wu P'ei-fu's generals with a peace agreement and an invitation to join the revolution. (Late in 1926, after the NRA had proven its endurance in the victory of Kiangsi, five Szechwan militarists became the commanders of the NRA's Twentieth, Twenty-first, Twenty-second, Twenty-third, and Twenty-fourth armies.) In early August, two KMT agents had convinced the generals that Szechwan would benefit by severing ties with Wu P'ei-fu.[17] Thus, by August 21 when Chiang ordered the Third and Sixth armies to the Hunan-Kiangsi border, diplomacy and subversion had considerably strengthened the NRA's position in Hunan and weakened Sun Ch'uan-fang's Kiangsi defense. When Sun gathered his subordinates together at his Nanking headquarters on August 25, he ordered the forces of his five provinces to contribute 100,000 troops for an attack on Hunan—but he could not be sure of their reliability.[18]

After the attack on Kiangsi began on September 1, the KMT used psychological warfare to weaken the morale and unity of Sun's clique. One tactic repeated was to offer Sun and his subordinates a truce and an invitation to join the revolution. The euphemism for defection was *kuei-fu*, which includes the sense of "returning to the fold" as in the case of rebels, thus implying the original legitimacy of the Canton government, which traced itself back to the 1917 split of the southern National Assemblymen from the Peking group. By keeping the door open to *kuei-fu*, the NRA deprived Sun's followers of the situation in which they would have no alternative but to fight. This tactic also harks back to one used by Sun Tzu, the military philosopher of the warring states era that so inspired Mao Tse-tung's military thinking. Upon the outbreak of the battle for Kiangsi, the KMT sent two representatives to Sun with proposals for a settlement—all publicized to Sun's subordinates through the Chinese press. Sun countered the offer with a telegram demanding the withdrawal of NRA units from Kiangsi (although the southern quarter of the province had already fallen).[19] During the peak of fighting in October, negotiation efforts continued,[20] and in November as Sun fell back out of Kiangsi, Chiang sent another two representatives to persuade him to defect in order to save China through unification.[21] Using a classmate of Sun's from the Shikan Gakko in Japan, the KMT made contact with Sun through Li Lieh-chün, who had been appointed the KMT's chairman of the Kiangsi provincial government and military committees.[22]

In April 1927 during the prolonged struggle for Kiangsu and following Sun's loss of Shanghai, the KMT again attempted negotiations.[23] By mid-June, Sun had been forced completely out of Kiangsu and still the KMT held out offers of a deal.[24] Sun continued to hold out against being absorbed into the revolutionary tide—perhaps because the KMT was so weakened from within that its momentum had slowed. Although he and his inner coterie refused to submit to the Party, the well-publicized invitations to defect and the resultant settlements did affect his *outer* ring of satellite militarists from the five provinces, as proved by the number of defectors.

SUBVERSIVE POLITICAL MOVEMENTS WITHIN SUN'S PROVINCES

While the KMT applied military and diplomatic pressure on Sun from without, the Party also promoted peace and autonomy movements within his provinces. In Chekiang, an association of gentry pressed Sun with peace proposals in early September 1926. Through the means of the All-Chekiang Association (Ch'uan-che kung-hui), the idea was circulated of the necessity for peace between Sun and Canton in order that the South might better defend its provinces against a pending invasion by the Manchurians of the Ankuochün.[25] Leaders in the All-Chekiang Association included KMT partisans Chiang Tsung-kuei, who had headed a Ningpo Independence Movement in 1924, and Ch'u Fu-ch'eng, a KMT member who in 1925, as the vice-speaker in Peking's National Assembly, had proposed a federation of autonomous Chinese provinces.[26] By September 1926, with Sun in communication with the Manchurian clique over a possible nation-wide military confederation against the southern "Reds," the nonpartisan Chekiang leadership began to weigh Sun's northern orientation against the Canton alternative. Under KMT influence, the group proposed a cease-fire followed by the joint Sun and Chiang defense against the rumored Manchurian intrusion.[27] In early October, those Chekiangese took part in a broader movement representing *all* of Sun's United Provinces. The movement again presented demands for peace and a coalition of Sun with the KMT against Chang Tso-lin and Chang Tsung-ch'ang of North China.[28] Although these civilian peace efforts did not achieve the apparent primary goal of peace, they did label Sun as a warlord, callous to the local interests of his provincial subjects.

In late 1926, this movement against Sun evolved effectively into movements for provincial autonomy within the five United Provinces. Some of the same persons who had been active in proposing peace took part in urging Sun to turn over more authority to provincial leaders and even to permit his provinces to defend themselves. Since the partisan affiliation was obvious, Sun rightly saw this as a pro-KMT rebellion. The first provincial movement to organize was in Chekiang. There, it peaked in the coup of Governor Hsia Ch'ao who proclaimed independence on October 16, 1926, and accepted from Canton the title of Eighteenth Army commander.[29]

Once Sun had the revolt nearly suppressed, he ordered a commander of a Chekiang division, Ch'en Yi, to return to his home province to replace Hsia as civil governor.[30] Sun's Chekiang commanders, Chou Feng-ch'i and Ch'en Yi, returned with their troops to Chekiang in late November 1926, and almost immediately became ambivalent toward Sun's suzerainty. Although their relationship with the KMT was still unclear, negotiations with Party agents like Ma Hsü-lun proceeded.[31]

Autonomy movements gained momentum in Anhui, Kiangsi, and even in the municipality of Shanghai, where activists promoted a free city.[32] The subversion was most effective in Chekiang where the KMT had responsive Chekiang troops. It was there that Sun had to send troops on December 19 to regain the authority lost when Ch'en Yi and a committee for provincial government declared its independence from Sun.[33] Sun's general, Meng Ch'ao-yüeh, entered Chekiang on December 22, quickly pushing pro-KMT rebels into the hinterland where they retained but a foothold in southwestern Chekiang (where the NRA was able to enter in mid-January).

In Kiangsu, Sun's governor threatened to resign if Sun invited his fellow Ankuochün leader, Shantung warlord Chang Tsung-ch'ang, to reinforce the province. On the same grounds, the commander of the Shanghai navy claimed he would take his fleet elsewhere if Chang brought Shantung troops into the delta area. The local autonomy movement had mixed results: in Chekiang the rebels provided the NRA with a place of entry and the movement allowed for effective anti-Sun propaganda. In other southeastern provinces the movement turned public sympathy toward local rule as an alternative to Sun—an issue that had appeal to Chinese with their strong provincial loyalties—and the spokesmen for local rule surfaced later as KMT partisans. Provincial military leaders, loosely tied to Sun's federation, also responded to the pull away from Sun. In Shanghai the idea of an autonomous municipality endured, later blossoming under the nurture of the CCP, who confronted the incoming NRA with the prospect of a city run by the GLU's soviets.

THE TACTIC OF ISOLATING WARLORDS FROM POLITICAL ALLIES

During the fall of 1926 and early 1927, while the KMT focused its military and political offensive against Sun Ch'uan-fang, the Party hoped to avoid a struggle with *all* the northern warlords. Easing its criticism of Sun's ally Chang Tso-lin, the KMT in Chiang's camp claimed it attacked only Sun, not Shantung or North China. However, since this tactic had been used earlier with Sun against Wu, it became less effective in separating Sun from Chang Tso-lin and Chang Tsung-ch'ang. By May 1927, after a year of NRA victories, the northern warlords finally saw sufficient danger to join forces against the KMT. The alliance was represented by the Ankuochün and not easily shaken by artful diplomacy. But, of the northern militarists, Chang Tso-lin had been the most sympathetic to Sun Yat-sen's movement. Chiang's part of the NRA therefore worked secretly to either lull Chang Tso-lin and Chang Tsung-ch'ang into a feeling of security, safe from KMT attack, or to convince them that they were opposing a just cause and should join the National Revolution. It was in response to this strategy that the Russians and the CCP directed their concern during the heat of the lower Yangtze campaign in February 1927.

To the Russians, Chang Tso-lin represented Japanese imperialism and any KMT strategy that relieved pressure on Japan was "incorrect." They did not want to see their mission be a part to Japan's gaining a sphere of influence over North China. Thus, the Russian advisors with the KMT ordered the CCP members to work against any rapprochement between the KMT and Chang Tso-lin, and to remove Chiang as a promoter of treasonous collaboration.[34] Since the CCP members in the KMT political structure could likely gain access to Chiang's plans, it is also probable that their fears of collusion were well founded. Nevertheless, on the basis of

Chiang's prior tactics and what later occurred, it would seem that the "softening" of Chiang and the KMT toward the northern militarists was a temporary device to dissuade them from reinforcing Sun in South China. With Chang Tso-lin, the stance of the Shanghai KMT may have influenced his decision not to transfer troops south to aid Sun's sector in mid-1927. By late July, rumors of a north-south settlement were well covered by the Chinese press. Although representatives at that time traveled between Peking and Nanking, neither side would compromise its ambitions for supremacy. [35] The KMT had also used its ally Yen Hsi-shan in June to urge Chang to compromise with Nanking, but to no avail. [36] However, Chang did avoid directly committing his Manchurian troops to the lower Yangtze as he had earlier in 1925.

During the last phase of the Northern Expedition in 1928, when the offensive aimed at three of the remaining warlords, the KMT continued negotiating and inducing the enemy leaders and subordinates to submit to the National Government. In January 1928, KMT agents operated in North China to win defections before the offensive began. Lu Ho-sheng was one then sent to Tientsin's foreign concessions to coordinate the subversion of the warlord infrastructure. Later, working behind enemy lines, men such as Nan Kuei-hsiang contacted officers of the Ankuochün, especially Sun's officer cadre (possibly even Sun himself). [37] Besides selling Nanking to the northern officers, the agents carried on an effective campaign of rumors, such as the one reporting that Chang Tso-lin's clique had already conceded defeat and therefore had sent their families home to Manchuria. In a family-centered society, a move like that would attain great significance. By early June 1928, Nan Kuei-hsiang was credited with gaining access to Sun Ch'uan-fang whom Nan persuaded to flee while still possible from the futile struggle with the victorious NRA. Thus, Sun pulled his forces out of the line defending Peking, thereby making possible the final NRA break-through toward the old capital—while Sun escaped to Japanese-held Dairen. [38]

Up to this final episode, Sun had resisted KMT efforts to gain his inclusion in the national revolutionary camp, which had welcomed a wide spectrum of military leaders. Wu P'ei-fu, Chang Tso-lin, and Chang Tsung-ch'ang had likewise resisted. However, the KMT had effectively approached their subordinates, those of Wu and Sun in particular, many of whom deserted to join with the victorious revolutionaries. Two prominent warlords, secure in their mountainous strongholds, did join with the KMT in the expedition—Feng Yü-hsiang and Yen Hsi-shan.

CHAPTER 29
The Winning Over of the Big Warlords: Feng and Yen

COURTSHIP OF FENG YÜ-HSIANG

Feng had long-standing personal ties with several leading KMT members. In 1925, both Feng and Canton were supported by Russia whose ancient passion for the East was reemerging through her efforts to increase her influence in as many parts of China as possible. The Soviet Union also could rationalize these efforts as a means of attacking world capitalism and imperialism through the markets of China. Since Canton's KMT was in no position, either economically or geographically, to provide him with needed aid in 1925, Feng remained ambivalent in his attitude toward the National Revolutionary Base, although Russia did encourage their cooperation.[1] They did have in common a set of enemies—various warlords in Central and North China—and sharing no contiguous territory they had, as yet, no conflict of interests. In early 1926, the KMT began the practice of assigning men to keep open channels of communication and to establish cooperation between Canton and Feng's Kuominchün.

Influenced by many political concepts and poorly indoctrinated in the classics, Feng, the "Christian General," spoke in March 1926 of being part of a movement to realize the principles of Sun Yat-sen.[2] He had, during his prior control of Peking, been unusually permissive toward the various KMT movements active there.[3] Other motives probably outweighed ideology in March 1926 when he suffered successive defeats in Honan and Hopei.[4] This was followed in April by his retreat from Peking, and then in July from Nan-k'ou—the last pass from which one could look down on the

North China Plain.[5] Following his loss in North China, a more compliant Feng traveled to Moscow to observe Russia's progress and also sent representatives to Canton to show his willingness (or desperation) to cooperate.[6]

To present his conditions for cooperation with the NRA, Feng sent to Canton the man who had provided liaison with the KMT, Hsü Ch'ien.[7] Hsü traveled to Canton via Shanghai, and on August 25, 1926, he presented Feng's views to the National Government Committee. Feng's submission included: the employment of the KMT's system of Party Representatives in his Kuominchün, the adoption of the KMT flag, the incorporation of the Kuominchün in the NRA, and the establishment in Canton of a liaison office. Much of this settlement was nominal in nature. Feng had some of his own reliables appointed as Party Representatives to his units, and his military organization, or chain of command, was not to be restructured until *after* the completion of the expedition.[8]

Along with his continued aid from Russia,[9] Feng received from allied Canton the appointments of military councilman, National Government committeeman, and the title of Party Representative to his own Kuominchün.[10] Returning from Russia to his mountain bastion of Shensi in September 1926, Feng was met by a KMT member who had been transferred from Shanghai to advise Feng in political matters.[11] This man was Yü Yu-jen, a native of Sanyuan, Shensi, an imperial degree holder, and considered a KMT intellectual for his calligraphy, and for his years in the presidency of Shanghai University in the 1920s. Yü had demonstrated his activism by founding several modern newspapers and by his recruitment of young revolutionaries and warlord defectors. Other KMT members assigned to communicate with Feng in late 1926 were Li Lieh-chün, Niu Yung-chien, and Huang Fu—associates of the Shanghai KMT. From mid-1926 to early 1927 Feng regrouped and recouped in the safety of Shensi. In September 1926, Feng joined the KMT.[12]

By December 11, 1926, when Feng moved his troops east from Shensi's T'ung-kuan Pass and entered Honan against the Manchurian Clique, Feng had already reached an agreement with Chiang Kai-shek to act as the commander of the Center Route of the Northern Expedition.[13] Upon reaching the agreement, the KMT sent a political expert from the NRA General Political Department to advise Feng and to head the proposed Political Department for the Kuominchün. Although Feng already enjoyed the services of a number of Russian advisors supervising the receipt of Russian aid, in December the CCP sent its agents as well.[14]

As the KMT moved deeper into polarized disintegration, Feng's attitude became ambiguous; during the spring of 1927 his attitude was that of watching and awaiting the opportunities offered on each side. The Mandate of Heaven would go to whichever faction was successful—pragmatic Chinese peasants like Feng do not knowingly back losers. Feng was in a good position with over 100,000 well-trained, battle-hardened troops in westernmost Honan, a strategic position to support an attack on North China, whether from Wuhan or Nanking.

Thus, during that spring of the Party split, Wuhan and Nanking wooed Feng with great ardor (and the granting of many titles). On April 6, Wuhan, where Feng's liaison man Hsü Ch'ien had been patronized, appointed Feng to the position of C-in-C of the Second Collective Army.[15] As Feng and Wuhan pressed their attack on Chang Tso-lin's forces in Honan, Feng appeared to be cooperating. But when the province was taken and Wuhan's badly mauled forces rested near exhaustion, Feng decided that he, rather than Wuhan, should administer the province of Honan. With the capture of Honan, Feng had access to Nanking's aid via the Lung-Hai Railroad. After hearing Wuhan's offerings at Ch'engchou, Honan, Feng traveled to Hsüchou, Kiangsu, to negotiate with Chiang and Nanking leaders on June 19, 1927.

Nanking could afford to be optimistic on several counts. Wuhan, with its economy crippled by the CCP's union movement, could offer Feng little but competition over authority in Honan. By this time many of Feng's old friends in the KMT had sided with Nanking where finances were in good enough shape to aid Feng with materiel and silver that could now be shipped via the Lung-Hai Railroad. Neighboring warlord Yen Hsi-shan also argued on Nanking's behalf with Feng.[16]

By Feng's second day of discussions at Hsüchou, he had decided to accept Chiang's "ideas," which were much more tangible than Wuhan's: the promise of war materiel and financial aid. Feng and Chiang issued a joint telegram stating that their armies would, together, finish the revolution against the imperialists.[17] National reunification was practically the sole ideological link holding together the proliferating National Revolution—although Feng had come to share with Chiang a reaction against the Communists. On June 21, Feng also wired Wang Ching-wei that he considered the CCP a threat to the National Revolution and that therefore Wuhan should exile Borodin and Teng Yen-ta to Russia.[18] As Feng resumed his offensive against Chang Tso-lin in early July 1927, he directed a purge from his ranks of Wuhan appointees (mainly Chinese Communists in the Political Department).[19]

On July 7, upon the resumption of Feng's campaign in eastern Honan, Nanking appointed Feng to its reorganized Military Council, and on the eighteenth the National Government made good Chiang's promise by voting support to Feng's army by the monthly sum of C$2 million.[20] As his offensive continued, Feng wired quickly his acceptance of the aid.[21] For Nanking, Feng's new dependence on aid, now that he had broken with Russia, meant that he would be forced to keep open the arterial railroad link with Nanking—the Lung-Hai Railroad. In particular, Feng would have to cooperate in defending the rail crossing at Hsüchou, Kiangsu, from northern counteroffensives. Once lost to the NRA in mid-1927, Hsüchou remained the focal point of Feng's military pressure—thus helping the NRA as it fought a desperate defense in southern Kiangsu in August. In this manner, Feng's pressure on the Ankuochün flank in Honan diverted strength from Sun Ch'uan-fang's last attempt to retake southeastern China. That same pressure aided the NRA as it fought its way back through

Kiangsu during November and December 1927 to retake Hsüchou (for the third time in 1927). Although Feng's political submission to Nanking proved to be nominal, he was a valuable *military* asset to the Northern Expedition. Without his cooperation during the last phase of the expedition in 1928, the campaign to take Peking would have lasted much longer or perhaps would have failed.

THE WOOING OF YEN HSI-SHAN, THE MODEL GOVERNOR

Another of the big warlords of North China to *kuei-fu* to the National Revolution and thus provide vital military support was Yen Hsi-shan. His rise as the ruler of mountainous Shansi went back before 1909, when he had become acquainted with the first generation of KMT members through his ties with the T'ung-meng hui. His military studies in Japan between 1904 and 1909 had provided him contacts with nationalism, new political techniques, and the modern-educated Chinese students there—many of whom later joined the KMT.[22] His subordinate, Shang Chen, who had long been a KMT member,[23] kept him aware of the wisdom of the Three People's Principles as well as the value of the KMT's military and financial power by late 1926. Yen, Feng, and the NRA shared a mutual enemy in Chang Tso-lin with his Manchurian army poised across North China. Yen's provincial defense differed from that of Feng in the northwest in that Yen had not taken his troops outside the protective border mountains of his fortress province. While Yen did not dash out into the contest for North China, he, nevertheless, had to defend himself against the giant Manchurian army.

On December 1, 1926, Yen's representative arrived at NRA headquarters to express Yen's interest in the National Revolution, which by that time had been victorious over Wu P'ei-fu in Hunan and Hupei, and against Sun Ch'uan-fang in Kiangsi and Fukien.[24] However, on December 20, Yen also accepted tactfully Chang Tso-lin's appointment as a vice-director of the Ankuochün—since the NRA was still far from North China and Chang Tso-lin, across Shansi's border, had to be kept at bay.[25] The following week, Yen's representative again called on Chiang[26] and presumably communications continued throughout early 1927. Located in pivotal Shansi province, which loomed above the invasion corridor of the North China Plain, Yen with his 100,000 troops had much to offer the National Revolution. From Yen's northern border with Hopei, he could concentrate troops less than 150 miles from Peking.

After the KMT split there was the same contention for the affections of Yen as have already been noted for Feng. On April 22, 1927, Wuhan's Military Council appointed Yen the C-in-C of the Third Collective Army (his own Shansi Army), just as Feng had earlier been legitimized as the C-in-C of his own Second Collective Army.[27] However, Yen leaned toward the faction at wealthy Shanghai, and so, on April 8, two days after Feng had been appointed by Wuhan to head the Second CA, Yen issued a declaration ordering his troops to follow the Three People's Principles *and* to be vigilant against disorders promoted by the CCP—thus siding with the anti-Communists.[28] Perhaps due to Chiang Kai-shek's reverses in

Kiangsu, Yen's declaration was suddenly canceled the following day, April 9, 1927, and he instituted instead martial law.[29] The nearby presence of the Manchurian giant had again forced Yen to back down from a public acceptance of the revolutionary banner.

By early June 1927, at the time of the first Japanese intervention in Shantung, Yen clarified his relationship with the KMT by flying the Party flag at his provincial capital, T'aiyüan, and by renaming his army the National Revolutionary Army. A June 6 mass meeting at T'aiyüan celebrated Yen's acceptance of Nanking's title of committee chairman of the Northern Route Army of the NRA. The title was one that had been offered Yen's representative earlier in December 1926 at a meeting at Nanchang, Kiangsi.[30] However, since the NRA was not within range to aid Yen, he had to placate Chang Tso-lin with the pledge that he would not invade Ankuochün territory. Yen's public fence-straddling in North China during June 1927 included his efforts to mediate between the KMT and Chang Tso-lin, a stance he maintained for the remainder of the summer.

On July 7, 1927, Nanking's Military Council made Yen a member, and the following day Chiang sent an ex-lieutenant of Sun Ch'uan-fang from Kiangsi to pressure Yen. Fang Pen-jen, who knew the benefits to be derived from defecting, discussed with Yen the details of cooperation with Nanking.[31] At that time Nanking urged both Yen and Feng to collaborate in attacking Chang Tso-lin through Hopei and Chahar. However, they were too jittery over the prospect that the other might occupy Peking and no action ensued. All they had in common was their enemy, Chang, in Peking, and straining their efforts at cooperation was their mutual desire for the territory of Hopei and Peking. However, Chang Tso-lin helped drive them together when, in late August 1927, he attacked Yen at Shih-chia-chuang and Feng in northern Honan. As Yen retreated back into Shansi in late September he became more willing to consider a coordinated campaign against the Manchurians.

At that point Yen wired Nanking his oath of battle against Chang Tso-lin and began to counterattack north along the Peking-Suiyüan Railroad.[32] By early October 1927, Yen was definitely committed against Chang Tso-lin as he fought him on two fronts, thereby lending support to Nanking's campaign to the south in Kiangsu. Chang Tso-lin was too distracted by Yen and Feng in North China to risk reinforcing Sun Ch'uan-fang in Kiangsu. Then during the final phase of the expedition in the spring of 1928, Yen's two-pronged attack out of Shansi was incalculably important in flanking the western end of the Peking-Tientsin line. In 1927 and 1928, it was definitely better for the NRA to have Yen and Feng as cooperative military allies than to have to face them as enemies.

It must be granted that both Feng and Yen provided invaluable military support to the Northern Expedition. There might have been no reunification of China had it not been for the inclusion of warlords of their breed. Unfortunately, the military conquest was only the first phase of the centralization that Nanking desired, just as had been the case with all Chinese regimes in their founding. While the expedition was in progress the allied warlords and the Party all stood to profit from the neutralization of Chang Tso-lin's power in North China. But, with the removal of Chang Tso-lin and his clique, Yen and Feng wanted to enjoy the privilege of having the last word in their respective territories, within some loose federation of autonomous provinces. Real subordination to the KMT at Nanking had no appeal. Neither Feng nor Yen had professed any devotion to Sun Yat-sen during the Party's *lean* days at Canton. Feng had begun to show interest during his desperate retreat from Hopei into the bleakness of Inner Mongolia, and pledged his support to Chiang only after Nanking proved able to deliver substantial aid. Yen Hsi-shan, more secure in the mountain fastness of Shansi, showed overt interest in the KMT's movement only *after* the NRA's victories in South China. Thus, the KMT policy of rallying beneath its flag any willing sources of military power was initially necessary and effective, but it also helped to weaken Nanking politically because of the ambiguous motivations of those it attracted. As with earlier Chinese regimes, after the tremendous task of pulling a disintegrated China back into a whole, there still remained the equally trying chore of consolidation of central power. The KMT's successors in the 1960s were still wrestling with "odd bedfellows" whom they had drawn into their movement during their rise in the 1930s and 1940s. Vast landed states, such as China, seem to be plagued by factionalism, by a lack of consensus, since, in order to pull them into a single entity, a heterogeneous base is demanded. Just as with the large extended Chinese family, harmony was the much sought after, but elusive, political ideal.

CHAPTER 30

The Defection of Warlord Subordinates

Beside the few big warlords who came to fight under the KMT banner, there was a larger number of subordinates who, with their units, defected to the National Revolution. These men did not have suzerainty over their territory, although some did have local control over a part of their superior's satrapy. Their status was due partly to their command of a body of troops and partly to their relationship to a higher military overlord; so the circumstances of their joining the NRA were different from those of Feng and Yen. Sometimes their superiors were not natives of their provinces, in which case they were not vassals by choice.

In such relationships there was the potential for strains from provincial interests and conflicting loyalties. In most cases, subordinates were tied to their leader by the need for a powerful protective patron. As long as the relationship seemed satisfactory, it remained in effect; but if the subordinate decided he was not receiving a fair return for the services of his troops, he felt little compunction about seeking a better deal, or about joining what appeared to be the winning side.[1] Chinese inclusiveness promoted compromises in the name of harmony, and Chinese practicality encouraged ideological flexibility. The KMT's term for defection, *kuei-fu*, implying a "return to the fold," bestowed a moral status on those who changed sides.

The stories of the many and vital defections have not been told. Because of the KMT propaganda against warlords as traitorous mercenaries—running dogs of the foreign devils—earlier warlord connections were so malodorous that those generals who defected and the KMT army that they entered both avoided reference to their past. Therefore, information on the defections is sketchy and incomplete. Most of the defections involved entire units with their commanders. They occurred at crucial times and places, since strategy dictated that the wavering force await an advantageous juncture before moving to the side of the NRA. Therefore, it is useful to study some of the circumstances in the defections that were most valuable to the progress of the expedition. From numbers alone, it can be seen that the NRA grew from eight corps when the expedition began to nearly fifty corps in the First Collective Army alone by 1928. In July 1926, NRA troops had numbered less than 100,000. In a February 1928 CEC report, the three collective armies (including those of Feng and Yen) were recorded at 1 million.[2] Since Yen and Feng are credited with the considerable figure of 100,000 troops each, Nanking's forces must have numbered around 800,000. This would present a growth of 700,000 in the NRA from all sources in 1½ years (July 1926 to February 1928). The bulk of these were forces drawn from the warlords; the rest were new recruits. These defections were valuable for more than the sheer weight of their numbers.

The first *kuei-fu* of large units took place in the early phase of the Hunan campaign. The defection of T'ang Sheng-chih's division, of course, helped the NRA launch the expedition and cross, unopposed, the difficult Nanling mountains. T'ang's case may have served as an example to other subordinates of Wu P'ei-fu and Sun Ch'uan-fang, of what could be gained from joining the revolution. T'ang had been the commander of one of the four Hunan divisions of Chao Heng-t'i—Wu's man in Hunan. Upon his defection on March 25, 1926 (once Chiang's coup was consolidated), T'ang was promoted from a division to an army command and received the title of provisional governor of Hunan, his home province.[3] Ideology notwithstanding, the promotion was attractive financially.

The unstable nature of warlord finances made uncertain the salaries of their subordinates, whereas Canton's Finance Ministry was efficient and dependable. Under the NRA pay schedule, officers received the following salaries:

Major General	C$450 to C$600 monthly
Lieutenant General	C$600 to C$750
Full General	C$800

An additional monthly command allowance was:

Regiment	C$150
Division	C$500
Army Corps	C$1,500[4]

There may also have been provisions for housing and a rice allowance. Under the NRA's system then, T'ang as Eighth Army Commander was due to receive C$1,500 plus the pay due his rank (also elevated) between C$450 and C$750 per month. If his duties as Hunan's provisional governor were salaried with an allowance the total would have been considerable—a secure monthly salary of nearly C$3,000 — even with the exchange value then of two Chinese silver dollars to one U.S. dollar. Since the cost of living was low in the 1920s—an urban resident could subsist on less than C$2 per month for room and board—there was hardly the financial sacrifice involved in defection that would have repelled an acquisitive Chinese.

Besides the attractive promotions in rank and salary, the KMT held out an ideology and propaganda that helped the opponents to rationalize their shift in loyalty. In some cases, a general may have been influenced by the response of his troops to the nationalistic propaganda. After T'ang "joined the revolution," efforts continued toward winning over the other members of Wu P'ei-fu's Hunan regime. Chiang wired Wu's governor of Hunan, Chao Heng-t'i, on July 5, 1926, at Changsha as the official attack began. In his appeal Chiang used patriotism and provincialism:

> . . . Since Hunan and Kwangtung have differences, the union in the southeast is broken, allowing the Northern warlords to be even more aggressive than before. There has been continual fighting in the past few years. [Sun Ch'uan-fang's] plan of self-government under the United Provinces can damage the nation. Now the fighting in Hunan . . . is ordered by Wu P'ei-fu, whose dream is to unify the nation by force. As imperialists treat barbarian chiefs in a colony, Wu treats the southern armies—causing them to fight each other to the death. The late Tsung-li [Sun Yat-sen] called for a Northern Expedition to attack Ts'ao K'un and Wu P'ei-fu. Now with Wu risen again, I will carry out the will of Tsung-li to attack Wu. Since you were a member of the Revolutionary Party, you cannot forget your past, and should respect the freedom and independence of the nation. The friendship between you and Wu is of lesser significance. We should be cooperating in an attack on him. . . . At your order . . . we can stop the fighting in Hunan at once and quickly carry out the National Revolution.[5]

Although the appeal was not immediately fruitful, it does serve as an example of those made to warlord subordinates. Eventually, two more of the four Hunan divisions did come over to the NRA, but not until early 1927.

To secure his western flank in Kweichow, Chiang and the Canton regime appealed to Kweichow military leaders who finally committed themselves on August 10 and 11, 1926, to oppose Wu P'ei-fu. The responses of P'eng Han-chang and Wang T'ien-p'ei came as the NRA was consolidating its strength for a final campaign to clear Hunan of Wu's forces. The month before, on July 20, 1926, they had been offered the titles of Ninth and Tenth army commanders in the name of the KMT's Central Executive Committee.[6] P'eng Han-chang accepted his title of Ninth Army commander in a telegram to the KMT's CEC:

> The calamity of war in China is mainly Wu P'ei-fu's fault. He has sacrificed the lives of our fellow countrymen to please the imperialists. He breached the dam when he assisted Ts'ao K'un to buy his presidency. I, being a long-time party member, will contact the generals of the Revolutionary Army in order to coordinate an attack against Wu.[7]

He replied on behalf of his three division commanders (including Ho Lung destined for fame in the Red Army). Both the Ninth and Tenth army commanders were promoted from division commanders, and their subordinates elevated from lower unit designations to division commanders (i.e., Ho Lung moved from brigade to division commander). Although the Ninth and Tenth armies saw little heavy fighting, their presence in western Hunan did allow the NRA to concentrate its forces elsewhere.

Chiang and the KMT were not completely naïve in their handling of the defectors. With the aid of Party Representatives and and political workers, it was possible for the C-in-C's headquarters to keep the new officers under some manner of surveillance, and if deemed guilty of malpractices the newcomers might, under the right circumstances, be purged. In the case of the Ninth and Tenth army commanders, they did not keep their positions long. Within a year, the commander of the Ninth Army was arrested on the charge of allowing his corps to exhibit poor revolutionary behavior toward civilians.[8] P'eng was relieved of his command along with some of his subordinates and replaced by officers of known Party experience and reliability from the Whampoa regiment of 1925.[9] In late July 1927, following his defeat in northern Kiangsu, the Tenth Army commander was arrested and charged with misuse of funds allocated for the salaries of his personnel. He too was relieved of command.[10] Thus, defected units were particularly vulnerable to later changes in top-level leadership in favor of officers with KMT pedigrees, especially if the KMT officers were from the units' home bases.

The title of Eleventh Army commander was involved in the offensive against Sun Ch'uan-fang in Kiangsi. Sun's Kiangsi man, Fang Pen-jen, may have crossed over into Hunan to meet with Chiang at his headquarters at Hengyang where, in late July, Fang was offered the title of Eleventh Army commander for his troops in southern Kiangsi and the governorship of Kiangsi's provisional government.[11] The appointment was made on August 10, 1926, while Sun Ch'uan-fang protested that the Kiangsi people wanted peace, and then on August 21, when Fang Pen-jen had his troops aligned at the strategic P'ing-hsiang Pass, he officially accepted the NRA affiliation.[12] His defection greatly speeded the passage of the NRA into Kiangsi in early September, and Fang began a career as a loyal supporter of Chiang.[13]

Another important link in Sun's Kiangsi defenses was the division of Lai Shih-huang, stationed in southern Kiangsi opposite the Kwangtung border. KMT agents had contacted Lai and on August 23 offered him the position of Fourteenth Army commander.[14] Accepting the title in late August, Lai proceeded to pass on to the NRA plans and information valuable to the invasion of southern Kiangsi, which fell quickly in early September.[15] However, by the 1928 phase of the expedition, neither Lai nor his army corps was listed under the NRA.[16]

On August 26, 1926, another defection took place as a division commander from the Hunan Army who had entered Kiangsi for asylum under Sun accepted an agreement with the NRA. Thus, Ho Yao-tsu's Hunan division became the Second Independent Division and joined in the NRA's campaign against Sun in northern Kiangsi. By proving his reliability during the campaign at Shanghai in March 1927, Ho gained the rank of general and saw his unit elevated from a division to the Fortieth Army. Loyal to Chiang during the disintegration of the KMT in mid-1927, Ho was still a commander in the NRA during the final phase of the expedition in 1928.[17]

In the Wuhan campaign of early September 1926, NRA agents worked hard to bring about defections among Wu P'ei-fu's defenders in order to free troops for the more crucial Kiangsi campaign. On September 5, Liu Tso-lung, commander of Wu's Hupei Army Second Division, ordered his troops to cease defense of their sector at Hanyang and join in the NRA offensive against the Hanyang Arsenal. Although in communication with the NRA for some weeks, Liu timed his defection to hasten the fall of the coveted arsenal.[18] By September 15, Liu received the appointment from the National Government of commander of the Fifteenth Army, a title Liu Tso-lung retained throughout the expedition despite his temporary subordination to the treasonous T'ang Sheng-chih.[19]

As Wu P'ei-fu's position in Hupei crumbled, the commanders of two of his Honan divisions on the Yangtze's north bank defected to the NRA. Promoted to army corps commanders, Jen Ying-ch'i and Fan Chung-hsiung accepted command of the Twelfth and Thirteenth armies under the NRA on September 12.[20] Further additions to these Honan units of the KMT occurred at the end of the siege of Wuchang. Then the Honan Army Third Division opened the city gate and surrendered, thereby allowing the capture of Wuchang under generous terms of surrender.[21]

In late September 1926, at a key border sector in the Fukien defense line, the defection of one of Sun Ch'uan-fang's brigades greatly speeded the invasion of the province. Secretly cooperating with the NRA, the brigade commander had provided the enemy's plan of defense and other military intelligence. In this case the reward was the promotion of the commanding officer from brigade level to the command of the NRA's new Seventeenth Army—an unusually rapid promotion that skipped the division level.[22] To this Seventeenth Army, the East Route of the NRA added other defectors in Fukien, in particular a brigade from Foochow, which allowed that provincial capital to be captured with little resistance. The Foochow brigade commander advanced to division commander in the Seventeenth Army.[23] Although the NRA and its Political Departments were constantly recruiting new troops, the advancement of unit designations, in many cases must have meant undermanned units according to accepted complements—and difficulties in assessing unit strength. This would mean that extra effort was necessary on the part of the new Political Department workers in the units (if assigned) and the NRA paymasters. In 1928, the Seventeenth Army was still listed under the First CA, commanded by Ts'ao Wan-hsün—the original defector.

The Chinese press in the fall of 1926 reported another KMT tactic within its newly conquered territories that may have influenced later defections. Following the occupation of Hupei in October and November 1926, the KMT confiscated the provincial properties of the defeated generals and officials of Wu P'ei-fu. The value of the confiscated property of five high-ranking members of Wu's regime in Hupei, alone, was estimated at between ten and twenty million silver dollars.[24] Some of this capital had been left in local banks and some was in movable property. The new occupation authorities in the larger cities moved into residences confiscated from the earlier military regime—such as the villa in Hankow where Borodin made his headquarters that had belonged to the Szechwan general, Yang Sen.[25] Borodin's car once had been Wu P'ei-fu's.[26] The knowledge that the property of the defeated clique would be confiscated on the one hand and that financial rewards were forthcoming to the defectors on the other hand must have acted as a spur to *kuei-fu*.

As Sun's Kiangsi defense met with defeat, his rapport with the provincial armies of his five United Provinces deteriorated, along with the morale of his subordinates. The Party propagandists effectively pointed up the folly of southeastern provincials sacrificing their lives for the benefit of a Shantung warlord who was not truly concerned with the people of Anhui, Chekiang, and Kiangsu. It can be seen, then, that the national revolutionaries were willing to use provincialism when necessary to appeal to the provincial military leaders.

The KMT's efforts to disintegrate the United Provinces through provincial autonomy movements were most effective in Chekiang. Chekiang men filled posts in the Canton administration, the NRA, and were active in the KMT in Shanghai. Many in the commercial sector of Shanghai were from Ningpo, Chekiang, Chiang's place of origin. Thus, KMT representatives and Chekiang leaders were able to communicate with Sun's governor, Hsia Ch'ao, during the summer of 1926. On October 16, Hsia announced that he would side with the KMT against Sun. On that day the KMT designated the troops under Hsia's command as the Eighteenth Army and ordered them toward the Chekiang border nearest Shanghai.[27] Concurrent with his military appointment was Hsia's appointment by the KMT as its provisional governor of Chekiang.[28] Although Sun quickly suppressed with Shangtung troops Hsia's revolt in Chekiang, the subversion of Sun's Chekiang units continued. In November 1926, Sun appointed Ch'en Yi, commander of his Kiangsu Army's First Division (manned by Chekiang troops), to be his next governor in Chekiang and ordered Ch'en from Kiangsu back to the province along with another Chekiang unit—Chou Feng-ch'i's Third Division of the Kiangsu Army.[29] Ch'en and Chou were to guard their own province for Sun, a concession to those Chekiangese demanding provincial autonomy and the ousting of Shantung troops.

Ch'en Yi had no sooner assumed his duties as Sun's Chekiang governor when he received visits from provincial leaders interested in further autonomy, many of whom were under KMT influence. The KMT involvement in the autonomy movement picked up momentum. A united meeting of leaders of Kiangsu, Anhui, and Chekiang heard an announcement by Chiang Kai-shek on December 11 stating that if they joined in the National Revolution their provinces would be assured provincial governments, each directed by people of that province. That day in Chekiang, Chou Feng-ch'i accepted the designation of his division as the Twenty-sixth Army and became its commander.[30] Next, on December 15, the KMT wired Ch'en Yi to maintain order in Chekiang in the name of the NRA until its arrival from Kiangsi and Fukien.[31] By December 17, Ch'en Yi had accepted from Chiang the KMT's designation of his division as the Nineteenth Army under his command, and had called a meeting of provincial luminaries in the Shanghai concessions. There they were to work out a list of Chekiang men who could create a new provincial government.[32] Sun moved troops into Chekiang to suppress the revolt but the rebels—then the Nineteenth and Twenty-sixth armies—did manage to defend themselves in an upland corner of Chekiang that bordered on Kiangsi and Fukien, which made a gateway for the NRA to cross the rugged border range.

Sun had moved quickly enough, however, to capture Ch'en Yi, so that with Hsia Ch'ao dead since October 1926, Chou Feng-ch'i received most of the rewards for defection to the NRA. As local commander for the NRA of the campaign in Chekiang, Chou had enough political influence that he was next appointed to the chairmanship of Chekiang's Military Committee and made a member of the Chekiang Government Committee.[33] Chou apparently retained his strong motivation as a prior provincial autonomist and the ambition to rule Chekiang personally.

Within months, by mid-1927, when the KMT and its military suffered from severe internal division and successive defeats on the northern front, Chou's true colors emerged. The most active civilian leaders in Chekiang's new provincial government were party stalwarts Chang Ching-chiang, who was theoretically the head of the province, and Ma Hsu-lün, who was acting chairman. Party problems and national affairs at Nanking took them away from Hangchow, allowing Chou Feng-ch'i the opportunity to realize his provincial ambitions.[34]

Gathering around him provincial opponents to KMT reforms and new taxes, Chou Feng-ch'i enjoyed dominance of Chekiang, and by placing his 12,000 troops along the Hangchow-Shanghai railroad he was able to rule Shanghai as well.[35] Chou reached this peak of his power as KMT fortunes dipped and Chiang Kai-shek resigned in mid-August 1927. When the massive counteroffensive of Sun Ch'uan-fang surged back across the Yangtze in late August, there were reports that Chou's supporters at Ningpo were preparing welcoming posters.[36] At least one source claimed that Chou conspired with T'ang Sheng-chih of Hunan to aid Sun's come-back in order to regain their positions of autonomy.[37]

After the bloody battle of Lung-t'an, Nanking's generals managed to repulse Sun's attack and then were able to turn their attention to Chou Feng-ch'i's recalcitrant autonomism. By late September 1927, unable to defend the province against attack from all sides, and with his civilian support dwindling, Chou fled Hangchow by train bound for the safety of the Shanghai foreign settlement.[38] Although many of our questions about the defecting commanders remain to be answered, we can afford to be quite skeptical of the level of Chou's commitment to a national government.

In the short run, since the three Chekiang defectors greatly eased the military operations of the NRA, they were valuable to the Northern Expedition. In 1926, Hsia Ch'ao's rebellion did distract Sun during the bitterly contested fight for Kiangsi. Chou Feng-ch'i had allowed the NRA to enter Chekiang through its highly defensible passes without shedding blood, and then guided its vanguard. Ch'en Yi as the current civil governor did help the KMT to alienate the Chekiangese from Sun's influence and added more local troops to the NRA. In that they speeded its military conclusion by 1928, it can be argued that negotiating these defections from regional overlords was vital.

On the other hand, in Chekiang the orientation of these provincial militarists toward goals broader than the attainment of self-rule seems weak. Among the three Chekiang commanders, Hsia Ch'ao and protégé Chou Feng-ch'i publicly stated their primary loyalty to be toward Chekiang autonomy. Even after the cadre of the NRA Political Department worked to reeducate the Chekiang divisions politically,[39] Chou retained control over the troops and soon turned them against Nanking's central authority.

In order of incorporation into the NRA, the next to join were several units in Anhui, in late 1926. Sun's defeat in Kiangsi had undermined the morale of his Anhui Army officers, in particular that of the military governor of Anhui, Ch'en T'iao-yüan. On December 5, 1926, a representative of Ch'en met with Chiang at his Nanchang headquarters, and by early February 1927, the Chinese press noted vaguely that Ch'en's "attitude was ambiguous."[40] Quite likely, Ch'en had been in contact with KMT agents since the November retreat out of Kiangsi, perhaps earlier, and had gained a reputation for changing sides.[41] In a play for Ch'en's continuing loyalty, Sun Ch'uan-fang and his Ankuochün allies had promoted Ch'en to the directorship of Anhui's defense on December 21.[42] Ch'en remained unconvinced and on February 19, 1927, gathered his subordinate Wang P'u and several other generals to discuss the prospects in Sun's United Provinces.[43]

The next day, February 20, a subordinate of Ch'en, Liu Pao-t'i, defected with his division to the NRA near Chih-teh, entry point to Anhui from upriver. Sun had earlier promoted Liu from brigade to division commander; but when Liu joined the NRA he came in as the commander of the "new" Third Army.[44] Liu's transfer provided the NRA with the chance to resume its offensive into Anhui without bloodshed. During the rest of February, that offensive hung fire while other Anhui officers met secretly with KMT agents over the details of their possible *kuei-fu* to the NRA.

When Chiang's NRA went on the march again in Anhui on March 4, it coincided with the defection of three of Sun's division commanders there. All three entered the NRA as army corps commanders: Ch'en T'iao-yüan as Thirty-seventh Army commander, Wang P'u as Twenty-seventh Army commander, and Yeh K'ai-hsin as "new" Third Army commander (redesignated as the Forty-fourth Army on March 19).[45] Ch'en and Wang's divisions had Anhui origins, while Yeh's had been one of Wu P'ei-fu's Hunanese units before his defeat in the fall of 1926. In the Anhui highlands bordering Hupei, local militia forces joined the NRA, reorganized as the

Thirty-third Army under Po Wen-wei, a longtime KMT leader from Anhui.[46] These defections in Anhui greatly aided in the capture of the provinces, in spite of Ankuochün efforts to rush in replacements. Anhui, south of the Yangtze, fell so quickly that Nanking's and Shanghai's defensibility were gravely prejudiced.

Apparently the defenders of Sun's choice plum, Shanghai, were also vulnerable to KMT persuasion. At least by August 1926, the KMT had appointed two agents to obtain the defection of the commander of Sun Ch'uan-fang's Shanghai navy. The agents shortly reported back to the KMT that Admiral Yang Shu-chuang was amenable to joining the National Revolution but had questions about the details. Yang wanted to know if the Canton government could pay the C$400,000 in monthly salaries his personnel required, and, if his navy defected, whether his officers were guaranteed their positions?[47] Part of Yang's fleet was attached to Fukien and during the campaign there, he dispatched a representative on November 26 to discuss further the *kuei-fu*.[48] In the meantime, the movement in Shanghai to resist the entry of Shantung troops into lower Kiangsu worked on the morale of Yang and his men. In early December 1926, Admiral Yang sent his plenipotentiary to Nanchang to settle with Chiang on the final terms. On December 14, Chiang was able to wire these terms to his East Route Commander, Ho Ying-ch'in, in Fukien.[49]

The actual defection was to coordinate with the planned siege of Shanghai. During the February uprising in Shanghai, Admiral Yang's hand was nearly tipped when two impetuous executive officers of his ships bombarded Sun's Kiangnan Arsenal in support of the rebels on shore.[50] Sun could not risk confronting Admiral Yang, whom he exonerated of responsibility for the bombardment but assigned a demerit. By early March 1927, Yang was collaborating with a high KMT political and military figure for the Shanghai area, Niu Yung-chien, with whom Yang arranged his defection to coincide with the general attack on Shanghai to begin on March 15. By March 9, Yang had already aided by threatening Sun Ch'uan-fang that his fleet of some twenty ships would resist any entry of Chang Tso-lin's Po Hai fleet into the Yangtze. In his dealings with the KMT, Yang became embroiled in the deepening polarization between the KMT and CCP. The CCP approached Yang independently through political workers who urged him to allow his sailors to be organized and represented in the Municipal Congress of Soviets that the CCP was promoting.[51] Through Niu Yung-chien's efforts, Yang ignored the CCP maneuvers and continued to cooperate with Niu and the KMT—Chiang's faction in particular. As the NRA offensive moved downriver in Anhui, three of Yang's ships slipped upriver from the Shanghai area to join in the bombardment of Tangt'u on March 11. On the twelfth, all the Shanghai fleet flew the KMT flag and a squadron steamed up the Yangtze to the Kiangsi headquarters of Chiang.[52] Although Admiral Yang secretly accepted his appointment as C-in-C of the National Revolutionary Navy on March 14, it was not publicized until his ships cooperated in the final taking of the Shanghai coast on March 21.[53]

Nui Yung-chien also succeeded in convincing the head of the Kiangsu

Waterway Police to add his boats and men to the revolutionary cause. Since the delta area around Shanghai is laced with canals and river channels, their control was of great value. In the final attack on the Shanghai defenses at Sungchiang, KMT units were able to flank Sun's forts there by use of the Whangpu River and its canals. In the battle, the defected head of the waterway police died, but through his defection saved the NRA a costlier assault on the remaining Shanghai defenses.[54]

Even the Ankuochün's appointee as Shanghai garrison commander, Pi Shu-ch'eng, who came south from Shantung, succumbed to the subversive atmosphere of Shanghai. Pi arrived in Shanghai on February 24 and helped direct the suppression of the second uprising, but was apparently disgruntled because Chang Tsung-ch'ang had not gained for him concurrently the title of mayor. By early March 1927, Niu Yung-chien, the local KMT chairman and agent of the C-in-C, who had been communicating with Pi had persuaded him to defect.[55] Apparently Pi was prepared to defect when the offensive neared Shanghai, and he also supplied the NRA's East Route commander, Ho Ying-ch'in, with plans and intelligence.[56] According to the set pattern, Niu offered Pi the title of commander of the Forty-second Army pending the peaceful surrender of the Shanghai garrison. However, as Shanghai's strategic position became untenable, Chang Tsung-ch'ang of the Ankuochün ordered Pi to withdraw on March 19 from Shanghai. Pi put off his retreat in order to join with the approaching NRA.[57] On March 20, as the NRA moved cautiously into Shanghai's suburbs, Pi dispatched a representative to General Ho to finalize the city's take-over.[58] Other units of the Ankuochün not included in the deal put up some resistance, which made for confusion.

The confusion was compounded by the attack of the CCP's GLU, which sought the weapons of the northern troops (see chapter 11). Pi's troops, in response to the attack and execution of northern soldiers, resisted and scattered. Some who did surrender to the GLU's armed pickets were later accepted into the picket corps—the large-bodied Shangtung soldiers were always in demand as policemen and the like. With the abortion of his planned defection, Pi Shu-ch'eng fled in panic into the French concession and from there escaped by sea to Shantung.[59] With the news of his planned defection receiving exposure in the press, Pi was untrusted—he was arrested in Tsingtao and executed on April 5 at Tsinan.[60]

THE DEFECTIONS AND THE KMT AS A SOUTHERN POWER

In that Pi Shu-ch'eng and his unit were part of the Shantung Army of Chang Tsung-ch'ang (an ally in the Ankuochün), his defection was unusual. From the record it appears that most of the other defectors and their units had southern origins and ties. The major defections to the NRA took place in South and Central China. The last significant defections before the completion of the expedition occurred as the NRA pursued the fleeing northern force across the Yangtze. In late March 1927, rather than face a dangerous battery dug in on the far side of the wide Yangtze, the NRA accepted the defection of Chang Kuo-wei's artillery regiment and Chang

Chung-li's brigade of Sun's Kiangsu Army. Therefore the NRA landing on the north bank at the entrance to the Grand Canal was easy.[61] Although small units of Sun's force entered the NRA in July 1927, and many surrendered before the last fight for Peking in 1928, defections in North China were much less a part of the expedition in its last phase. Feng Yü-hsiang did gather in some Honanese troops of Wu P'ei-fu and a few small Manchurian units, but these have not been publicized. It may have been that with the four collective armies of the NRA in 1928 totaling around 1 million Chiang and Nanking made no further effort to reward defections.

It would seem that the KMT was most influential in winning over *southern* enemy troops stationed in their *southern* provinces. The fact was that more of the KMT membership was from the Yangtze basin and the southern coast than from the north. Thus, in contacting southern officers there were available more men with valuable school ties, mutual friends, and family relations. Furthermore, in their dealings with the northern warlords and their officer cadres, the KMT was handicapped by the cultural and educational differences. In general, the northern officers were from more lowly, narrowly provincial origins—many rose to high positions through the experience of fighting with "irregular" military bands. This had been the case with Chang Tso-lin, Chang Tsung-ch'ang of Shantung, and many of Chang Tso-lin's subordinates. There were few KMT available who could act as middlemen in starting a dialog with them. Their lack of a modern education also made these warriors less susceptible to the rationale of nationalism. Of the leading institutions of modern higher education in China then listed, sixteen were located in southern China while only eight were in the north.

The stories of major defections have yet to be told, but would give a fascinating insight into the mentality of twentieth-century China. There are still present numbers of the defectors active in both Chinas. Interestingly their presence is at the same time both a help and a hindrance in researching the circumstances of their pasts. There is no doubt, however, that those commanders who did *kuei-fu* were of great military value in the *short-run*, bringing, as they did, badly needed troops and firepower to the expedition. Knowing the significance of their contribution to the KMT's unification campaign, the later-surfacing problems of disunity and lack of ideological direction can be better understood. The founding of a Chinese regime by an inclusive movement, even after its apparent military victory, must face the equally massive task of consolidating a central power by subordinating its military allies. Sharing this problem with Chiang Kai-shek have been such great unifiers as Ch'in Shih-huang-ti, Liu Pang, and now Mao Tse-tung.

CHAPTER 31
Conclusion:
Military or Political Victory?

What was the significance of the Northern Expedition? With the study of this great period of genesis only in its formative stage, conclusions must be tentative and more on the order of questions. The two modern political parties of contemporary China and their members learned many lessons—many of them bitter—and gained much experience in warfare and politics during this phase of China's era of civil war. Much of what occurred reflected *new* trends and universal ideas, while other aspects show striking parallels with timeless patterns of Chinese state building. The Nationalists won on the battlefield, but then suffered from the problems that were the consequence of the heterogeneous coalition they had thrown together to achieve victory. The Communists seemed to have lost out, but learned much from their experiences in the Revolutionary Base and the expedition. A generation of leaders, who are still in control of China, emerged from the period 1925 to 1928 as from a training ground. Not only did Chiang Kai-shek and a multitude of KMT luminaries pass through the halls of Whampoa, but Mao Tse-tung, Chou En-lai, Liu Shao-ch'i, and Lin Piao also served in some way. In that period, they turned from discussion and intellectualization of Marxism and nationalism to a phase of experimentation, implementation, and development of their maturing political styles. What they were involved in was the movement that was carrying China away from its ancient status of a dynastic state or empire toward a modern nation state—a goal from which the Chinese people have not been diverted.

There are many elements that contributed to the military success of the expedition. The importance of the Revolutionary Base from which the National Revolution spread cannot be overemphasized. In a way it was so like the ancient base areas from which dynastic founders sallied forth to gather allies and conquer the empire. There had been the Wei River valley, the "land within the passes," in North China where Feng Yü-hsiang ruled; Yen's Shansi; and the Manchurian basin where the Manchus had organized and consolidated their power before they defeated their rivals within the empire and where, in the 1920s, Chang Tso-lin had built up his military machine. All of these base areas had in common their outer border of defensible mountains and their inner plains that were productive enough to at least support the launching of a campaign outward into other basins. The topography of China acted as a centrifugal force continually pulling China apart, but then, when the countering force rose to pull it back together, the same topography allowed the build-up of the new regime within the protective cover of some province's mountains. For the revolutionaries, there was a parallel with the conquering dynasties who had built up power beyond the wall and the authority of the prior regime's armies; in the 1920s the foreign concessions were sanctuaries where revolutionaries hiding from warlord executioners and partisans could blend in with the compradors and Chinese workers. Thus, the KMT not only set up its regime in the fertile, defensible Kwangtung basin, but also used the concessions as its distant outposts. Kwangtung, the first point of entrance of modern ideas and trade, was a logical seedbed for the national movement. Provincials, such as Sun Yat-sen, had been quite active in anti-Manchu subversion and were more open to innovation and progressive trends.

Out of the city of Canton where the KMT made its headquarters grew the Revolutionary Base. The growth was slow and often frustrating, but productive of valuable experience. By the time of Sun's death, the movement seemed to have finally taken root and showed promise of bearing fruit. The modern elites who had begun to gravitate to Canton by the mid-1920s tried to make the province into a model state, using rationalized, modern techniques spiced with nationalism. By 1926, Kwangtung did stand as an exemplary alternative to the warlord states. There glistened shining hopes and idealism, which many of the new breed of Chinese could not find elsewhere. Returned students, exuberant with energy and the desire to put to work their new-found modern skills in reconstructing China, found opportunities awaiting them at Canton. Elsewhere, given the instability of warlord states and their arbitrary rulers, the modern-educated elite had felt frustrated. Many graduates and faculty members lacked suitable employment. Bringing their ideas to Canton, the new elites made it a laboratory of nationalism, rationalism, and socialism. None of these foreign ways passed through Kwangtung intact. The need of the KMT for foreign aid and technical advice had forced the Party to take into its bed the eager Russian mission and its CCP followers. The nationalism of the KMT became socialistic through Russian and Chinese Marxist pollination. Chinese Marxism at Canton began to take on nationalistic traits as it blossomed alongside the KMT's ideology. In 1926, Mao Tse-tung came under criticism from his comrades for being too much under KMT influence. The activists planted foreign concepts at Canton, but what spread outward and influenced contemporary China were hybrid Chinese movements: a nationalism emphasizing a Confucian harmony in the all-class union and a Marxist class struggle led by the peasants.

The first "united front" of a nationalistic party and a Communist party provided a heady mixture and some hangovers. As in the extended Chinese family, harmony was an ideal that was more often preached than practiced. The dependence of both the KMT and the CCP on Russian support and guidance was subconciously a galling experience for both, and each reacted against it—the KMT in its anti-Communist excess from 1927 on, and in the later anti-Russian resentments among Mao's faction after Stalin's blunders. The movement in Kwangtung fed on anti-foreignism (perhaps even xenophobia) in the May 30 Incident, the Shameen Affair, and the exciting Hong Kong-Kwangtung Strike. Foreigners were, once again, the scapegoats and outlets for Chinese frustrations. All of these ideas and feelings brewed in the Revolutionary Base and then spilled over into a disintegrated China thirsting for some new life-giving elixir. Although Kwangtung was but one province in China, the movement there claimed to be a national one—though it was simultaneously manipulating provincialism elsewhere.

Another element in the Northern Expedition's success was the national image that the movement was eventually able to project. The National Revolution was able to stand in contrast to the more narrow, personal movements of the various military regimes elsewhere. What made the Kwangtung movement seem less Cantonese was a political party that had evangelized throughout China and could boast a membership that was at least nominally representative of all the regions, although showing a preponderance of southern Chinese. The KMT ideology, mainly some rather loosely gathered ideas of Sun Yat-sen, did stress the needs of the Chinese people and nation rather than provincialism. There were KMT branch headquarters, or cells, in most of the major provincial cities, and especially in all the growing new port cities. The modern Chinese elites, infected with nationalistic pangs from their exposure to foreign patriotism, came in contact with the Kwangtung message and then read press reports of the KMT-promoted demonstrations against the foreign powers in such widely flung points as Peking, Shanghai, and Canton. By 1926 there was a growing pantheon of KMT martyrs enshrined with Sun Yat-sen, who was apotheosized as a patriarchal spirit of a national family.

Modern-educated intellectuals, students, and businessmen could all identify with the nationalism that the KMT strove to symbolize. Thus, as the Northern Expedition moved into the Yangtze basin, it was able to travel with less of the colorings of an alien invasion. In many areas, there were with the National Revolutionary Army and ahead of it natives of that area who could communicate with the provincials. The proliferating KMT and CCP student organizations throughout urban China provided agents, spies, guides, and recruits for both parties and the NRA.

Since the national revolutionary movement was built on the base of a party rather than a charismatic individual, there was a broader structure of leadership and greater resources in brainpower and economic power available. Although the rather inclusive KMT was weakened by factional strife, the diversity did allow for more creativity than the regimes topped only by a military ruler. Leadership and decision-making in the KMT were more the result of merit and expediency than they were in the other regimes dependent on personal ties and mercenary arrangements. At least during the buildup toward the expedition this was the trend, although personal obligations and mercenary considerations increasingly plagued the KMT from early 1927 on, once the incorporated defectors became indispensable. In the democratic centralism adopted from the Russians, there was some chance for partisans to personally identify with a movement for which they had given their consent. This kind of broader, more progressive nationalism appealed to those Chinese most susceptible to ideology. An urban coalition of modern-educated intellectuals and treaty port businessmen with their economic power gave their support to the National Revolution.

Another conclusion as to the success of the expedition relates to the military contribution. Mao's reflection that power grew out of the barrel of a gun is just as relevant to the Northern Expedition that he supported in 1926 as it was to his revolution in the 1930s and 40s. The expedition was not merely masses of propagandists armed with ideological slogans moving ahead of the NRA to which they joyfully gave over the cities and the countryside they had won. From 1926 through to the final campaign on the great North China Plain, there were junctures at which the battles were desperate and waged with great sacrifice in blood. Those tens of thousands who died deserve recognition. Mao's partnership with Lin Piao, head of the Red Army, may have been the indirect recognition of the military side to Chinese politics as practiced in the expedition. The expedition succeeded through combining the military advantages enjoyed by the KMT with its political efforts.

The KMT's Whampoa Military Academy taught many of the skills that the NRA needed. There too was blended the rationalized *modern* military science of the Russians and the Japanese-trained Chinese with the *Confucian* ideals of Tseng Kuo-fan regarding dealings with civilians. Like the Party and its model provincial government, the military nucleus of Whampoa attracted thousands of bright cadets and a crew of energetic instructors. Within the Revolutionary Base, the inner core of the NRA-to-be studied, drilled, and gained experience in the Eastern Expeditions that expanded authority into distant valleys of Kwangtung. Engineering students and apprentice artillerymen put into practice their military lessons in the siege of Huichou, which forced Ch'en Chiung-ming out of his lair. The political indoctrination of new recruits and civilian passersby prepared cadet workers for their significant contributions in the Political Departments of the NRA.

The Political Departments did become almost a special weapon of the NRA and one that the warlords failed to match. Through efforts with its soldiery, NRA morale and fighting spirit far surpassed that of the opposing forces, which were for the most part comprised of mercenaries. Although ideology instilled a new level of patriotism in Chinese troops, the political work included practical benefits that cheered them. Steadier pay, regular meals, and the promise of promotions based on merit all exemplified the value of a rationalized approach. The political workers also contributed to the creation of a good name, or "face," for the army and its soldiers. Traditionally the ubiquitous poor of China were attracted to army life out of desperation and, once enlisted, were doomed to a frustrating existence as the pariahs of society. The KMT and its cadre instilled pride by teaching the soldiers that they were to be the saviors of the people—the only means for China to achieve vital unification. As the NRA became known for its exemplary behavior, the social status, so much a concern of the Chinese psyche, of its members rose. This good reputation was of inestimable value for the NRA in its dealings with the teeming Chinese populace through which it moved. In China, Mao's analogy of the people as a sea is well taken.

Where warlord armies had been avoided, fled from, and despised, the NRA was made welcome because of its astute dealings with natives. Not fearing the NRA, peasants and workers came to agents of the Political Departments to volunteer for well-paying jobs as porters and guides. Peasants brought their rice and produce to *sell* to the troops moving through their area rather than hiding those needed commodities in the hills as they had done with the rapacious warlord troops. Carrying away with them good silver dollars and information about the NRA, the local people became the best propagandists the KMT had. Recruits and defectors swelled the ranks once the pragmatic NRA policy became known. Belief that they were involved with a morally upright cause glamorized dealings with the KMT's army in a way unshared by the warlord forces. Ideology *and* pragmatism were combined in the NRA policies. The northern regimes of Yen Hsi-shan and Feng Yü-hsiang had both incorporated ideologies, but in practice their operations reflected the one-man operations of the leaders. Their movements were much more region-oriented and did not capture the nationalistic imagination of the modern elites, although political techniques of Feng and Yen must have influenced the national revolutionaries.

Another military advantage enjoyed by the NRA was its pragmatic approach to strategy and tactics. This, too, grew from the broader base of leadership in the Party and its army. The NRA leadership attempted to use means of modern rationalized and systematized warfare: structuring their organization to include engineering units and logistics, artillery, and Political Departments. In other ways, the styles of operating were reminiscent of the methods of Sun Tzu, the great military philosopher who was such an influence on Mao and most likely colored the thinking of all his generation. The KMT did not launch a nationwide war, but rather attacked warlords *one* by *one*. While Wu P'ei-fu was in the sights of the NRA, the Party propagandists and diplomats sought to placate, divide, and isolate other rivals. Neither did the leaders of the expedition, which maintained a high pitch of antiforeign, anti-imperialist rhetoric, promote war against the powers. The memory of the first Sino-Japanese war and the Boxer debacle was still too fresh, the presence of the powers' military might too threatening. Rather, the KMT trod a narrow path between the skillful manipulation of the righteous wrath of the Chinese people against the foreigners and the policy of prudence in only pushing the powers, singly, and not to the point of forcing a belligerent response. Wherever Chiang was in control, this was followed, but other factions failed to avoid dangerous incidents such as at the Hankow and Kiukiang concessions, at Nanking, and perhaps at Tsinan in 1928.

Japan proved to be the most unbending in these confrontations, and the interventions in Shantung in 1927 and again in 1928 foreshadowed the future trend of Sino-Japanese relations. Although the 1928 intervention slowed the progress of Chiang's Collective Army, the emotional furor against the imperialists and their warlord "running dogs" helped generate steam for the last push to take North China.

Chiang's political style, established during the expedition, placed a higher priority on internal domestic unification than on external defense—China would have to present itself as a strong whole if it were to defend its interests against the rapacious foreigners. After the expedition, this attitude influenced the KMT's domestic and foreign policy from the Manchurian Incident of 1931 through to the final opening of Japanese aggression in 1937. In that later period, Mao's call to all Chinese to forget their differences and fight Japan harked back to the propaganda used against Chiang during the Tsinan intervention during May and June 1928. Similarly, Mao's Cultural Revolution may have set out to accomplish, among many aims, the weeding out of unorthodox domestic factions—one of which was pro-Russian—before a confrontation with Russia.

Another broad military strategy that paid off, in the short run, was the inclusive synthesis of the national movement. First, the CCP was incorporated in the KMT operation. As the Revolutionary Base became a reality, the Party drew in seven regional armies to fight along with Whampoa's First Army. Then as the expedition began, T'ang Sheng-chih's unit became the Eighth Army, and the gathering in continued through to the last phase when the old NRA opened up to include a total of four massive Collective Armies. The rationale was that in attracting as many of the militarists as possible, there would be that many fewer to fight.

The problem with the inclusive policy, and the emphasis on harmony, is that it put off until some future time decisions as to the goals of the new "nation." The struggle could not be put off indefinitely—witness the KMT-CCP split, the KMT division, T'ang Sheng-chih's revolt, and then the struggle in the 1930s against Yen, Feng, and the warlords taken in earlier who resisted cooperation with Nanking's centralization of Chinese political power. China's vastness, topographic barriers, and cultural and linguistic differences were not to be easily overcome by the KMT's manner of nation building. Following the apparent reunification of China in 1928, upon the completion of the Northern Expedition, there remained to be accomplished the centralization of political power.

Even while gathering in heterodox military allies, KMT members and their CCP collaborators did concern themselves with political orthodoxy.

In 1925 and 1926, the Revolutionary Base witnessed a succession of struggles between and among politicians attempting to set the Party on the
"correct" course. First the KMT Left and CCP had neutralized the Right,
then Chiang, as centrist allied with the anti-Communists, countered the
Left. By late 1926, an anti-Chiang movement worked for the Left and the
CCP, followed by a KMT split and the purge of the CCP. Sun Yat-sen's
metaphorical reference comparing Chinese society to a dish of sand was
borne out in the divisiveness—even within the ranks of the revolutionaries. The evidence builds toward a conclusion: that in the 1920s
and later, China required the firm hand of a strong man to keep up the
momentum of centripetal force needed to maintain unity.

Tactically, the NRA was forced to make do with what it had. It had
mobility in the countryside off the main byways and railroads through its
utilization of civilian carriers and guides. Time and time again, the NRA
moved quickly and with daring around the enemy's flanks to threaten the
railroad that provided its lifeblood. This tactic avoided confronting the
superior firepower of the warlords. Where the NRA did not have the heavy
cannon to level city walls, the Ankuochün had long-range artillery
mounted on trains and manned by crack White Russian teams. The ability
to strike out across the friendly countryside with hard-working porters
helped to compensate for the initial inaccessibility of rail communications.
Eventually through capture and aid from workmen, the NRA did acquire
engines and rolling stock, so that from late 1926 on the communications gap
narrowed. To the mobility of the NRA should be added its emphasis on
keeping on the offensive. By moving quickly ahead, keeping the enemy off
guard, and attacking where the enemy seemed weakest, the NRA made the
most of its discipline and high spirit. Focusing on the enemy's
weakness—known through civilian informants—harkened back to the
teachings of Sun Tzu. Chiang's desire for the rapid expansion of the NRA
through the drawing in of warlord forces sprang from the need to unify
China quickly, but it also shows the ancient Chinese proclivity toward mass
armies, another trait Chiang shared with his associate Mao Tse-tung. The
result of Chiang's desire was a loosely allied force of 1 million that had been
added to his model regiment in the years from 1925 to 1928. Many of these
troops had defected from the warlords; many were recruited on the basis of
the NRA's reputation.

One of the most intriguing questions about the Northern Expedition has
been the role of civilians—individuals and organized masses. Because of
the Marxist requirement that history fit its ideological formulas, the Communist writers, Chinese and Western, have credited the organized proletariat and peasantry with achieving the victories. That Trotskyite thesis
prompted this study. However, there is certainly enough evidence to
question this conclusion although in the Revolutionary Base there were
times and places where unionized workers and organized peasants did
weigh the balance in favor of the KMT, there were more numerous and
crucial junctures when the mass organizations under CCP direction
threatened or distracted the military campaign.

The Hong Kong Strike organization and the General Labor Union that it nurtured were the CCP's most prided creations. The CCP managed to capture the leadership of the strike, and then, in the compromise with the Russians after the March 20 Coup, Chiang and his supporters turned over organizing the masses to the CCP. By the launching of the expedition, the strike apparatus was powerful and autonomous of KMT direction. Its diametrically opposed aims were a challenge to the KMT's leadership of the United Front. The CCP unions continually disrupted the economy of the Revolutionary Base with strikes and union clashes, a situation repeated again as the workers and peasants' movements followed the NRA to Wuhan. There the CCP's proletariat undermined the KMT Left and ruined its chance of capturing the leadership of the KMT military machine. At Shanghai, contrary to the CCP version, the GLU's General Strike in March 1927 was not so much to capture the city *for* the NRA as it was to take advantage of the vacuum of military power to seize Shanghai, arm the unions, and create a soviet enclave from which to combine with the upriver comrades.

The real significance for the CCP of the United Front with the KMT was not so much its contribution to the military victory as it was the unprecedented opportunity for the CCP to practice its organizational techniques on the workers and peasants. In this respect the CCP was able to change from a tiny debating society of educated elites into a burgeoning mass movement with over 50,000 disciplined members and literally millions of affiliated workers and peasants. However, the tiny Chinese proletariat and the vast peasantry seem to have been at a very backward stage of political awareness in Marxist terms. Had the proletariat and the peasantry of Hunan, Kiangsi, and Kwangtung been as awakened to social revolution as the CCP had convinced itself they were, would there have been the debacles of Changsha, Nanchang, Swatow, and finally the Canton soviet?

Another element in the polemic over mass participation in the expedition has been the timing and placing of its contribution. The small-scale propagandizing and scouting that preceded the NRA behind warlord lines was nowhere near as significant as the massive effort of the CCP cadre, many of whom were Political Department workers, in the wake of the NRA under the KMT regime. That was where the mass organizations sprang up and gathered power unto themselves. In contemporary CCP accounts, as late as 1926, there were admissions that the union and peasants' association movements *behind* the warlord lines had *declined*. This conclusion as to the role of the organized masses in the expedition must not detract from the contributions of the cooperative *individual* farmers and coolies who aided the NRA in so many ways. The exemplary behavior and good repute of the NRA eased the way for that beneficial relationship. The unions and peasants' associations helped defeat the warlords, but even more the success of the expedition must be credited to military means.

The organizing of peasant and labor masses from 1925 into 1927 provided invaluable experience for the CCP and lessons to both the CCP and the KMT. A lesson that the CCP began to digest was that the Chinese workers and ubiquitous peasants seemed to be most energized by issues that directly related to their economic betterment—economic incentives that encouraged the later economism of Liu Shao-ch'i in the 1960s. The proletariat, few in number, proved to be weak when most needed. The three Shanghai uprisings accomplished little more than martyrdom for the GLU workers. The organized power of the workers in Shanghai, where there was the largest concentration of unionized proletariat, was not equal to the combined strength of the NRA garrison and the members of the Green Society. When Chiang unleashed the purge in Shanghai, the unionized workers were far more numerous than the KMT troops and allies, but, even with their caches of arms, they were not equal to the military. The same weakness was revealed in the purge that the KMT Left carried out in Wuhan, and again after the failure of the Canton soviet of December 1927. The inescapable conclusion was that, ideology aside, the proletariat and the rural masses could not stand alone to topple a hostile Chinese regime supported by troops. Even where Mao's peasants' movement was strongest—in Hunan where he had ecstatically praised the millions of affiliated peasants ". . . who have risen to fulfill their historic mission"—the CCP's peasants failed to protect the party from the opposing military. Mao must have been premature when he claimed in February 1927 that ". . . in a few months the peasants have accomplished what Dr. Sun Yat-sen wanted, but failed to accomplish . . . ," but within the year, the lesson had been driven home that the CCP needed its *own* Red Army. Political power would have to grow out of the barrel of a gun for the CCP, not out of the bullhorns of propagandists or from the spears of peasants.

The violence unleashed in the warlord era would not subside without its suppression by brute armed force. Thus, the trend for the CCP moved toward collaboration between Mao and warrior Lin Piao rather than toward the peasant-worker combine of Mao and Liu Shao-ch'i. The KMT had reviewed the same lesson during its traumatic, often suicidal, careenings. Controlling the powerful centrifugal forces that wracked China would take military might as well as political technique. The KMT failed to gain the aid of organized workers. In its reaction to what it viewed as labor and peasant excesses in 1926 and 1927, the KMT veered sharply from developing the mass movements for social revolution toward organizing as a means of holding down such disruptions. Rather than risk the loss of the gentry's support of KMT preeminence, the KMT had to put off indefinitely a thorough rural reform and, instead, rely on an urban coalition for progress, protected by the massive KMT military machine. The Northern Expedition may have accomplished fewer political aims than its KMT promoters had envisioned, but the military victory did achieve the first phase in the reintegration of a Chinese state—the phase of unification. What remained was the towering task of centralization.

Appendix

Chiang Kai-shek, February 25, 1927.

. . . the only purpose of this propaganda is to force out their opponents. . . . As Chairman of the highest political organization I support the Party's power even more than the others do. . . . The only dictator is Hsü Ch'ien himself. He has no basis of authority but has made himself chairman of Hankow's Joint Council and has thereby disobeyed the regulations of the KMT. He is nothing but a dictator. . . . I, myself, carry out the decisions of the [Central Executive] Committee. Our Party has its *own* history, its *own* purposes, and its *own* principles. Merely criticizing without careful consideration is action against the revolution and seeks destruction of our Party. A member of this Party should cooperate with his comrades in guarding our Party power. Impulsive, excessive criticism is wounding our Party.

My hope is that Wang Ching-wei will return to his duties. I have strongly proclaimed our friendship, but there have been words that aim to break up our friendship and ruin the chances of Wang Ching-wei's return. . . . therefore broadening the power of the Party is not a question of personality but of beliefs. Our Party members now are so confused and distrustful that issuing *one* order stirs questions. We cannot give too much attention to this!

I have not said that we couldn't cooperate with the CCP. I was the first to advocate mutual cooperation. Recently it has been said that I disbelieve the CCP and want to be rid of them, but this is not the truth. In the past I was asked to especially protect the CCP. Then I answered that we should aid the weak among the revolutionary body in order to strengthen the revolution. At that time CCP members were few in number and loyal to the KMT. I, as with KMT members, was not permitted to suppress the CCP, but I also said that should the CCP in the future become coercive they should be restrained. Now the CCP is quite unruly and wants to damage the KMT organization; thus, we cannot treat them as before.

My function is to focus the power and spirit of the revolution. My attitude is necessarily open and frank. Some say that I am neither Left nor Right and am without ideology. In fact my principles are those of the revolution and must be neither Left nor Right. In the end, if our revolution fails then I will die with the KMT. If we struggle amongst *ourselves*, we can only lose. I am the leader of the revolutionary party and should consider this basis of both parties. Furthermore, I am not an anti-Communist, I have long sympathized with them, but I must make CCP *members* take heed not to oppress KMT members. If they do, the two parties will through attacking each other ruin the revolution.

Some denounce me for dictatorial tendencies. I have been given the position of general, and the burden of this responsibility is heavy indeed. In carrying out my duties I must have a certain amount of authority. On the one hand I must bear the heavy responsibilities, while on the other I am for this suspected and envied by others. How can we hope for the revolution's success? If people are dissatisfied with the way I am conducting affairs I, myself, can resign.

(Kuowen [March 13, 1927], n. p.)

Notes

Shortened forms to the literature cited have been employed in the notes. To aid the reader in locating the corresponding bibliographic entries, the following list is provided.

Akimova. See Akimova.
Boorman. See *Biographical Dictionary of Republican China*.
Borodin. See Chiang Yung-ching.
Canton Uprising. See *Kuang-chou p'ao-tung-chih yi-yi yü chiao-hsün*.
CCP before the War. See *K'ang-chan yi-ch'ien-te Chung-kuo Kung-ch'an-tang*.
CCP History. See *Chung-kuo Kung-ch'an-tang chien-ming li-shih*.
CCP Martyrs. See *Chung-kuo Kung-ch'an-tang lieh-shih chuan*.
CCP 2nd Enlarged CEC Meeting. See *Chung-kuo Kung-ch'an-tang ti-ssu-chieh erh-chung ch'uan-hui erh-ts'e chung-yang k'uo-ta chih-hsing wei-yüan-hui yi-chüeh-an*.
Chang Kuo-t'ao. See Chang Kuo-t'ao.
Chapman. See Chapman.
Ch'en Kung-po. See Ch'en Kung-po.
Ch'en Kuo-fu. See Ch'en Kuo-fu.
Chiang before 1926. See Mao Szu-ch'eng.
China Yearbook 1928. See *China Yearbook 1928*.

Chinese Peasant Monthly. See *Chung-kuo nung-min yüeh-k'an.*

Ch'ü Ching-pai. See Ch'ü Ching-pai.

CKHT. See *Chung-kuo hsien-tai ko-ming yün-tung shih.*

CKYS. See *Chung-kuo kung-jen yün-tung shih-kao.*

Documents. See Wilbur, C. Martin, and How, Julie Lien-ying.

F.F. Liu. See Liu, F.F.

1st Peasants' Movement. See *Ti-yi-tz'u kuo-nei ko-ming chan-cheng shih-ch'i-te nung-min yün-tung.*

1st Workers' Movement. See *Ti-yi-tz'u kuo-nei ko-ming chan-cheng shih-ch'i-te kung-jen yün-tung.*

History of Political Work. See *Kuo-chün cheng-kung shih-kao.*

HKDP. See *Hong Kong Daily Press.*

HTSL. See *Hsien-tai shih-liao.*

Huston, "Sketch." See Huston, J.C.

Ko-ming wen-hsien. See *Ko-ming wen-hsien.*

Kuo Mo-jo. See Kuo Mo-jo.

Kuowen. See *Kuowen chou-pao.*

MacNair. See MacNair.

Ma Hsü-lun. See Ma Hsü-lun.

Ma, *Labor.* See Ma Ch'ao-chün.

NCH. See *North China Herald.*

N. Exp. See *Pei-fa chan-shih.*

Roots, "Canton Idea." In *Asia* (27[4]:285-288).

Russia in China. See Chiang Kai-shek.

Schram. See Schram.

SCMP. See *South China Morning Post.*

Seized Documents are from U.S. National Archives, Military Records Division, file no. 2657-I-281(111), document no. 30.

Shameen White Paper. See "Papers relating to the First Firing in the Shameen Affair of June 23, 1925."

Sheean. See Sheean, Vincent, "Some People from Canton".

Sheean, "Moscow." See Sheean, Vincent, "Moscow and the Chinese Revolution".

Su Chao-cheng. See *Su Chao-cheng.*

Sun Lien-chung. See Sun Lien-chung.

T'ang Leang-li. See T'ang Leang-li.

Ta-shih chi. See *Chung-hua min-kuo ta-shih chi.*

Teng Chung-hsia. See Teng Chung-hsia.

Trotsky. See Trotsky.

TSKY. See Chang Ch'i-yün.

Wang Chien-min. See Wang Chien-min.

Wang Ching-wei. See Wang Ching-wei.

Warlord: Yen Hsi-shan. See Gillin.

Wu Hsiang-hsiang. See Wu Hsiang-hsiang.

CHAPTER 1

1. Emanuel Hsü, *The Rise of Modern China* (New York: Oxford University Press, 1975), pp. 582, 587, 623.

2. From an interview with Sun Fo, son of Sun Yat-sen, on May 25, 1966, at Yangmingshan, Taiwan.

3. James P. Harrison, *The Long March to Power* (New York: Praeger, 1972), p. 52. Chang Kuo-t'ao, *The Rise of the Chinese Communist Party 1921-1927*, vol. 1 of his autobiography (Lawrence: University of Kansas Press, 1971), p. 306. Hereafter cited as Chang Kuo-t'ao.

4. From an interview with a member of the early Whampoa Political Department, Li Shao-lin.

5. *Chung-hua Min-kuo ta-shih chi* [Record of major events of the Republic of China], ed. by Kao Yin-tzu (Taipei: Shih-chieh Book Co., 1957), p. 176. Hereafter cited as *Ta-shih chi*.

6. Papers Relating to the First Firing in the Shameen Affair of June 23, 1925, *China* No. 1 (1926), *House of Commons*, XXX, *Accounts and Papers* No. 15, p. 12. Hereafter cited as *Shameen White Paper*.

7. *Shameen White Paper*, p. 12 (pt. 2). *Ti-yi-tz'u kuo-nei ko-ming chan-cheng shih-ch'i-te kung-jen yün-tung* [The workers' movement during the first period of the national revolutionary war] (Peking: People's Publishing Association, 1958), pp. 121-122. Hereafter cited as *1st Workers' Movement*.

8. *Shameen White Paper*, p. 7.

9. From an interview with General Ho Ying-ch'in, Taipei, Taiwan, 1966. Ho was an instructor at Whampoa, regimental commander, and then First Army commander in the Northern Expedition. Both Ho and Chiang Kai-shek were Tokyo Shikan Gakko Military Academy graduates.

10. *Su Chao-cheng* (Shanghai?: China National General Labor Union, 1930), pp. 3-13. Hereafter cited as *Su Ch'ao-ch'eng*. Also in *Chung-kuo kung-ch'an-tang lieh-shih chuan* [Biographies of the Chinese communist martyrs] (Peking: Youth Publishing Society, 1951), pp. 49-52. Hereafter cited as *CCP Martyrs*.

11. *1st Workers' Movement*, p. 122. Copied from Teng Chung-hsia, *Sheng-kang pa-kung k'ai-kuan* [Hong Kong-Kwangtung strike] (Canton: Hong Kong-Kwangtung Strike Committee Propaganda Dept. August 1926. Hereafter cited as Teng Chung-hsia.

12. From an interview with General Leng Hsin, May 17, 1966, Taipei, Taiwan. Teng Chung-hsia, p. 122.

13. Teng Chung-hsia, p. 123.

14. *Ko-ming wen-hsien* [Revolutionary documents], vol. 11, p. 298, ed. by Lo Chia-lün (Taipei: Historical Materials Editing Committee of the Party History of the KMT, 1956). Hereafter cited as *Ko-ming wen-hsien*.

15. *L'Humanité* (April 2, 1926), p. 3.

16. *1st Workers' Movement*, p. 165, table of Kwangtung's tariff revenues, 1924/25.

17. *Chung-kuo hsien-tai ko-ming yün-tung shih* [History of the modern Chinese revolution] (Shanghai?: Committee on Study of Chinese Modern History, 1938), pp. 162-163. Hereafter cited as *CKHT*.

18. *South China Morning Post*, (July 10, 1926), p. 8. Hereafter cited as *SCMP*.

19. Teng Chung-hsia, p. 126.

20. *Hong Kong Daily Press* (May 10, 1926), p. 1. Hereafter cited as *HKDP*.

21. Teng Chung-hsia, pp. 133-134.

CHAPTER 2

1. *Kuowen chou-pao* (February 26, 1927), "Biography of the Week." Hereafter cited as *Kuowen*. *China Yearbook 1928*, ed. by H.E.W. Woodhead (Tientsin, December 1927), p. 1157. Hereafter cited as *China Yearbook 1928*. Vincent Sheean, "Some people from Canton," *Asia* 27(10):815-817. Hereafter cited as Sheean. *Biographical Dictionary of Republican China*, ed. by Howard L. Boorman (New York: Columbia University Press, 1970), vol. 3, pp. 149-150. Hereafter cited as Boorman.

2. John M. Roots, "The Canton Idea," *Asia* 27(4):285-288. Hereafter cited as Roots, "Canton Idea." *1st Workers' Movement*, p. 165. This CCP study does not mention T.V. Soong

but compliments "the ability of the finance officials" of the Canton government.

3. Boorman, vol. 3, pp. 162-165.

4. *China Yearbook 1928*, pp. 1155, 1178. Boorman, vol. 3, pp. 412-413.

5. Roots, "Canton Idea," p. 346. The author cites his interview with Mayor Sun Fo.

6. From a 1966 interview with Sun Fo, who stressed that Russian advisory assistance was more valuable than was their aid in arms or money.

7. T'ang Leang-li, *The Inner History of the Chinese Revolution* (New York: E.P. Dutton & Co., 1930), p. 340. Hereafter cited as T'ang Leang-li.

8. *Kuowen* (July 25, 1926), "Canton Labor Unions," pp. 9-10.

9. From a 1966 interview with General Ho Ying-ch'in, Taipei.

10. Ch'en Kuo-fu, *Huang-p'u chien-chün shih-hua* [Short history of establishing the army at Whampoa] (n.p.:1944). Hereafter cited as Ch'en Kuo-fu. Also included as a selection in *Ko-ming wen-hsien*, pp. 27-36.

11. From a list of entrance examinees for Whampoa's first class, the photostat of which, showing the Kuomintang headquarters letterhead, is held at the National Military Historical Museum, Taipei.

12. From an interview in Taipei, 1966, with Lu Chün-yüeh, brother of Peking KMT leader Lu Yu-yü who was garroted by Chang Tso-lin after the raid on the Russian Embassy in April 1927.

13. From an interview in Taipei, 1966, with Liu Tsu-ch'iang who was a KMT student activist in Peking during the mid-1920s when he worked on a popular student newspaper.

14. *Hsien-tai shih-liao* [Contemporary historical materials], vol. 3 (Shanghai: Hai T'ien Publishing Society, 1934), p. 81. Hereafter cited as *HTSL*.

15. *K'ang-chan yi-ch'ien-te Chung-kuo Kung-ch'an-tang* [The Chinese Communist Party before the war of resistance] 2nd ed. (Chungking?: Sheng-li Publishing Agency, 1942), p. 26. Hereafter cited as *CCP before the War*.

16. *CCP before the War*, p. 26. At least as early as 1925, tension between the KMT-CCP collaborators was evident at Shanghai where Yeh Ch'u-ts'ang and CCP activists Ch'en Tu-hsiu, Ch'ü Ch'iu-pai, and Mao struggled for status in Shanghai University's leadership and on the Shanghai KMT Executive Committee. See also *HTSL*, p. 81. *Kuowen* (May 15, 1927), "Biography of the Week."

17. Interview in Taipei, 1965, with Liu Chü-ch'üan, head of the KMT's Peking branch Women's Department in 1926.

18. Ch'en Kuo-fu, passim.

19. Interview with General Leng Hsin, in Taipei, 1966, who studied and then taught in the Political Department at Whampoa from 1925 to 1926.

20. C. Martin Wilbur and Julie Sien-ying How, *Documents on Communism, Nationalism, and the Soviet Advisors in China 1918-1927* (New York: Columbia University Press, 1956), p. 191. Kisanka's report on the KMT military from the documents seized in 1927 at the Russian Legation. Hereafter cited as *Documents*. See R. Landis, "Training and Indoctrination at the Whampoa School," chapter in *Nationalism and Revolution: China in the 1920's*, ed. by F.G. Chan and T. Etzold (New York: New Viewpoints, 1976).

21. Interview with Sun Fo.

22. *HKDP* (October 2, 1926), p. 1.

23. *Documents*, p. 169. Many additional reports of aid to Canton also in U.S. National Archives, Military Records Div. collection seized in the 1927 raid on the Soviet Embassy, MRD file no. 2657-I-281, items 20, 69, 79, 120 and others. See also U.S. Canton Consul Jenkins reports to State Department, such as May 29, 1925 (893.00/6393).

24. *HKDP* (April 6, 1926), p. 5.

25. Interview with Sun Fo, Yangmingshan, Taiwan, 1966, and in the *HKDP* (October 15, 1926), p. 5.

26. *Documents*, p. 150.

27. As late as 1938, as a wartime emissary to Moscow, Sun Fo was instructed by Chiang to request Galen's return to China as an advisor. Initially, Stalin did not respond to that name until an aide remembered that General Bluecher had been known as Galen. Stalin then told Sun that Galen had been "liquidated" that year for allowing Far Eastern Army secrets to leak out via Japanese female spies who lived with him. See also Vera V. Akimova, *Two Years in*

Revolutionary China, 1925-1927 (Cambridge, Mass.: Harvard University Press, 1971), pp. 223-225. Hereafter cited as Akimova.

28. Roderick L. MacFarquhar, "The Whampoa Military Academy," *Papers on China* IX (August 1955), p. 157.

29. According to Sun Fo, this expertise was more valuable than Russia's materiel aid.

30. Vincent Sheean, "Moscow and the Chinese Revolution," *Asia* 27(6):468-486. Hereafter cited as Sheean, "Moscow."

31. From an interview with Li Ch'ao-ying in Taipei, 1965, who traveled secretly in this manner for the KMT during 1925 and 1926. This is corroborated by the intelligence gathered by the U.S. military attaché in Peking, report dated September 9, 1926, in U.S. National Archives Military Records Div., file no. 2657-I-281(64).

32. *China Yearbook 1928*, p. 1283. By late 1925, Russian military advisor Kisanka reported to the Russian military attaché at Peking that the arsenal produced 125,000 cartridges weekly. From a translated document seized in the 1927 raid on Russian's Peking Legation, *Documents*, p. 193.

33. *Ch'en Kuo-fu*, chap. 5.

34. *China Yearbook 1928*, p. 1282, includes data from 1926 and 1927.

CHAPTER 3

1. *China Yearbook 1928*, p. 1158.

2. Chang Kuo-t'ao, vol. 1, p. 224.

3. *Kuowen* (March 14, 1926), p. 44. Interview with Leng Hsin, Taipei, 1966.

4. U. S. Peking Legation report of January 17, 1925, Department of State 893.00/6049.

5. *Documents*, p. 195, also in an interview with Leng Hsin.

6. T'ang Leang-li, p. 251. F.F. Liu, *A Military History of Modern China 1924-1929* (Princeton: Princeton University Press, 1956), p. 41. Hereafter cited as F.F. Liu.

7. *CCP Martyrs*, p. 222.

8. "Yeh T'ing t'ung-chih lieh-li" [A history of comrade Yeh T'ing]. May 5, 1946. Short mimeographed biography held at the Bureau of Investigation, Research Center on Communism, Ch'ing-t'an, Taiwan.

9. T'ang Leang-li, p. 251.

10. *Documents*, p. 192.

11. *SCMP* (March 5, 1926). *Kuo-chün cheng-kung shih-kao* [History of political work in the national military] (Taipei: History Bureau of Ministry of Defense, 1960), vol. 1, p. 267. Hereafter cited as *History of Political Work*.

12. *Ta-shih chi*, p. 191.

13. *Kuowen* (November 21, 1926), n. p.

14. T'ang Leang-li, p. 251.

15. *Documents*, pp. 389, 392.

16. F.F. Liu, p. 26. *Ta-shih chi*, p. 201.

17. *Ta-shih chi*, p. 202.

18. *SCMP* (March 20, 1926), p. 8.

19. *SCMP* (March 18, 1926), p. 8.

20. *Pei-fa chan-shih* [Military history of the northern expedition] (Taipei: National Defense Ministry Historical and Political Bureau, 1959), vol. 1, p. 69. Hereafter cited as *N. Exp.*

21. *History of Political Work*, vol. 1, p. 267, and the observations of Leng Hsin.

22. *Ta-shih chi*, p. 201.

23. Ibid., p. 202.

24. *SCMP* (March 9, 1926), p. 8.

25. *Ta-shih chi*, pp. 203, 206.

CHAPTER 4

1. *History of Political Work*, vol. 1, p. 361.

2. *Documents*, p. 163.

3. *Ta-shih chi*, pp. 162, 177.

4. *1st Workers' Movement*, p. 127; and Teng Chung-hsia.

5. *Ta-shih chi*, p. 182.

6. Ibid., p. 179.

7. *1st Workers' Movement*, p. 127; *Ta-shih chi*, p. 183; and Harley F. MacNair, *China in Revolution* (Chicago: University of Chicago Press, 1931), p. 98. Hereafter cited as MacNair.

8. *Ta-shih chi*, pp. 184-193; and Teng Chung-hsia, pp. 133-134.

9. *Huang-pu chien-chün san-shih-nien kai-shu* [A summary of thirty years of creating the army at Whampoa], ed. by Kuomintang Party Historical Materials Compilation Committee (Taiwan: Huang-pu Publication Society, 1954), p. 13.

10. Ibid.

11. Chang Ch'i-yün, ed., *Tang shih kai-yao* [Outline of the party's history] (Taipei: Central Committee on Culture Supply Association, 1953), vol. 2, p. 623. Hereafter cited as *TSKY*.

12. Ibid.

13. *Ta-shih chi*, pp. 198-199.

14. Ibid. Chang Kuo-t'ao recalls that Chiang at the Congress ". . . showed himself to be a man of extraordinary achievement. . . . attracted great attention. . . . exhibited the pose of an important military bulwark" (vol. 1, p. 479).

15. Wang Chien-min, *Chung-kuo kung-ch'an-tang shih-kao* [History of the Chinese Communist Party] (Taipei: by the author, 1965), vol. 1, p. 154. Hereafter cited as Wang Chien-min.

16. T'ang Leang-li, p. 240.

17. *Ta-shih chi*, p. 200.

18. Ibid.

19. T'ang Leang-li, p. 242.

20. *SCMP* (March 1, 1926), p. 8.

21. T'ang Leang-li, p. 242.

22. Chang-Kuo-t'ao, vol. 1, pp. 496-497, which is corroborated by a report signed by Kisanka that was seized in the April 1927 raid on the Russian Embassy, U.S. National Archives, Military Records Div., file 2657-I-281(111), no. 7, and the U.S. military attaché's intelligence report from May 2, 1925, MRD 2675-I-281(51).

23. Leon Trotsky, *Problems of the Chinese Revolution*, reprint (New York: Paragon, 1966), pp. 76-77.

CHAPTER 5

1. Wang Chien-min, vol. 1, p. 154. Stuart Schram, *Mao Tse-tung* (New York: Penguin Books, 1967), p. 89fn. Hereafter cited as Schram.

2. Wu Hsiang-hsiang, *O-ti ch'in-lieh Chung-kuo shih* [The history of the Russian empire's invasion of China] (Taipei: Cheng-chung Shu-chü, 1954), p. 328. Hereafter cited as Wu Hsiang-hsiang.

3. Chiang Kai-shek, *Soviet Russia in China* (New York: Farrar, Straus and Giroux, 1965), p. 28. Hereafter cited as *Russia in China*.

4. *SCMP* (March 1, 1926), p. 8.

5. *Ta-shih chi*, p. 202.

6. Wu Hsiang-hsiang, p. 328.

7. *SCMP* (March 2, 1926), p. 8. Wang Chien-min, vol. 1, p. 154.

8. *1st Workers' Movement*, p. 182, copies of *Chung-kuo hai-yüan* [Chinese seaman], Canton, 4 (March 1, 1926).

9. *1st Workers' Movement*, p. 152.

10. *Ko-ming wen-hsien*, vol. 11, p. 298.

11. Teng Chung-hsia, p. 126.

12. *1st Workers' Movement*, p. 165, table of tariff revenue for Kwangtung, 1924/25.

13. Chang Kuo-t'ao, vol. 1 p. 483. U.S. Peking military attaché report of Borodin's promotion of the strike against the advice of Ilyin of the Russian Embassy, but with Moscow's approval. Peking, July 30, 1925; April 8, 1926, in file of MRD 2657-I-281, U.S. National Archives.

14. *SCMP* (March 24, 1926), p. 12.

15. Teng Chung-hsia, p. 137.

16. Ibid., p. 141.

17. Roots, "Canton Idea," p. 287. Based on information and interviews gathered in July 1926.

18. *HKDP* (March 5, 1926), p. 5.

19. *SCMP* (March 6, 1926), p. 11, and (March 17, 1926), p. 9.

20. *SCMP* (March 15, 1926), p. 8.

21. Wu Hsiang-hsiang, p. 328.

22. *SCMP* (March 6, 1926), p. 8, and (March 12, 1926), p. 8.

23. *SCMP* (March 11, 1926), p. 8.

24. Wang Ching-wei, "Wuhan fen-kung-chih ching-kuo" [Wuhan's split with the CCP] *Kuo-li Chung-shan ta-hsüeh jih-pao* [National Chung-shan University daily] *Supplement* (Canton, November 9, 1927), p. 4. Hereafter cited as Wang Ching-wei. Chang Kuo-t'ao admits that Communist insubordination to the KMT leaders was provocative, but was told by CCP comrades there upon his arrival at Canton on March 30 that the *Chung-shan* movement was engineered by the Sun Yat-senist Society as a pretext for an anti-Communist coup (pp. 494-500). Akimova, although not in the highest circle in the Russian mission, recalls the coup as a surprise to the advisors (pp. 210-211). The reports of the U.S. Peking military attaché, based on informants in the Russian Embassy and intelligence gathered at Kalgan at Feng Yü-hsiang's headquarters, indicate that there was considerable divergence of opinion within the Russian group in China, and considerable "adventurism" conducted by factions (MRD 2657-I-281 [5, 57]), so that a conspiracy against Chiang directed secretly by a small group is not inconceivable.

25. *SCMP* (March 22, 1926), p. 8. T'ang Leang-li, pp. 244-245.

26. *SCMP* (March 29, 1926), p. 12. Akimova claims that Kuybyshev (Kisanka) and his associates departed by ship on March 24, (pp. 212-213). Chang Kuo-t'ao, vol. 1, pp. 496-499.

27. *CCP before the War*, pp. 27-28. *SCMP* (March 23, 1926), p. 8.

28. *CKHT*, p. 165; *Kuowen* (April 11, 1926), n. p.

29. *SCMP* (March 23, 1926), p. 8; *HKDP* (March 23, 1926), p. 5.

30. *Ko-ming wen-hsien* (vol. 9, p. 86) reproduces Chiang's telegram to Wang Ching-wei of March 25.

31. *HKDP* (March 30, 1926), p. 5.

32. *Russia in China*, p. 29.

33. *Documents*, no. 23, p. 248.

34. *HKDP* (March 23, 1926), p. 5, and (March 25, 1926), p. 5.

35. Akimova, p. 213.

CHAPTER 6

1. Teng Chung-hsia, and also in *HKDP* (March 26, 1926), pp. 4-5.

2. Teng Chung-hsia, p. 144.

3. *SCMP* (March 29, 1926), p. 10.

4. *HKDP* (March 31, 1926), p. 5.

5. *HKDP* (March 30, 1926), p. 5.

6. *HKDP* (April 2, 1926), p. 5.

7. *Ta-shih chi*, p. 207.

8. *SCMP* (June 3, 1926), p. 9.

9. *HKDP* (April 14, 1926), p. 5.

10. Teng Chung-hsia, p. 144, which agrees with *HKDP* (April 5, 1926), p. 5.

11. *1st Workers' Movement*, p. 144. Ma Ch'ao-chün, ed., *Chung-kuo lao-kung yün-tung shih* [History of the Chinese labor movement] (Taipei: Chung-kuo Lao-kung Fu-li Ch'u-pan She, 1959), p. 762. Hereafter cited as Ma, *Labor*.

12. *HKDP* (April 10, 1926), p. 5.

13. *SCMP* (June 3, 1926), p. 9, and (June 5, 1926), p. 8.

14. *Ta-shih chi*, p. 208.

15. *SCMP* (December 7, 1926), p. 8.

16. See Trotsky. See also Ho Kan-chih, *Chung-kuo hsien-tai ko-ming shih* [A history of the modern Chinese revolution] (Peking: Higher Education Publishing Society, 1957).

17. Wu Hsiang-hsiang, p. 330.

18. *Ta-shih chi*, p. 211.

19. *Documents*, no. 23, p. 248. Notes of the meeting between the Soviet mission and the CCP Kwangtung Branch following the March 20 Coup.

20. *HKDP* (May 17, 1926), p. 5.

21. *Kuowen* (April 24, 1927), n. p. quotes proposals and resolutions of the CEC meeting on May 15, 1926.

22. *Ta-shih chi*, p. 211; *SCMP* (May 22, 1926), p. 3.

23. *HKDP* (May 18, 1926), p. 5, quotes regulations published in the official *Canton Gazette.*

24. Akimova, pp. 213-219.

25. Chang Kuo-t'ao, vol. 1, p. 530. Chang recollects that the CCP Central Committee was dominated by "scholarly-type persons" who could only write "meaningless articles." At that time Chang was chairman of the Labor Movement Committee, but gained, at the launching of the expedition, the new post of chairman of the Military Department of the CCP at Wuchang.

26. *HKDP* (April 21, 1926), p. 5, and (April 22, 1926), p. 5.

27. Ch'en Tu-hsiu, "Chinese Revolutionary Strength, the Policy of Unity and the Canton Coup," *Hsiang Tao* (April 3, 1926), n. p.

28. *L'Humanité* (April 10, 1926), p. 3.

29. *HKDP* (May 11, 1926), p. 5.

30. *HKDP* (May 18, 1926), p. 5, and (May 12, 1926), p. 5.

31. *Ta-shih chi*, pp. 206-207; *HKDP* (April 1, 1926), p. 5.

32. *Ta-shih chi*, p. 207.

33. *HKDP* (April 19, 1926), p. 5.

34. *Kuowen* (May 15, 1927), "Weekly Biography."

35. Wang Chien-min, vol. 1, p. 155; *SCMP* (May 19, 1926), p. 8.

36. *SCMP* (May 21, 1926), p. 8. Chang Kuo-t'ao claims that Wang Ching-wei probably left Canton on May 9 on the same ship that carried Rightist Hu Han-min (vol. 1, p. 709fn. 8).

37. *Kuowen* (February 20, 1927), "Weekly Biography" on last page. *China Yearbook 1928*, p. 1095. *Tang-tai Chung-kuo Ming-jen Chih* [A record of famous men of contemporary China] (Shanghai: 1940), pp. 201-202.

38. *HKDP* (May 22, 1926), p. 5.

CHAPTER 7

1. Akimova, p. 215fn. 15.

2. *HKDP* (April 5, 1926), p. 5, and (April 14, 1926), p. 5.

3. *1st Workers' Movement*, p. 192.

4. *Kuowen* (July 25, 1926), p. 12, pt. 10.

5. *HKDP* (April 8, 1926), p. 5.

6. *HKDP* (April 27, 1926), p. 5.

7. *SCMP* (June 15, 1926), p. 8.

8. *HKDP* (April 14, 1926), p. 5.

9. *Kuowen* (July 25, 1926), pp. 11-17.

10. *HKDP* (April 14, 1926), p. 5.

11. Akimova, p. 192.

12. *SCMP* (March 6, 1926), p. 1.

13. *Kuowen* (July 25, 1926), p. 10.

14. *HKDP* (April 14, 1926), p. 5.

15. *SCMP* (June 1, 1926), p. 9.

16. *Kuowen* (January 23, 1927), "Weekly Biography" on last page. *China Yearbook 1928*, p. 1106. Sheean, pp. 854-858.

17. From an interview with Sun Fo, May 25, 1966, in which Sun recalled that Borodin was assigned to Canton because of his proficiency in English, and because there were more KMT leaders who knew English than knew Russian.

18. *SCMP* (June 21, 1926), p. 8.

19. *SCMP* (July 22, 1926), p. 8.

20. *1st Workers' Movement*, p. 146.

21. Chang Kuo-t'ao lists the original demands of mid-1925, which had been more political in nature (vol. 1, p. 471). *1st Workers' Movement*, p. 148.

22. *1st Workers' Movement*, p. 148, and *SCMP* (July 26, 1926), p. 10.

23. *Kuowen* (July 25, 1926), p. 26, reproduces his address.

24. *SCMP* (July 12, 1926), p. 8.

25. *HKDP* (April 23, 1926), p. 5.

26. *SCMP* (June 9, 1926), p. 9.
27. *SCMP* (June 11, 1926), p. 8.
28. *SCMP* (June 22, 1926), p. 9.
29. *SCMP* (June 30, 1926), p . 8.

CHAPTER 8

1. *HKDP* (May 10, 1926), p. 1, quotes from the *Canton Gazette*.
2. *Su Ch'ao-ch'eng*, p. 26.
3. *Ko-ming wen-hsien*, vol. 11, p. 298.
4. *HKDP* (April 17, 1926), p. 5.
5. Lo Sheng, "Ti-san-ts'e ch'uan-kuo lao-tung ta-hui-chih ching-kuo chi-ch'i chieh-kuo" [Results of the third national labor assembly], *Hsiang Tao* (May 30, 1926), pp. 1500-1501.
6. *HKDP* (April 20, 1926), p. 5.
7. Chang Kuo-t'ao, vol. 1, p. 525. Ch'en Tu-hsiu's letter to Chiang in *Hsiang Tao* (June 9, 1926), pp. 1526-1529.
8. *Ta-shih chi*, p. 210.
9. *HKDP* (May 1, 1926), p. 5.
10. *Ta-shih chi*, p. 212; *CCP Martyrs*, p. 222.
11. *CKHT*, pp. 168-169. Ho Kan-chih, *A History of the Modern Chinese Revolution* (Peking, 1960), p. 129. Hereafter cited as Ho Kan-chih, *Chinese Revolution*.
12. *SCMP* (May 24, 1926), p. 9. Estimate of the number of strikers varies. Chang Kuo-t'ao claims there were over 100,000 (vol. 1, p. 43). *Su Ch'ao-ch'eng*, p. 12, claims 120,000. Akimova, p. 232, states there were 50,000 in Canton and 100,000 in Hong Kong. *Hong Kong Daily Press* interview with Ch'en Yu-jen (Eugene Ch'en) (October 6, 1926), p. 5, cites 60,000 strikers in Kwangtung.
13. *SCMP* (June 2, 1926), p. 10; *Ta-shih chi*, p. 212.
14. *Ta-shih chi*, p. 213.
15. *SCMP* (June 7, 1926), p. 8, and (June 8, 1926), p. 8, and (June 9, 1926), p. 8.
16. *1st Workers' Movement*, p. 146.
17. Roots, "Canton Idea," p. 347. *SCMP* (June 10, 1926), p. 10, and (June 11, 1926), p. 10.
18. *SCMP* (June 26, 1926), p. 10.
19. *SCMP* (June 9, 1926), p. 8.
20. *SCMP* (June 16, 1926), p. 10.
21. *SCMP* (June 21, 1926), p. 8.
22. *Su-Ch'ao-ch'eng*, p. 12.
23. *SCMP* (June 25, 1926), p. 9, and (June 28, 1926), p. 7.
24. *SCMP* (June 26, 1926), p. 10.
25. *SCMP* (July 5, 1926), p. 8.
26. *1st Workers' Movement* cites Teng Chung-hsia's "Hong Kong Strike Story," p. 146.
27. *Su Ch'ao-ch'eng*, p. 12.
28. *SCMP* (June 25, 1926), p. 9.
29. *SCMP* (June 18, 1926), p. 9.
30. *SCMP* (June 28, 1926), p. 9.
31. *SCMP* (June 14, 1926), p. 8.
32. *Kuowen* (July 25, 1926), p. 13.
33. *SCMP* (July 3, 1926), p. 8.
34. *SCMP* (July 7, 1926), p. 8, and (July 8, 1926), p. 8.
35. *Hsiang Tao* (July 7, 1926), pp. 1584-1585. According to Wang Chien-min's reading of CCP reports to the Soviet ambassador after the July meeting of the Second Conference of the Enlarged Central Committee, the CCP not only opposed the expedition but hoped to use the peasants, workers, and soldiers movements to overthrow Chiang's leadership by force.
36. *History of Political Work*, p. 286. Quoted from Mao Szu-ch'eng, *Min-kuo shih-wu-nien yi-ch'ien-chih Chiang chieh-shih hsien-sheng* [Chiang Kai-shek before 1926] (Hong Kong: Lung-men Book Store, 1965). Hereafter cited as *Chiang before 1926*.
37. *L'Humanité* (July 3, 1926), p. 3; *SCMP* (July 3, 1926), p. 8.
38. From the photograph of a document held at the National Military Museum, Taipei.
39. *Ko-ming wen-hsien*, vol. 12, p. 831.

CHAPTER 9

1. Chang Kuo-t'ao, vol. 1, p. 525, describes the pessimism of Galen and Borodin.
2. Lucian W. Pye, *Warlord Politics* (New York: Praeger, 1971), p. 129.
3. J.C. Huston, U.S. consul general at Hankow, MS report to State Department. "General Historical Sketch of Political Conditions in the Hankow Consular District from the Revolution of 1911 to March 1925," April 4, 1925, State Dept. no. (SD) 893.00/6206, pp. 39-41, 143-144. Hereafter cited as Huston, "Sketch."
4. Boorman, vol. 2, pp. 419-420. Ch'en Ming-shu's biography is in vol. 1, pp. 213-214.
5. Boorman, vol. 1, p. 281 on Ch'eng Ch'ien. *China Yearbook 1928*, p. 1106.
6. Chiang's telegram to Chao, dated July 5, 1926, in the collection of the National Military Museum, Taipei.
7. U.S. Changsha Consul C.D. Meinhardt to State Department, March 12, 1925, SD 893.00/6148. Consul Meinhardt to State Department, March 12, 1926, SD 893.00/7314.
8. From a report of the Russian mission at Canton in early 1926 entitled "Characteristics of Prominent Men of the Kuomintang," included in the documents seized in the Russian Legation at Peking in April 1927. Translated by the staff of the Army Attaché of the U.S. Legation. U.S. National Archives, Military Records Division (MRD), file no. 2657-I-281(111), document no. 30. Hereafter cited as *Seized Documents* with MRD numbers.
9. U.S. Changsha Consul C.D. Meinhardt to State Department, March 5, 1926, SD 893.00/7319, MF 329-51, probably in Chinese dollars, which were valued at approximately 2/U.S. dollar.
10. *Seized Documents*, MRD 2657-I-281(111), no. 30.
11. *Ta-shih chi*, p. 202.
12. U.S. Changsha Consul C.D. Meinhardt to State Department, March 5, 1926, SD 893.00/7319.
13. *SCMP* (March 1, 1926), p. 8.
14. U.S. Changsha Consul C.D. Meinhardt to State Department, March 5, 1926, SD 893.00/7319.
15. U.S. Canton Consul Douglas Jenkins to State Department, March 10, 1926, SD 893.00/7293.
16. U.S. Changsha Consul C.D. Meinhardt to Secretary of State, April 3, 1926, SD 893.00/7372.
17. Ibid.
18. U.S. naval attaché Peking to Department of Navy, April 29, 1926, SD 893.00/7448.
19. *Hsiang Tao*, July 14, 1926, p. 1606, "Hunan in the Midst of the Noise of the Northern Expedition," published by the CCP in Shanghai.
20. Report of U.S. naval attaché, May 7, 1926, SD 893.00/7466.
21. *SCMP* (June 1 and 8, 1926) reports the movement of large NRA units across the border.
22. *SCMP* (July 7, 1926), p. 8, and (July 8, 1926), p. 8, in which reports state that the vanguard including Yeh T'ing had been defeated and was awaiting reinforcements. Ko T'eh, "pei-fa sheng-chung-chih Hunan" [Hunan in the midst of the northern expedition], *Hsiang Tao* (July 14, 1926), p. 1608, where the official CCP organ states that the fighting had stopped in preparation for an "official battle of North versus South."
23. *Ta-shih chi*, p. 213.
24. Jean Chesneaux, "The Federalist Movement in China, 1920-3," in *Modern China's Search for a Political Form*, ed. by Jack Gray (London: Oxford University Press, 1969), chap. 4, p. 107, which translated Chesneaux's article in *Revue Historique*, October-December, 1966.
25. See *China Yearbook 1926*, pp. 1038-1043.
26. *N. Exp.*, vol. 2, pp. 350-351.
27. *SCMP* (July 27, 1926), p. 9. Some recruits went first to Kwangtung for training and then returned north to combat.
28. Ch'en Kung-po, *Han feng chi* [Collection of the north wind] (Shanghai: Association of Local Government, 1945), p. 40. Hereafter cited as Ch'en Kung-po. Akimova, p. 242.
29. Akimova, p. 242.
30. *Kuowen* (August 5, 1926), p. 3.

31. *SCMP* August 5, 1926), p. 9. *Ta-shih chi*, p. 219, states ⸜hiang arrived on August 9.
32. *Kuowen* (August 5, 1926), p. 23.
33. *Ko-ming wen-hsien*, vol. 12, pp. 162-163. *Ta-shih chi*, p. 219, claims Chiang on August 6 ordered P'eng's Ninth Army and Wang's Tenth Army to concentrate at Ching-li.
34. *SCMP* (August 18, 1926), p. 9.
35. *New York Times* (August 24, 1926), p. 4.
36. Ch'en Kung-po, pp. 45-46.
37. Ibid.
38. *TSKY*, vol. 2, p. 524.
39. Ibid.
40. *SCMP* (August 20, 1926), p. 8.
41. *Pei-fa chien-shih* [Simple history of the northern expedition] (Taipei, May 1961), pp. 53-54.
42. *SCMP* (August 26, 1926), p. 9.
43. *SCMP* (August 29, 1926), p. 8.
44. *Kuowen* (August 29, 1926), p. 8.
45. *SCMP* (August 28, 1926), p. 10.
46. *N. Exp.*, vol. 2, p. 4.
47. *TSKY*, vol. 2, p. 525.
48. Ibid., pp. 411-412.
49. Ch'en Kung-po, pp. 54-55.
50. *N. Exp.*, vol. 2, p. 426.
51. Ibid., pp. 423-430.
52. *TSKY*, vol. 2, p. 525.
53. *N. Exp.*, vol. 2, p. 427.
54. *New York Times* (September 1, 1926), p. 7. Huo Jan "Chin-shu yüeh lai Hunan-te kung-jen yün-tung" [The Hunan workers' movement in recent months], *Chan-shih chou-pao* [Soldiers' Weekly] (November 14, 1926), quoted in *1st Workers' Movement*, pp. 323-324.
55. *Kuowen* (September 5, 1926) n. p. *N. Exp.*, vol. 2, p. 405.
56. *N. Exp.*, vol. 2, pp. 414, 430-433.
57. *Kuowen* (September 12, 1926), p. 4. *SCMP* (September 8, 1926), p. 8. *N. Exp.*, vol. 2, p. 443. Akimova, pp. 245-246.
58. *N. Exp.*, vol. 2, p. 434.
59. *SCMP* (September 16, 1926), p. 9. *N. Exp.*, vol. 2, p. 464.
60. *N. Exp.*, vol. 2, p. 433.
61. *Kuowen* (September 19, 1926), p. 2.
62. *Kuowen* (January 2, 1927), n. p. in the published diary of a minor administrator besieged in Wuchang.
63. *Ko-ming wen-hsien*, vol. 13, p. 2003, quotes from *Chiang before 1926*.
64. *Documents*, pp. 367-368.
65. Letter in the National Military Museum, Taipei, collection from Chiang Kai-shek to Li Chi-shen dated August 6, 1926.
66. *Kuowen* (August 8, 1926), n. p.
67. *Documents*, pp. 367-368.
68. *Kuowen* (September 12, 1926), "The Situation in Fukien and Kiangsi."
69. Ibid., p. 4, agrees with *N. Exp.*, vol. 2, chap. 6.

CHAPTER 10

1. *Ta-shih chi*, p. 221.
2. *Kuowen* (October 3, 1926), n. p.; *SCMP* (September 30, 1926), p. 9, and (October 20, 1926), p. 9.
3. *Kuowen* (October 3, 1926), n. p.; *SCMP* (September 22, 1926), p. 9.
4. *SCMP* (September 25, 1926), p. 9. *HKDP* (October 5, 1926), p. 7. *N. Exp.*, vol. 2, pp. 455-456.
5. *Kuowen* (October 3, 1926), n. p. *China Mail* (October 5, 1926), p. 9. *SCMP* (October 21, 1926), p. 9. *New York Times* (September 28, 1926), p. 9.
6. *SCMP* (September 30, 1926), p. 9, and (October 20, 1926), p. 9.

7. *SCMP* (September 25, 1926), p. 8, and (September 30, 1926), p. 8. *HKDP* (October 7, 1926), p. 5.

8. *Kuowen* (October 3, 1926), n. p.

9. *HKDP* (October 1, 1926), p. 7. *China Mail* (October 5, 1926), pp. 1, 9. *Kuowen* (January 2, 1927), "Diary from the Siege of Wuchang," quotes Sun's press releases.

10. *SCMP* (December 2, 1926), p. 9. Wang, a member of the Whampoa faculty, is considered to have been a friend of Chiang.

11. *China Mail* (October 5, 1926), p. 9. *N. Exp.*, vol. 2, p. 456.

12. *Kuowen* (September 19, 1926), p. 2.

13. *Kuowen* (October 3, 1926), n. p. *SCMP* (September 17, 1926), p. 9, and (September 30, 1926), p. 9.

14. *Kuowen* (October 3, 1926), n. p.

15. *N. Exp.*, vol. 2, p. 456.

16. *China Mail* (October 5, 1926), p. 1. *HKDP* (October 8, 1926), p. 7. *N. Exp.*, vol. 2, p. 467.

17. *HKDP* (October 13, 1926), p. 7. *N. Exp.*, vol. 2, p. 518.

18. *New York Times* (October 8, 1926), p. 9.

19. *SCMP* (October 19, 1926), p. 9.

20. *Kuowen* (January 2, 1926), "Diary from the Siege of Wuchang."

21. *Kuowen* (October 10, 1926), n. p.

22. *Kuowen* (September 19, 1926), p. 2.

23. *Kuowen* (October 24, 1926), n. p.

24. Hsia Ch'ao was born in Ch'ing-t'ien about 1881 (*Kuowen* [Aug. 22, 1926]). Chou Feng-ch'i was born in either 1880 or 1882 in Chang-hsing, northeastern Chekiang, according to the *Tang-tai chung-kuo ming-jen lu*, p. 134, or *Chung-kuo kuan-shen jen-ming lu*, p. 230.

25. Edwin S. Cunningham, U.S. Consul-General Shanghai, "A Brief Historical Sketch of the Political History of Chekiang Province since the Year 1911," (Shanghai, 1925), p. 11.

26. Ma Hsü-lun, *Wo tsai liu-shih-sui i-ch'ien* [My life sixty years ago] (Shanghai: Sheng-huo Book Store, 1947), p. 96. Ma was a provincial KMT member who was a friend of Hsia and worked to gain his defection in 1926. Hereafter cited as Ma Hsü-lun.

27. *Chung-kuo kuan-shen jen-ming lu* [Lives of Chinese officials and gentry] (Tokyo, 1918), p. 366. *Min-kuo chün-fa ch'ü-hsien* [Interesting anecdotes on the warlords of the republic] (n. p.: Hsien-tai Pub. Co., ca. 1937), pp. 195-197.

28. *North China Herald* (September 20, 1925), p. 452, reported from Shanghai that Hsia had 10,000 armed police, while the British Consul at Ningpo, Chekiang, H.F.H. Derry, in "Quarterly Report to the Foreign Office" April 31, 1925, states Hsia had 5,000 police, and in Ch'en Pu-lei's *Kuo-min ko-ming chün chan-shih* [A history of the battles of the National Revolutionary Army] (Nanking, 1936), chap. 2, p. 9, the number is set at 15,000 in 1926.

29. British Foreign Office report, series 405/231 no. 180, April 1, 1921.

30. Ch'en was born ca. 1883 in Shaohsing *hsien* according to Boorman, vol. 1, pp. 251-253.

31. U.S. Shanghai Consul Edwin S. Cunningham, October 29, 1924 (893.00/5801).

32. *Tung-fang tsa-chih* (January 25, 1926), vol. 23, no. 2, publishes the entire constitution, which is dated January 1, 1926.

33. U.S. Shanghai Consul-General Cunningham to Peking Legation, January 26, 1926 (893.00/7108).

34. U.S. Shanghai Consul-General Cunningham, November 20, 1926 (893.00/5853).

35. *Shen Pao* (June 14 and later September 11, 1926). *Tung-fang tsa-chih* [Eastern miscellany], vol. 24, no. 16, p. 4, "The Situatiion with the Farmers of Ch'ü-chou, Chekiang."

36. In an interview at Yangmingshan, Taiwan, 1966, Sun Fo emphasized the vital significance of the subversion of provincial commanders, work with which he had experience as an intermediary carrying the prestige of his father's name. *Hong Kong Daily Press* (April 19, 1926), p. 5, reports Sun Fo's visit to Sun Ch'uan-fang.

37. *Hsin chung-kuo jen-wu chih: Fen-sheng* [The record of the personalities of new China: by provinces], edited and published by Huang Hui-ch'üan (Hong Kong: 1930), p. 272. U.S. Nanking Consul J.K. Davis, October 30, 1926 (893.00/7913).

38. Ma Hsü-lun, pp. 95-96.

39. State Department Diplomatic vol. 1237 on Chekiang Affairs, U.S. National Archives.

40. *North China Herald* (Shanghai) (October 23 and 30, 1926). Hereafter cited as *NCH*. Reuter reports from Canton dated October 19 and 23. *SCMP* (October 21 and 28, 1926), p. 8.

41. U.S. Shanghai Consul Cunningham to Peking Legation, November 2, 1926. U.S. National Archives (893.00/7876).

42. Ma Hsü-lun, pp. 96, 110. U.S. Shanghai Consul Gauss to Secretary of State, December 6, 1926. U.S. National Archives (893.00/7990).

43. *Kuowen* (September 19, October 10, 24, 1926), n. p.

44. U.S. Nanking Consul J.K. Davis, October 15, 1926, reported the "mutiny" firsthand from the neighboring consulate. Report to U.S. Legation, Peking, U.S. National Archives (893.00/7838).

45. *Ta-shih chi*, p. 228. Ch'en Pu-lei, *Min-kuo ko-ming chün chan-shih* [A history of the battles of the National Revolutionary Army], vol. 2, p. 103. U.S. Naval Intelligence Report, C.O. of U.S.S. *Isabel* to Yangtze patrol at Shanghai, October 21, 1926, WA-7: *Isabel*, U.S. National Archives.

46. U.S. Nanking Consul J.K. Davis to F. Mayer at the Peking Legation, October 25, 1926, U.S. National Archives (893.00/7925).

47. *Min-kuo chün-fa ch'ü-hsien* [Interesting anecdotes on the warlords of the republic], p. 199, report of Shanghai Consul Cunningham, October 21, 1926. *Shen Pao* (October 20, 1926), p. 5. Story reported in Boorman, vol. 1, p. 252.

48. U.S. Nanking Consul Davis to Peking Legation, October 25 (893.00/7925).

49. Boorman, vol. 1, p. 252.

50. *Shen Pao* (October 22, 1926), p. 6.

51. *Ta-shih chi*, p. 228.

52. *Shen Pao* (October 20, 1926), p. 5. *Ta-shih chi*, p. 228, claims the Political Affairs Committee included the KMT's contact, Ma Hsü-lun.

53. U.S. Shanghai Consul Cunningham to Peking Legation, October 17, 1926, U.S. National Archives (893.00/7755).

54. *Min-kuo chün-fa ch'ü-wen* [Interesting anecdotes about the warlords] (Shanghai, n.d.), pp. 201-202.

55. *SCMP* (October 30, 1926), p. 9. *TSKY*, vol. 2, pp. 534-535.

56. *N. Exp.*, vol. 2, p. 551. *SCMP* (October 26, 1926), p. 9.

57. *N. Exp.*, vol. 2, pp. 554-556.

58. *History of Political Work*, vol. 1, p. 296.

59. *TSKY*, vol. 2, pp. 528-529. *SCMP* (December 2, 1926), p. 9.

60. *SCMP* (November 19, 1926), p. 9, cites Chu P'ei-teh's telegram to Canton.

CHAPTER 11

1. *Kuowen* (August 30, 1926), n. p.

2. *SCMP* (September 9, 1926), p. 9.

3. *SCMP* (September 20, 1926), p. 9.

4. *Ta-shih chi*, pp. 226-228.

5. *N. Exp.*, vol. 2, pp. 575-576.

6. Ibid., pp. 574-590.

7. Interview with Liao Wen-yin, December 22, 1965, Taipei. See also *N. Exp.*, vol. 2, pp. 592-593.

8. *N. Exp.*, vol. 2, pp. 592-593.

9. Liu Chien-ch'ün, "Pei-fa ch'ien-hou ku-jen ch'ün" [Old friends from the northern expedition], *Chüan-chi wen-shüeh* [Biographical literature] (Taipei, 1966), pp. 22-27.

10. *Kuowen* (November 7, 1926), p. 3. *N. Exp.*, vol. 3, p. 588.

11. *Kuowen* (November 21, 1926), n. p.

12. *N. Exp.*, vol. 2, pp. 589-590. *Kuowen* (December 5, 1926), n. p., and (December 12, 1926), n. p.

13. *New York Times* (December 3, 1926), p. 4.

14. From an interview with Liao Wen-yin, December 22, 1965, Taipei.

15. *Ta-shih chi*, p. 234. *N. Exp.*, vol. 2, p. 593.

16. *Kuowen* (November 28, 1926), n. p.

17. *Kuowen* (December 12, 1926), n. p. *SCMP* (November 26, 1926), p. 12, and (November 27, 1926), p. 12.

18. *Ta-shih chi*, p. 233.

19. *Kuowen* (November 28, 1926), n. p.

20. *Kuowen* (December 5, 1926), n. p.

21. *CKHT*, p. 176, and *HTSL*, vol. 3, pp. 174-176.

22. *1st Workers' Movement*, pp. 329-330, copied from "Yueh-Han t'ieh-lu kung-jen ta pa-kung" [The Canton-Hankow railroad workers' strike], *Chan-shih chou-pao* (November 21, 1926). See also *SCMP* (November 22, 1926), p. 8, and *CCP before the War*, p. 28.

23. *SCMP* (November 29 and 30, and December 10, 1926), n. p.

24. *Min-kuo shih-wu-nien yi-ch'ien-chih Chiang chieh-shih hsien-sheng*, vol. 20, p. 19.

25. *SCMP* (December 10, 1926), p. 9. *New York Times* (December 10, 1926), p. 4.

26. *New York Times* (December 1, 1926), p. 1.

27. Chiang Yung-ching, *Pao-lo-t'ing yü Wuhan cheng-ch'üan* [Borodin and the Wuhan regime] (Taipei: Chung-kuo Hsüeh-shu Ch'u-tso Chiang-tsu Wei-yüan Hui, 1963), p. 33. Hereafter cited as *Borodin*. *L'Humanité* (December 4, 1926) on the general strike plan.

28. *SCMP* (December 7, 1926), p. 8.

29. *Kuowen* (December 12, 1926), p. 1. *SCMP* (December 8, 1926), p. 9.

30. *New York Times* (December 1, 1926), p. 1.

31. *Kuowen* (December 12, 1926), p. 1.

32. *SCMP* (December 7, 1926), p. 8.

33. U.S. Shanghai Consul C.E. Gauss to the Peking Legation, December 6, 1926 (State Dept. Record Group 84, 800: Chekiang).

34. *Kuowen* (November 28, 1926), "Report on the War, Nov. 19-25."

35. *Shen Pao* (November 26, 1926), p. 6.

36. U.S. Shanghai Consul C.E. Gauss to the Secretary of State, December 6, 1926 (893.00/7990), in which Gauss interpreted the movement as one coordinated by the KMT to weaken Sun's hold on the United Provinces. See also *HTSL* vol. 3, pp. 174-176.

37. U.S. Nanking Consul J.K. Davis to Minister MacMurray, December 15, 1926, U.S. National Archives (893.00/8033).

38. *Shen Pao* (December 14, 1926), p. 5.

39. *Kuowen* (November 28, 1926), n. p.

40. U.S. Nanking Consul J.K. Davis reported to Minister J. MacMurray, December 11, 1926 (893.00/8032), that the Manchurian allies were to receive C$250,000 monthly from Chekiang (plus similar amounts from Kiangsu and Anhui) for their reinforcements.

41. *Hsin chung-kuo jen-wu chih: Fen-sheng* [A record of personalities of new China: by provinces] (Hong Kong, 1930), p. 272.

42. *NCH* (April 4, 1925), p. 2.

43. *Ta-shih chi*, p. 235.

44. U.S. Shanghai Consul Gauss to Minister MacMurray, December 14, 1926, U.S. National Archives (893.00/8036).

45. U.S. Shanghai Consul Gauss to Secretary of State, December 6, 1926, U.S. National Archives (893.00/7990).

46. *Ta-shih chi*, p. 236.

47. *Kuowen* (December 26, 1926), n. p.

48. *Kuowen* (January 2, 1927), p. 3. U.S. Shanghai Consul Gauss to Minister MacMurray, December 28, 1926, National (893.00/8109). *Ta-shih chi*, p. 237.

49. *HTSL*, vol. 3, pp. 26-27.

50. *Kuowen* (January 16, 1927), n. p. *New York Times* (January 24, 1927), p. 1. *N. Exp.*, vol. 2, pp. 629-631.

51. *Kuowen* (January 23, 1927), n. p.

52. *N. Exp.*, vol. 2, pp. 623-627.

53. Ibid., pp. 627-628; *Kuowen* (February 13, 1927), n. p.

54. *Kuowen* (February 20, 1927), n. p.

55. Ibid.; *N. Exp.*, vol. 2, p. 628.

56. *Kuowen* (February 20, 1927), "The War in Chekiang."
57. Ibid., and *Kuowen* (February 27, 1927), n. p.
58. *Kuowen* (March 13, 1927), "A Week's Record of the Disorderly Retreat through Chiahsing." *HTSL*, vol. 3, pp. 34-35.
59. Ma Hsü-lun, pp. 106-107. *Ta-shih chi*, p. 246.

CHAPTER 12

1. *Kuowen* (March 6, 1927), n. p. See discussions of intervention in State Department and consular reports from Shanghai, January, February 1927, U.S. National Archives series, 893.00/8200-8600s.
2. *New York Times* (December 1, 1926), p. 1.
3. U.S. Shanghai Consul Gauss' report on Sun's "Secret Service Corps," January 17, 1927 (893.00/8264). *Kuowen* (January 16, 1927), n. p.
4. *HTSL*, vol. 3, p. 177.
5. *Kuowen* (November 28, 1926), n. p.
6. *SCMP* (March 18, 1927), p. 10.
7. Shih Ying, "The Record of the Shanghai General Strike," *Hsiang Tao* (February 28, 1927).
8. *HTSL*, vol. 3, p. 178.
9. *CCP before the War*, p. 31.
10. *Kuowen* (February 27, 1927), n. p.
11. Ibid.
12. *Hsiang Tao* (February 28, 1927), n. p.
13. *Kuowen* (February 27, 1927), n. p.
14. *Kuowen* (March 8, 1927), n. p.
15. Ibid.
16. *Documents*, p. 382.
17. *Documents*, p. 389.
18. *Kuowen* (January 16, 1927), n. p.
19. *Kuowen* (May 1, 1927), n. p.
20. Ibid.
21. *Borodin*, p. 43, cites the record of the sixty-fourth session of the Central Political Meeting, Nanchang, February 1927.
22. *Ch'ing-tang yün-tung* [The party purification movement] (Nanking: Ch'ing-tang Committee, 1927), pp. 16-19.
23. *Documents*, p. 395.
24. U.S. Nanking Consul J.K. Davis' reports of late November and early December 1926, State Department series in National Archives (893.00/7997, 8002, 8031). *Ta-shih chi*, p. 234.
25. *N. Exp.*, vol. 2, p. 648.
26. Ibid.
27. *Kuowen* (March 6, 1927), n. p.
28. *SCMP* (March 17, 1927), p. 11.
29. *Kuowen* (March 20, 1927), n. p.
30. *SCMP* (March 21, 1927), p. 10.
31. *N. Exp.*, vol. 2, p. 660.
32. *Kuowen* (March 27, 1927), n. p.
33. *Kuowen* (March 27, 1927), "Weekly News."
34. Ibid. *SCMP* (March 21, 1927), p. 10, and (March 22, 1927), p. 10. *CCP before the War*, pp. 31, 32.
35. *N. Exp.*, vol. 2, p. 635.
36. *SCMP* (March 22, 1927), p. 10. *N. Exp.*, vol. 2, p. 636.
37. *Pei-fa chien-shih*, chap. 3, Map 42.
38. Ibid.
39. *1st Workers' Movement*, p. 16.
40. *Kuowen* (March 27, 1927), n. p.
41. Ibid.

42. *SCMP* (March 25, 1927), p. 10, General Pai's order to organized labor prohibiting strikes in essential public services, and his call for an end to the general strike. *SCMP* (April 9, 1927), p. 12, United Press release from Shanghai.

43. *SCMP* (April 8, 1927), p. 12.

44. Ibid.

CHAPTER 13

1. Wang Chien-min, vol. 1, p. 253. *Documents*, p. 393.

2. *Kuowen* (April 3, 1927), "Record of the CEC Meeting."

3. *Kuowen* (March 20, 1927).

4. *Ta-shih chi*, p. 251. *SCMP* (April 4, 1927), p. 10.

5. *History of Political Work*, vol. 1, pp. 303-313.

6. *SCMP* (March 19, 1927), p. 13.

7. Translation from the photograph of the original in the National Military Museum, Taipei, collection. A brush written "828" appears on the top margin and a stamped "00904" in the bottom margin.

8. *Documents*, pp. 400-401. T'ang Leang-li, p. 264.

9. *SCMP* (April 6, 1927), p. 10. Originated in *Nan-chung pao* [S. China daily]. *Kuowen* (April 10, 1927), n. p.

10. *SCMP* (April 4, 1927), p. 12. Wang Chien-min, vol. 1, p. 275.

11. Harold R. Isaacs, *The Tragedy of the Chinese Revolution* (Stanford: Stanford University Press, 1951), p. 166. Hereafter cited as Isaacs.

12. *Kuowen* (April 3, 1927), "Weekly News Diary." *SCMP* (April 6, 1927), p. 11.

13. *SCMP* (April 4, 1927), p. 12.

14. H. Owen Chapman, *The Chinese Revolution 1926-27: A Record of the Period under Communist Control as Seen from the Nationalist Capital, Hankow* (London: Constable & Co., 1928), p. 66. Hereafter cited as Chapman.

15. Hsü Wen-t'ien, ed., *Chung-kuo kung-jen yün-tung shih-kao* [A history of the Chinese workers' movement] (Chungking: Central Social Department, 1940?), p. 101. Hereafter cited as *CKYS*.

16. *SCMP* (April 2, 1927), p. 12.

17. *SCMP* (April 8, 1927), p. 10, and (April 12, 1927), p. 12.

18. Letter published in *Ch'ing-tang yün-tung* [The party purification movement], ed. by the Committee to Encourage Party Purification (Nanking: 1927), pp. 38-39.

19. *Kuowen* (April 10, 1927), n. p.

20. Borodin, p. 78.

21. *Kuowen* (April 10, 1927), n. p.

22. Wang Ching-wei, pp. 5-6. See also Wang's letter quoted in *Ch'ing-tang yün-tung*, pp. 39-40.

23. *SCMP* (April 13, 1927), p. 10, and (April 9, 1927), p. 10.

24. Isaacs, p. 172. *SCMP* (April 8, 1927), p. 12.

25. Isaacs, p. 172. *History of Political Work*, vol. 1, p. 312.

26. *Documents*, p. 403.

27. *SCMP* (April 4, 1927), p. 12. See Wu T'ien-wei, "Chiang Kai-shek's April Twelfth Coup d'Etat of 1927," in *Twentieth Century China*, vol. 1 of Nationalism and Revolution: China in the 1920's, ed. by F. Gilbert Ch'an (New York: New Viewpoints, 1976).

28. Wang Chien-min, vol. 1, p. 229, quotes extensively from Wu Chih-hui's report.

29. *1st Workers' Movement*, pp. 494-500.

30. *Kuowen* (April 10, 1927), n. p.

31. *SCMP* (April 12, 1927), p. 10, and (April 18, 1927), p. 12.

32. *Kuowen* (May 15, 1927), n. p.

33. Sheean, pp. 815-817.

34. *SCMP* (March 31, 1927), p. 12.

35. *SCMP* (March 31, 1927), p. 12. *Kuowen* (April 2, 1927), "Diary of Weekly News."

36. *Ta-shih chi*, p. 251.

37. *Kuowen* (April 3, 1927), n. p.

38. *Chiang Chieh-shih Yao-lun Chi* (Taipei: Shih-chieh Book Co., 1955), p. 37.

39. *SCMP* (April 1, 1927), p. 10.
40. *SCMP* (April 2, 1927), p. 10.
41. *SCMP* (April 20, 1927), p. 12.
42. *Ta-shih chi,* p. 252.
43. *Kuowen* (May 1, 1927), n. p.
44. Schram, p. 126.
45. *Borodin,* p. 175.
46. *Ta-shih chi,* p. 255. *Kuowen* (April 24, 1927), n. p.
47. *Kuowen* (May 1, 1927), n. p.

CHAPTER 14

1. *Kuowen* (May 1, 1927), n. p.
2. *N. Exp.,* vol. 3, p. 678.
3. *SCMP* (April 20, 1927), p. 12.
4. *Ta-shih chi,* p. 258. *Kuowen* (May 22, 1927).
5. *N. Exp.,* vol. 3, p. 731.
6. *Kuowen* (May 15, 1927), n. p.
7. *Kuowen* (June 5, 1927), n. p. *N. Exp.,* vol. 3, p. 748.
8. *Kuowen* (July 12, 1927), n. p.
9. *N. Exp.,* vol. 3, p. 678.
10. *Kuowen* (June 5, 1927), n. p.
11. *Kuowen* (June 26, 1927), n. p. MacNair, p. 124
12. *Kuowen* (July 10, 1927), n. p.
13. *Kuowen* (June 12, 1927), n. p.
14. *Kuowen* (June 5, 1927), n. p.
15. *Kuowen* (July 10, 1927), n. p.
16. *Kuowen* (May 29, 1927), n. p.
17. *Russia in China,* p. 43.
18. *Kuowen* (July 17, 1927), n. p. *Ta-shih chi,* p. 263.
19. *Ta-shih chi,* p. 262.
20. *Kuowen* (July 10, 1927), n. p.
21. *Kuowen* (July 17, 1927), n. p.
22. See Wu T'ien-wei, "A Review of the Wuhan Debacle," *Journal of Asian Studies* 29(1):125-143.
23. Wang Ching-wei, p. 6.
24. *Kuowen* (August 21, 1927), n. p.
25. T'ang Leang-li, p. 292.
26. MacNair, p. 125. According to S. Okamoto's unpublished research, Temple University.
27. *Ta-shih chi,* pp. 270, 274.
28. *Kuowen* (August 21, 1927), n. p.
29. T'ang Leang-li, p. 290.
30. *Kuowen* (August 28, 1927), n. p.
31. *N. Exp.,* vol. 3, pp. 868-869.
32. Ibid., pp. 873-875.
33. *Kuowen* (September 4, 1927), n. p.
34. Ibid.; *N. Exp.,* vol. 3, p. 894.
35. *N. Exp.,* vol. 3, pp. 897-899.
36. Ibid.
37. *Huang-pu chien-chün san-shih-nien kai-shu.* p. 24. TSKY, vol. 2, p. 561.
38. *N. Exp.,* vol. 3, pp. 900-903.

CHAPTER 15

1. Arthur N. Holcombe, *The Chinese Revolution* (Cambridge, Mass.: Harvard University Press, 1930), p. 238.
2. *CKHT,* p. 121. *Kuowen* (June 5, 1927), "Weekly News Diary."
3. CCP Central Committee emergency meeting recorded in *Chung-yang t'ung-hsin* [Communiqué from the headquarters], vol. 2 (August 23, 1927), pp. 14-15.

4. *N. Exp.*, vol. 3, pp. 1089-1102.

5. *N. Exp.*, vol. 3, pp. 1106-1108.

6. *Ta-shih chi*, p. 274.

7. *N. Exp.*, vol. 3, p. 1024.

8. Ibid., p. 1047.

9. Wang Ching-wei, pp. 1-10.

10. T'ang Leang-li, pp. 309-310.

11. *Kuang-chou p'ao-tung-chih yi-yi yü chiao-hsün* [The significance and lessons learned from the Canton uprising] (CCP Central Committee, 1928), pp. 6-11. Hereafter cited as *Canton Uprising*.

12. Interview in 1966 with Teng Hui-fang, a women's movement leader of the KMT, who was in Canton during the coup.

13. *Canton Uprising*, p. 10.

14. *SCMP* (May 4, 1928), p. 10. Conrad Brandt, *Stalin's Failure in China: 1924-1927* (Cambridge, Mass.: Harvard University Press, 1958), pp. 162-163. Akimova, p. 337.

15. *Ta-shih chi*, p. 278.

16. T'ang Leang-li, p. 319. *Ta-shih chi*, pp. 278-279.

17. *Ko-ming wen-hsien*, vol. 18, pp. 10-11, quotes the telegram in full.

18. *Ta-shih chi*, p. 281.

CHAPTER 16

1. *N. Exp.*, vol. 4, pp. 14-28. *TSKY*, vol. 2, p. 570.

2. *Ta-shih chi*, p. 285.

3. MacNair, p. 132.

4. *Ta-shih chi*, p. 281.

5. *Ko-ming wen-hsien*, vol. 18, p. 13, quotes the public announcement from Nanking to Hsüchou.

6. *Ta-shih chi*, p. 287.

7. *TSKY*, vol. 2, p. 571. *History of Political Work*, vol. 1, p. 333.

8. *Kuowen* (April 8, 1928), n. p.

9. Ibid., p. 10.

10. Ibid. cites the *Chung-yang jih-pao* [Central daily news], Shanghai, KMT, 1928.

11. *History of Political Work*, vol. 1, p. 351.

12. Ibid., p. 344.

13. *N. Exp.*, vol. 4, pp. 1227-1229.

14. *TSKY*, vol. 2, p. 575; Hugh Borton, *Japan's Modern Century* (New York: The Ronald Press, 1955), pp. 312, 319.

15. U.S. military attaché, Peking, report of May 2, 1928 (National Archives MRD file 2055-2622(82).

16. *N. Exp.*, vol. 4, pp. 1262-1265.

17. *N. Exp.*, vol. 4., p. 1265.

18. Ibid., pp. 1246-1250.

19. *Kuowen* (May 6, 1928), n. p.

20. *Kuowen* (April 29, 1928), n. p.

21. *History of Political Work*, vol. 1, pp. 370-371. *SCMP* (May 2, 1928), p. 12.

22. *SCMP* (May 5, 1928), p. 12, cites the Shanghai *Hua-ch'iao jih-pao* [Overseas Chinese daily] of May 4.

23. *SCMP* (May 2, 1928), p. 12.

24. *SCMP* (May 7, 1928), p. 12.

25. Ibid., and *SCMP* (May 16, 1928), p. 11.

26. *SCMP* (May 7, 1928), p. 12. David Bergamini in *Japan's Imperial Conspiracy* (New York: Simon and Schuster, 1972, p. 381) concludes that Japanese agents provoked the outbreak.

27. *SCMP* (May 8, 1928), p. 12.

28. Ibid.

29. Donald G. Gillin, *Warlord: Yen Hsi-shan in Shansi Province 1911-1940.* (Princeton: Princeton University Press, 1967), p. 109. Hereafter cited as *Warlord: Yen Hsi-shan.*

30. *SCMP* (May 9, 1928), p. 12, cites a Shanghai release of May 7.
31. *History of Political Work*, vol. 1, pp. 381-382, quotes report from a Foreign Ministry official returned from Tsinan, published in *Chung-yang jih-pao* (May 19, 1928). See *Ko-ming wen-hsien*, vol. 19, p. 5661. David Bergamini (p. 381) claims that the Japanese wanted to slow the NRA but that Chiang bypassed Tsinan and agreed to give Japan Manchuria.
32. *SCMP* (May 5, 1928), p. 14.
33. *Kuowen* (May 13, 1928), n. p. *SCMP* (May 18, 1928), p. 12.
34. *SCMP* (May 11, 1928), p. 10, which uses a Reuter release from Peking of May 10.
35. *SCMP* (June 2, 1928), p. 16, cites evidence used in a Hong Kong sedition trial.
36. *SCMP* (May 22, 1928), p. 10.
37. *Pei-fa chien shih*, p. 265.
38. *SCMP* (May 15, 1928), p. 10, cites Shanghai's *Hua-ch'iao jih-pao* of May 14.

CHAPTER 17

1. *N. Exp.*, vol. 4, pp. 1980-1982. *SCMP* (May 14, 1928), p. 10, cites the Shanghai *Hua-ch'iao jih-pao* of May 13.
2. *N. Exp.*, vol. 4., battle map no. 2 following p. 1356.
3. Ibid., p. 1352.
4. *Kuowen* (May 27, 1928), n. p.
5. *N. Exp.*, vol. 4, p. 1381, and battle map on p. 1380a.
6. Ibid., p. 1402.
7. *SCMP* (May 31, 1928), p. 22, cites Reuter, Tokyo. *TSKY*, vol. 2, p. 578. *Kuowen* (June 2, 1928), n. p. *N. Exp.*, vol. 4, pp. 1386-1389, includes a list of casualties and ammunition consumed in the battle.
8. *N. Exp.*, vol. 4, p. 1409. *SCMP* May 15, 1928), p. 10, and (June 2, 1928), p. 16.
9. *SCMP* (May 21, 1928), p. 10.
10. *Kuowen* (June 10, 1928), n. p. *Ko-ming wen-hsien*, vol. 19, p. 1410.
11. *Kuowen* (June 10, 1928), n. p.
12. *N. Exp.*, vol. 4, p. 1427. Dispatch to U.S. Secretary of State from Minister J. MacMurray at Peking, July 3, 1928, U.S. National Archives (893.00/10174), and the July 7, 1928, report from Consul General C.E. Gauss of Tientsin, U.S. National Archives (893.00/10185).
13. *SCMP* (June 12, 1928), p. 10. *N. Exp.*, vol. 4, p. 1428.
14. *SCMP* (June 2, 1928), p. 16, quotes from *Hua-ch'iao jih-pao*, May 31.
15. *SCMP* (June 13, 1928), p. 10. *N. Exp.*, vol. 4, p. 1428.
16. *N. Exp.*, vol. 4, p. 1431.
17. Ibid., pp. 1450-1456.
18. *Ta-shih chi*, p. 320.
19. *SCMP* (June 13, 1928), p. 10.

CHAPTER 18

1. *Kuowen* (July 25, 1926), pp. 11-15. Paul Monroe, *China: A Nation in Evolution* (New York: Macmillan, 1928), p. 192, cites his observations of China in 1920 and 1921. *1st Workers' Movement*, pp. 187-188.
2. Wang Chien-min, vol. 1, p. 161. Chang Kuo-t'ao, vol. 1, pp. 228-230.
3. *Kuowen* (July 10, 1927), n. p.
4. *Ma Ch'ao-chün chuan-chi* [The biography of Ma Ch'ao-chün] (Taipei, 1966, mimeographed), printed to honor Ma on his eightieth birthday.
5. Ma, *Labor*, vol. 1, p. 136.
6. Ibid., pp. 102-103.
7. Sheean, "Moscow," pp. 468-486.
8. Interview with Sun Fo at Yangmingshan, Taiwan, May 25, 1966.
9. Ma, *Labor*, vol. 2, p. 401.
10. *1st Workers' Movement*, p. 182, copies *Chung-kuo hai-yüan* [Chinese seaman], 4 (March 1, 1926).
11. Teng Chung-hsia, p. 131.
12. Ibid.
13. *SCMP* (March 24, 1926), p. 12.

14. *SCMP* (March 5, 1926), p. 1.
15. *SCMP* (March 6, 1926), p. 1.
16. Akimova, p. 233.
17. Teng Chung-hsia, p. 137.
18. Ibid., p. 141.
19. *SCMP* (March 22, 1926), p. 8.
20. *HKDP* (March 25, 1926), p. 5. *SCMP* (March 22, 1926), p. 8.
21. *SCMP* (March 25, 1926), p. 8.
22. *HKDP* (March 23, 1926), p. 5.
23. *HKDP* (March 25, 1926), p. 5.
24. *Chung-kuo Kung-ch'an-tang ti-ssu-chieh erh-chung ch'uan-hui erh-ts'e chung-yang k'uo-ta chih-hsing wei-yüan-hui yi-chüeh-an* [Decisions of the 2nd enlarged central committee of the CCP, 4th session] (Shanghai?: CCP July 12, 1926), p. 4. Hereafter cited as *CCP 2nd Enlarged CEC Meeting*.
25. Ibid., p. 5.
26. *Ti-yi-tz'u kuo-nei ko-ming chan-cheng shih-ch'i-te nung-min yün-tung* [The peasant movement during the first national revolutionary war] (Peking: People's Press Agency, 1953). Hereafter cited as *1st Peasants' Movement*.
27. Ibid.
28. Interview with Ma Ch'ao-chün, Taipei, Kwangtung Provincial Association Hall, July 15, 1966.
29. *1st Peasants' Movement*, p. 38, copies in its entirety a passage from *Chung-kuo nung-min yüeh-k'an* [Chinese peasant monthly], No. 9 (November 1926). Hereafter cited as *Chinese Peasant Monthly*. The same passage is copied in *Kung-fei huo-kuo shih-liao hui-pien* [Collection of historical materials on the betrayal of the nation], vol. 1 (Taipei, 1961), pp. 133-136.
30. *1st Peasants' Movement*, p. 20.
31. Interview with Wang Chien-min, April 21, 1966, Mu-chia, Taiwan. According to the *1st Peasants' Movement*, p. 20, 318 graduated.
32. *CCP Martyrs*, pp. 79-81, gives Yün Tai-ying's biography. Wang Chien-min recalled Yün as a leader of the Student Union of Wuhan during the preceding year of 1925.
33. *Chinese Peasant Monthly*, p. 21.
34. *1st Peasants' Movement*, p. 36, includes a photograph of the official admittance pass issued for the conference.
35. *Chinese Peasant Monthly*, p. 21, which presents the tally during July when those enrolled totaled 313; 14 more joined, but then 9 withdrew.
36. *1st Peasants' Movement*, p. 436, copies "Report on the Chinese Peasant Question," dated January 1927.
37. *SCMP* (March 25, 1926), p. 12, and (March 26, 1926), p. 9, and (March 27, 1926), p. 9.
38. *1st Workers' Movement*, p. 188, copies Chang Ch'iu-jen, "Kuo-min cheng-fu-hsia-ti kung-jen yün-tung" [The workers' movement under the national government] in *Cheng-chih chou-pao*, no. 10 (May 3, 1926).
39. *HKDP* (March 26, 1926), pp. 4-5. Teng Chung-hsia, p. 144.
40. *HKDP* (April 2, 1926), p. 5.
41. *HKDP* (April 17, 1926), p. 5.
42. *SCMP* (June 7, 1926), p. 8.
43. *SCMP* (July 26, 1926), p. 8. *1st Workers' Movement*, p. 148.
44. *Kuowen* (July 25, 1926), p. 26. *SCMP* (July 26, 1926), p. 8.
45. *1st Workers' Movement*, p. 148.
46. *HKDP* (April 5, 1926), p. 5, and (April 14, 1926), p. 5.
47. *HKDP* (April 8, 1926), p. 5.
48. *Kuowen* (July 25, 1926), pp. 11-17.
49. *HKDP* (April 17, 1926), p. 5.
50. *HKDP* (April 14, 1926), p. 5.
51. Ibid.
52. *SCMP* (June 1, 1926), p. 9.
53. *SCMP* (June 9, 1926), p. 9.

54. *SCMP* (June 11, 1926), p. 8.
55. *SCMP* (June 14, 1926), p. 8.
56. *Kuowen* (July 25, 1926), p. 13.
57. *Su Ch'ao-ch'eng*, p. 12.
58. *SCMP* (June 16, 1926), p. 10.
59. *SCMP* (June 22, 1926), pp. 8-9, and (June 30, 1926), p. 8.
60. *SCMP* (July 26, 1926), p. 8.
61. *SCMP* (July 9, 1926), p. 8.
62. *SCMP* (July 12, 1926), p. 8.
63. *SCMP* (July 1, 1926), p. 8.
64. *SCMP* (July 6, 1926), p. 8.
65. *SCMP* (July 2, 1926), p. 8.
66. *SCMP* (June 28, 1926), p. 9.
67. Chang Kuo-t'ao, vol. 1, pp. 528-530.

CHAPTER 19

1. *SCMP* (May 24, 1926), p. 9.
2. *SCMP* (June 26, 1926), p. 10.
3. *SCMP* (June 28, 1926), p. 9.
4. Ibid.
5. *Kuowen* (March 27, 1926), n. p.
6. Ch'en Tu-hsiu, "Kei Chiang chieh-shih-ti yi-feng-hsin" [Letter to Chiang Kai-shek], *Hsiang Tao*, (June 9, 1926), pp. 1526-1529.
7. Ch'en Tu-hsiu, "Lün kuo-min cheng-fu-chih pei-fa" [On the northern expedition of the national government], *Hsiang Tao* (July 7, 1926), p. 1584.
8. *CCP 2nd Enlarged CEC Meeting*, p. 2A.
9. *Chung-kuo Kung-ch'an-tang chien-ming li-shih* [A simple history of the CCP] (Shanghai?: CCP Central, 1926). Hereafter cited as *CCP History*. Chang Kuo-t'ao (vol. 1, pp. 528-529) criticized his CCP comrades for their "passive attitude" from May until Hunan had been taken in August.
10. *SCMP* (July 5, 1926), p. 8.
11. *SCMP* (July 6, 1926), p. 8, and (July 9, 1926), p. 8, and (July 10, 1926), p. 8.
12. Teng Chung-hsia, p. 146.
13. *SCMP* (July 8, 1926), p. 8.
14. Ch'en Kung-po, pp. 41-42.
15. Ibid.
16. Teng Chung-hsia, p. 146.
17. Ibid., and *SCMP* (August 13, 1926), p. 9.
18. *SCMP* (August 13, 1926), p. 9.
19. From an interview with General Ho Ying-ch'in, June 4, 1966, in Taipei.
20. *1st Workers' Movement*, pp. 321-322, copies letter to the Hunan Union as published in *Chan-shih chou-pao* (November 14, 1926), n. p.
21. Ibid.
22. *SCMP* (September 30, 1926), p. 9.
23. Interview with Wang Chien-min, April 21, 1966.
24. *1st Peasants' Movement*, p. 21.
25. Ch'en Kung-po, pp. 45-46. Chang Kuo-t'ao (vol. 1, p. 537) recalls similar information gained in interviews with Yeh T'ing, CCP commander of the Independent Regiment.
26. *N. Exp.*, vol. 2, pp. 337-339.
27. *1st Peasants' Movement*, *1st Workers' Movement*, and *Hsiang Tao* reports from July through November 1926.
28. *1st Peasants' Movement*, p. 293, copies an article in the *Chan-shih chou-pao*, (September 19, 1926), n. p.
29. *1st Workers' Movement*, pp. 329-330.
30. "Hunan during the Northern Expedition," newsletter from Hunan dated July 6, *Hsiang Tao* (July 14, 1926), p. 608.
31. *1st Peasants' Movement*, p. 293. *N. Exp.*, vol. 2, pp. 337-355. Chang Kuo-t'ao (vol. 1,

pp. 594, 610-614) recalls the CCP's mistrust of Eighth Army commander T'ang, who had become the equivalent of the governor of Hunan-Hupei.

32. *1st Peasants' Movement*, pp. 329-330.

33. *N. Exp.*, vol. 2, pp. 380-382.

34. Article from *Min-kuo jih-pao* (September 28, 1926), an official KMT organ, which *Hsiang Tao* reproduced (November 4, 1926, n. p.).

35. *1st Peasants' Movement*, p. 330.

36. Ko T'eh, "Pei-fa sheng-chung-chih Hunan" [Hunan during the northern expedition], Hunan communiqué of July 7, *Hsiang Tao* (July 14, 1926), p. 1606. Shu Chien, "Ts'ung kuang-chou suo-hsin pei-fa-chün-chih sheng-li yü min-chung" [News from Canton on the victories of the northern expeditionary army and the masses], *Hsiang Tao* (November 4, 1926), 1843-1844. Quotes from the Canton *Kuo-min jih-pao* (September 20, 1926), n. p. The *SCMP* (March 23, 1926, p. 8) reports that the *Min-kuo jih-pao* and *Kuo-min hsin-wen* were both *temporarily* suspended for their known CCP affiliations. *Chan-shih chou-pao* (September 19, 1926) article copied in *1st Peasants' Movement*, p. 273.

37. *N. Exp.*, vol. 2, pp. 347-348.

38. Ibid.

39. *Hsiang Tao* (November 4, 1926, n. p.), in which Shu Chien quoted from the Hong Kong *Hua-ch'iao jih-pao* (September 7, 1926).

40. Kuo Mo-jo, *Wuch'ang ch'eng-hsia* (Shanghai, 1933), translated by Josiah W. Bennet as "A Poet with the Northern Expedition," *Far Eastern Quarterly* 3(1-4) (February 1944-August 1944):144-145, 165. Hereafter cited as Kuo Mo-jo.

41. *SCMP* (August 13, 1926), p. 9.

42. *New York Times* (September 1, 1926), p. 7.

43. Interview with Sun Fo on May 25, 1966.

44. Interview with Li Shao-ling, January 1966, ex-Political Department cadre.

45. *N. Exp.*, vol. 2, p. 393.

46. Ma, *Labor*, vol. 2, p. 575.

47. *Hsiang Tao* (November 4, 1926), p. 1843.

48. *SCMP* (September 13, 1926), p. 9.

49. *SCMP* (September 16, 1926), p. 9.

50. Chang Kuo-t'ao, vol. 1, pp. 530, 539.

51. *Kuowen* (January 2, 1927), n. p. Akimova, p. 247.

52. Pai T'ien, "Wuhan tsui-chin-ti chi-ts'e kung ch'ao" [Recent labor tides in Wuhan], communiqué from Hankow July 16, 1926, *Hsiang Tao* (August 6, 1926), pp. 1665-1666. *CKHT*, p. 163.

53. *L'Humanité* (September 27, 1926), n. p.

54. Chang Kuo-t'ao, vol. 1, pp. 547-549.

CHAPTER 20

1. Ma, *Labor*, vol. 2, pp. 575, 607.

2. *SCMP* (November 20, 1926), p. 9.

3. *L'Humanité* (October 31, 1926), n. p.

4. *SCMP* (October 20, 1926), p. 9.

5. *SCMP* (September 30, 1926), p. 9. Akimova, p. 251.

6. *HKDP* (October 5, 1926), p. 7.

7. *SCMP* (October 29, 1926), p. 9. *Kuowen* (October 31, 1926), p. 3.

8. *Ch'ing-tang yün-tung kai-lün* [A summary of the party purification movement] (Shanghai: Chun-chiung T'u-shu Co., 1927), p. 114. Interview with Liao Wen-yin, December 22, 1965.

9. *Pei-fa chien-shih*, p. 98, and chart no. 15.

10. *Hsien-tai p'ing-lün* (December 11, 1926), p. 2.

11. *New York Times* (December 3, 1926), p. 4.

12. Interview with General Ho Ying-ch'in, then commander of the East Route Army.

13. Interview with Liao Wen-yin, January 1966.

14. *HTSL*, vol. 3, pp. 26-29.

15. *Kuowen* (March 13, 1927), n. p.

CHAPTER 21

1. *1st Workers' Movement*, p. 449; *SCMP* (November 25, 1926), p. 8.
2. *SCMP* (October 26, 1926), p. 9.
3. *1st Workers' Movement*, p. 449. Chang Kuo-t'ao (vol. 1, p. 585) claims that the CCP led the insurrection on October 24.
4. *SCMP* (October 18, 1926), p. 9.
5. *New York Times* (October 20, 1926), p. 14.
6. *Kuowen* (October 24, 1926), n. p.
7. *SCMP* (October 18, 1926), p. 9; *New York Times* (October 17, 1926), p. 22. *1st Workers' Movement*, p. 448, quotes from Ch'ü Ching-pai, *Chung-kuo chih-kung yün-tung ts'ai-liao* [Selected materials on the Chinese labor movement] (Shanghai?: CCP, March 1931). Ch'ü was the brother of CCP leader Ch'ü Ch'iu-pai. Hereafter cited as Ch'ü Ching-pai.
8. *SCMP* (October 18, 1926), p. 9.
9. Ch'ü Ching-pai, p. 448.
10. Ibid., and *SCMP* (October 19, 1926), p. 9.
11. *SCMP* (October 23, 1926), p. 9.
12. *SCMP* (October 26, 1926), p. 9.
13. *SCMP* (October 29, 1926), p. 3.
14. *CCP before the War*, p. 46.
15. Ibid.
16. "Record of the Shanghai General Strike," *Hsiang Tao* (February 28, 1927), n. p.
17. *CKYS*, pp. 39-40.
18. *China Yearbook 1928*, pp. 996-997; *Kuowen* (February 27, 1927), n. p.
19. Ibid. lists thirteen demands. Chesneaux claims there were seventeen.
20. Ibid.
21. *Kuowen* (February 27, 1927), n. p.
22. *Kuowen* (March 6, 1927), n. p.
23. *CKHT*, pp. 176-177.
24. Jean Chesneaux, *The Chinese Labor Movement* (Stanford: Stanford University Press, 1968), p. 360; Chang Kuo-t'ao, vol. 1, p. 589.
25. *Kuowen* (March 13, 1927), n. p.
26. Chang Kuo-t'ao (vol. 1, p. 530) says that he ordered agents to Hupei to seize enemy arms "to arm ourselves."
27. *HTSL*, vol. 3, p. 182. Chang Kuo-t'ao (vol. 1, p. 589) claims there were 5,000 armed pickets.
28. *Kuowen* (April 10, 1927), p. 1.
29. *CKYS*, pp. 16-17; *CKHT*, p. 178; *Kuowen* (March 27, 1927), n. p. *SCMP* (March 23, 1927), p. 10, cites Reuters release.
30. *SCMP* (March 25, 1927), p. 10.
31. *SCMP* (March 24, 1927), p. 12.
32. *Su Ch'ao-ch'eng*, p. 13.
33. Ma, *Labor*, p. 679.

CHAPTER 22

1. *CCP Martyrs*, p. 60.
2. *HKDP* (May 11, 1926), p. 5.
3. *Kuowen* (July 25, 1926), pp. 13-14.
4. *1st Workers' Movement*, p. 148.
5. *Kuowen* (July 25, 1926), p. 10.
6. *SCMP* (August 4, 1926), p. 9.
7. *SCMP* (August 5, 1926), p. 8.
8. *SCMP* (August 4, 1926), p. 9.
9. *SCMP* (August 10, 1926), p. 8.
10. *SCMP* (August 23, 1926), p. 10.
11. *1st Workers' Movement*, p. 39.
12. "Condition of the Kwangtung Peasants during the Northern Expedition," *Hsiang Tao*

(September 20, 1926), n. p. Chang Kuo-t'ao (vol. 1, p. 603) indirectly refers to the *min-t'uan* resistance, under landlord leadership, to the peasants' associations of Kwangtung.

13. Akimova, p. 252.
14. *Kuowen* (November 7, 1926), p. 1.
15. *SCMP* (September 30, 1926), p. 8. *HKDP* (October 7, 1926), p. 5.
16. *Kuowen* (November 7, 1926), n. p.
17. *HKDP* (October 7, 1926), p. 5.
18. *HKDP* (October 9, 1926), p. 5.
19. *HKDP* (October 13, 1926), p. 5.
20. *HKDP* (October 14, 1926), p. 5.
21. *SCMP* (November 2, 1926), p. 8.
22. Ibid., p. 9.
23. *SCMP* (November 9, 1926), p. 8. Akimova, p. 256, recalls that the pickets helped to police Canton as late as December 1926.
24. Akimova, p. 252.
25. *SCMP* (November 16, 1926), p. 9.
26. *SCMP* (November 17, 1926), p. 10.
27. Ibid.
28. *SCMP* (November 26, 1926), p. 9.
29. *SCMP* (November 22, 1926), p. 8, and (November 30, 1926), p. 9.
30. *SCMP* (December 6, 1926), p. 9, and (December 9, 1926), p. 10.
31. Marius B. Jansen, *The Japanese and Sun Yat-sen* (Cambridge: Harvard University Press, 1954), pp. 170-172.
32. *CCP before the War*, p. 25. Akimova, p. 255.
33. *SCMP* (December 10, 1926), p. 10.
34. *1st Workers' Movement*, p. 400, published the report of the Hupei GLU's First Congress.
35. Ch'en Kung-po, pp. 103-104.
36. *L'Humanité* (November 20, 1926), p. 1; *New York Times* (December 1, 1926), p. 1.
37. *SCMP* (December 9, 1926), p. 11. Chang Kuo-t'ao, vol. 1, pp. 550-552.
38. Chang Kuo-t'ao, vol. 1, p. 541.
39. Akimova, p. 256, describes Canton in November-December 1926.
40 *1st Workers' Movement*, pp. 383-384, which reproduces an article from Canton's *Min-kuo jih-pao* (January 10, 1927).
41. *SCMP* (December 6, 1926), p. 10; *Su Chao-cheng*, pp. 3-13.
42. Ch'en Kung-po, pp. 103-104.

CHAPTER 23

1. Wang Chien-min, vol. 1, p. 163. Chang Kuo-t'ao, vol. 1, p. 548.
2. *1st Workers' Movement*, p. 187.
3. *Chan-shih chou-pao* (September 19, 1926) published the report, which the *1st Peasants' Movement* reproduces on p. 273.
4. The report of the Hunan peasants' delegation to the Sixth Hunan CCP Assembly included in the Hunan Executive Committee report, reproduced in *1st Workers' Movement*, pp. 372-374. Chang Kuo-t'ao, (vol. 1, p. 609), claimed to the contrary that in mid-1926 there were 200,000; in December, 1,360,000.
5. *CKHT*, p. 172.
6. Chang Ch'iu-jen, "Report on the Progress of the Labor Movement in China," *Cheng-chih chou-pao* (May 3, 1926), reproduced in *1st Workers' Movement*, pp. 194-198.
7. *CKHT*, p. 172.
8. "Letter from Hunan's CCP Executive Committee," *Chan-shih chou-pao* (September 5, 1926), reproduced in *1st Workers' Movement*, pp. 316-318.
9. *CKHT*, p. 172.)
10. *1st Peasants' Movement*, p. 275.
11. Chang Kuo-t'ao, vol. 1, p. 609, p. 714fn. 36.
12. *Documents*, p. 376. *1st Peasants' Movement*, p. 400, claims there were 100,000 organized workers in all Hupei prior to its liberation and 300,000 three months later.

13. *CKHT*, p. 172. Chang Kuo-t'ao, vol. 1, p. 609, however, claims there were 280,000 by December 1926.

14. *CKHT*, p. 192.

15. *Chung-kuo nung-yeh ching-chi ts'ai-liao* [Materials on China's agricultural economy] (Nanking?, 1934), reproduced in *1st Peasants' Movement*, pp. 412-420. Chang Kuo-t'ao, (vol. 1, p. 609) claims Kiangsi's movement was inferior to that in Hupei.

16. *Chung-kuo nung-min wen-t'i* [The Chinese peasant question] (January 1927), reproduced in *1st Peasants' Movement*, pp. 922-924.

17. Ibid. Chang Kuo-t'ao, (vol. 1, p. 410) recalled CCP plans to transform Honan's Red Spears into peasants' associations in 1925.

18. "Hunan Newsletter," datelined May 25, 1926, in *Hsiang Tao* (July 16, 1926), pp. 1545-1546.

19. *Kuowen* (July 17, 1927, n. p.), which claims the Comintern recently decided to make better use of the Red Spears and to place more emphasis on peasant power.

20. *CCP History*, p. 19A.

21. Ibid., p. 1, and other CCP sources.

22. *Yün-yung t'ung-yi chan-hsien yi-ch'ien Chung-kung-chih chien-shih* [A short history of the CCP before the united front] (Yenan: Chinese Communist Central Committee, 1939), pp. 37-38. C. Martin Wilbur's interpolation in *Documents*, pp. 94, 110.

23. Figures from the staff of the CCP Studies Research Center, Taipei *hsien*, which agree with Ch'en Tu-hsiu's compilation in April 1927 cited in James P. Harrison, *The Long March to Power* (New York: Praeger, 1972), p. 99.

CHAPTER 24

1. *History of Political Work*, vol. 1, p. 361.

2. Ibid., p. 80.

3. R. Landis, "Training and Indoctrination at Whampoa," in *Nationalism and Revolution: China in the 1920's*, vol. 1 of Twentieth-Century China (New York: New Viewpoints, 1976).

4. *Huang-p'u hsün-lien chi* [A collection of training materials from Whampoa], ed. by Teng Wen-yi (Nanking: National Defense Ministry Information Bureau, 1947), pp. 21-35. See also *History of Political Work*, vol. 1, pp. 93-96.

5. *History of Political Work*, vol. 1, p. 80.

6. Ibid., p. 99.

7. *Ko-ming hua-pao* [Revolutionary pictorial], cover of May 1926 issue.

8. Chang Kuo-t'ao, vol. 1, p. 540.

9. Kuo Mo-jo, p. 7.

10. Interview with Li Hsiao-ling, a retired KMT Political Department worker, January 1966.

11. *History of Political Work*, vol. 1, p. 106.

12. Interview with Li Hsiao-ling, January 1966.

13. Interview with Leng Hsin who served both as a military officer and a Political Department worker.

14. *History of Political Work*, vol. 1, p. 267. *Documents*, p. 370. Kuo Mo-jo, p. 7. *China Yearbook 1928*, p. 1161. Chang Kuo-t'ao., vol. 1, p. 540.

15. *History of Political Work*, vol. 1, pp. 270-271.

16. Interview with Ho Ying-ch'in June 4, 1966.

CHAPTER 25

1. *History of Political Work*, vol. 1, p. 461.

2. Ibid., p. 97. Li Hsiao-ling recalled the song in an interview. *Ai-min Ko* is published in *Tseng Wen-cheng kung ch'üan-chi* [Collected works of Duke Tseng] (Shanghai: World Book Co., 1932, 1st edition; second reprint in Taiwan, 1956), vol. 10, pt. 2, pp. 71-72.

3. Schram, pp. 51-52.

4. Interview with Wang Chien-min, who experienced the political activities of student life in the mid-1920s. See Ka-che Yip "Student Activism in the 1920's" in *Nationalism and Revolution: China in the 1920's*, vol. 1 of Twentieth-Century China (New York: New Viewpoints, 1976).

5. *CCP Martyrs,* pp. 79-81.
6. Interview with ex-Political Department workers Liao Wen-yin and Li Hsiao-ling, and in *History of Political Work,* vol. 1, p. 289.
7. *Kuowen* (April 4, 1926), n. p.
8. Ch'en Kung-po, p. 53.
9. *SCMP* (September 30, 1926), p. 8.
10. Interview in 1966 with journalist Liu Tsu-ch'iang, who had been a student leader in 1926.
11. Wang Jih-hsin's editorial in *Hsien-tai p'ing-lün* (November 20, 1926), pp. 18-20.
12. For example, the *Kuowen chou-pao* cited in this study was, from 1926 through 1928, published alternately in the international concession at Shanghai and in the Japanese concession at Tientsin.
13. *Kuowen* (March 13, 1927), n. p.
14. Interview with Liao Wen-yin in Taipei, December 22, 1965.
15. Ibid.
16. Chang Kuo-t'ao (vol. 1, p. 603) implied that people's militias were generally set up by the landholding gentry, another reason why radical land reform was not preached in Fukien by the NRA.
17. Ibid., and *History of Political Work,* vol. 1, p. 291.
18. *China Yearbook 1928,* p. 981, and disseminated earlier through other press agencies.
19. *HKDP* (April 7, 1926), p. 5; another 2,300 "propagandists" were assigned to work within Kwangtung-Kwangsi. Chang Kuo-t'ao, head of the CCP's Military Department in mid-1926, remembers the tiny scale of his operation and an "insurrection corps" of eight that he sent to join forces with other partisans in Wuhan to "harass the rear lines of the enemy, to incite desertions and uprisings, and to seize the arms of the enemy troops in order to arm ourselves." He then found his men inside Wuchang after its long siege ended (Chang Kuo-t'ao, vol. 1, pp. 530, 538).
20. *History of Political Work,* vol. 1, p. 370.

CHAPTER 26

1. Interview in Taipei with Liao Wen-yin in 1966.
2. Ibid., and interviews in 1966 with Li Hsiao-ling and Leng Hsin in Taipei.
3. Interview in Taipei with Li Hsiao-ling in 1966.
4. Photographs in *Asia* 27(6):485.
5. Chapman, *The Chinese Revolution 1926-1927,* p. 23.
6. *Kuowen* (November 14, 1926), p. 2.
7. Interview with Leng Hsin on June 22, 1966, in Taipei.
8. *History of Political Work,* vol. 1, p. 291.
9. Interview in Taipei with Ho Ying-ch'in, June 1966.
10. Kuo Mo-jo, p. 157.
11. Interview in Taipei with Ho Ying-ch'in in June 1966.

CHAPTER 27

1. Liao Wen-yin interview, and in *N. Exp.,* vol. 2, pp. 574-596.
2. Liao Wen-yin interview.
3. *SCMP* (November 3, 1926), p. 8. Chang Kuo-t'ao (vol. 1, p. 537) recalls the large number of recruits added to combat units at the front in Hunan and Hupei.
4. *SCMP* (November 20, 1926), p. 11; *L'Humanité* (November 26, 1926), p. 3.
5. *History of Political Work,* vol. 1, p. 267. *Documents,* p. 217.
6. Wang Chien-min, vol. 1, p. 303; *History of Political Work,* vol. 1, p. 312.
7. *History of Political Work,* vol. 1, p. 328.
8. Ibid.
9. *Ta-shih chi,* p. 366.
10. *History of Political Work,* vol. 1, pp. 345-346.
11. Ibid., p. 371.
12. *History of Political Work,* vol. 1, p. 366 quotes from *Pei-fa ch'üan chün tso-chan chi-hua, ming-ling, ching-kuo ho-pien* [Complete collection of military plans, orders and

experiences in battles of the northern expedition]. No bibliographic data and the work is not accessible in Taiwan.

13. *Kuowen* (July 3, 1927), n. p.
14. *SCMP* (May 1, 1928), p. 12.
15. *History of Political Work*, vol. 1, pp. 383-384.
16. *SCMP* (May 17, 1928), p. 9.
17. *SCMP* (May 11, 1928), p. 8, a Reuters agency release.
18. Ibid.
19. *SCMP* (May 15, 1928, n. p.) quotes *Hua-ch'iao jih-pao* (May 14, 1928).
20. *SCMP* (June 12, 1928), p. 8.
21. *1st Peasants' Movement*, p. 430.
22. *N. Exp.*, vol. 4, p. 1299.
23. *History of Political Work*, vol. 1, pp. 375-377.
24. *History of Political Work* (vol. 1, p. 376) quotes a report in the Shanghai *Chung-yang jih-pao* (April 14, 1928).
25. Liao Wen-yin interview.
26. *Kuowen* (November 14, 1926), p. 2.
27. *Kuowen* (April 10, 1927), n. p.
28. *Kuowen* (March 6, 1927), n. p.
29. *Kuowen* (November 14, 1926), n. p. Interview with Liu Chü-ch'üan in 1965 in Taipei.
30. *History of Political Work*, vol. 1, p. 356.
31. Ibid., p. 431.
32. Ibid., p. 432, quotes a report in the Shanghai *Chung-yang jih-pao* (June 10, 1928).

CHAPTER 28

1. T'ang Leang-li, p. 242. *Ta-shih chi*, under February 16, 1926, p. 201.
2. *Ta-shih chi*, pp. 196, 200. U.S. Canton Consul D. Jenkins report of February 20, 1926 (State Dept. 893.00/7291).
3. Intelligence report gathered by U.S. naval attaché, March 1, 1926 (State Dept. 893.00/7277).
4. *Kuowen* (August 8, 1926), n. p.
5. *Ta-shih chi*, p. 201.
6. Interview (May 25, 1966, Yangmingshan, Taiwan) with Sun Fo, who negotiated for the KMT with many of the warlords.
7. *SCMP* (March 6, 1926), p. 3.
8. *HKDP* (April 19, 1926), p. 5.
9. *Kuowen* (August 8, 1926), n. p.
10. Ibid.
11. National Military Historical Museum collection, Taipei.
12. *Kuowen* (August 29, 1926), p. 23.
13. *Ta-shih chi*, p. 219.
14. *SCMP* (August 16, 1926), p. 8. *Ko-ming wen-hsien*, vol. 20, p. 1690.
15. *Ko-ming wen-hsien*, vol. 20, p. 1690. Interview in Taipei with Liao Wen-yin, January, 1966.
16. *Ko-ming wen-hsien*, vol. 12, p. 162 and vol. 20, p. 1689. *SCMP* (August 16, 1926), p. 8.
17. *Kuowen* (August 29, 1926), n. p.
18. *Ta-shih chi*, p. 219.
19. *Kuowen* (September 12, 1926), p. 4.
20. *Documents*, p. 373.
21. *History of Political Work*, vol. 1, p. 294.
22. *SCMP* (November 5, 1926), p. 8.
23. *Kuowen* (May 1, 1927), n. p.
24. *Kuowen* (June 19, 1927), n. p.
25. *SCMP* (September 10, 1926), p. 9.
26. *NCH* (October 23, and 30, 1926), Reuter reports from Canton dated October 19 and 23. *SCMP* (October 21 and 28, 1926).
27. *Kuowen* (September 19, 1926), p. 2; *SCMP* (September 10, 1926), p. 9.

28. *Kuowen* (October 10, 1926), n. p.
29. *Kuowen* (October 24, 1926), n. p.
30. *SCMP* (October 23, 1926), p. 9; *Ta-shih chi,* p. 229.
31. *Kuowen* (November 28, 1926), n. p.
32. *HTSL,* vol. 3, pp. 174-176; *SCMP* (October 18, 1926), p. 9; *Kuowen* (November 21, 1926), n. p.; Chang Kuo-t'ao, vol. 1, p. 586.
33. *Kuowen* (December 26, 1926), n. p.
34. *Documents,* p. 389; Robert C. North, *M.N. Roy's Mission to China* (Berkeley: University of California Press, 1963), p. 50.
35. *Kuowen* (August 7, 1927), n. p. The negotiations between Nanking and Chang Tso-lin repeated Sun Yat-sen's attempts in 1922 to gain Chang's acquiescence to a northern expedition against Wu. *Sheng ching Daily* (Mukden, March 3, 1922); *North China Daily News* (Shanghai, March 14, 1922); U.S. Vice-Consul to Canton's interview with KMT diplomats C.C. Wu and Wu T'ing-fang on April, 1, 1922 (State Dept. report of April 4, 1922 in National Archives microfilm series 329, roll no. 29).
36. *Kuowen* (June 19, 1927), n. p.
37. *N. Exp.,* vol. 4, p. 1428.
38. Ibid.

CHAPTER 29

1. Chang Kuo-t'ao (vol. 1, p. 496) recalls that Kisanka (Kuybyshev) was the leading messenger of that combination at Canton.
2. *L'Humanité* (April 3, 1926), p. 3.
3. Interview with Liao Wen-yin in Taipei, December 22, 1965.
4. *Ta-shih chi,* pp. 202-203.
5. *China Yearbook 1928,* pp. 1221-1222.
6. Sun Lien-chung, *Sun Lien-chung hui-i-lu* [Memoirs of Sun Lien-chung] (Taipei: Hai T'ien Printing Co., 1962), p. 22. The author was one of Feng's leading generals during the Northern Expedition. Hereafter cited as Sun Lien-chung.
7. Akimova, p. 82. Chang Kuo-t'ao, vol. 1, p. 561.
8. *SCMP* (August 28, 1926), p. 10.
9. Reports and Feng's signed obligation to Moscow for aid received are among the documents seized from the Russian Embassy in April 1927, in U.S. National Archives, Military Records Division series 2657-I-281, dated April 15, 1925, to July 8, 1926; copy of the loan agreement signed August 15, 1926, in Moscow and held at the Soviet military attaché's office. British Foreign Office Report of October 27, 1925 (371/10957-424).
10. Sun Lien-chung, p. 22.
11. Ibid.
12. *Documents,* p. 334.
13. *Ta-shih chi,* p. 235. Sun Lien-chung, p. 22.
14. Sun Lien-chung, p. 22.
15. *Kuowen* (April 24, 1927), n. p. *Ta-shih chi,* p. 253. Chang Kuo-t'ao (vol. 1, p. 561) claims Hsü had been favored due to his connections with Feng.
16. *Kuowen* (June 12, 1927), n. p. Chang Kuo-t'ao, vol. 1, p. 642.
17. Sun Lien-chung, p. 23.
18. *Kuowen* (July 3, 1927), n. p. Henry F. Misselwitz (*The Dragon Stirs* [New York: Harbinger House, 1941] pp. 123-124) saw the telegram from Feng and noted Borodin's shock upon hearing its contents.
19. Sun Lien-chung, p. 24. See also James E. Sheridan, *Chinese Warlord: The Career of Feng Yü-hsiang* (Stanford: Stanford University Press, 1966).
20. *Kuowen* (July 24, 1927), n. p.
21. Sun Lien-chung, p. 24.
22. Donald G. Gillin, "Portrait of a Warlord: Yen Hsi-shan in Shansi Province, 1911-1930," *Journal of Asian Studies* 19(3):291. See also his *Warlord: Yen Hsi-shan.*
23. *Kuowen* (July 3, 1927), n. p.
24. *Ta-shih chi,* p. 234.
25. Ibid., p. 236.

26. Ibid., p. 237.
27. Ibid., p. 255.
28. Ibid., p. 253.
29. *Kuowen* (April 17, 1927), n. p.
30. *Kuowen* (June 12, 1927), n. p.
31. *Kuowen* (July 10, 1927), n. p.
32. *Ta-shih chi*, p. 270.

CHAPTER 30

1. Lucian W. Pye, *Warlord Politics* (New York, 1971).
2. *History of Political Work* (vol. 1, p. 256) quotes the CEC's "Outline of Propaganda" dated February 1928 from the *Collection of Military Plans, Orders, and Accounts of the Northern Expeditionary Forces*.
3. *Ta-shih chi*, p. 206.
4. *HKDP* (March 31, 1926), p. 5.
5. Photographic reproduction of the original letter before or after the telegraphic translation. Held in the National Military Historical Museum collection, Taipei.
6. *Ko-ming wen-hsien*, vol. 20, p. 1689.
7. *Ko-ming wen-hsien*, vol. 12, p. 162.
8. *Kuowen* (March 20, 1927), n. p.
9. *N. Exp.*, vol. 4, chart no. 78, and *N. Exp.*, vol. 1, p. 150.
10. *Kuowen* (August 21, 1927), n. p.; *N. Exp.*, vol. 4, chart no. 78.
11. *SCMP* (August 16, 1926), p. 8.
12. *Ta-shih chi*, p. 219. *Ko-ming wen-hsien*, vol. 20, p. 1690.
13. *Who's Who in China*, 4th ed. (Shanghai, 1931), p. 122.
14. Interview with Liao Wen-yin, January 1966, Taipei. *Ko-ming wen-hsien*, vol. 20, p. 1690.
15. *Ta-shih chi*, p. 221.
16. *Pei-fa Chien-shih*, chart no. 22, dated March 1928.
17. *Ta-shih chi*, pp. 221, 224, 250. Boorman, vol. 2, pp. 77-78.
18. *N. Exp.*, vol. 2, p. 464. U.S. Hankow Consul F.P. Lockhard to Minister J. MacMurray at Peking describes Liu's post in the Hanyang-Hankow defense, August 30, 1926 (SD 893.00/7742). Paul Wakefield, "A Story of the Seige of Wuchang" (SD 893.00/7781), p. 3.
19. *Ta-shih chi*, p. 244.
20. *Ko-ming wen-hsien*, vol. 20, p. 1690.
21. *N. Exp.*, vol. 2, p. 470. U.S. Hankow Consul F.P. Lockhard to Peking, October 23, 1926 (SD 893.00/7866), which presented the terms under which the Honanese were incorporated into the Fifteenth Army.
22. *Ko-ming wen-hsien*, vol. 20, p. 1690; and interview with Liao Wen-yin.
23. *Pei-fa Chien-shih*, p. 97.
24. *Hsien-tai p'ing lün* [Contemporary review] 5(107):1; *SCMP* (December 8, 1926), p. 11.
25. Interview with Lo Chia-lün in Taipei, 1966.
26. Akimova, p. 275.
27. *Ko-ming wen-hsien*, vol. 20, p. 1690; *SCMP* (October 18, 1926), p. 9.
28. *SCMP* (October 21, 1926), p. 8.
29. *Kuowen* (November 28, 1926), n. p.
30. *Ta-shih chi*, p. 235.
31. *Kuowen* (December 26, 1926), n. p.
32. *Ta-shih chi*, p. 234. *Kuowen* (December 26, 1926), n. p.
33. Ma Hsü-lun, pp. 106-107. *Ta-shih chi*, p. 246.
34. Ma Hsü-lun, p. 110.
35. *NCH* (September 24, 1927), pp. 514, 525.
36. *NCH* (October 10, 1927), p. 10.
37. Lo Yü-t'ien (*Chün-fa i-wen* [Anecdotes of the warlords] [Taipei: Hu-p'o Publishing Soc., 1967]) claims that Chou colluded with T'ang and was supported from Ningpo.
38. *NCH* (October 15, 1927), p. 91. *China Yearbook 1928* vol. 2, p. 1269.
39. *HTSL*, vol. 3, pp. 26-28.

40. *Ta-shih chi*, p. 234. *Kuowen* (February 13, 1927), n. p.

41. U.S. Nanking Consul to Washington, January 17, 1925, pp. 10-12 (893.00/6104).

42. *Ta-shih chi*, p. 237.

43. *Kuowen* (February 27, 1927), n. p.

44. *N. Exp.*, vol. 2, pp. 626, 646, 648.

45. *Ta-shih chi*, p. 247. *Kuowen* (March 13, 1927) "News Diary."

46. *N. Exp.*, vol. 2, p. 647. John K. Davis, "Historical Sketch of Political Conditions in Anhui Province from the Revolution of 1911 to the end of 1924" (Nanking U.S. Consulate, February 28, 1925; SD 893.00/6135).

47. Photographic reproduction of translated telegram in handwritten form, held in the collection of the National Military Historical Museum, Taipei.

48. *Ta-shih chi*, p. 233.

49. *Ta-shih chi*, p. 236. *TSKY* vol. 2, p. 531.

50. U.S. C-in-C Asiatic Fleet Intelligence Report to OPNAV Washington, February 23, 1927 (SD 893.00/8308).

51. Soviet military attaché, "Minutes of the Meeting of the Military Section," undated but approximately March 13, 1927. Photographs of original documents and translation by the U.S. military attaché, Peking, held in National Archives, Modern Military Records Division, Washington, D.C., file no. 2657-I-281(122-A46).

52. *Kuowen* (March 20, 1927), n. p.

53. *TSKY*, vol. 2, p. 530.

54. *N. Exp.*, vol. 2, p. 636. *SCMP* (March 22, 1927), p. 10.

55. Among Russian documents seized in Peking, April 1927, U.S. National Archives, Military Records Div. file no. 2657-I-281(83-22).

56. *N. Exp.*, vol. 2, p. 631.

57. *Kuowen* (March 27, 1927), n. p. U.S. Shanghai Consul C.E. Gauss to Peking, March 18, 1927 (SD 893.00/8405).

58. *SCMP* (March 21, 1927), p. 10; *China Weekly Review* 40 (March 26, 1927):112.

59. *Kuowen* (March 27, 1927), n. p.

60. *Kuowen* (April 10, 1927), n. p.

61. *Kuowen* (April 3, 1927), n. p. *Ta-shih chi*, p. 251.

Bibliography

Boldface parenthetical interjections presented with some of the entries are the shortened citation forms employed in the text and notes.

BOOKS AND ARTICLES

Abend, Hallet Edward. *My Life in China 1926-1941.* New York: Harcourt, Brace and Co., 1943.

Akimova, Vera Vladimirovna (Vishnyakova). (**Akimova**). *Two years in Revolutionary China, 1925-1927.* Cambridge, Mass.: Harvard University Press, 1971.

Bergamini, David. *Japan's Imperial Conspiracy.* New York: Simon and Schuster, 1972.

Biographical Dictionary of Republican China. Vols. 1, 2, and 3. Edited by Howard L. Boorman. (**Boorman**). New York: Columbia University Press, 1967 (vol. 1), 1968 (vol. 2), 1970 (vol. 3).

Borton, Hugh. *Japan's Modern Century.* New York: The Ronald Press, 1955.

Brandt, Conrad. *Stalin's Failure in China: 1924-1927.* Cambridge, Mass.: Harvard University Press, 1958.

Carey, F.W. "China: A Survey of the Present Position," *Journal of the Central Asian Society* 15(4):399-415.

Ch'an, F. Gilbert, ed. *Nationalism and Revolution: China in the 1920's.* Vol. 1 of Twentieth-Century China. New York: New Viewpoints, 1976.

Chang Ch'i-yün. *Tang-shih kai-yao* [Outline of the party's history]. (**TSKY**). Taipei: Central Committee on Culture Supply Association, 1953.

Chang Hsing-ping. *"Peiching kung-jen yün-tung shih-liao"* [Historical materials on the Peking workers' movement]. Mimeographed. Taiwan: ca. 1960s.

Chang Kuo-t'ao. (**Chang Kuo-t'ao**). *The Rise of the Chinese Communist Party 1921-1927*, vol. 1. Lawrence: University of Kansas Press, 1971.

Chapman, H. Owen. *The Chinese Revolution 1926-27, A Record of the Period under Communist Control as Seen from the Nationalist Capital, Hankow.* London: Constable & Co., 1928.

Ch'en Kung-po. (**Ch'en Kung-po**). *Han feng chi* [Collection of the north wind]. 4th ed. Shanghai: Association of Local Government, 1945.

Ch'en Kuo-fu. (**Ch'en Kuo-fu**). *Huang-p'u chien-chün shih-hua* [Short history of establishing the army at Whampoa]. N. p., 1944.

Ch'en Pu-lei. *Kuo-min ko-ming chün chan-shih* [A history of the battles of the National Revolutionary Army]. Nanking: KMT(?), 1936.

Ch'eng Hao-sheng. *Chung-hua min-kuo chien-kuo shih* [The history of the establishment of the Chinese republic]. Chungking: Cheng-chung Publishers, 1943.

Chesneaux, Jean. *The Chinese Labor Movement, 1919-1927.* English translation: Stanford: Stanford University Press, 1968.

———. "The Federalist Movement in China, 1920-3." In *Modern China's Search for a Political Form*, edited by Jack Gray. New York: Oxford University Press, 1969.

Chiang Chieh-shih yao-lun chi [A collection of Chiang Kai-shek's important discourses]. Taipei: Shih-chieh Book Co., 1955.

Chiang Kai-shek. *Soviet Russia in China: A Summing-Up at Seventy.* (**Russia in China**). New York: Farrar, Straus and Giroux, 1965.

Chiang Yung-ching. *Pao-lo-t'ing yü Wuhan cheng-ch'üan* [Borodin and the Wuhan regime]. (**Borodin**). Taipei: Chung-kuo Hsüeh-shu Ch'u-tso Chiang-tsu Wei-yüan Hui, 1963.

Ch'ing-tang yün-tung [The party purification movement]. Edited by the Committee to Encourage Party Purification. Nanking: Ch'ing-tang Committee, 1927.

Ch'ing-tang yün-tung kai-lün [A summary of the party purification movement]. Shanghai: Ch'ün-chung T'u-shu Co., 1927.

Ch'ou Ch'ing-chüan. *Min-tsu chan-shih Ch'ou Ch'ing-chüan* [Ch'ou Ch'ing-chüan: national warrior]. Taipei: Pa-t'i Book Co., 1959.

Ch'ü Ching-pai. (**Ch'ü Ching-pai**). *Chung-kuo chih-kung yün-tung ts'ai-liao* [Selected materials on the Chinese labor movement]. Shanghai: CCP, March 1931.

Chung Hsia and K'ang Sheng. *Su Chao-ch'eng, Lo Teng-hsien chuan* [The biographies of Su Chao-ch'eng and Lo Teng-hsien]. Shanghai: International Publishing Co., 1940.

Chung-hua Min-kuo ta-shih chi [Record of major events of the Republic of China]. (**Ta-shih chi**). Edited by Kao Yin-tzu. Taipei: Shih-chieh Book Co., 1957.

Chung-kung Nanch'ang pao-tung chi-yao [Sketch of the CCP's Nanch'ang uprising]. Chungking(?): Central Investigation Statistics Bureau, 1944.

Chung-kuo hsien-tai ko-ming yün-tung shih [History of the Modern Chinese revolution]. (**CKHT**). 2nd. ed. Shanghai(?): Committee on Study of Chinese modern History, 1938.

Chung-kuo kuan-shen jen-ming lu [Lives of Chinese officials and gentry]. Tokyo: China Research Soc., 1918.

Chung-kuo Kung-ch'an-tang chien-ming li-shih [A simple history of the CCP]. (**CCP History**). Shanghai(?): CCP Central, 1926.

Chung-kuo Kung-ch'an-tang lieh-shih chuan [Biographies of the Chinese communist martyrs]. (**CCP Martyrs**). Peking: Youth Publishing Society, 1951.

Chung-kuo Kung-ch'an-tang shih-lieh [Brief history of the CCP]. 2nd ed. Chungking: United Publishing Society, 1942.

Chung-kuo Kung-ch'an-tang ti-ssu-chieh erh-chung ch'uan-hui erh-ts'e chung-yang k'uo-ta chih-hsing wei-yüan-hui yi-chüeh-an [Decisions of the second enlarged central committee of the CCP; fourth session]. (**CCP 2nd Enlarged CEC Meeting**). Shanghai(?): CCP, July 12, 1926.

Chung-kuo kung-jen yün-tung shih-kao [A history of the Chinese workers' movement]. (**CKYS**). Edited by Hsü Wen-tien. Chungking: Central Social Department, 1940(?)

Chung-kuo nung-min yüeh-k'an [Chinese peasant monthly]. Canton: CCP, 1926.

Cunningham, Edwin S. "A Brief Historical Sketch of the Political History of Chekiang Province since the Year 1911." Shanghai: U.S. Consul General Report, 1925. U.S. National Archives.

Davis, John K. *Historical Sketch of Political Conditions in Kiangsu Province from the*

Revolution of 1911 to the End of 1924. Nanking Consulate, 1925. U.S. National Archives 893.00/6104.

Gillin, Donald G. *Warlord: Yen Hsi-shan in Shansi province 1911-1940.* (**Warlord: Yen Hsi-shan**). Princeton: Princeton University Press, 1967.

Harrison, James P. *The Long March to Power.* New York: Praeger, 1972.

Ho Kan-chih. *Chung-kuo hsien-tai ko-ming shih* [A history of the modern Chinese revolution]. Vol. 1. Peking: Higher Education Publishing Society, 1957.

Holcombe, Arthur N. *The Chinese Revolution.* Cambridge, Mass.: Harvard University Press, 1930.

Hsien-tai shih-liao [Contemporary historical materials]. (**HTSL**). Vols. 3 and 4. Shanghai: Hai T'ien Publishing Society, 1934.

Hsin Chung-kuo jen-wu chih [The record of the figures of new China]. Hong Kong: Chou-muo Pao She-hang, 1950.

Hsin Chung-kuo jen-wu chih: fen-sheng [A record of the personalities of new China: by provinces]. Edited and published by Huang Hui-ch'üan. Hong Kong, 1930.

Hsü, Emanuel. *The Rise of Modern China.* New York: Oxford University Press, 1975.

Hsü En-ts'eng. *Wo ho kung-tang tou-cheng ti hui-yi* [Recollections of my struggle with the CCP]. Taipei: n. p., 1953.

Huang-pu chien-chün san-shih-nien kai-shu [A summary of thirty years of creating the army at Whampoa]. Edited by the Kuomintang Party Historical Materials Compilation Committee. Taiwan: Huang-pu Publication Society, 1954.

Huang-p'u hsün-lien chi [A collection of training materials from Whampoa]. Edited by Teng Wen-yi. Nanking: National Defense Ministry Information Bureau, 1947.

Hu Ch'iao-mu. *Chung-kuo Kung-ch'an-tang-te san-shih nien* [Thirty years of the Chinese Communist Party]. Peking: Jen-min Ch'u-pan She, 1951.

Hung-seh wen-hsien [Red documents]. Shanghai(?): Chieh Fang She Liberation Society, 1938.

Huston, J.C. "General Historical Sketch of Political Conditions in the Hankow Consular District from the Revolution of 1911 to March 1925." U.S. Hankow Consul General report, 1925, U.S. National Archives 893.00/6206. (**Huston, "Sketch"**).

Isaacs, Harold R. (**Isaacs**). *The Tragedy of the Chinese Revolution.* Stanford: Stanford University Press, 1951.

Jansen, Marius B. *The Japanese and Sun Yat-sen.* Cambridge, Mass.: Harvard University Press, 1954.

June Twenty-third. Canton: Commission for the Investigation of the Shakee Massacre, 1925.

June Twenty-third, The Truth. Canton: 1925. Included by U.S. Canton Consul Jenkins in report of March 15, 1926 (SD 893.00/7384).

K'ang-chan yi-ch'ien-te Chung-kuo Kung-ch'an-tang [The Chinese Communist Party before the war of resistance]. (**CCP before the War**). 2nd ed. Chungking(?): Sheng-li Publishing Agency, 1942.

Ko-ming wen-hsien [Revolutionary documents]. (**Ko-ming wen-hsien**). Edited by Lo Chia-lün. Taipei: Historical Materials Editing Committee of the Party History of the KMT, from 1950 onward as a series.

Ko T'eh (pen name). "Pei-fa sheng-chung-chih Hunan" [Hunan in the midst of the noise of the Northern Expedition]. *Hsiang Tao* (July 14, 1926), p. 1606.

Kuang-chou p'ao-tung-chih yi-yi yü chiao-hsün [The significance and lessons learned from the Canton uprising]. (**Canton Uprising**). N. p.: CCP Central Committee, 1928.

Kung-fei-te kung-jen yün-tung [Communists' workers movement]. Taipei: Bureau of Investigation, 1962.

Kuo-chün cheng-kung shih-kao [History of political work in the national military]. (**History of Political Work**). Vols. 1 and 2. Taipei: History Bureau of Ministry of Defense, 1960.

Kuo Mo-jo. (**Kuo Mo-jo**). *Wuch'ang ch'eng-hsia* (Shanghai: 1933) appears as "A Poet with the Northern Expedition," translation and notes by Josiah W. Bennett. *Far Eastern Quarterly* 3(1-4) (November 1943-August 1944):144-145, 165.

Lei Hsiao-ch'en. *San-shih nien tung-luan chung-kuo* [Thirty years of turmoil in China]. Vol. 1. Hong Kong: Asia Publishing Co., 1955.

Liang Han-ping. *Chung-kuo hsien-tai ko-ming shih chiao-hsüeh ts'an-k'ao t'i-kang* [History of

China's modern revolution—reference outline for teaching]. Tientsin: Tientsin T'ung Publishing Society, 1955.

Li Chien-nung. *The Political History of China 1840-1928*. Princeton: D. VanNostrand Co., 1956.

Liu Chien-ch'ün, "Pei-fa ch'ien-hou ku-jen ch'ün" [Old friends from the Northern Expedition], *Chüan-chi wen-hsüeh* [Biographical literature]. Taipei, 1966, pp. 22-27.

Liu, F.F. (**F.F. Liu**). *A Military History of Modern China 1924-1949*. Princeton: Princeton University Press, 1956.

Lo Sheng, "Ti-san-ts'e ch'uan-kuo lao-tung ta-hui-chih ching-kuo chi-ch'i chieh-kuo" [Results of the third national labor assembly], *Hsiang Tao* (May 30, 1926), pp. 1500, 1501.

Lo Yü-t'ien. *Chün-fa i-wen* [Anecdotes of the warlords]. Taipei: Hu-p'o Publishing Soc., 1967.

MacFarquhar, Roderick L. "The Whampoa Military Academy," *Papers on China* 9 (August 1955):146-163.

Ma Ch'ao-chün, ed. (**Ma, Labor**). *Chung-kuo lao-kung yün-tung shih* [History of the Chinese labor movement]. 4 vols. Taipei: Chung-kuo lao-kung Fu-li Ch'u-pan She, 1959.

"Ma Ch'ao-chün chuan-chi" [The biography of Ma Ch'ao-chün]. Mimeographed. Taipei, 1966.

MacNair, Harley Farnsworth. (**MacNair**). *China in Revolution: An Analysis of Politics and Militarism under the Republic*. Chicago: University of Chicago Press, 1931.

Ma Hsü-lun. (**Ma Hsü-lun**). *Wo tsai liu-shih-sui i-ch'ien* [My life sixty years ago]. Shanghai: Sheng-huo Book Store, 1947.

Mao Szu-ch'eng. *Min-kuo shih-wu-nien yi-ch'ien-chih Chiang Chieh-shih hsien-sheng* [Chiang Kai-shek before 1926]. (**Chiang before 1926**). Reprint. Hong Kong: Lung-men Book Store, 1965.

Ma Yün. *Chung-kuo fan-kung yün-tung shih* [History of the Chinese anti-CCP movement]. T'ai-chung: Tung-nan Co., 1957.

Miao Ch'u-huang. *Chung-kuo kung-ch'an-tang chien-yao li-shih* [The simple outline history of the CCP]. Peking: Hsüeh-hsi Tso-chih She, 1956.

Min-kuo chün-fa ch'ü-hsien [Interesting anecdotes on the warlords of the republic]. N. p.: Hsien-tai Publishing Co., ca. 1937.

Misselwitz, Henry F. *The Dragon Stirs*. New York: Harbinger House, 1941.

Monroe, Paul. *China: A Nation in Evolution*. New York: Macmillan, 1928.

North, Robert C. *Kuomintang and Chinese Communist Elites*. Hoover Institute Studies, Series B. Elite Studies No. 8 (July 1952). Stanford: Stanford University Press, 1952.

———. *M.N. Roy's mission to China: The Communist-Kuomintang Split of 1927*. Berkeley: University of California Press, 1963.

Pao Tsun-p'eng. *Chung-kuo chin-tai ch'ing-nien yün-tung shih* [History of the modern Chinese youth movement]. Chungking: Shih-tai Publishing Association, 1943.

Pei-fa chan-shih [Military history of the northern expedition]. (**N. Exp.**) 4 vols. Taipei: National Defense Ministry Historical and Political Bureau, 1959.

Powell, John B. *My Twenty-five Years in China*. New York: Macmillan, 1945.

Pye, Lucien. *Warlord Politics: Conflict and Coalition in the Modernization of Republican China*. New York: Praeger, 1971.

San-shih nien lai te Shanghai kung-yün [The thirty-year Shanghai labor movement]. Shanghai: Department of Culture and Education, Shanghai General Labor Union, 1951.

Schram, Stuart. (**Schram**). *Mao Tse-tung*. New York: Penguin Books, 1967.

Sheean, Vincent. "Some People from Canton," *Asia* 27(10):815-817. (**Sheean**).

———. "Moscow and the Chinese Revolution," *Asia* 27(6):468-486. (**Sheean, "Moscow"**).

Sheridan, James E. *Chinese Warlord: The Career of Feng Yü-hsiang*. Stanford: Stanford University Press, 1966.

Su Chao-cheng. (**Su Chao-cheng**). Shanghai(?): China National General Labor Union, 1930.

Sun Lien-chung. (**Sun Lien-chung**). *Sun Lien-chung hui-i-lu* [Memoirs of Sun Lien-chung]. Taipei: Hai T'ien Printing Co., 1962.

Tang-tai Chung-kuo ming-jen chih [A record of famous men of contemporary China]. Shanghai: Shih-chieh P'ing-lun Publ. Soc., 1940.

Tang-tai Chung-kuo ming-jen lu [A listing of famous men of contemporary China]. Edited by Fan Yin-nan. Shanghai: N. p., 1931.

T'ang Leang-li. (**T'ang Leang-li**). *The Inner History of the Chinese Revolution.* New York: E.P. Dutton & Co., 1930.

Teng Chung-hsia. (**Teng Chung-hsia**). *Sheng-kang pa-kung k'ai-kuan* [Hong Kong-Kwangtung strike]. Canton: 1926.

Ti-yi-tz'u kuo-nei ko-ming chan-cheng shih-ch'i-te kung-jen yün-tung [The workers' movement during the first period of national revolutionary war]. (**1st Workers' Movement**). Peking: People's Publishing Association, 1958.

Ti-yi-tz'u kuo-nei ko-ming chan-cheng shih-ch'i-te nung-min yün-tung [The peasant movement during the first national revolutionary war]. (**1st Peasants' Movement**). Peking: People's Press Agency, 1953.

Toynbee, Arnold J. *Survey of International Affairs.* London: Oxford University Press, 1929.

Trotsky, Leon. *Problems of the Chinese Revolution.* Reprint. New York: Paragon, 1966.

Tseng Wen-cheng kung ch'üan-chi [The collective works of Duke Tseng]. Vol. 10. Shanghai: World Book Co., 1932. Reprinted in Taipei, 1956.

Wang Chien-min. (**Wang Chien-min**). *Chung-kuo Kung-ch'an-tang shih-kao* [History of the Chinese Communist Party]. 2 vols. Taipei: by the author, 1965.

Wang Ching-wei. (**Wang Ching-wei**). "Wuhan fen-kung-chih ching-kuo" [Wuhan's split with the CCP]. *Kuo-li Chung-shan ta-hsüeh jih-pao* [National Chung-shan University daily] *Supplement* (Canton, November 9, 1927).

Who's Who in China. Edited by M.C. Powell. Shanghai: The China Weekly Review, 1925, and 4th edition of 1931.

Wilbur, C. Martin, and How Julie Lien-ying. *Documents on Communism, Nationalism and Soviet Advisors in China 1918-1927.* (**Documents**). New York: Columbia University Press, 1956.

Wu Hsiang-hsiang. (**Wu Hsiang-hsiang**). *O-ti ch'in-lieh chung-kuo shih* [The history of the Russian empire's invasion of China]. Taipei: Cheng-chung Shu-chü, 1954.

Wu T'ien-wei. "Chiang Kai-shek's March Twentieth Coup d'etat of 1926," *Journal of Asian Studies* 27(3):585-602.

———. "A Review of the Wuhan Debacle," *Journal of Asian Studies* 29(1):125-143.

Yeh T'ing t'ung-chih lieh-li [A history of comrade Yeh T'ing]. CCP, May 5, 1946. Short, mimeographed biography held at the Bureau of Investigation, Research Center on Communism, Ch'ing-t'an, Taiwan.

Yün-yung t'ung-yi chan-hsien yi-ch'ien Chung-kung-chih chien-shih [A short history of the CCP before the united front]. Yenan: Chinese Communist Central Committee, 1939.

DOCUMENTS

British Foreign Office confidential prints, "Quarterly reports to the Foreign Office", London, F.O. 405/230 series on China.

Chung-kuo Kung-ch'an-tang ti-szu-chieh erh-chung ch'üan hui erh-ts'e chung-yang k'uo-ta chih-hsing wei-yüan-hui yi-chüeh-an [The decisions of the fourth session of the entire second enlarged central executive committee]. N. p.: CCP Central Enlarged Executive Committee, 1926.

Chung-yang lin-shih cheng-chih-chü k'uo-ta hui-yi chüeh-yi an [Decisions of the enlarged meeting of the central provisional political bureau]. N. p.: CCP Central Political Bureau, 1927.

Chung-yang t'ung-hsin [Communiqué from the headquarters]. Shanghai(?): CCP Central Party Headquarters(?), periodic series of 1926 and after.

Kwangchou paotung chih yi-yi yü chiao-hsün [The significance and the lesson learned from the uprising in Canton]. N. p.: CCP Central Committee, 1928.

National Military Historical Museum collections of pictorial photographs and photographs of documents. Taipei.

Papers relating to the First Firing in the Shameen Affair of June 23, 1925 (**Shameen White Paper**): *China* No. 1 (1926) Cmd. 2636, *House of Commons*, London, 1926, XXX, *Accounts and Papers* No. 15.

Papers relating to the Nanking Incident of March 24 and 25, 1927: *China* No. 4 (1927) Cmd. 2953, *House of Commons*, London, 1927, XXVI, *Accounts and Papers* No. 14.
U.S. State Department Records, National Archives, Washington, D.C.
U.S. National Archives, Military Records Division: intelligence reports on China from foreign military commands and U.S. Army military attachés stationed in China.

PERIODICALS

Asia. Concord, N.H., 1926-1927.
Chan-shih chou-pao [Soldiers' weekly]. Changsha, 1926.
Cheng-chih chou-pao [Political weekly]. Canton, Kuomintang.
China Christian Year Book 1928. Shanghai, 1928.
China Mail. Hong Kong, 1926-1928.
China Yearbook 1926. (**China Yearbook 1926**). Edited by H.E.W. Woodhead. Tientsin, 1927.
China Yearbook 1928. (**China Yearbook 1928**). Edited by H.E.W. Woodhead. Tientsin, 1927.
Chung-kuo hai-yüan [China seaman]. Canton: China Seamen Industrial Union, January 1926.
Chüan-chi wen-hsüeh [Biographical literature]. Taipei, 1960s.
Chung-yang jih-pao [Central daily news]. Shanghai: KMT, 1928.
Hong Kong Daily Press. (**HKDP**). 1926-1928.
Hong Kong Telegraph. 1926-1928.
Hsiang Tao [The guide weekly]. Shanghai: CCP, September 1922-July 1927.
Hsien-tai p'ing-lün [Contemporary review]. Shanghai and Peking: Hsien-tai p'ing-lün Soc., December 1924-December 1928.
Ko-ming hua-pao [Revolutionary pictorial]. Canton: Whampoa Academy, 1926.
Kuowen chou-pao [National news weekly]. (**Kuowen**). Shanghai and Tientsin: Kuowen Chou-pao Soc., August 1924-December 1928.
Le Monde. Paris, 1926-1928.
L'Humanité. Paris, 1926-1929.
North China Herald. (**NCH**). Shanghai, 1920-1941.
Sheng ching jih-pao [Sheng Ching daily]. Mukden, 1922.
Shen pao [Daily]. Shanghai.
South China Morning Post (**SCMP**). Hong Kong, 1926-1928.
Tao-chih hsün-pao [Punish Reds weekly]. Hong Kong: Ch'en Keng Huan Book Store, nos. 1-9, July-October 1926.
Tu-li ch'ing nien [Independent youth]. Shanghai: Tu-li ch'ing-nien Magazine Soc., 1926-1927.
Tung-fang tsa-chih [Eastern miscellany]. Shanghai: Commercial Press, 1920s.

Index

About the Author

DONALD A. JORDAN, associate professor of East Asian History at Ohio University, Athens, Ohio, first became interested in Sinology during a two-year residence in Taiwan where he studied the Chinese language and worked as a naval advisor. He later spent another year in Taiwan and Hong Kong completing his graduate work and researching the controversial Northern Expedition on a Fulbright grant, in cooperation with the University of Wisconsin Asian Studies Committee.

OH   R-12 OWLJ
      Jordan